SCOTTISH
GENEALOGY

SCOTTISH
GENEALOGY

BRUCE DURIE

First published 2009

The History Press
The Mill, Brimscombe Port
Stroud, Gloucestershire, GL5 2QG
www.thehistorypress.co.uk

British Library Cataloguing in Publication Data.
A catalogue record for this book is available from the British Library.

ISBN 978 0 7509 4568 4

Typesetting and origination by The History Press
Printed in Great Britain

Contents

Preface

This book emerged from courses in genealogy, family history, heraldry and related subjects at the universities of Strathclyde and Edinburgh. It is not a list of sources, although a great many sources are mentioned. There are other places to get lists of books, archive holdings and websites. It is, rather, intended as a working manual for genealogists with an interest in Scottish records, firmly based in the praxis of a genealogical educator, with worked examples, templates and methodologies. It is aimed at all those interested in pursuing proper research into Scottish records and archives for genealogical purposes. This includes:

– anyone wishing to trace ancestors of a particular person of Scottish descent, including the vast numbers in countries which accepted the Scottish diaspora – principally the USA, Canada, Australia, New Zealand and India.
– archivists, librarians and others who guide the use of records and archives.
– those with a professional interest in Scottish genealogy – lawyers, records agents, researchers in archives and, of course, genealogists.
– anyone needing a suitable textbook for a preparatory course on Scottish genealogy.

There are subjects here not routinely covered in most introductory genealogy books – for instance, the interpretation of medieval documents, Latin inscriptions and palaeography. Where possible and relevant, parallels and differences have been drawn between Scottish genealogy and that of England, Ireland and other countries. As the basic family history sources – censuses, vital records and the various registers of property, electors and membership – become widely available, genealogists will seek to push their research further back in time to the 1500s and earlier. There is much in this book which, with luck, will be of wider interest than the records of Scotland, but as these are so rich and go back so far, there is a great deal every genealogist can learn from their study and careful application.

Finally, thanks are due to Paul Parr, Deputy Registrar General of Scotland for permission to use images, and to his staff and those at NAS, TNA, many local libraries and archives, and to the numerous long-suffering university colleagues and family members who put up with the process of authorship.

To quote an old Scots toast, particularly appropriate to the study of those long gone:

Here's tae us
Wha's like us?
Dam' few
And they're all deid!

Introduction

History is the great destroyer – it destroys reputations, illusions, myths and vanities; it reminds us that we are all mortal, and passing; it teaches us that we have little control over our actions and their consequences, our destinies and even our motives. We have no choice over our ancestors, and little over our descendants' choices of friends and spouses. Each of us is the product of our genes, our immediate family environment, our society and the influence of the wider world. Even our deepest-held beliefs, prejudices and bigotries dissolve when put under the microscope of history, and our seemingly complex human world is much like an ant-hill when viewed from a sufficient distance. But where genealogy differs from history *per se* is that it moves the focus away from the grand sweep of civilisations and larger social groups to the lives and actions of individuals and immediate families. It is often as far from the 'Great Man' view of history the way it used to be taught (lists of kings and battles) as a cat is from a queen. Those interested in history itself often find it is best illuminated when seen through the life of one person, an ancestor with whom we have some commonality of feeling, by virtue of no more than a shared surname or a family story.

Almost all sources of demography and biography come from collision with the authorities. This tends to be for purposes of registration (birth, marriage, death, census, taxes, poor relief etc.) or for legal reasons, whether criminal (arrests, trials, executions, witness statements) or civil (law suits, divorce, wills, property transfers). All of these generate records, which may still exist in some form, or at least as indexes or abstracts.

Scotland has possibly the most complete and best-kept – and certainly the most comprehensively digitised – set of vital records, land registers and other documents on the planet. This stems from the ancient Scottish tradition of writing everything down (especially property transfers and inheritances), and the nation's unreasonable love of lawyers. But it has served us well. Being a small country, the set of records available is approximately one-tenth of that of England, and therefore of manageable proportions. Scottish genealogy is, to that extent, easier. However, there is far more to Scottish genealogy than merely searching for vital data in the old parish registers (OPRs – baptism, marriage and burial records from the 1560s to the 1850s) and statutory records (births, marriages and deaths from 1855 and the decennial census from 1841).

The OPRs, by definition, only start with the birth of the Church of Scotland at the Reformation in the 1560s, and only deal with that church (called 'The Kirk'). Catholics, dissenters and those who simply chose not to take part in parish registration (the nobility, often) are completely ignored until much later. Equally, records of burials were not considered important until well after the Reformation, since it was only after that time that bodily resurrection at the last trump became an issue; before this, the location of physical remains hardly mattered except for royalty or anyone likely to achieve sainthood (and therefore be a source of relics and object of veneration). Even then, the OPRs are incomplete.

So, before the 1560s, family history can become murky. However, names were often recorded in Charters, especially when feudal lands were passed on, or where grants of land, title or other inheritances held of the sovereign had to be recorded. These are a rich source of name and place information.

Most genealogical research stalls somewhere in the seventeenth or eighteenth centuries. Between the 1560s and 1854, not everyone will be recorded, especially the nonconformists. Remember that it was not births which were noted in the OPRs, only Church of Scotland baptisms, and the same goes for the other sacraments – proclamation of marriage (banns) rather than the marriage itself, and burial or mort-cloth (shroud) rental rather than death. Happily, there are sasines – records of land and property transfer and mortgage. Also, Scotland is fortunate (and lawyers more fortunate still) that inheritance was not automatic and had to be 'proved', which required a record of actual immovable property (land, houses) and other 'incorporeal hereditaments', (i.e. heritable but intangible rights, titles, honours, obligations etc.). The Retours of Services of Heirs are therefore another rich but neglected source of family information. Testaments (which may include wills) record moveables (money and other possessions).

Even after 1841 (the first proper nationwide census) and 1855 (statutory recording of BMD) the records are incomplete. Not everyone was captured; there were considerable movements into and furth of Scotland; surname variants were commonly recorded haphazardly – so they give a partial picture of an individual life. At best, the researcher can get a person's given name at birth plus a date and place, and the names, address and (possibly) occupations of the parents and their date of marriage; the announcement of banns (pre-1855) or registration of a marriage, may include the place, the names and occupations of both spouses and those of both sets of parents, plus names of witnesses; and at death, the place and time of death are given, and often the cause, with the names and occupations of the deceased's parents and of the registrant (witness). This can be filled in with census information every decade from 1841 to 1901 (and, from 2012, to 1911). For example, for someone born in 1840, married in 1862 and who died in 1902, it will usually be possible to identify that person, the parents, spouse and spouse's parents from BMD records, and all of these people can be further identified in the snapshots from the censuses of 1841 to 1901. But it leaves much to be told. Were they rich or poor? Owned land or rented it? Had children or otherwise? The accessible vital records give a very bare-bones account. Precisely because much of this data is digitised and available on-line, it is possible to imagine, as is often claimed, that 'all of Scottish genealogy is on the Internet'.

This is where most people stop looking. In truth, it may be enough for them to start building a family tree with a reassuringly complete and impressively precise set of dates and places. But there are many pitfalls: a child born a year or more after a dead sibling might be given the same name; there may be inconsistencies in ages across the various censuses leading to inaccurate linkages of completely separate individuals; children of 'Scottish' marriages (i.e. irregular, based on the principle in Scots Law that marriage was constituted by mutual consent) may not be recorded; anyone could be away from home on census night; there is emigration and re-immigration; and we find seemingly identical individuals, stemming from the understandable but infuriating practice of naming children after parents, grandparents, uncles and aunts, leading to complete families with children of the same names, married to other people of the same names, probably their near-relatives and in the same parish. To take only one example, a number of villages in Fife had a high proportion of congenital diseases, such as spina bifida, caused by the number of intermarriages between same-surnamed families. (For a long time, this was blamed on eating potatoes with the eyes in!)

Fortunately, that's not all there is to it. There are other sources of information, which fill out the details of individual lives, allow the grouping of individuals by family group, locality or occupation. These include: charters; wills and testaments (not the same thing!); dissenting and Catholic church records; lair records (for churches or municipal cemeteries); local electoral and valuation rolls; commissariot (court) records; military lists; Poor Law records; Kirk Session minutes; registers of trades and guilds; and many others.

Then there are the Landed. They may be nobility (whether of the Scottish, English, Irish or British peerages); baronial (the place and the purpose of a baron in Scotland is wildly different from the English baronage, which is part of the peerage), and baronetage (which is a kind of hereditary knighthood); or merely landowning (but often tied up with a barony). And this has all changed somewhat with the enactment of the Abolition of Feudal Tenure etc. (Scotland) Act 2000 in 2004, but the older records exist and are of great value. Often, these people will have had Coats of Arms, so heraldry is a useful adjunct to 'standard' genealogy.

This book is intended to show researchers how to get beyond the standard BMD and census search and dig deeper into genealogy and the social history surrounding an individual or family. Necessarily, there will be a discussion on other archives outside Scotland: National Archives of England; Irish records; US and Canadian census data, ships' passenger lists and so on.

Is genealogy the same as family history?

Not really, but they have a lot in common, and each informs the other. Genealogy (as the term is used in this book) is the study and construction of familial relationships, mainly from vital records (birth, marriage, death, censuses etc.). Family history concerns itself more with events and their social context. To that extent, genealogy is the Who and Where, while family history is the What and When. Sociology would doubtless claim to be concerned with the Why, although much sociological investigation centres on the collection of the sort of data used by family historians and genealogists, but tends to turn it into statistical summaries. Perhaps it is better to think by analogy to the sciences – genealogy is more like mathematics while family history is chemistry and sociology is nature study or population biology. Or, genealogy is the bones, and family history is the flesh on the bones, and each needs the other.

Frankly, such discussions are rather fruitless. Everyone knows a straightforward piece of genealogy when they see it (a family tree, for instance) and a family history (such as a biography). It is rather pointless, or at least unilluminating, to collect only the dates of birth, marriage, death and so on, and the locations of these for a family tree or pedigree, without understanding something of why great-grandfather gave up cottage weaving to work in a mill, grandfather was a coal miner and father left for Canada. Equally, it is difficult to understand a complex family history without a simple table of relationships and dates. A good example of this is the intermarriages of European royalty in the nineteenth and twentieth centuries, many of whom were related by descent from Queen Victoria and Prince Albert. But just having the rather useful charts at the back of such books tells us little about the politics or the social conditions of the time.

It is generally agreed that family history is more about who people were and how they lived, why they did this job or married that spouse, the circumstances in which they were born, worked, loved, fought, died and the wider social and economic milieu when they did it. Like all narratives, it is open to speculation and interpretation. Genealogy is, in a sense, more precise than that, as it deals largely with concrete parameters – dates and places, for example. Genealogy is about tracing (and proving) ancestry and descent, or what is sometimes called 'pedigree'.

Definitions

Properly, pedigree charts start with one individual and trace the ancestry backwards through time. These are sometimes called 'birth briefs' and end up looking like an ice-cream cone (if laid out vertically) or a megaphone (if set down horizontally). Descendant charts or trees take the other approach – from one pair of ancestors at the top fanning out to a confusing tangle of distantly related nth cousins at the bottom. Each of these is a useful visual aid – but no more than that. The end point of any research project is information, not merely a diagram.

Be clear about your aims

One thing is certain about genealogy and family history – it can become an all-consuming passion. However, it can also swamp you with information, paper, file boxes and computerised data. Everything you discover will lead you on to more tantalising snippets, interesting ancestors, new connections and ultimately the whole sweep of human history. It is utterly absorbing, but can also be maddeningly complicated.

Every genealogist or family historian has discovered, or will at some point, that there is simply no sensible way to fit hundreds of interlinked individuals onto one chart the size of a roll of wallpaper, and no filing system that works without bursting at the seams. Even if you only search back five generations from yourself, and each generation has two siblings on each side of the family, that's over 250 people, without worrying about the children of your great-aunts and great-uncles etc.

Imagine the documentation associated with these, if you had the certificates for every birth, marriage and death, every census, military service and occupational record and every will. You would need a library.

There is a solution, though, and it requires three things:

1. know where you want to go and stick to it. If your aim is to track the male line back to a certain point, then do just that. If you want to find all descendants of one person, then make that your goal. If you decide to find every instance of a surname back to a particular year or in a particular place (a one-name study), then decide that's it, and stick to it. Do not get sidetracked by interesting byways. Note them, and come back to them as a separate project.
2. the best way to swallow an elephant is one bite at a time. If it all seems too much (and it will) then concentrate on solving one aspect. If it defies solution, shelve it, move on and come back to it later.
3. organisation is all. Keep good records, have a decent but simple filing system, organise your computer files properly and above all, buy a robust genealogy database program.

Do these things, following the recommendations in this book, and you just might save your life, sanity, marriage or whatever you value most (after your genealogy project, of course).

STEP ONE – Start with what you know

Almost every genealogy book, course and how-to guide starts with this advice. Generally, it's sensible – you and your family are already the experts on your family history. It is likely that you will be able to get reliable dates and places for births, marriages and deaths back to grandparents and even further. There may well be documents (certificates, wills, letters, inscriptions in family bibles) as well as diaries, newspaper clippings and photographs. By talking to older relatives and family friends, and showing them photographs and records, you may trigger memories and elicit more information. Ask where deceased relatives are buried and visit the graves, to photograph or record the headstone information or lair records. But there are dangers, complications and pitfalls.

First, memory is a very good if selective editor. A family story, repeated by many relatives, may be wrong in detail, embroidered over time or just plain invented. What seems a crucial piece of information, repeated by a number of those you talk to, may turn out to be no more than hearsay, or even a carefully constructed lie. One family had spent years trying to trace a great-uncle who had 'gone abroad to work' and they were less than delighted to be told he had in fact died while serving time in the local prison.

Second, different family members may have very different views of an ancestor. The grandfather who seemed stern but upright to one may have been a brutal bully to another. A beloved aunt may have been an appalling mother or an ungrateful daughter.

Third, you may well discover a long-buried secret or an inconvenient piece of information that certain family members may prefer to forget or have spent years assiduously covering up, and they won't thank you for bringing it to the light of day. An illegitimacy, a dead child, an earlier marriage, an abandoned family, disinherited offspring, debts, bankruptcies, collapsed business ventures, dishonourable war service, problems with drink, police records, illnesses, suspicious deaths, murders, suicides, the important job that turns out to be not what was claimed, violence, child abuse, disagreements over a will, stolen property – all of these may emerge, and other long-suppressed skeletons. You run the risk of alienating as many people as you delight. On the other hand, your researches may be the instrument for bringing together branches of a family who haven't spoken for years over some now-forgotten slight or misunderstanding.

Fourth, if you choose to start from some supposed distant ancestor ('we're all descended from Bonnie Prince Charlie' is not untypical) and work forwards to try to establish the link with living persons, it is more than likely you will hit a brick wall or end up researching some other family entirely. If the presumed great-great-great-grandfather had seven children, and so did each of them, which of these forty-nine branches do you track? Generally it is better to research backwards in time, one generation at a time. You can always explore collateral branches later, as a new project.

Fifth, check it hasn't been done before. Another family member may have been an amateur or professional genealogist and collected a great deal of information. But re-check every statement and assumption! Also, there may be a printed or manuscript family history out there in some local library or archive. Finding these will save time and effort.

Lists of family histories are held in various places – the Scottish Genealogy Society, the Guild of One Name Studies, the Office of the Lord Lyon, the Society of Genealogists (England), local libraries and archives, the National Library of Scotland, university libraries. Check catalogues such as *The Genealogist's Guide*, available via the public library. And, of course, check on the Internet.

STEP TWO – Get charting

As early as possible, start sketching out a family tree. You will probably need two versions – a 'drop-line' pedigree chart for yourself (or whoever is the starting point) working backwards; and a descendant tree from a specific ancestor. This should show, where possible, full names (with maiden surnames for the females), dates and places of birth, marriage and death, address at census dates and occupations. Use a large piece of paper, use a pencil, leave room for additions and be prepared to redraw it often. Or, use a genealogy program to organise the data and print charts.

Don't wait until the end of your research to produce a final, definitive family tree or family history narrative. Genealogical projects are never finished, and there is always more information to add.

Be prepared to copy or print ongoing versions of the work in progress and send it to relatives and others. This may itself jog further memories.

STEP THREE – Arrange your material

Note everything you find, even the blind alleys and false leads. This will save time and effort later when you find yourself heading off up the same garden path again. Document every source as fully as possible and photocopy, photograph or transcribe fully every document and record you find, writing the reference number on it.

Keep all of this in a flexible, easy to access form. A filing cabinet will probably be essential at some point. Until then, a system of folders, ring-binders and file boxes should do; but use a bound (not loose-leaf) book for your notes, which you will type up or copy later into your filing system. (See chapter 19).

Don't forget the female line

For a variety of reasons – to do with land and property inheritance, the transfer of a name, the way documents are recorded and so on – family trees often concentrate on the male line. But there is no reason not to follow the female line too, if you wish. It is half of everyone's genetic inheritance, after all.

Using the Internet

There is no question that the Internet has transformed genealogy and family history studies. Apart from more and more records and indexes to records appearing online, it is also possible to track down and keep in contact with a vast network of family and contacts around the world. With an e-mailing list of relatives and others interested it is possible to share and contribute information. More and more surnames and areas have their own dedicated family history websites, online newsgroups and bulletin boards. To find the local Family History Society (FHS) for your area of interest, see the website of the Scottish Association of Family History Societies (www.safhs.org.uk) or, for the rest of Britain, the Federation of Family History Societies (www.ffhs.org.uk).

Above All…

Remember that genealogy is the history of the future – and you are writing it. You are not just doing this for your own amusement. Your research is part of your family's legacy and future generations will either praise you or curse you depending on how good your work is and whether it can be accessed.

If you are intending to conduct professional genealogical research, you will naturally be expected to produce correct, well-indexed, properly assembled material with all 'facts' checked and documented and all records presented neatly and accessibly. But even if this is just a hobby, start with the same professional attitude, and your hard work will stand the test of time.

www.scotlandspeople.gov.uk – the 'official' source for BMD, censuses, testaments, Arms and other records (pay-per-view)

www.ancestry.co.uk and the international version www.ancestry.com – a huge finding aid with access to many records and links and growing all the time (subscription)

www.familyrecords.gov.uk – the UK government gateway to public records and more

www.familysearch.org – a global resource linked to the International Genealogical Index (IGI compiled by the Church of Jesus Christ of the Latter-Day Saints (the Mormons)

www.genesreunited.co.uk – a major UK family tree and genealogy website; useful for linking with others who are also currently researching names of interest

www.genuki.org.uk – UK and Ireland Genealogy site, providing a virtual library of information and links

www.one-name.org – website of the Guild of One-Name Studies (GOONS); good for clans, families and more unusual surnames (membership)

www.rootsweb.com – a huge resource linked to www.ancestry.com; designed to connect people doing genealogical research; excellent forum and discussions

www.sog.org.uk – the Society of Genealogists (England) with details of thousands of submitted family histories and more (requires Society membership for full access)

Public records

Despite the scale of Internet genealogical material, it still represents only a fraction of the totality. Ultimately, if you want to pursue family history to the next level of detail and precision, you are going to have to look at original records. You may be able to see them online, on microfilm or microfiches, or you may have to seek out the real thing, such as original parish registers – wonderful historic documents, hand-written in copperplate script (if you're lucky!) and redolent of the past.

Britain has an extraordinary depth and breadth of public records. For family history, the most important are the records of birth, marriages and deaths (BMD). A key date here is 1837. This is the date that the formal 'civil registration' began in England and Wales. Before 1837, baptisms, marriages and burials were recorded in parish registers; some of these go back to the sixteenth century. (It is hard to trace back family history beyond this – unless you belong to a well-documented line of nobility or royalty.)

A similar system of civil registration was inaugurated in Scotland in 1855. In Ireland the records are patchier, because many of the national archives were destroyed during the Civil War in 1922, but there is some civil registration information from about 1854. Such civil records will help you to fix the precise details (if not always 100% accurate) about your ancestors: dates, occupations, where they lived – the bare bones of their histories, if not much else. You can consult the indexes to births, deaths and marriages and order photocopies of the certificates; for English and Welsh records, you can do this through The National Archives in Kew, by going in person or via the Internet (www.familyrecords.gov.uk). A large proportion of the indexes for England and Wales has been transcribed, and is accessible through www.freebmd.org.uk or www.ancestry.co.uk.

You can get further details of your ancestors from the census returns. A national census has taken place in Britain every decade since 1801 (except 1941) and they are available up to 1901 (1911 for various Irish censuses). Census returns provide a fascinating snapshot of households, the names and ages of the residents, the relationships between them, their occupations and where they were born. The census returns are released to the public after a century has elapsed. The 1901 census can now be consulted (for a fee) on www.1901census.nationalarchives.gov.uk. You can see census returns for 1851 through to 1901 on microfilm at County Records Offices, or, for a modest fee, you can download them from licensed websites; some of these records have also been transcribed into print. Scottish records are at www.scotlandspeople.gov.uk.

There are many other forms of records beyond this, any of which could help you to fill in vital gaps in your knowledge (military records, wills, tax records, company records, electoral rolls, overseas civil records, and so on). Most of these cannot be seen on the Internet, but you can find out where they are located by using websites such as:

www.nas.gov.uk (National Archives of Scotland)
www.nas.gov.uk/nras (National Register of Archives for Scotland)
www.scan.org.uk (Scottish Archive Network)
www.nationalarchives.gov.uk (Britain)
www.archon.nationalarchives.gov.uk/archon (UK government gateway to repositories of archives)
www.a2a.org.uk (the English strand of the UK archives network)

A useful source for service personnel who died in the two world wars is the Commonwealth War Graves Commission (www.cwgc.org).

1

The Scottish Censuses of 1841 to 1911

The best place to start with any genealogical research is knowing where people were at a particular time. From there it is possible to work backwards to births and marriages, forward to marriages and deaths and laterally to other information such as occupations and land ownership.

The background to the various censuses will be covered later. For now, if we look at an example of a census return, we can see how much information can be gleaned. The one shown is for Cupar, Fife, in 1901 and specifically the household of James Bremner, Chief Constable of Fife at the time.

We can see that at Sandilands, in Cupar, lived James Bremner, aged seventy-five; his wife Isabella aged sixty-eight; and two single daughters, Mary, thirty-four and Keith, thirty-two. Furthermore, we have Bremner's occupation as Chief Constable of Fife and Kinross, and while he was born in Kirkcaldy (some 20 miles to the south) his wife and daughters were natives of Cupar. The headquarters of Fife police were in Cupar, so we might assume Bremner moved there because of his work, where he met and married Isabella; but that would need to be checked. Notice also that their house has ten rooms with windows and that the family employed two servants who lived in (or at least, were there overnight on the census date) and came from smaller towns nearby. Neither Mary nor Keith worked (except 'at home') and this, along with the large house, suggests a well-off family with the Head of Household on a good salary, as might be expected of Fife's senior police official. We are not told whether the household members spoke Gaelic (or indeed English!), but none, it seems, was deaf and dumb, blind, a lunatic or 'feeble-minded'.

Among the things we do not know are whether the Bremners had any other children, not living at home (they did, in fact), or had any other living relatives. But what inferences can we draw? Assuming a 'regular' marriage and no hanky-panky beforehand (not as unusual as we are sometimes led to believe in Victorian times), the Bremners had wed at least thirty-five years before, when James was about forty and Isabella thirty-three or so, and thus in or before 1866. We can also give approximate birth years: James in 1825–27 (he might be just seventy-five or almost seventy-six), Isabella in 1832–34, and the two daughters some time between 1866 and 1870 – although we might remember that unmarried ladies slightly past their first bloom would occasionally misremember their true ages when the census came around.

Already we have quite a picture of the Bremners – well-to-do, living in a comfortable house with servants, James still working as Chief Constable even though seventy-five and therefore (presumably) in reasonable health, married to a lady some seven years his junior and with at least two children.

Yet, if anyone had looked for these individuals in the General Register Office for Scotland (GROS) or on ScotlandsPeople, they might have been missed, as they were indexed as follows:

Taken from the 1901 Census for Cupar, Fife, GROS 420/00 009/00 015, with permission. For explanations of Civil Parish, Ward, Ecclesiastical Parish, School Board D, Quoad Sacra Parish etc.

Taken from the 1891 Census for Cupar, Fife, GROS 420/00 009/00 007, with permission.

Surname	Forename	Sex	Age	District	City/County	GROS Data
BRUNNER	ISABELLA	F	68	CUPAR	FIFE	420/00 009/00 015
BRUNNER	JAMES F	M	45	CUPAR	FIFE	420/00 009/00 015
BRUNNER	KEITH	F	32	CUPAR	FIFE	420/00 009/00 015
BRUNNER	MARY	F	34	CUPAR	FIFE	420/00 009/00 015

Not only had the names been transcribed wrongly from admittedly hard-to-read handwriting, Bremner's age is wrong by thirty years. An incautious researcher might assume this really was a family called Brunner, and a widowed mother and two younger sisters living with an elder son, James, aged 45. (The spelling has now been amended, but not the age.) But compare this with the 1891 census for the same address: Ten years before, we see James Bremner (65); his wife Isabella (58); daughters Mary (24) and Keith (22); and also two sons, Herbert (20) and Louis Rae (17), both students, unmarried and living at home (on the census night at least). The servants are different.

This confirms our presumed birth dates and marriage year ranges for the Bremners, and adds to our knowledge two boys, who were likely away and married by 1901, or else dead. We still do not know if there were any older children. Further searches would confirm these details, and we will return to the Bremners as a full case study later.

The point is there is a great deal of information in a census which makes it a good jumping-off point for a genealogical investigation. The other point is, that not all records are indexed properly (some not at all) and that it is necessary always to consult the original sources – although, as we shall see, not even these can be fully trusted.

Incidentally, GROS is always happy to correct mistakes, if notified.

How the census came about

The first census of England had been carried out under William I (William the Conqueror) and the results collated as the Domesday Book in 1086. There were later census-like exercises, for example, in the sixteenth century when bishops enumerated the number of families in their dioceses. The first national census in Britain took place in 1801, and there has been a further census every ten years since, except for 1941 when the Second World War took priority. However, the earliest four censuses (1801, 1811, 1821, 1831) were rather different in aim and character from the later ones, and it was only from 1841 that these are of much use to genealogists, as names were recorded.

The 1801 census

The first modern census, in 1801, was considered necessary because of growing unease about the demand for food in Britain, especially in the aftermath of the publication of Thomas Robert Malthus's *Essay on the Principle of Population* in 1798. The upshot was the Census Act or Population Act 1800 (An Act for taking an Account of the Population of Great Britain, and the Increase or Diminution thereof 41 Geo. III c.15), which legislated for a Census of Scotland, England and Wales, the Channel Islands and the Isle of Man. Ireland was not included until 1821. The process was remarkably swift, which underlines the importance attached to it – the Census Bill was presented to parliament on 20 November 1800, was passed on 3 December and received Royal Assent from King George III on 31 December. The first census was held just fourteen weeks later, on Monday 10 March 1801. This was possible because a House of Commons clerk called John Rickman was passionate about the idea and was prepared to take on the analysis of the results and the preparation of abstracts and reports, which he did for the 1801 census and the next three.

The 1801 census collected two sorts of information: the first was the numbers of families and houses, the numbers of individuals and their occupations; the second collection the numbers of marriages, christenings (not births) and burials, which allowed those who followed the new science of population statistics to estimate the rate at which the population was growing or declining, what proportion was of working age and so forth.

In an earlier century, it might have fallen to the Church to collect such data. Even at this time, in Scotland, it was parish registers collated by the local minister which recorded individual baptisms, banns and burials (see chapter 3), just as they largely wrote the Statistical Accounts. But this exercise would take a greater army of recorders than the Church could muster, and in any case it was seen as a secular exercise and the province of government. Luckily, there was already an administrative infrastructure in place. In England, the local census enumerators were usually the Overseers of the Poor. In Scotland, it tended to be the local schoolmaster (often known 'the Dominie'), along with other literate, educated and trustworthy individuals – doctors, clergymen, lawyers, merchants –acting as the army of paid volunteers. These enumerators would visit each household, institution or ship within their allocated district just before the census date and deliver a form (called a Schedule) to the Head, or the person in charge of the house, who was required to complete it for collection on the day after the night of the census. The enumerator would check the completed forms – or complete them if they were not, by questioning whoever was in – copy the information into pre-printed books of blank forms and take them to the local Registrar, who checked the data again and forwarded it on to the central office in London, where it was checked again, collated and published in summary as a Parliamentary Paper. The individual details of households and people, which would have been of great value to later generations of historians, sociologists and genealogists, were destroyed in the vast majority of cases. The summaries include the totals of:

Houses: Inhabited, By how many families occupied, Uninhabited
Persons: Males, Females
Occupations: Persons chiefly employed in agriculture, Persons chiefly employed in Trade, Manufactures, or Handicraft, All other Persons not comprised in the two preceding Classes
Total of persons: England, Wales, Scotland, Army, Navy, Seamen and Convicts

As well as the overall national summaries there were county tables organised by Hundred, Parish, Township or Extra-parochial place, and separate tables for the Cities of London and Westminster.

The diligent Mr Rickman managed to complete his work and publish the *Enumeration of England and Wales* by 21 December 1801 with Scotland following on 9 June 1802.

The 1801 census estimated the population of England at 8.3 million; Wales at 541,000; Scotland at 1.6 million; the number of those in the army, navy and merchant marine about 370,000; and 1,410 'convicts on hulks' (see box on p. 18). This made almost 11 million souls, plus a further 4 million in Ireland (estimated from hearth tax returns) and 80,000 on the Channel Islands, the Scilly Isles and the Isle of Man.

Local censuses

Some local libraries and Family History Societies have census information from 1801 for certain parishes. They can be obtained from the FHS in question, or the Scottish Genealogy Society.

PRISON HULKS

These were decommissioned warships, and were originally used to relieve overcrowding in English prisons in the 1700s. The Industrial Revolution at the end of the eighteenth century led to mass movements of people into the cities, with a consequent increase in petty crime. There were more and more debtors, and towards the end of the century, French prisoners of war. The problem the authorities had was that there were no 'national' prisons, only local gaols. Misdemeanours could be dealt with locally and the miscreants imprisoned there, but for more severe crimes (felonies) prisoners had to be transported to London. This was carried out by private contractors, who also had the idea of keeping the prisoners on derelict ships or 'hulks' in the Thames, in the Medway, off south coast ports and elsewhere. (There were also hulks in Bermuda.)

The conditions on these floating prisons were appalling, but there was no desire to go back to the old days of execution for minor crimes, so a more humane idea developed – transport them to the North American colonies. Some 50,000 transportees were settled there, but after the War of Independence in 1776 America decided it didn't want any more, thank you. Fortunately, Australia was discovered about then and provided an alternative. The first fleet (775 prisoners) went in 1786, followed by another three large transports between 1787 and 1791. They weren't all thieves and brigands. Transportees included the radical intellectual William Skirving who was arrested in Scotland with three others – Thomas Muir, John Fyshe Palmer and Maurice Margarot – for writing and publishing pamphlets on parliamentary reform. They were put on prison hulks on the Thames in preparation for their journey to Australia in 1793.

There is a persistent story that transportees temporarily housed at Millbank prison wore jackets with POM (Prisoner of Millbank) stencilled on the back, which explains why to this day Britons in Australia are called 'Poms'.

There were no prison hulks in Scotland, although the overseer of the Thames hulks was one Duncan Campbell, son of the Principal of Glasgow University, a major tobacco shipper, prisoner-transporter and slave-runner, and the man who put Captain Bligh in charge of the *Bounty* for that notorious voyage to bring breadfruit from Tahiti as cheaper food for the slaves.

Prison ships have been used since, notably for internment of Republicans during the Irish 'troubles' of 1922 and for internees during the Second World War. In 1997 the first prison ship for 200 years off mainland UK was opened off Portland, Dorset, but within ten years was due to be closed as 'unsuitable, expensive' and 'in the wrong place'. However, severe prison overcrowding again meant that the idea was revived in 2006. Interestingly, detaining prisoners of war on hulks was outlawed by the 1949 Geneva Convention.

The 1811, 1821 and 1831 censuses

The next three censuses used the same model as the 1801 census. Again, there is little individual information and no names.

More information and images of statistical summaries are available at the website of the Great Britain and Ireland Historical GIS Project based at the Centre for Data Digitisation and Analysis, The Queen's University of Belfast (www.qub.ac.uk/cdda/gis/eandw.html). There is also some limited statistical information at county and, in some cases, parish level at A Vision of Britain (www.visionofbritain.org.uk/gbhdb/index.jsp). It may be useful to know how a particular area's population changed in these years, in terms of total number, age distribution or occupations. Scottish parishes tend to have population statistics and other data available more so than for burghs, where the amount of information (and whether it was collected at all) depended to some extent on size.

For instance, the parish and royal burgh of Auchtermuchty in Fife had a population of around 2,000, and the same or fewer from 1900 to 1950. But in 1851 it peaked at over 3,700. The number of houses followed exactly the same trend (435 in 1801 and 587 in 1901 but a high of 794 in 1851), so the population surge wasn't due to the same number of families having twice as many children. Nor did the parish or burgh boundaries suddenly grow and shrink again in the nineteenth century. The answer, or a clue towards it, is in *Slater's Directory*, published in 1852, which says: 'A considerable trade is carried on here in manufacturing linen & cotton goods for Dunfermline, Dundee and Kirkcaldy houses, and this forms the principal business of the place'. Cottage handloom weaving was a major enterprise in Fife and elsewhere in the mid-1800s, but although Auchtermuchty had perhaps a thousand looms in its heyday, making linen from the flax grown in the surrounding Howe of Fife, the introduction of the steam loom and large factory-mills ended the time of hand weavers with their white trousers and blue-striped carseckie (a canvas over-shirt) working for less than 5s. (25p, about 50 cents) a week.

Census dates 1801–1911

1801 – 10 March	1811 – 27 May	1821 – 28 May	1831 – 30 May
1841 – 7 June	1851 – 30 March	1861 – April 7	1871 – 2 April
1881 – 3 April	1891 – 5 April	1901 – 31 March	1911 – 2 April

The 1841 census

With the passing of the Population Act 1840 (Act 3° & 4° Victoria, Cap. 99, intituled 'An Act for taking an Account of the Population of Great Britain'), there was a new form of census. The responsibility for this (in Scotland) lay with the Sheriff Substitute in each county, and for the first time individual names were recorded. There were stiff penalties for giving misleading information (see p. 20). As still happens today, the census enumerators delivered forms to each household, which they would later collect, check and enter into their printed book of forms. The census information we have today is from the enumerators' transcript books, as the original schedules were destroyed.

Census returns were collected according to enumeration districts (roughly equivalent to parishes, but not always exactly) and larger ones further divided into sub-districts. This was to ensure that an enumerator could reach every household on the same day, so reducing the chance of a duplicate or missed entry if someone happened to be in another house. The enumerator entered a mark to show where each household and/or building ended, and indicated whether the house was uninhabited (U) or being built (B).

Since 1855, when civil registration began, each Registration District (RD) has been given a number and this has been applied retrospectively to the 1841 and 1851 censuses, and to the pre-1855 parishes. The numbers run roughly north to south and east to west by county, and within a county are numbered by alphabetical parish or RD name. Therefore, a complete reference for an 1841 census record includes, the Parish/RD Number, Enumeration District (ED) Number, Entry Page Number, Parish/RD Name, County Name, and Census Year, such as 405/00 001/00 007 Auchterderran Fife 1841. In this case 405 is the parish or RD (Auchterderran); there may be a suffix (in this case there isn't, so it is given as /00); 001/00 is the ED, with a supplement if an additional book was required (/00 if not); 007 is the page number, but remember that this refers to the first page of a double-page, so the entry in question may in fact be on page 8 (as is the example on p. 25). A description of the district and its boundaries is given at the beginning of each new enumeration district in the records.

Understanding GROS data – example 709/01 005/00 007

Component	709	/01	005	/00	007
Refers to	Registration District (RD)	RD suffix, to locating the relevant register (not always present)	Enumeration District (ED) assigned to an enumerator	Enumeration District supplementary book, opened if necessary. 00 indicates none exists	Page Number. But check the adjacent page as a household could spread over two
In this case	Haddington, East Lothian	Haddington Burgh (/02 is Haddington Landward)			

Remember that a household may appear across two pages, so if the relevant entries are near the top or bottom of a page, check the page before or after. Genealogists should remember that not everyone listed at an address actually lived there, and not everyone who lived at an address was necessarily there on census night – this would include travellers and visitors.

The following information was recorded about every person staying at the address on the census night:

Address

Surname and first name: If, as happened in lodging-houses, hotels and inns, a person who slept there the night before went away early and the name was not known, 'NK' was written where the name should have been

Age: Correct if fifteen or under, but rounded down to nearest five years if over fifteen

Sex: Indicated by the column in which the age is recorded

Profession, trade, employment or if of independent means: Occupations were recorded as abbreviations, e.g., Ag. Lab. (agricultural labourer), Coal M (coal miner) or H.L.W. (handloom weaver). See Table 2, p. 22

Born in the county of the census: Yes, No or Not Known (NK)

Born in the country of the census: Yes or No, or sometimes S for Scotland, E for England and Wales, I for Ireland or F for Foreign Parts

---

EXTRACT from the Act 3° & 4° Victoria, Cap. 99, intituled
'An Act for taking an Account of the Population of Great Britain'
Penalty for refusing Information, or giving false Answers

XX. And the better to enable the said Commissioners, Enumerators, Schoolmasters and other Persons employed in the Execution of this Act to make the said Inquiries and Returns, be it enacted. That the said Commissioners, Enumerators, Schoolmasters and other Persons shall be authorized to ask all such Questions as shall be directed in the Instructions to be issued by the said Commissioners, with the Approval of One of Her Majesty's Principal Secretaries of State, which shall be necessary for making the preliminary Inquiries and for obtaining the Returns required by this Act; and every Person refusing to answer, or wilfully giving a false Answer to such Questions, or any of them, shall for every such Refusal or wilfully False Answer, forfeit a Sum not more than Five Pounds, nor less than Forty Shillings, at the Discretion of any Justice of the Peace or Magistrate before whom Complaint thereof shall be made.

The above may be shown by the Enumerator to any person refusing to answer, showing his authority to require an Answer, or giving an Answer which he suspects is false.

There were stiff penalties for evading or misleading the census-takers.

Problems with the 1841 census

Some parishes are known to be missing from the records. A lot of these are in Fife (See Table 1) because the records were lost overboard during their transit by boat to Edinburgh. Even though people might have moved after census night, and therefore could be counted twice, it was impossible to repeat the exercise for these fourteen Fife parishes, which represented about 30% of Fife's census data, much to the fury of genealogists ever since.

The other major problem with 1841 is the rounding error in adult ages. Ages of anyone over fifteen were rounded down to the nearest five. If someone aged thirty made a mistake, or lied, and said twenty-nine, this would be recorded as twenty-five, giving later researchers a headache when trying to establish a birth date. Someone aged thirty-four would go down as thirty. Sometimes, however, the householders or enumerators ignored this and inserted the actual age.

The 1851–1901 censuses

From 1851 on, the Head of Household was asked to provide more information which is a boon to family historians. In particular, each household was given a schedule number, the relationship of each individual to the head of the family was collected, correct ages were taken instead of adults being rounded down and there was more birthplace detail – including the place and parish of birth. (In the 1891 and 1901 census taken in Wales, there was also a question on language spoken.)

Table 1. Missing Enumeration Districts from the 1841 Scotland census. Entries for Number 93, Cromdale, Moray, can be found under Inverallan. St Kilda was also missed out, possibly because the Regional Manager did not want to travel all the way there to count the 109 souls on the island. However, a later voyager made good the omission (www.scotlandspeople.gov.uk/content/images/Inhabitants of St Kilda.pdf).

Parish Number	Parish Name	County	Parish Number	Parish Name	County
93	Cromdale	Moray★	423	Dunbog	Fifeshire
167	Seafield	Banffshire	439	Kinghorn	Fifeshire
324	Aberfeldy	Perthshire	440	Kinglassie	Fifeshire
367	Kinloch Rannoch	Perthshire	442	Kirkcaldy	Fifeshire
400	Abdie	Fifeshire	444	Leslie	Fifeshire
406	Auchtermuchty	Fifeshire	509	Cumlodden	Argyllshire
409	Balmerino	Fifeshire	535	Tarbert	Argyllshire
415	Ceres	Fifeshire	556	Lochranza	Buteshire
416	Collesie	Fifeshire	557	North Bute	Buteshire
418	Creich	Fifeshire	577	Auchinleck	Ayrshire
419	Cults	Fifeshire	776	Kirkhope	Selkirkshire
420	Cupar	Fifeshire	809	Teviothead	Roxburghshire
421	Dairsie	Fifeshire	862	Corsock Bridge	Kirkcudbrightshire

Table 2. Taken from the Instructions to Enumerators at the 1841 census. 'Alphabetical List of Abbreviations which may be used and no others, unless a large class occurs in any Enumerator's District, when, if he uses another abbreviation, it must be carefully noticed in the page left for observations of Enumerators.'

Agricultural Labourer	Ag. Lab.	To signify all Agricultural Labourers, whether in the fields, or as Shepherd, Ploughman, Carter, Waggoner, or Farm Servant generally.
Apprentice	Ap.	The letters Ap., which must be accompanied by the name of the trade, will signify Apprentice.
Army	Army.	All persons of whatever rank in the Military Land Service of Her Majesty, whether Cavalry, Infantry, Artillery, Engineers, &c. must be inserted Army – add for half-pay, H.P; for Pensioners, P.
Calico Printer	Cal. Prin.	Insert Cal. Prin. as the sign for all persons engaged in that trade.
Clerk	Cl.	All persons employed as Clerks or Book-keepers, &c. may be inserted Cl.
Factory		(See Manufacturer)
Hand Loom	H.L.W.	Always add H.L.W. to each person engaged in Weavers Hand Loom Weaving, after the words Silk, Cotton, &c. as the case may be.
Journeyman	J.	The letter J. following the name of the trade or handicraft will signify Journeyman.
Male Servant	M.S.	All Male Servants may be entered M.S. This class to include, without further distinction, all Bailiffs, Game-keepers and Domestic Servants; Butlers, Coachmen, Footmen, Grooms, Helpers, Boys, &c.
Maid Servant	F.S. (Female Servant.)	This classs to include all females emplyed in houses as House Keeper, Ladies Maids, Nurses, &c.
Maker	m.	The letter J. following the trade of any person designated as a maker.
Manufacturer	Manf.	Master Manufacturers to have Manf. following the name of the staple commodity in which they are engaged.
Merchant Seaman	Mer. S.	Add Mer. S. as the designation of all persons engaged in Merchant Service, whether in the Coasting or Foreign Trade.
Miners	M.	Always add the name of the Mineral in which each person is employed to the occupation in which he is engaged. If only general work add M. as Coal M., Copper M., Iron M.
Navy	Navy.	All persons, of whatever rank, engaged in the Sea Service of Her Majesty, whether in the Navy or Marines; must be inserted as Navy – adding H.P. for half-pay; and P. for Pensioner.
Operatives		Insert the staple commodity in which workmen are employed, as Cotton, Flax or Hemp, Silk, Woollen, Worsted, Linen, &c. &c., along with the particular designation of the branch of the trade in which the person is engaged, as Silk Throwster, Cotton Weaver, Wool Carder, &c. &c.

Power Loom Weavers	P. L. W.	Always add P.L.W. to the name of each person engaged in Power Loom Weaving, after the words Silk, Cotton, &c. as the case may be.
Shopman	Sho.	All persons employed by retail traders in their shops, must have the name of the trade prefixed to this abbreviation.
Spirit Dealers	Sp. Deal.	Add Sp. Deal. to the trade of all persons who are also engaged in vending spirits.

Data requested in the 1851, 1861, 1871, 1881, 1891 and 1901 census was as follows:

Address

Names: Surname and first name, and sometimes middle name or initial

Age (exact)

Occupation

Born (county): Name of county given

Born (country): Name of country given

Relationship to Head of Household

Condition as to marriage: Married, single, widowed, widower

Disability: Blind, deaf-and-dumb, imbecile or lunatic

DIRECTIONS

Respecting the manner in which Entries should be made in this Book.

The process of entering the Householder's Schedules, in this book should be as follows:–

The Enumerator should first insert, in the spaces at the top of the page, the name of the Parish, Quoad Sacra Parish, City or Burgh, Town or Village, to which the contents of that page will apply, drawing his pen through all the headings which are inappropriate.

He should then, in the first column write the No. of the Schedule he is about to copy, and in the second column the name of the Street, Square, &c. where the house is situate, and the No. of the house, if it has a No., or, if the house be situate in the country, any distinctive Name by which it my be known.

He should then copy from the Schedule into the other columns, all the other particulars concerning the members of the family (making use if he please of any contractions authorised by his Instructions); and proceed to deal in the same manner with the next Schedule.

Under the last name in any house he should draw a line across the page as far as the fifth column. Where there is more than one Occupier in the same house, he should draw a similar line under the last name of the family of each Occupier; making the line, however in this case, commence a little on the left hand side of the third column, as in the example on page vi. By the term 'House', must be understood 'a distinct building separated from other buildings by party-walls'. Flats, therefore, must not be entered as houses.

Where he has to insert an uninhabited house or a house building, this may be done, as in the example, by writing in the second column on the line under the last name of the last house inhabited, 'One house uninhabited', 'Three houses building', as the case may be, drawing a line underneath as in the example.

At the bottom of each page for that purpose, he must enter the total number of HOUSES in that page, separating those inhabited from those uninhabited or building. If the statement regarding any one inhabited house is continued from one page to another, that house must then be reckoned in the total of the page on which the first name is entered. He must also enter on the same line the total number of males and of females included in that page.

When he has completely entered all of the Schedules belonging to any one Parish or Quoad Sacra Parish, he should make no more entries on the LEAF on which the last name is written, but should write across the page, 'End of the Parish [or Quoad Sacra Parish] of ——'; beginning the entry of the next Schedule on the subsequent LEAF of his book. The same course must be adopted with respect to any isolated or detached portion of a distant Parish; which portion, for the sake of convenience, may have been included in his district. When he has entered all the Schedules belonging to any Burgh, Village, &c., he should make no more entries on that PAGE, but write underneath the line after the very last name, 'End of Burgh [or Village &c.] of ——'; making his next entry on the first line of the following PAGE.

In this way he will proceed until all his Householders' Schedules are correctly copied into his Book; and he must then make up the statement of totals, at page ii of this book, in the form there specified. He must also, on page iii, make up the summaries mentioned, in the form according to the instructions there given.

Directions for enumerators from the 1851 census.

Problems with the 1851 Census
MISSING CENSUS DATA

The following Registration Districts are missing from the GROS records:

277, Careston, Angus
278, Cortachy & Clova, Angus
279, Coupar Angus, Angus
280, Craig, Angus
281, Dun, Angus
597, Kilmarnock, Ayrshire
268, Strachan, Kincardineshire

There are some missing data from Bower, Canisbay, Dunnet and Halkirk, Caithness

From the census for Kirkcaldy, Fife (p. 27), we can see that one James F. Bremner, unmarried male aged twenty-five, is living at 28 High Street with his father, John, fifty, a widower, and a live-in domestic. John is a sailcloth manufacturer, originally from Arbroath, employs twenty-four men and fourteen women and is Dean of Guild. James is clerk to the local MP. The rest of that census page (not shown here) gives the occupations of the nearest neighbours – a minister and his family; a lady and her sisters and brother who are all teachers of English and Music; a confectioner; and a gentleman of private means and property. The Bremners live at the genteel end of town. Clearly John Bremner is a man of some wealth and worth in the town, and James has secured a good position with one of the most important men in Kirkcaldy and has good prospects. All he lacks is a wife.

Parish of *Auchterderran*

8

1			2			3		4	
PLACE	HOUSES		NAME and SURNAME, SEX and AGE, of each Person who abode in each House on the Night of 6th June.			OCCUPATION		WHERE BORN	
Here insert Name of Village, Street, Square, Close, Court, &c.	Uninhabited or Building	Inhabited	NAME and SURNAME	AGE		Of what Profession, Trade, Employment, or whether of Independent Means.			
				Male	Female				
Whitehall	1		Jas. Birrell	36		Ag. Lab		Y	
			Isabell Do		25			Y	
			Helen Do		6			Y	
			Ann Do		3			Y	
Sunny Side	1		Ann Greig		75			Y	
			Henry Forrester	30		Coal M		Y	
			Henry Do	8				Y	
Do	1		Agnes Bettingall		55			Y	
			Wm Bowman	15		Coal M		Y	
			Cecil Do		15			Y	
Do	1		Thos Younger	35		Coal M		Y	
			Jean Do		35			Y	
			Jean Do		5			Y	
			Wm Do	4				Y	
			Thos Do	1				Y	
			Jas Bremner	15					✓
Do	1		Janet Irvine		50			Y	
			Helen Forrester		30	Out door work		Y	
			Ann Do		25	Out door work		Y	
			Alex Do	20		Coal M		Y	
			Janet Do		20	Out door work		Y	
			Jas Do	15		Coal M		Y	
			John Do	15		Coal M		Y	
			Robt Do	5				Y	
			Robina Stark		2			Y	
TOTAL in Page 8	5			12	13				

✓ B 3

Example of an 1841 census record, in this case for Auchterderran, Fife. Notice the tally marks made by the clerks who checked and collated the census data – sometimes written over the information making it difficult to read – and the single slash (/) between households (families) within a building and the double slash (//) separating buildings. GROS 405/00 001/00 007, used with permission. Notice also James Bremner, aged 15 (and thus born about 1826), apparently living in the same building as a coal miner called Thomas Younger and his family. This is a different James Bremner – the Kirkcaldy records were lost.

PERSONS NOT IN HOUSES, AND COMPLETION OF THE ENUMERATION BOOK.

After having completed the entry of all the Enumeration Schedules according to the above directions, commence a fresh page, and writing across the top 'List of Persons not in Houses', proceed to copy from your 'Memorandum Book' the particulars contained in the list of Persons who slept in Barns, Sheds, &c. When marking up the totals at the foot of that page, the column headed 'Houses' must be left blank, as Barns, Sheds &c. are not to be reckoned as houses. Then, having satisfied yourself of the correctness of your book, fill up the tables on pages iv and v, and sign the Declaration on page vi.

CONTRACTIONS TO BE USED BY THE ENUMERATOR

ROAD, STREET, &c. – Write 'Rd.' for Road; 'St.' for Street; 'Pl.' for Place; 'Sq.' for Square; 'Ter.' for Terrace.

NAMES – Write the First Christian Name in full; Initials or first letters of the other Christian names of a person who has more than one may be inserted.

When the same surnames occur several times in succession, write 'do.' for all such surnames except the first, which should be written out in full.

When the name or any particular is not known, 'n. k.' should be entered in its place.

In the column 'RELATION TO HEAD OF FAMILY', write 'Head' for head of family; 'Daur.' for daughter; 'Serv.' for servant.

In the column 'CONDITION', write 'Mar.' for married; 'Un.' for unmarried; 'W.' for widow; 'Widr.' for widower.

In the column for AGE, write the number of years carefully and distinctly in the proper column for 'Males' or 'Females' as the case may be; in the case of Children under One Year of age, as the age is expressed in months write 'Mo.' distinctly after the figure.

In the column for 'RANK, PROFESSION, or OCCUPATION', the following contractions may be used: 'Ag. Lab.' for agricultural labourer; 'Ap.' for apprentice; 'Cl.' for clerk; 'Serv.' for servant.

Further Instructions to the enumerator, taken from the 1861 census.

Censuses after 1851

There are no further surprises in the structure of censuses from 1861 to 1901 – all ask more or less the same information and use the same layout to record the answers. However, after 1861 the administrative arrangements were different. The new Registrar General for Scotland had been appointed as a result of the 1854 Registration of Births, Deaths and Marriages (Scotland) Act and the responsibility for the censuses, as with statutory registration, fell to him. Thus, the 1861 census was the first carried out by the office of the Registrar General and the new network of local Registrars.

Generally, the census information gets more and more detailed over the years. By 1861, the number of rooms with windows was recorded. In 1871 there is information on those with, what would now be called, disabilities (deaf, dumb, blind etc.), mental health problems or learning difficulties. From 1891 we can learn employment status (employee, self-employed, employer, of independent means) and whether the individual was a Gaelic or English speaker.

Part of the 1851 census for Kirkcaldy, Fife, GROS 442/00 011/00 008, used with permission.

Part of the 1861 census for Kirkcaldy, Fife, GROS 442/00 016/00 003, used with permission.

Part of the 1871 census for Cupar, Fife, GROS 420/00 003/00 007, used with permission.

Table 3. Images of the 1881 census records are not currently available from GROS. The website produced a transcribed table similar to this. Notice that Cupar, Fife, is considered to be 'Highlands'.

Road, Street, Address &c.	Given Name	Surname	RELATION to Head	CONDITION as to Marriage	AGE	SEX	OCCUPATION	BIRTHPLACE
Sandilands	James F.	BREMNER	Head	Married	55	M	Chief Constable Of Fife	Kirkcaldy, Fife, Scotland
Sandilands	Isabella	BREMNER	Wife	Married	48	F		Kirkcaldy, Fife, Scotland
Sandilands	James F.	BREMNER	Son	Unmarried	16	M	Scholar	Cupar, Fife, Scotland
Sandilands	Mary	BREMNER	Daughter	Unmarried	14	F	Scholar	Cupar, Fife, Scotland
Sandilands	Frederick R.	BREMNER	Son	Unmarried	13	M	Scholar	Cupar, Fife, Scotland
Sandilands	Keith	BREMNER	Daughter	Unmarried	12	F	Scholar	Cupar, Fife, Scotland
Sandilands	Herbert	BREMNER	Son	Unmarried	10	M	Scholar	Cupar, Fife, Scotland
Sandilands	Lewis	BREMNER	Son	Unmarried	7	M	Scholar	Cupar, Fife, Scotland
Sandilands	Charles M.	KEITH	Boarder	Unmarried	46	M	Income From Dividends	Edinburgh, Scotland
Sandilands	Janet	MILLER	Servt	Unmarried	23	F	General Servant	Springfield, Fife, Scotland

Source: FHL Film 0203519 GRO Ref Volume 420, EnumDist 9, Page 13, 262767, Cupar, Fife, Scotland, Highlands/Lowlands. Used with permission.

The only other issues to be aware of are:

– certain 1881 Dumfriesshire records are unavailable – 821 Dumfries (Enumeration Districts 13–27) and 822 Dunscore;
– if searching the 1881 census on the GROS Scotland's People website only, images of typed transcripts are available and extracts of the original record have to be ordered. However, the whole 1881 census is being re-digitised and will be available as images in 2009.

Tracking James Bremner, we see him ten years later in 1861, a widower living alone in a large house (nine rooms with windows and in a rather good location at 14 Wemyssfield) with only a domestic servant for company. He appears to be working as a merchant of some sort.

But by 1871, James Fleming Bremner is married with children: James Fleming (aged 6); Mary (4); Frederick Russell (3); daughter Keith (2); and Herbert John (11 months). There are two nurses and a cook (Isabella obviously needs them, having children at almost annual intervals and little Louis Rae expected soon) in a large house at Cupar, where Bremner is now Chief Constable. Life has turned considerably for him in the intervening decade.

We have already seen the 1891 and 1901 censuses (page 15). We could have tracked the four sons in the same way. And there are two more clues that we might follow for more information of the Bremner genealogy – James has the middle name Fleming, which might be his mother's maiden surname or that of a close relative; and daughter Keith Bremner is obviously named for the family of Charles Maitland Keith, given as a cousin (1871) and a boarder (1881), which may be a hint as to Isabella's or James's ancestry.

Limitations on the census

Because of the need to protect the privacy of living individuals, census records are released only 100 years after they were recorded. The 1911 census will be available in 2012.

Making sense of the census

Bear in mind the following when you hit the inevitable 'brick wall':

– the census records for the parish of your interest may just be missing.
– married women were usually, but not always, recorded by the married surname. However, if the maiden surname is given, it is not necessarily the case that the couple was unmarried. Also, widows sometimes reverted to their maiden names and children often took the name of the stepfather if the mother remarried. Check married and maiden surnames if at all possible.
– if the birthplace of a child (especially the eldest) is different from that of the parents or the census place, it may be that the mother had gone back to her family for her first birth. This can be a valuable clue as to the address of her parents.
– it is often said that people did not move around much in the nineteenth century. But it only took the opening or closing of a mine or a mill, or better work available in a nearby parish, for someone to disappear from one district and turn up in another. Especially if the district is near a county boundary, check the neighbouring county, and always check adjoining parishes.
– it is also worth checking nearby workhouses, hospitals, asylums, prisons, barracks, and prison hulks, and any ships or other vessels.

Finding census records

The census is available in various forms – on the web, as microfilm and in print.

Online

The most convenient source of census information is via the web.

Scotland's People, the 'official' GROS website, has indexes and digital images (where available) from all censuses from 1841 to 1901, with 1911 to be added in 2012. It is necessary to buy credits in blocks of 30 for £6 which must be used within a certain time limit. After this time, unused credits cannot be redeemed unless more credits are bought. It costs 1 credit to view a page of up to 25 results and 5 credits (= £1) to view an image (one credit for an 1881 transcript). So a search which produced 250 results would cost 10 credits and viewing four digital images (which can be printed or downloaded) would cost a further 20 credits. Bear in mind that all family or household members are likely to be on one page. So if you happened to want every image of the 34 Lumsdens recorded in Dysart in the 1891 census, it would cost 2 credits for the two pages (25 + 9) and 40 credits for the eight images on which they appear, a total of 42 credits. You would most likely have to buy 60 credits at a cost of £12, and £1.50 is a reasonable average amount to pay per image. However, if you only wanted one image, it would have cost you £6 (30 credits, but only 2 + 5 used), and the remaining 23 credits would become unavailable after 90 days unless another 30 were purchased. The best advice is to save up searches for when 30 will be needed, or share a session with someone else. If you happened to want many more images of records for a more popular surname, it would be expensive. However, once a search or an image is purchased with credits, it can be visited again and again at no additional cost. Where there is no image available, or if you want an extract★ sent to you, this can be ordered online, at an additional cost of £10/$20. To view and download a digital image of an original will, testament or inventory (actual size) costs £5/$10 per document regardless of its length. Be aware that these require a separate credit card transaction and are not covered by credits.

Ancestry.co.uk has indexed transcriptions (no images) of the Scottish census returns. The cost of this unlimited-download subscription service – which also allows address and keyword searches – should be balanced against the cost of pay-per-view at Scotland's People. A good and cost-effective technique is to find the required person or family at Ancestry or FreeCen (www.freecen.org.uk) then access the image at Scotland's People.

Where to find census data

Census returns for 1841–1901 can be consulted at the General Register Office for Scotland in Edinburgh. The LDS Family History Centres worldwide have copies on microfilm and microfiche indexes to the 1881 census returns. GROS also has statistical data on more recent censuses (e.g. 1991 and 2001) and SCROL (Scottish Census Results On Line) has an impressive array of statistical and demographic information from the 2001 census, but nothing at the individual level. See www.scrol.gov.uk.

The indexes for the 1851, 1861, 1871, 1881, 1891 and 1901 censuses have been computerised and are available at the Scotland's People Centre in Edinburgh, and online (after registration and payment) at Scotland's People (www.scotlandspeople.gov.uk). At the time of writing this includes images of the 1851, 1861, 1871, 1891 and 1901 censuses and facsimile or full transcript for 1881, with indexes and images for 1841 being added. Typically, an index entry will give the surname, forename, age, registration district name and number, enumeration district and

---

★ There is a difference between a Statutory Record and an extract – a digital image is merely a copy of the register page containing the entry you specified (and possibly several others), whereas an extract is a certified, legal copy of one specific register entry for one named individual. There may be circumstances where this is necessary – proving inheritance in court, for instance – but for most genealogical purposes the information in the image (or even the data in the index entry) will be enough.

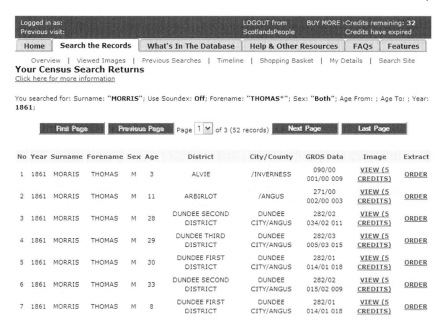

Part of the results page from an 1861 census search for MORRIS, THOMAS. The full search produced 52 results over 3 pages, with a maximum of 25 per page. Reproduced with permission.

page number and therefore indicates the full household entry on microfilm. At the Scotland's People site an initial surname search is free and covers all records, including the available census, OPR and statutory indexes and the index of wills and testaments. This has the merit of showing how many records are in the various datasets before committing to pay.

What you get for your money

A 25-name search produces a listing as above. The search was in the 1861 census for MORRIS, THOMAS and produced fifty-two results, over three pages (only the top of page 1 is shown, with seven of the first twenty-five results). There is also a printer-friendly version which strips out the navigation aids at the top and has the added advantages that it can be printed as a paper record (ALWAYS DO THIS!), and cut-and-pasted into a spreadsheet, database or Word document, but not without some re-formatting.

A digital image of a selected name (5 credits) is shown on p. 32. Bear in mind that an image shows a household (and neighbouring households) so you may find all the family members you want on one or two images. Notice the ability to zoom, save, print and other options. As a matter of course, both save the image (the options are PCX, TIFF or CALS Type I, and you will have to specify the directory path to wherever you store your document images) and print it (remembering to specify landscape format and the appropriate quality). Printing the web page directly or saving a snapshot of it to a graphics file will produce a low-resolution image. Save and print it in as high a resolution as possible (usually 600 dpi).

Other census resources

The Scotland's People website, although excellent, is considered expensive by many who undertake regular searches. Fortunately there are other options, though not, as yet, so complete.

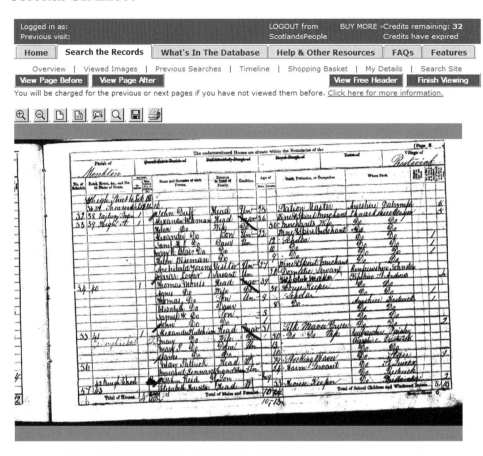

The full page containing a view of an 1861 census register entry. Reproduced with permission.

Scotland census finder (www.censusfinder.com/scotland.htm) is a website listing other sites which offer free census records online. Part of Brenda Hay's commendable the Censusfinder site (www.censusfinder.com), this carries lists of census indexes, organised by county, with hyperlinks. It is particularly useful for 1841 and 1851 returns, but of course, is only as good as the records themselves, which are produced and maintained by others. For example, the listing for Fife as of January 2006 was:

FIFE .

1841 Census Index of Scoonie Parish

1841 Census of Scoonie Parish

1851 Census Downloads

1851 Census (partial)

1851 Census of Dysart (partial)

1851 Census of Saline Parish

1851 Census of Schoonie Parish Part 1

1851 Census of Schoonie Parish Part 2

1851 Census of Strathmiglo ED 1–3

1851 Census of Strathmiglo ED 4–6

1851 Census of Wemyss Parish, Buckhaven (East)

1851 Census of Wemyss Parish, Buckhaven (West)

1851 Census of Wemyss Parish, Coaltown of Wemyss

1851 Census of Wemyss Parish, Kirkland

1851 Census of Wemyss Parish, Methilhill

1851 Census of Wemyss Parish, Methil

1851 Census of Wemyss Parish, Wemyss (East)

1851 Census of Wemyss Parish, Wemyss (West)

1851 Census Strays Found in England

OTHER RECORDS

Kingdom of Fife Surnames List

Fife, Scotland: Parish and Probate Records Search at Ancestry

© 2002–2005 Brenda Hay and reproduced here with permission.

This should not lead you to believe that each link is to a complete census set. Many of these are in the process of being transcribed, or are census data samples. The link to the 1841 Census Index of Scoonie Parish (member.melbpc.org.au/~andes/scooniex.html) is to a website maintained by Australian genealogist Alexander Romanov-Hughes, and he is to be applauded for it. An example of his Surname Index (below) gives enough information to see if an individual can be tentatively identified, and gives a reference to the Enumeration District and page, which should save time in searching a microfilm or fiche.

Name	Age	Enumeration District	Page Number
ADAMS, Isabella	14	E.D.6	6
ADAMS, Benjamin	40	E.D.5	17
ADAMS, Elizabeth	5	E.D.5	17
ADAMS, Janet	30	E.D.5	17
ADAMS, John	8	E.D.5	17
ADAMSON, Agnes	20	E.D.3	6
ADAMSON, Agnes	60	E.D.2	5
ADAMSON, Alexander	20	E.D.3	14
ADAMSON, Andrew	40	E.D.3	2
ADAMSON, Ann	6	E.D.5	3
ADAMSON, Ann	14	E.D.2	8

© 2002–2005 Alexander Romanov-Hughes and reproduced here with permission.

Mr Romanov-Hughes has only transcribed certain parishes in Kinross and one in Fife, and has no plans to do more. But step forward Drew Heggie, who has done a masterful job in marshalling vaious early censuses (members.aol.com/drewhss/drew.htm), and David Stuart, who has pulled over 64,000 names from the 1851 census into a searchable database, though not always with complete accuracy, as Mr Stuart is the first to admit (hometown.aol.co.uk/ Genealogyscot/Page80.html). Bear in mind that the population of Scotland in 1851 was almost 2.9 million, so this represents just over 2%. It does, however, have the merit of including more than just names, for example:

County	Surname	Given Name	Relation	Marriage Status	Age	Occupation	Birth County	Birth Parish	Address
AYR	DOSK	EUWAR	Wife	Mar	49		AYR	IRVINE	91 MONTGOMERIE LANE
AYR	DOSK	JANET	Daur	UN	15	Muslin sewer	AYR	IRVINE	91 MONTGOMERIE LANE
AYR	DOSK	THOMAS	Grd son		4		AYR	SALTCOATS	91 MONTGOMERIE LANE

© 2005 David Stuart and reproduced here with permission.

There are many other worthy amateurs (in the original and honourable meaning of the word) beavering away to get census data online.

FreeCen Scotland (freecen.rootsweb.com) is part of the larger FreeUKGEN project, which aims, in time, to have all registration data and other primary (or near-primary) records of genealogical relevance available free online. There are equivalent FreeBMD (civil registrations of births, marriages and deaths) and FreeREG (church records) projects, all transcribed by a network of over 2,000 volunteers worldwide. FreeCen Scotland concentrates on the 1841 and some 1851 records, and while not yet complete, is subject to a high degree of checking and error trapping. Searches are by surname, but can be narrowed down by census places and counties, age, occupation and other filters. The output is the basic information, viz:

Surname	First name(s)	Sex	Age	Occupation	Where Born	Census Place
DURIE	(Mrs)	F	40		Outside Census County (1841)	Barony
DURIE	(Mrs)	F	40		Outside Census County (1841)	Gorbals
DURIE	Adam	M	18	Agricultural Labourer	Midlothian	Cranston

But there is the option of showing an entire household:

Piece: SCT1841/622 Place: Barony-Lanarkshire Enumeration; District: 30
Civil Parish: Barony Ecclesiastical Parish; Village or Island: Anderston
Folio: 30; Page: 5
Address: Clyde Street

Surname	First name(s)	Sex	Age	Occupation	Where Born	Remarks
DURIE	(Mrs)	F	40		Outside Census County (1841)	
DURIE	Margaret	F	15	Straw Hat Maker	Outside Census County (1841)	
DURIE	Isabella	F	10		Lanarkshire	
CAMPBELL	William	M	15	Baker	Outside Census County (1841)	

Other sources of census data

Gordon Johnson of KinHelp (www.kinhelp.co.uk) has produced the highly useful *Census Records for Scottish Families at Home and Abroad* (ISBN 0 947659 74 9, £6/$12 plus P&P). This is available from many Family History Societies and elsewhere, including Aberdeen & N.E. Scotland FHS (www.anesfhs.org.uk) and the Scottish Association of Family History Societies (www.safhs.org.uk). It includes a listing of census holdings in Scottish libraries and archives and details of census records in other countries.

There is also Peter Ruthven-Murray's small booklet *Scottish Census Indexes, 1841–1871* available from many Family History Societies (22pp, £2/$4 plus P&P). It contains lists of the counties and parishes as they existed in the nineteenth century and up to the local government reorganisations in May 1975.

Many Family History Societies have compiled indexes of local censuses. Most will send a list on request, or have such lists available on their websites. But do remember that information so copied can only be used for your personal use, and not republished or put on a website without the formal permission of the Queen's Printer for Scotland.

Ancestry has now indexed all Scottish censuses up to 1901 from GROS microfilms as transcripts. Digital images of the records may be added. The advantage to using Ancestry is that once the subscription is paid, all searches and downloads are free thereafter. The annual fee for the British-only Ancestry site is about £70, £10 for a one-month trial or £5 for 10 record views within fourteen days. The World Deluxe annual subscription is £200 (useful if US or other country sources are required) which may be worthwhile compared with £6 per session from GROS. See www.ancestry.com or www.ancestry.co.uk.

Others include individuals who have transcribed census details of: one county or a sample of that county (e.g. 1841 Kinross & Fife at www.member.melbpc.org.au/~andes); one or more parish or town (e.g. 1861 Strathdon, Aberdeen at www.mywebpages.comcast.net/dcoreilly); a single surname (e.g. BAIRD at www.bairdnet.com); or all of one person's relatives wherever they may be (e.g. Terry's Relative Finder at www.freepages.genealogy.rootsweb.com/~relys4u).

There are lists of such resources maintained at UKBMD (www.ukbmd.org.uk) and at CensusFinder (www.censusfinder.com/scotland.htm).

You searched for: Surname: **LUMSDEN**; Use Soundex: **Off**; Forename: ★★★★; Sex: **Both**; Age From; Age To; Year: **1891**; County: **FIFE**; District: **DYSART**;

Table 4. The printed output from an 1891 census search at www.scotlandspeople.gov.uk sorted by GROS Data and Age; this allows for easy identification of likely family groups or households (which will be on the same page) and the identities of the parents. If you only need the basic information (Name, Age, GROS Data) then the search results pages can be printed or cut-and-pasted into a document or spreadsheet.

No	Year	Surname	Forename	Sex	Age	District	City/County	GROS Data
24	1891	LUMSDEN	JOHN	M	53	DYSART	/FIFE	426/00 003/00 016
25	1891	LUMSDEN	JOHN	M	18	DYSART	/FIFE	426/00 003/00 016
20	1891	LUMSDEN	JAMES	M	16	DYSART	/FIFE	426/00 003/00 016
11	1891	LUMSDEN	ELIZABETH	F	13	DYSART	/FIFE	426/00 003/00 016
22	1891	LUMSDEN	JANE	F	11	DYSART	/FIFE	426/00 003/00 016
17	1891	LUMSDEN	GEORGE	M	8	DYSART	/FIFE	426/00 003/00 016
9	1891	LUMSDEN	DAVID	M	5	DYSART	/FIFE	426/00 003/00 016
28	1891	LUMSDEN	ROBERT	M	3	DYSART	/FIFE	426/00 003/00 016
10	1891	LUMSDEN	DAVID	M	2	DYSART	/FIFE	426/00 005/00 006
7	1891	LUMSDEN	DAVID	M	27	DYSART	/FIFE	426/00 005/00 025
12	1891	LUMSDEN	EUPHEMIA	F	25	DYSART	/FIFE	426/00 005/00 025
29	1891	LUMSDEN	THOMAS	M	3	DYSART	/FIFE	426/00 005/00 025
13	1891	LUMSDEN	EUPHEMIA	F	0	DYSART	/FIFE	426/00 005/00 025
33	1891	LUMSDEN	WILLIAM	M	29	DYSART	/FIFE	426/00 010/00 001
27	1891	LUMSDEN	MARY	F	24	DYSART	/FIFE	426/00 010/00 001
14	1891	LUMSDEN	EUPHEMIAW	F	4	DYSART	/FIFE	426/00 010/00 001
2	1891	LUMSDEN	ALEXIS	F	41	DYSART	/FIFE	426/00 013/00 004
31	1891	LUMSDEN	WILLIAM	M	40	DYSART	/FIFE	426/00 013/00 004
34	1891	LUMSDEN	WILLIAM	M	21	DYSART	/FIFE	426/00 013/00 004
4	1891	LUMSDEN	ANDREW	M	18	DYSART	/FIFE	426/00 013/00 005
	1891	LUMSDEN	AGNES	F	16	DYSART	/FIFE	426/00 013/00 005
16	1891	LUMSDEN	GEORGE	M	14	DYSART	/FIFE	426/00 013/00 005
8	1891	LUMSDEN	DAVID	M	11	DYSART	/FIFE	426/00 013/00 005
18	1891	LUMSDEN	HELEN	F	9	DYSART	/FIFE	426/00 013/00 005
3	1891	LUMSDEN	ALEXIS	F	7	DYSART	/FIFE	426/00 013/00 005
26	1891	LUMSDEN	MAGGIE	F	6	DYSART	/FIFE	426/00 013/00 005
30	1891	LUMSDEN	THOMAS	M	2	DYSART	/FIFE	426/00 013/00 005
19	1891	LUMSDEN	JAMES	M	23	DYSART	/FIFE	426/00 014/00 017
5	1891	LUMSDEN	ANN	F	22	DYSART	/FIFE	426/00 014/00 017
6	1891	LUMSDEN	ANN	F	0	DYSART	/FIFE	426/00 014/00 017
32	1891	LUMSDEN	WILLIAM	M	37	DYSART	/FIFE	426/00 014/00 028
23	1891	LUMSDEN	JANET	F	32	DYSART	/FIFE	426/00 014/00 028
21	1891	LUMSDEN	JAMES	M	2	DYSART	/FIFE	426/00 014/00 028
15	1891	LUMSDEN	FRED	M	0	DYSART	/FIFE	426/00 014/00 028

Local Family History Societies often have census indexes for parishes in their areas, either printed or available online at the relevant FHS site. Consult SAFHS or the Scottish Genealogy Society for lists of these.

Microform

Census images are available as microfilm or microfiche at various places, chiefly New Register House in Edinburgh, local libraries, Family History Society premises and LDS Family History Centres. Bear in mind that local facilities may only have census data for that parish, area or county, and perhaps those adjoining. These films and fiches cannot be searched by name, only by place, so the first best step is to identify the individuals in question through an Internet search or other index (see below), then use the GROS data to identify the correct reel for that parish, enumeration district and page.

Using the 1881 Census Index on microfiche

Remember that there are, at the time of writing, no images available for this census, only indexes. There are four parts to the fiche version.

People Index – individuals listed in alphabetical order by surname, given name, and age, plus other details including relationship to Head of Household

Birthplace Index – people in alphabetical order by surname and birthplace, for example, all Bremners born in Abbotshall, Fife, will be grouped together, regardless of whether they are related. This index does not contain all the other census information

Census Place Index – individuals in alphabetical order by surname and census place, for example, all Bremners recorded in Abbotshall, Fife, will be grouped together, regardless of relationship. Again not all enumerators' information is in this index

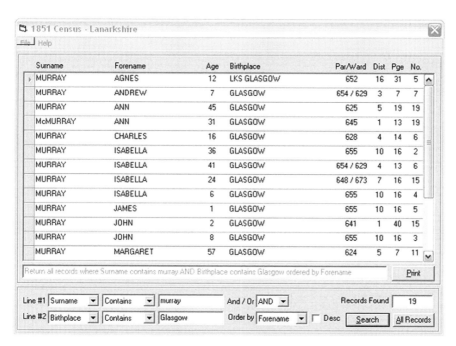

An honourable exception: the 1851 census for Lanarkshire (which included Glasgow) from the Lanarkshire FHS. Note the flexibility of searching in the interface.

Enumerators List – places and individuals in the order in which they appear on the Census. Use the reference numbers from the other indexes to find the page. This shows complete households, not just family members

Printed and CD versions

Local Family History Societies often have census indexes and street indexes available for purchase as printed booklets, parish by parish, and sometimes as whole counties on CD-ROM. Again, the SAFHS or the Scottish Genealogy Society may have these for sale, or details of the FHS in question. They are usually available at the many Family History fairs up and down the country and for sale online.

LDS Family History Centres and local libraries may have these booklets or CDs available for consultation free of charge.

There are also commercial companies who produce census records on CD, and as good a place as any to start is S&N Genealogy Supplies www.genealogysupplies.com, although the local FHS may also have them for sale. The image quality and indexing on CDs is variable, so try to see one in use first.

General difficulties with census records

Genealogists are always advised to consult original records where possible, However, even original sources can be incomplete or just wrong and census records are no different. Add to this the inevitable errors that will creep in during indexing and transcribing, and it is clear why nothing can be taken at face value. Knowing what the likely problems are and how they occur should help in recognising them when they arise.

NOT COLLECTED OR LOST

As seen above, various Fife parish records for the 1841 census were lost. Others are missing for different reasons.

INFORMATION PARTIAL

The 1841 census contains much less information than later exercises – little or no birthplace information, for example, and adults' ages rounded down. In all censuses, there are individuals for whom some information is simply not recorded.

INFORMATION NOT GIVEN OR WRONGLY GIVEN

Despite the severe warnings and penalties for giving wrong or no details, it still happened. Unmarried women claimed to be married and took the surname of the 'husband'; ages were given wrongly, especially when there were implications of eligibility for military service, factory work or marriage. Some individuals were simply unclear about where or when they were born.

Enumerators, officials at institutions, ships' captains and proprietors of boarding houses made mistakes when recording information, but they may have been given wrong information in the first place and transmitted it in good faith. Someone living in a hotel with a good reason not to provide a true name, age and occupation could easily provide alternatives. In prisons, asylums and hospitals, and in the armed services, there must have been many who either did not know, or had changed or simply invented details about themselves.

Many women were prostitutes in the nineteenth century, but few would have recorded that on the form. 'Dressmaker' and 'Of independent means' were common euphemisms. Children listed as 'scholars' (i.e. at school) may have in fact been sent out to work; if under-age, their parents were breaking the law.

INFORMATION WRONGLY RECORDED OR TRANSFERRED

Illiteracy was common, especially in the earlier nineteenth century, and many individuals asked friends, neighbours or enumerators to help them complete the forms. Any spelling or numerical errors may not have been spotted. Where the official in charge of a ship, hospital, school, prison etc. took notes and transferred the information onto the census form, there was the possibility for errors at both stages. Typical mistakes were in spelling names, recording ages or writing down occupations. Occasionally, enumerators misheard (see below).

A likely example of an enumerator mishearing. Christian and David 'Dairy' were in fact Durie. It is known (from other records) that the son, David, was illiterate and perhaps his mother was too, and so unable to correct the mistake. Her maiden name was, in fact, Laing. 'Unmarried' obviously means 'widowed' here. Taken from the 1851 census for Dysart, Fife, with permission.

INFORMATION WRONGLY TRANSCRIBED OR KEYED

There is many a slip between record and transcription. Genealogists are eternally grateful to all the volunteers and commercial organisations who have indexed and transcribed the various censuses plus other records, but despite checks, error-trapping and validation routines, glitches do still get through. There are examples of 'John Smith Senior' being indexed as if 'Senior' were the surname.

Taken from the 1841 Scottish census, Dunfermline – Durie.

Two examples of mis-transcription are shown on p. 40, with the index data from both Ancestry.com and GROS given for comparison. In the first example (Table 5), the Ancestry transcribers have mistaken Durie (correct) for Dwire and have completely missed David's occupation (Coal Miner). That said, at least their transcript gives the address and occupation, and helpfully works out the likely birth year; in GROS, such information has to be paid for by buying the image.

In the second example, also from 1841 (p. 41), the major error is a simple misreading of the form. Andrew Durie (third from bottom) has been correctly identified, but his wife and daughter have had their 'Ditto' confused with that of the family above, and listed as Wattsons.

Census Headers

At the beginning of each census book is a description of the district concerned. This can be helpful in deciphering the names of streets or finding the position of addresses which

Table 5. – ANCESTRY.COM

| Mary Dwire | abt 1821 | Fife, Scotland | Dunfermline | Fife | 424 | 26 | 4 | 20 | Golfdrum Str | | Female |
| David Dwire | abt 1821 | Fife, Scotland | Dunfermline | Fife | 424 | 26 | 4 | 20 | Golfdrum Str | Con C W | Male |

Table 6. – GROS

| DURIE | MARY | F | 20 | DUNFERMLINE | /FIFE | 424/00 026/00 003 |
| DURIE | DAVID | M | 20 | DUNFERMLINE | /FIFE | 424/00 026/00 003 |

Table 7. – ANCESTRY.COM

| Mary Wattson | abt 1786 | Fife, Scotland | Kettle | Fife | 435 | 4 | 11 | 55 | Kettle | | Female |
| Margret Wattson | abt 1831 | Fife, Scotland | Kettle | Fife | 435 | 4 | 11 | 10 | Kettle | F S | Female |

Table 8. – GROS

DURIE	ANDREW	M	65	KETTLE	/FIFE	435/00 004/00 011
DURIE	MARY	F	55	KETTLE	/FIFE	435/00 004/00 011
DURIE	MARGRET	F	16	KETTLE	/FIFE	435/00 004/00 011

Taken from the 1841 Scottish census, Kettle – Durie.

have disappeared in the years since. On microfilm, check the beginning of each district. On www.scotlandspeople.gov.uk click the 'View Free Header' tab above a census image.

Onomastics

No, it isn't some kind of dental cement; onomastics is to do with naming, which is the very stuff of genealogy.

First, there is the spelling issue. This was standardised, especially for names, only comparatively recently. Even when almost everyone could read and write, many simply spelled what they heard. The David Durie who appeared as 'Dairy' in the census above later managed to get himself married under the name 'Derry'. Quite possibly, he mumbled. The Mc/Mac controversy rolls on, with some writers even suggesting that one is Scottish and one Irish. This is nonsense. All Scottish surnames of this type are Mac (meaning son of) but were often abbreviated at Mc or even M' so that MacKay could be written as McKay, M'Kay, Mackay etc. Spelling was largely a toss of the coin until names got recorded somewhere official (such as in a birth record after Statutory Registration, or in an earlier sasine for example); and so the same could be said for Johnson/Johnston/Johnstone or Thomson/Thomsson/Thompson. Check all variants.

Marriage and re-marriage are obvious reasons for a name change. But there are also professional, personal and political reasons for this. A bigamist, convicted felon or fraudster would have good reason to find a brand new surname. The celebrated Victorian novelist and detective story author James Edward Muddock, living in Dundee in the 1880s, changed his first names to Joyce Emmerson Preston (Muddock), which has led to him being included in several databases of female authors. For similar professional reasons Diana Fluck became Diana Dors, and who can blame her?

Others again changed their names from Gaelic to a more anglicised form, either for convenience (Rory O'Connor is a great deal easier to spell than Ruaidhri O Conchobhair, but sounds the same), or to suit the political milieu.

Given names

The Scots have always used interchangeable first names and diminutives, such as Meg, Maggie and Peggy for Margaret; Eliza, Lizzie, Liza, Lisbet, Beth or Betty for Elizabeth; Isa, Bel, Isabelle or Issie for Isobel; and Janet, Jean, Jane or Jessie for each other. Jackie may have been christened John; Andy was almost certainly baptised Andrew; Tam, Tom and Tommy are really Thomas.

Adding to that confusion, enumerators (or the individuals themselves) would abbreviate names – Thos for Thomas; Jas for James; Rbt for Robert; Alexr for Alexander.

Remember also that in the decade between two censuses a lot may have happened to a person or a family – a marriage or even two resulting in a wholesale name change, not just for the wife but all the children; or a radical change in fortune (up or down) necessitating a change in surname. When James Oswald Murray (surname Murray) decided that Oswald Murray had a better ring to it as a surname for a portrait painter, he confused art historians and others for over a century.

Scottish naming patterns

This is one instance where the Scots' adherence to tradition is useful. Often an eldest son would be named for the paternal grandfather, an eldest daughter for the maternal grandmother, the next son for the maternal grandfather, the next daughter for the paternal grandmother, the third son after the father, third daughter after the mother and other children after aunts and uncles etc. This is confusing where a number of families live in close proximity, especially if they share an ancestor, but can sometimes give a valuable clue as to family relationships. It is quite possible for a whole set of first cousins, and their uncles, to have the same first name. However, an unusual first name might repeat itself every other generation down a single line.

There was also a tradition to give children two or three names, but call them after the last of these. So, a David John Brian Dempster may be recorded (officially) as David but called Brian throughout his life. He may appear as David John Brian, David J. B. etc. on birth, marriage and death records, but Brian on census returns.

Remember, too, that often when a child died young, a later child was given the same name. So a Tom Morris, aged 1 in the 1871 census should not be confused with a Tom Morris born to the same family in 1873. Check birth and death records to confirm.

Moving around

It was noted earlier that people did move around to a degree, whether it was agricultural labourers who changed from farm to farm on term days, fee'd themselves at markets to different farmers and moved to different rented accommodation on quarter days. There was seasonal work, and times when mills, mines or new factories opened up or closed. Miners and weavers in particular moved around the country. And, of course, there was a great deal of migration in the late eighteenth and early nineteenth centuries – from the Highlands to industrial cities, for example, as well as transportation and, after that, mass emigration to the USA, Canada, South America, Australia, New Zealand and elsewhere. Many people went to work in India, or joined the armed services and moved abroad.

For this reason, if no other, a genealogist might have to delve into English or Irish records, or even into the murky waters of ships' passenger lists, immigration records and overseas census and death records.

Young, unmarried women were often in domestic service and living with their employers rather than their families. Young, unmarried agricultural labourers would frequently live in a communal dormitory or bothy and be counted as part of the farm household on census night. It was not uncommon for assistants in large department stores to live on the premises, or together in accommodation provided by the employer.

A sailor may have been at sea on the census night – both the Royal Navy and Merchant Service lists will appear under 'shipping' rather than a county – or in dock elsewhere in Scotland or at an English port, in which case he would be recorded at the ship's address.

Medical staff working in hospitals, prison wardens, policemen, factory night-shift workers and others would be recorded at those institutions instead of their home addresses. The same is true of schoolchildren, if at boarding school, and university students.

People who were not where they 'should' be on a particular census night – working away from home, visiting friends, staying at an hotel – were collectively known as 'Census Strays'. There are websites and other resources dedicated to identifying these, such as in Tommy Manson's *Fife Post* (www.thefifepost.com/censusstraysinengland.htm).

Sometimes it is only by cross-referring to birth, marriage and death records that an individual missing from a census can be tracked down. But fortunately, there are also census substitutes (see chapter 4).

English Censuses

These are extremely similar to Scottish censuses. They are available as partial transcripts and images at ancestry.co.uk or ancestry.com by agreement with The National Archives (www.nationalarchives.gov.uk/census) for 1841 to 1891, and at www.1901censusonline.com for 1901, which allows search by Person, Address, Vessel or Institution. All of the census years are free to search, but image downloads are charged. FreeCen has many of the censuses transcribed.

Most local and county record offices in England have microfilm or microfiche copies of the census returns for their areas, as do many large libraries, and the LDS Family History Centres have or can obtain all of these. In addition, IGI and familysearch.org have the 1881 censuses for the whole British Isles.

Irish Censuses

Remember that until 1922 Ireland was one country, and part of the Unitd Kingdom. Therefore, do not necessarily expect records relating to the (present-day) Northern Ireland to be in Belfast or Republic records to be in Dublin.

The census started in Ireland in 1821. That sounds like good news, but almost all nineteenth century census returns were pulped for paper during the First World War (1861, 1871, 1881 and 1891), or destroyed during the Easter uprising (1821, 1831, 1841 and 1851). However, a few census fragments and surnames indexes exist for some areas, chiefly Co. Fermanagh for 1821, Co. Londonderry for 1831 and Co. Antrim for 1851. The 1901 and 1911 censuses can be seen at The National Archives of Ireland in Dublin. The normal 100 year rule for census availability has been relaxed because all but 1901 and 1911 are intact.

The National Archives of Ireland has a project to digitise and put online all of the 1901 and 1911 Irish censuses. Dublin, Kerry, Antrim and Down for 1911 are already available at www.census.nationalarchives.ie and other counties will follow throughout 2009. Ireland is unusual in that the original household manuscript returns – the forms filled in by the head of the household – still survive, as well as the Enumerators' books. The records are organised by County; District Electoral Division; and Townland or Street. Irish censuses are particularly detailed. As well as the usual name, address, occupation, age and other details familiar to anyone looking at Scottish or English censuses, the Irish also recorded religion, the number of years women had been married, the number of their children born alive and the number still living.

Old age pension records, which have some of the information from the 1841 and 1851 censuses, are at the Public Record Office, Dublin and the Public Record Office of Northern Ireland (PRONI) in Belfast.

Bibliography

SPECIFICALLY SCOTTISH

Escott, Anne, *Census Returns and Old Parochial Registers on Microfilm: A directory of public library holdings in the West of Scotland*, Glasgow District Libraries (1986).

Johnson, Gordon, *Census Records for Scottish Families at Home and Abroad*, 3rd edn, Aberdeen: Aberdeen & North East Scotland Family History Society (1997).

Ruthven-Murray, Peter, *Scottish Census Indexes: Covering the 1841–1871 Civil Censuses*, Aberdeen: Scottish Association of Family History Societies (1998).

GENERAL

Christian, Peter and Annal, David, *Census: The Expert Guide*, The National Archives (2008).

Gibson, Jeremy and Hampson, Elizabeth, *Marriage and Census Indexes for Family Historians*, 8th edn, Bury: Federation of Family History Societies (2000).

——, *Census Returns 1841–1881 in Microform: A directory to local holdings in Great Britain; Channel Islands; Isle of Man*, 6th edn, Bury: Federation of Family History Societies (2001).

Gibson, Jeremy and Medlycott, Mervyn, *Local Census Listings, 1522–1930: Holdings in the British Isles*, 3rd edn, Bury: Federation of Family History Societies (2001).

Higgs, Edward, *A Clearer Sense of the Census, the Victorian Censuses and Historical Research*, Public Record Office Handbooks, No. 28, London, HMSO (1996).

Mills, Dennis and Schurer, Kevin (eds), *Local Communities in the Victorian Census Enumerators' Books*, Oxford: Leopard's Head Press (1996).

Riggs, Geoff, *Distribution of Surnames in the 1881 British Census*, London: Guild of One-Name Studies (2001).

Using Census Returns, Richmond: Public Record Office (2000) – Public Record Office pocket guides to family history.

Wood, Tom, *An Introduction to British Civil Registration*, 2nd edn, Bury: Federation of Family History Societies (2000).

OTHER RESOURCES

GROS has a downloadable list of Registration Districts from 1855 in Excel (spreadsheet) and PDF versions at www.gro-scotland.gov.uk/famrec/hlpsrch/list-of-parishes-registration-districts.html.

There is useful information on individual Registration Districts (actually, parishes) in the Statistical Accounts of Scotland (see page xxx), mainly written by the parish minister, in the 1790s and 1830s–1840s. These are available in print in most large libraries and online from EDINA, a national datacentre based at Edinburgh University Data Library www.edina.ac.uk/stat-acc-scot (requires registration).

Official GROS site: www.scotlandspeople.gov.uk
Ancestry: www.ancestry.com or www.ancestry.co.uk
FreeCen: www.freecen.org.uk
UKBMD: www.ukbmd.org.uk
Census Finder: www.censusfinder.com/scotland.htm
Scottish Association of Family History Societies: www.safhs.org.uk

Of Kingborn. 229

NUMBER XIX.

TOWN AND PARISH OF KINGHORN.

(COUNTY AND SYNOD OF FIFE, PRESBYTERY OF KIRKCALDY.)

By the Rev. Mr. JOHN USHER.

Situation, Name, Extent, Soil, &c.

THE town of Kinghorn, is pleafantly fituated upon a de-
clivity on the N. fide of the Frith of Forth, nearly
oppofite to the town of Leith, and diftant from it about 7
miles. At what time this town was firft built, it is perhaps,
impoffible for us, at prefent, to determine. It is not impro-
bable, that the aborigines of the country, would fettle here,
at a very early period, for the conveniency of fifhing *, even
before either commerce, or agriculture, or pafturage, had
become objects of attention to their uncultivated minds. However this may be, it is next to certain, that when Edinburgh
began to rife into a capital, and to become a place of refort,
fifhermen

* There was formerly a confiderable quantity of fifh caught between the
town of Kinghorn and the ifland of Inch-Keith; but of late the fifh have retired nearer to the mouth of the Frith.

The Statistical Account of Scotland, 1791–99, vol. 12, p. 229: Kinghorn, Fife. Notice the 'Frith of Forth'
and the antique 's' as in 'fifhing' and 'refort'. This, and the new Statistical Account (1830s), are a useful
adjunct to the censuses.

2

Statutory Registers of Birth, Marriage and Death Post-1855

In 1837 the formal civil registration of births, marriages and deaths (BMD) began in England and Wales. Scotland followed on some eighteen years later, with the Registration of Births, Deaths and Marriages (Scotland) Act 1854. Compulsory civil registration started on 1 January 1855, taking over from the voluntary registration system operated by the Church of Scotland. Before these dates, baptisms (not usually births), proclamations of marriage (sometimes marriages themselves) and records of burials or mort-cloth records (occasionally deaths) were recorded in parish registers, known in Scotland as the Old Parish Registers (OPR) – See chapter 3.

Statutory Registration (SR) was the province of the newly formed General Register Office for Scotland (GROS) and a network of local Registrars, under a Registrar General. In 1855 GROS also took in the OPRs up to 1819 and those from 1820 to 1854 were given over to the local Registrars, but sent to GROS thirty years later. Thus, GROS has control of all BMD records back to the beginning of the Church of Scotland in 1563 or thereabouts. The earliest parish record available is for Errol, Perthshire in 1553, but this is an exception. It can be difficult to trace family history back beyond this unless the family concerned already had a well-documented pedigree, was connected to nobility or royalty or owned land.

A similar system of civil registration was started in Ireland in 1845 for non-Roman Catholic marriages, and for all births, marriages and deaths since 1864. This was an outgrowth of the Irish public health system, which was in turn based on the poor relief for the destitute, using the areas covered by the Poor Law Unions. For that reason, the responsibility for registration in the Republic of Ireland is still with the Department of Health. Local Health Boards have the original registers and the General Register Office of Ireland (GROI, 8-11 Lombard St, Dublin) has the master indexes to all thirty-two counties up to 1921, and to the twenty-six counties of the Republic from then. For Northern Ireland, the indexes and registers from 1921 and after are at Oxford House, Chichester St, Belfast. Originally, local registrars forwarded records to Dublin for copying, after which they were returned. GROI has microfilms of the copy registers as well as the master indexes. The registers can be consulted at the offices of the local registrars (at their discretion). Some of the local heritage centres have transcripts on databases. The Latter-Day Saints have copies of almost all GROI indexes and registers, accessible at LDS Family History Centres, and the indexes of some of these (primarily birth registrations from 1864 to 1875 inclusive) are in the IGI – searchable online at www.familysearch.org – and on the LDS British Isles Vital Records CDs.

The often-repeated story that most of the records were lost when the Four Courts in Dublin were destroyed during the Easter Uprising of 1922 is simply untrue.

BMD registration after 1855 – the coming of GROS

At the end of 1854, there were some 900 Church of Scotland parishes. For the purpose of the registration of births, deaths and marriages, over 900 parishes in Scotland were replaced in 1855 by 1,027 Registration Districts (RDs). Amalgamations and the closure of Registrars' Offices over the years reduced the number to 360 by 1994. Most of the new RDs were coterminous with the existing parishes, but some were divided in two halves – Burgh (urban) and Landward (rural), although many of these were reunited before 1860. In some cases, certificates will bear the registrar's mark B or L in the margin for some years after, but this is of no real significance other than it may give a clue as to the location of a now-disappeared farm, house or village.

Each RD was allocated to a county, but some sat astride county boundaries and would therefore include registrations from two (in a few cases, three) counties. The allocated county was the one in which the largest part of the RD's population lived. There were a few attempts to tidy this up over the years, sometimes by moving county boundaries so as to include entire RDs, or by reallocating certain areas from one RD to another, or by merging smaller RDs together. Some of this was piecemeal, but there was a wholesale exercise of boundary changes in 1892/3 as a result of the Local Government (Scotland) Act 1889. The new counties are called the Administrative Counties, and are the old versions the Historic Counties.

This was also a time of industrial growth, which meant expansion of the cities as the rural population flocked to large centres in search of work. The growing cities incorporated existing

Table 9. The various RDs in Aberdeen city over the years. Dundee is equally complicated. Edinburgh and Glasgow, just because of their greater sizes and growths, are more complicated still.

	OPR	Date from	Date to	
Aberdeen	168	1560	1854	
Registration Districts after 1855		**Date from**	**Date to**	**Notes**
St.Nicholas	168/01	1855	1930	
Old Machar	168/02	1855	1863	
Old Machar, Aberdeen Burgh	168/02	1864	1875	
Old Machar, Landward	168/03	1864	1875	
Old Machar	168/02	1876	1885	
Old Machar Parish	168/02	1886	1897	
Woodside	168/03	1886	1913	See Woodside, below
Old Aberdeen	168/04	1886	1913	
St Machar	168/02	1898	1930	Same area as Old Machar
Rubislaw	168/03	1914	1930	Note change from previous Woodside number
Woodside	168/04	1914	1930	
Old Aberdeen	168/05	1914	1930	
Aberdeen, Northern District	168/01	1931	1967	
Aberdeen, Southern District	168/02	1931	1967	
Aberdeen, Eastern District	168/03	1931	1967	
Aberdeen	168	1968	1971	
Aberdeen	300	1972	current	

Registration District	From County	RD	To County	RD	Cause
Carbrach	1892-1893	Aberdeenshire	177	Banffshire	149b	Local Government (Scotland) Act 1889
Coupar Angus	1892-1893	Angus	279	Perthshire	341b	Local Government (Scotland) Act 1889
Arisaig	1899-1900	Argyllshire	505/2	Inverness-shire	91b	
Kilmallie	1910-1911	Argyllshire	520	Inverness-shire	98b	
St Fergus	1892-1893	Banffshire	166	Aberdeenshire	237c	Local Government (Scotland) Act 1889
Arngask	1892-1893	Fife	404	Perthshire	328c	Local Government (Scotland) Act 1889
Cromdale & Advie	1869-1870	Inverness-shire	93/1	Moray	128b/1	Inverness and Elgin County Boundaries Act 1870
Inverallan	1869-1870	Inverness-shire	93/2	Moray	128b/2	Inverness and Elgin County Boundaries Act 1870
Banchory Devenick	1931-1932	Kincardineshire	251/1	Aberdeenshire (Nigg & Banchory Devenick)	266	
Nigg	1931-1932	Kincardineshire	266	Aberdeenshire (Nigg & Banchory Devenick)	266	
Plantation	1912-1913	Lanarkshire	646/1	Glasgow (Burgh)	646/20	Glasgow Boundaries Act 1912
Govan	1912-1913	Lanarkshire	646/2	Glasgow (Burgh)	644/21	Glasgow Boundaries Act 1912
Partick	1912-1913	Lanarkshire	646/3	Glasgow (Bergh)	644/22	Glasgow Boundaries Act 1912
Cathcart	1926-1927	Lanarkshire	633b	Glasgow (Burgh)	644/24	
Maryhill, Glasgow	1906-1907	Lanarkshire (Barony)	622/1	Glasgow (Burgh)	644/14	
Shettleston, Glasgow	1912-1913	Lanarkshire (Barony)	622/2	Glasgow (Burgh)	644/19	Glasgow Boundaries Act 1912
Portobello	1896-1897	Midlothian	684/1	Edinburgh (Burgh)	685/6	Burgh Reform Act 1896
Duddingston	1902-1903	Midlothian	684	Edinburgh (Burgh)	685/7	Edinburgh Corporation Act 1900
Colinton	1920-1921	Midlothian	677	Edinburgh (Burgh)	685/14	City of Edinburgh Extension Act 1920
Corstorphine	1920-1921	Midlothian	678	Edinburgh (Burgh)	685/13	City of Edinburgh Extension Act 1920
Cramond	1920-1921	Midlothian	679	Edinburgh (Burgh)	685/12	City of Edinburgh Extension Act 1920
Leith North	1920-1921	Midlothian	692/1	Edinburgh (Burgh)	685/10	City of Edinburgh Extension Act 1920
Leith South	1920-1921	Midlothian	692/2	Edinburgh (Burgh)	685/11	City of Edinburgh Extension Act 1920
Liberton	1920-1921	Midlothian	693	Edinburgh (Burgh)	685/15	City of Edinburgh Extension Act 1920
Newcraighall	1920-1921	Midlothian	695b	Edinburgh (Burgh)	685/16	City of Edinburgh Extension Act 1920
Abernethy & Kincardine	1869-1870	Moray	128	Inverness-shire	90a	Inverness and Elgin County Boundaries Act 1870
Duthil	1869-1870	Moray	132/1	Inverness-shire	96b/1	Inverness and Elgin County Boundaries Act 1870
Rothiemurchus	1869-1870	Moray	132/2	Inverness-shire	96b/2	Inverness and Elgin County Boundaries Act 1870
Boharm	1892-1893	Moray	128a	Banffshire,	147b	Local Government (Scotland) Act 1889
Megget	1892-1893	Peebles-shire	765/2	Selkirkshire	779/2	Local Government (Scotland) Act 1889
Culross	1892-1893	Perthshire	343	Fife	418b	Local Government (Scotland) Act 1889
Fowlis Easter	1892-1893	Perthshire	356	Angus	288b	Local Government (Scotland) Act 1889
Logie	1892-1893	Perthshire	374	Stirlingshire	485b	Local Government (Scotland) Act 1889
Tulliallan	1892-1893	Perthshire	397	Fife	458b	Local Government (Scotland) Act 1889
Cathcart	1912-1913	Renfrewshire	560	Lanarkshire	633b	Glasgow Boundaries Act 1912
Scotstoun & Yoker	1925-1926	Renfrewshire	575/2	Glasgow (Burgh of)	644/23	Glasgow Boundaries Act 1925
Eastwood	1926-1927	Renfrewshire	562	Glasgow (Burgh of)	644/25	
Ladhope (see also 1892-1893)	1872-1873	Roxburghshire	799/2	Selkirkshire	776b	
Ashkirk	1892-1893	Roxburghshire	781	Selkirkshire	773b	Local Government (Scotland) Act 1889
Ladhope (Became Langshaw in 1894)	1892-1893	Selkirkshire	776b	Roxburghshire	799/2	Local Government (Scotland) Act 1889
Roberton	1892-1893	Selkirkshire	777	Roxburghshire	802b	Local Government (Scotland) Act 1889
Alva	1892-1893	Stirlingshire	470	Clackmannanshire	465b	Local Government (Scotland) Act 1889

RDs from their surrounding hinterland, but new housing also meant new RDs. There were other times when RDs were merged or given new names. Remember that the censuses from 1861 on were also based on the RDs. All of this makes life difficult for historians, as it can look like whole families moved about through the years while in fact, they may have stayed put as the RD boundaries changed around them.

By 1972, the number of RDs had contracted from 1,000 or more to just over 400. This left a number of gaps and a few sub-divisions in the RD numbering system, so it was decided to re-number them completely. They should have waited, because as if this wasn't bad enough, the Local Government (Scotland) Act 1973 was just around the corner. On 16 May 1975 the thirty-three counties and four cities were replaced by a system of nine large regions subdivided into fifty-three districts, plus three single-level island authorities. No one lived in a county any more. Not content to leave the system alone (or, more likely, recognising that this change had been unwelcome, unworkable and unpopular) some twenty years later local government was overhauled again. The Local Government (Scotland) Act 1994 replaced the regions, districts and island authorities with thirty-two Unitary Authorities (which actually took place on 1 April 1996). In 1999 the Scottish parliament was re-established, the previous one having been abolished in 1707 with the Act of Union.

The old parishes did not have numbers as such. But after 1855 they were retrospectively given OPR numbers, which coincided for the most part with the RD code. Take Aberdeen for example. From the original OPR parish, given the number 168, it became two RDs – St Nicholas as 168/01 (until 1930) and Old Machar as 168/02 (which changed its name a few times until then and was subdivided for a while). Later, additional RDs (Old Aberdeen, Rubislaw and Woodside) were swept away by the administratively tidier but hardly imaginative Northern, Southern and Eastern RDs. In 1968 all the RDs were incorporated into one, still numbered 168 etc. and four years later Aberdeen became RD 300. Table 9 on p. 47 makes this as clear as it can be. The message for researchers is: don't assume continuity of name or number across the years. However, since most research will be pre-1901, the 1931, 1968 and 1972 changes won't matter much, unless you are trying to match up an Aberdeen death in, say,

Table 10. A number of parishes are named for Scotland's patron saint

St Andrew, Dundee	282/4	1868	1918	Now in 353
	282/3	1919	1951	
	350 & 353	1952	now	
St Andrew, Edinburgh (Midlothian)	685/2	1859	1971	Now in 734
	734	1972	now	
St Andrews and St Leonards, St Andrews, Fife	OPR 453	1627	1854	Now in 413
	453	1856	1967	
St Andrews Burgh, Fife	453/1	1855	1855	
St Andrews Landward, Fife	453/2	1855	1855	
St Andrews, Fife	413	1968	now	
St Andrews, Orkney	OPR 25	1657	1854	Now in 144
	25	1855	1971	
St Andrews Lhanbryde, then in Elgin	OPR 142	1701	1854	Now in 280
St Andrews Lhanbryd, then in Moray	142	1855	1954	

1973 with a marriage in Aberdeen Southern in 1920, a census in St Machar in 1901, another census in Old Machar Parish in 1891 and a birth in Old Machar in 1885.

Table 11. Logie as a name is so widespread because it simply means 'a hollow' (*lagaidh* in Gaelic)

Logie, Fife	OPR 446	1660	1854	Now in 417
	446	1855	1967	
Logie, then in Perthshire	OPR 374	1688	1854	Now in 386 & 473
	374	1855	1892	
Logie, then in Stirlingshire	485	1893	1970	
Logiealmond, Perthshire	OPR 375, 380, 382			Now in 390
	304	1855	1963	
Logierait, Perth	OPR 376	1650	1854	Now in 386
	376	1855	1971	
	386	1972	now	
Logie Buchan, Aberdeen	OPR 216	1698	1854	Now in 316
	375	1855	1967	
Logie Coldstone, Aberdeen	OPR 217	1716	1854	Now in 330
Logie Coldstone and Cromar, Aberdeen	216	1855	1967	
Logie Easter, Ross & Cromarty	OPR 77	1665	1854	Now in 193
	217	1855	1967	
Urquhart and Logie Wester, Ross & Cromarty	OPR 84	1715	1854	Now in 196
Logie Pert, then in Forfarshire	OPR 304	1717	1854	Now in 367
Logie Pert, then in Angus	77	1855	1965	

Bear in mind, too, that the cities were in counties. Aberdeen was in Aberdeenshire, but Dundee was in Forfarshire (later called Angus), Edinburgh was in Midlothian (at one time called Edinburghshire and from 1921 including Leith) and Glasgow spread over parts of Lanarkshire and Renfrewshire.

REMEMBER
Many Parishes and RDS in different counties had the same name. Don't confuse the various St Andrews parishes with the town in Fife (in its various permutations through the years) and watch for the county change from Elgin to Moray. See Table 10.

Be equally careful with the various places called Logie – in Fife, in Perthshire (later in Stirlingshire), two in Aberdeenshire, two in Ross and one in Forfarshire (which became Angus). See Table 11.

Note
The Scotland's People website (www.scotlandspeople.gov.uk) now has BMD indexes available more or less up to the present day, as is the case in England. The current provision (as at 1 January 2009) is:
– births index 1855 to 2007, images to 1908
– marriages index and images 1855 to 1933
– deaths index 1855 to 2007, images to 1958
[Where no image is available, order an extract (£10, $20) if necessary. See p. 56.]

3

Old Parish Registers

Statutory civil registration started in 1855 and the earliest census with any genealogically useful information is that of 1841. The next obvious step in this trip back through time is to consult the Old Parish Registers (OPRs). Each of the 900 or so Church of Scotland parishes kept registers of baptisms and/or births, of marriages and/or the proclamations of banns and of deaths and/or burials. This was a rather haphazard system for a number of reasons:

1. It only applied to Church of Scotland members – after 1560 or so, Presbyterianism was the predominant denomination of the population, but there were still Catholics, Episcopalians and those of other faiths such as Judaism, but very much in the minority (although some nonconformists did choose to be so registered).
2. There is no absolute starting date for these records – the earliest is from 1553, but not many date so far back and the majority started in the seventeenth or even the eighteenth century; some are even later and some parishes have no records at all.
3. There was also no standard format, with the individual ministers deciding how to keep them; many have no death or burial registers.
4. Not everyone chose to register a birth, marriage or death, or to have the event itself celebrated in church, as it generally cost money; in particular, the imposition from 1783 to 1794 of a 'stamp duty' of three pence on each registration was a serious inhibition.
5. As the population grew, and people moved from villages and hamlets to the larger towns towards the end of the eighteenth century, people's ties with their local church become less firm and registration was less likely
6. As usual, some registers have just become lost, or are damaged beyond recovery.

That said, it is always worth inspecting the OPRs first, not least because the births and marriages are very accessible and searchable online, or on microfilm at many libraries and LDS Family History centres. Some caveats, though:

– quite often you will find two people married in a certain parish, but be unable to find their births there, or in any other parish. Sometimes a will or testament throws up names of children when their births – and the parents' marriage itself – seems not to be registered;
– the amount of information in OPRs is often less than ideal. Baptisms will usually give the name of the child and the date, but the parents' names, place of residence and occupations are not always documented. The mother's name may be unrecorded (as happened in the Perthshire parish of Alyth between 1742 and 1786), or the baptised child's sex not given (which will be U for 'Unknown' in the index);
– remember that a date of baptism is not a date of birth; one of the pitfalls of IGI is that many well-meaning people uploading information have assumed that one is the same as the other, but

a birth could precede a baptism by some weeks or months; do not accept any date given as either Born or Baptised/Christened without checking the original document;

– sometimes there appear to be double entries, the same child apparently 'born' on two different dates; this is usually because one is a birth date and the other the date of baptism, but could be due to the proud parents being from different parishes and wishing to having the baby baptised at both;

– much the same is true of marriage entries, which are usually a record of the proclamation of banns, which again might be made in two parishes, those of the bride *and* groom; one OPR entry may give more details than the other but typically the names of the parties to be wed, their places of residence and the date of the proclamation are given, sometimes with a statement that the marriage took place (which it need not have);

– burial records often have no more details than the name of the deceased and the date of interment but often a child's age is given.

Every so often a particular minister – whether because he thought it was his religious duty, or just because he had a tidy mind – would choose to give other information, such as a maiden name in a baptismal entry, or those of godparents (at a baptism) or witnesses (at a marriage), or a cause of death. You may even be told the fee paid in caution (pronounced 'cay-shun', essentially a bond or surety), whether a child was legitimate or illegitimate and the relationships of witnesses or godparents to the married couple or child. Witnesses and godparents may well be relatives, so that could be useful to the family historian. Ages are rarely recorded, except in the case of child burials, but a surviving spouse might be mentioned.

The single major hazard of consulting OPRs is over-enthusiastic identification. A small town or isolated parish may have a number of individuals with the same name and of a similar age – cousins, for instance, all christened with the grandfather's first name – who married others with common or locally predominant names.

Here are two examples of Rolland marriage entries:

   1. BESSIE ROLLAND – Marriage: 23 FEB 1712 Culross, Perth, Scotland
   2. BESSIE ROLLAND – Marriage: 21 MAR 1712 Torryburn, Fife, Scotland

Is this the same person, married twice a month apart? No, but it could be banns read in two parishes. Or are these two individuals with the same name and similar marriage dates, just a coincidence? The husbands in each case are: 1. ROBERT NUCLE; 2. ROBERT NICOLE. There is no further information about names of parents, even when the original registers are consulted. Given that Torryburn and Culross are only a couple of miles apart and the similarity of the spouses' surnames (which could be due to idiosyncratic spelling by one or both ministers, or a transcriptional error), it is likely that this is one couple, having the proclamations made in the parishes of both. (Incidentally, although Culross is given as a parish in Perthshire, it is really in Fife; a sort of detached enclave of Perthshire up to 15 May 1891, kept so that county would have access to the River Forth.) It would require more information to decide.

By consulting OPR births, we find:

   George Nicol – Male Christening: 01 NOV 1713, Torryburn, Fife, Scotland
   George Nicole – Male Christening: 11 NOV 1713, Torryburn, Fife, Scotland
   Robert Nicol – Male Christening: 07 NOV 1714, Torryburn, Fife, Scotland
   John Nicol – Male Christening: 17 FEB 1717 Torryburn, Fife, Scotland

William Nickol – Male Christening: 21 JUN 1719, Culross, Perth, Scotland

Charles Nicol – Female Christening: 10 DEC 1721, Culross, Perth, Scotland

Margaret Nicol – Female Christening: 10 DEC 1721, Culross, Perth, Scotland

George Nicoll – Male Christening: 14 DEC 1724, Culross, Perth, Scotland

Agnes Nicol – Female Christening: 29 OCT 1727, Culross, Perth, Scotland

Notice:

1. the multiple christenings for some children, sometimes in two parishes
2. the multiple spellings
3. two children called George, eleven years apart
4. that Charles is possibly incorrectly listed as female

The sceptical genealogist will wonder if this does indicate two families after all (one in Torryburn, one in Culross) or whether the Nicol-Rollands moved around 1718; and whether the first George died young and his name given to a later child, as was common. The way to check would be to look for the deaths of the children, and see if the parents' names and occupations were given. Sadly, OPR death and burial records are few and far between, and do not appear at all on the Scotlands People website (although some indexes are available in book form at GROS). However, some Family History Societies have burials indexes, and a few of these are online. There is the possibility of Scotland's People including some of this data as a 'thin' index on the website. IGI does not include burials and deaths, except where that information has been uploaded by an individual from another source, and should be treated with caution. Again, two different people might be mistakenly identified as one and a death tagged to the wrong individual.

Conversely, sometimes, it is possible to assume the same person is two or more different individuals. If John Anderson from Leven, Fife, has his occupation listed, in the births of four children, as Ag. Lab., HLW (handloom weaver), Fisherman and Flax Cutter, and his wife's name given as Elisabeth, Elsbeth, Bess and Elspet, it could still be the same family.

As with any genealogical study, always look at the original entry. Granted, in 2009 that means a trip to Edinburgh, but one day the whole OPR– deaths and burials included will be online, images and all. In the meantime, indexes and some images can be found online or in microform.

Searching OPRs on-line

Scotlands People (www.scotlandspeople.gov.uk) is a wonderful resource but expensive to use, especially if copies of the original records are wanted. Unlike with post-1855 Statutory Registration records (see chapter 2), not all OPR images are available for download. Instead, it is possible to order an extract (see p. 56).

A useful aspect of the site is the possibility of searching with wildcards. For instance, a search for MO*BRAY, ROB* in OPR Births for the date range 01/01/1685 to 31/12/1740 yields twelve results (p. 54). A Soundex-enabled search is also possible.

It is also possible to specify the parish, or to select more than one for the search (by using ctrl+left-click); specify a date range, and indicate the names of one or both parents. A search just by parish and date (i.e., without a surname) is not yet possible, which is a shame.

IGI

The International Genealogical Index (www.familysearch.org) has the twin disadvantages of an unforgiving search facility and many flawed entries. However, it is a rapid and (above all)

No	Date	Surname	Forename	Parent Names/Frame No.	Sex	Parish	GROS Data	Image	Extract
1	22/10/1689	MOUBRAY	ROBERT	THOMAS MOUBRAY/MARY TWEEDY FR3215	M	EDINBURGH	685/01 0011	No Image	**ORDER**
2	31/03/1699	MOUBRAY	ROBERT	JAMES MOUBRAY/ISOBELL PUNTON FR304	M	CRAMOND	679/00 0001	No Image	**ORDER**
3	20/07/1702	MOUBRAY	ROBERT	ROBERT MOUBRAY/ELIZABETH SAWER FR637	M	AYR	578/00 0002	No Image	**ORDER**
4	30/10/1704	MOUBRAY	ROBERT	ROBERT MOUBRAY/ELIZOBETH KRINGLIE FR4023	M	EDINBURGH	685/01 0014	No Image	**ORDER**
5	27/04/1707	MOUBRAY	ROBERT	ROBERT MOUBRAY/ELIZABETH HENDERSON	U	INVERKEITHING	432/00 0001	No Image	**ORDER**
6	18/05/1731	MOUBRAY	ROBERT	JOHN MOUBRAY/CHRISTIAN DICK FR89	U	QUEENSFERRY	670/00 0001	No Image	**ORDER**
7	17/09/1732	MOUBRAY	ROBERT	ROBERT MOUBRAY/MARY DUDGEON	M	DALGETTY	422/00 0002	No Image	**ORDER**
8	12/08/1734	MOUBRAY	ROBERT	JOHN MOUBRAY/AGNES MAKAY FR5320	M	EDINBURGH	685/01 0019	No Image	**ORDER**
9	10/06/1736	MOUBRAY	ROBERT	JOHN MOUBRAY/ISOBEL HOGG	M	DALGETTY	422/00 0002	No Image	**ORDER**
10	12/07/1736	MOUBRAY	ROBERT	ROBERT MOUBRAY/CATHARINE LINN FR5555	M	EDINBURGH	685/01 0020	No Image	**ORDER**
11	18/10/1691	MOWBRAY	ROBERT	JAMES MOWBRAY/RACHELL COOK FR183	M	NEWTON	696/00 0001	No Image	**ORDER**
12	04/04/1699	MOWBRAY	ROBERT	JAMES MOWBRAY/ISOBELL PONTINE FR93	M	DALMENY	665/00 0001	No Image	**ORDER**

Notice that the search returned multiple surname variants by using a 'wildcard' (see p. 53).

free way to do an initial quick search. Take the results with a pinch of salt. There is a new pilot site under development which will improve the search capabilities.

Ancestry

The OPRs do not appear on Ancestry.com or Ancestry.co.uk, but in time they may, and it is likely that the search possibilities will be better than those of Scotland's People or IGI – searching entire parishes, for instance, would be a boon to those researching an area or village.

Using New Register House

The original parish registers are kept at the Scotland's People Centre in Edinburgh and, after paying a day fee, there is free access to computerised indexes to the baptisms and marriages, to some paper indexes for burials, to images of the records on microfilm and access to the original books where necessary. Print-outs are available, at a modest cost (50p to £1.00), as are downloads to a USB memory stick.

LDS and other libraries

The Family History Centres of the Mormon Church and some libraries have the indexes on microfiche and may have the record book images on microfilm.

The deceased John Mowbray of Hartwood, Esq., Writer to the Signet, and Mrs Patricia Hodge or Mowbray, his spouse, had the children after-named born to them on the respective dates underwritten, viz:

A son born on the 26th day of August 1813 – John Marshall
A daughter born on the 2nd day of March 1817 – Patricia
A son born on the 7th day of March 1819 – George Cranstoun

> A son born on the 25th day of March 1821 – Henry
> A son born on the 11th day of June 1823 – Archibald Cuthill
> A son born on the 18th day of March 1825 – Seymour
> A daughter born on the 9th day of September 1826 – Margaret Higgins
> A son born on the 5th day of February 1829 – Richard
> Asserted by Patricia Hodge before the Justices of the Peace of Edinburgh

The marriage of John Mowbray/Moubray and Patricia Hodge is in the Extract on p. 56. This transcription from the OPR Births of 16 February 1847, St Cuthbert's Parish, Edinburgh (685/02 0036 FR9422) shows that the Mowbrays never got round to registering the births of their children until Mrs Mowbray eventually did so when the eldest was well over thirty. Or it may be that she discovered the original entry had been lost, and chose to get the births on the record. This may have mattered, as her husband had died by then, possibly in 1838. In which case, why wait so long? Perhaps there was a succession issue.

Parish registers still exist

The parish registers did not go away overnight in 1855. Parishes still maintain these, and it can be fruitful to contact a parish church or church authority and ask to consult the Baptism Rolls ('Cradle Rolls'), Marriage Registers, Burial lists and so on. Churches may also have lists of war dead from the parish. BMD information is also often in Kirk Session records.

Kirk Sessions

Since the Reformation, every congregation of the Church of Scotland has had a Kirk Session, essentially the lowest (and local) court of the Church of Scotland. It consisted of the minister(s) and senior elders and its main duties were to maintain order. When the congregation was effectively everyone in the parish, this was the unit of social control, and the Kirk Session could not help but to enquire into the moral status of the parishioners.

Kirk Session records are essentially the business records of a parish, and contain a vast amount of information valuable to the genealogist. If your ancestor was chastised for some reason (non-attendance, squabbling with a neighbour, misbehaving before marriage, having a child out of wedlock and even witchcraft) or was involved with the Kirk Session in some other way, it will likely be recorded here. The illegitimacy records in particular are a rich vein for genealogists unable to find an individual in other records. Kirk Session minutes (or separate accounts) might also include details of monies raised, bequeathed and disbursed, often with lists of recipients. These minutes survive from the late sixteenth century for some parishes, and in unbroken runs for most from the late seventeenth century. Many are in print or available on the Internet.

The Kirk Session and the Heritors (local landowners) ran the parish and often had responsibility for Poor Law, the school, hospital, alms house and other parochial resources. The records, along with those of presbyteries, synods and the General Assembly of the Church of Scotland, are deposited at the National Archives of Scotland (NAS) in Edinburgh and over five million pages covering the period from 1500 to 1901 have been digitised by a partnership between the NAS, the Church of Scotland and the Genealogical Society of Utah. The timetable for their online availability is at www.scottishdocuments.com, but the plan is to have them available by the end of 2009.

Heritors' minutes

Heritors were landowners living in the parish who were bound by law to contribute to the maintenance of a church (capable of accommodating two-thirds of the population aged over

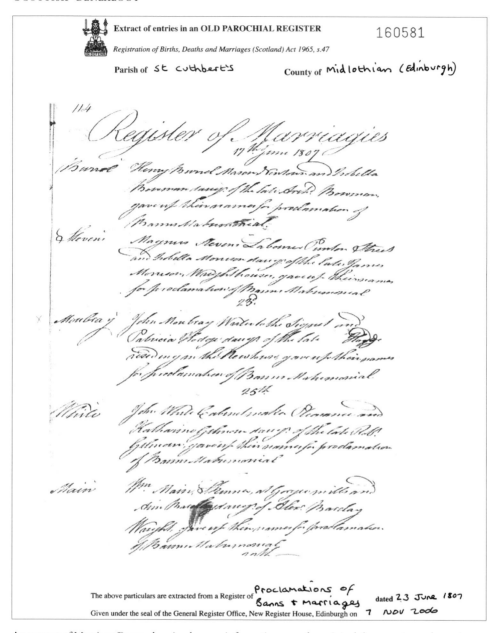

An extract of Marriage Banns, showing how uninformative even the original documents can be at times.

12), the stipend of the minister plus a manse and a glebe (garden, orchard or farmland), a school and the salary of the 'Dominie' (schoolmaster) as well as other public works. Although there was a system in place for the formal assessment of heritors' payments towards Poor Relief, they often just made voluntary contributions to the parochial structure. They paid according to the size of their estates, so the largest landowners had the majority of the costs and also, therefore, the greatest influence. Since the same people were likely to be elders of the Kirk, and also Commissioners of Supply (p. 63) as well as holding other burgh or county duties, they exercised considerable sway over the parish and area.

Table 14. An extract from the Kirk Session minutes of 1639/40 of various parishes within the Presbytery of Kirkcaldy, showing the degree to which the Kirk elders took witchcraft seriously at the time, and acted as local court in such matters. It also shows what a rich source of names, offices, occupations and other genealogical information such a record can be.

Kirkcaldie, December 27	Kirkcaldy, December 27 1639 (modernised)
Mr Georg Gilespie Minister at Weyms, declaried to the brethern sundrie presumptiouns of witchcraft aganest ane Janet Durie in Weyms. The brethern desyres him first to try the saids presumptions befoir his sessioun and thairafter to bring them to the Presbytrie.	Mr George Gillespie Minister at Wemyss, declared to the brethren sundry presumptions of witchcraft against one Janet Durie in Wemyss. The brethren desire him first to try the said presumptions before his [Kirk] Session and thereafter to bring them to the Presbytery.
Dysert, Januarii 10	Dysart, January 10
Janet Durie to be sowmonti to the nixt day.	Janet Durie to be summoned to the next day.
Dysert, Januarii 17	Dysart, January 17
Compeired Janet Durie in Weyms challenged of witchcraft: denyes all: sowmonit apud acta to compeir the nixt day in Dysert.	Compeired [appeared in court] Janet Durie in Wemyss challenged of witchcraft: Denies all: summoned at the time of the proceedings to appear the next day in Dysart.
At Dysert, 24 day of Januarii, 1639	At Dysart, 24th day of January, 1639 [1640 by modern calendar]
Compeired Janet Durie challangit anent sundrie poynts of witchcraft; denyed the same. Sundrie witnesses compeireand aganest hir being admittit and deiplie sworne deponed as follows:– In primis Adam Blaikwood Reider at Weyms deponed that he comeing to visit James Kedie in Weyms being sick the said James said to him that Janet Durie was the causs of his death he having stickit ane swine to the said Janet Durie befoir for whilk she had professit to causs him rewit.	Compeired Janet Durie challenged about various points of witchcraft; denied the same. Various witnesses appeared against her being admitted and truly sworn testified as follows:– In the first, Adam Blackwood Reader [Minister] at Wemyss testified that he coming to visit James Keddie in Wemyss being sick, the said James said to him that Janet Durie was the cause of his death, he having hit with a stick a pig [belonging] to the said Janet Durie before for which she had professed to cause him to rue it.
Compeired John Walker who deponed that Robert Bennett he being sick and dead (as was thought) for he was streakit said that Janet Durie had the wyte of it.	Compeired John Walker who testified that Robert Bennett, he being sick and dead (as was thought), for he was laid out [presumably unconscious], said that Janet Durie had knowledge of it.
Compeired Geills Thomson relict of Umqll James Keddie who deponit that hir husband was sick of the disease whereof he died, hee said to Adam Blaikwood that Janet Durie was the causs of his death for when he stickit hir swine she said that she would causs him repent it. Compeired Kathren Courtier deponed that James Keddie being sick laid his death upon Janet Durie. The Presbytrie considering the things alledgit aganest hir thinks it is reason that she be wardit to abyd further tryell.	Compeired Geills Thomson, relict of deceased James Keddie, who testified that her husband was sick of the disease whereof he died, he said to Adam Blackwood that Janet Durie was the cause of his death, for when he hit her pig she said that she would cause him [to] repent it. Compeired Kathren Courtier testified that James Keddie being sick laid his death upon Janet Durie. The Presbytery considering the things alleged against her thinks it is reason that she be held to wait further trial.

Although heritors had no responsibility for the religious, moral or pastoral care of the parishioners, they did share the duties of Poor Relief. They often held joint meetings with the Kirk Session and usually had their own meetings in the parish church. (The situation in burghs was different, and where the parish church was burghal, that is, wholly within the burgh, the magistrates were the heritors.)

After the 1845 Poor Law Act the new parochial boards did impose assessments on landowners and occupiers, and the place of heritors in the scheme of things dwindled away to nothing.

Parochial board and parish council minutes

When parochial boards were established in 1845 they had a rather complex structure. In rural areas, if they imposed a poor rate, they had to elect a number of local members to sit alongside the heritors and Kirk Session. If there was no poor rate, it was business as usual. The balance shifted gradually from 1845 to the 1860s and, in any case, the parochial boards were replaced by wholly elected parish councils and a Local Government Board for Scotland by the Local Government (Scotland) Act 1894; the parish councils themselves were abolished by the Local Government (Scotland) Act 1929 when the county, district and town councils took up their responsibilities.

The minutes of parochial boards and parish councils are usually manuscript (although some have been printed or transcribed) and have a particular structure. They generally begin with a sederunt (a list of those 'sitting') and go on to the whole panoply of board business including applications for Poor Relief, brought to the board by the Inspector of the Poor. Most minutes are in local authority archives (or whoever inherited the responsibility for the county council records) but are not always indexed.

The influence of parochial boards and parish council Poor Relief is still felt to this day in Scotland, where applying for unemployment benefit is still known half-jokingly as 'going to join the parish'.

4

Census Substitutes

The obvious 'genealogical' records (birth, marriage, death, census etc.) are not the only sources of information available to the genealogist and family historian. Particularly for family history, there are rich seams of data and detail in other places. These can be thought of in a number of categories, for instance, where individuals interact with officialdom, the criminal and civil law, employment, the armed services and so on. Not only do these record significant events in individuals' lives, and provide details not available in vital records, they also provide additional useful information – names of parents, children and other relatives, occupations, financial and work status plus addresses at particular times. Addresses are particularly useful, especially where a whole family is recorded as living there, and they may provide the stepping stone to track down someone who has apparently 'disappeared' between censuses, moved between birth and marriage or death, or changed name. Since the census records are a decade apart and BMD records twenty-five, fifty or more years from each other, these accessory records are crucial for completing the understanding of an entire life and the surrounding social conditions.

Among the most complete and best organised are tax records, and for obvious reasons – the collecting authority wants to know what it can expect to receive, and from whom. There are essentially two forms of taxation: taxes on individuals, levied per head ('poll' taxes, income taxes etc.); and those on fixed assets such as land or houses (land taxes, death duties, hearth taxes and so on).

VALUATION ROLLS AND STENT ROLLS

Valuation rolls for Scotland have been compiled since at least the early seventeenth century. The main purpose initially was to record who owned property worth more than £100 Scots, what each property was worth (in terms of annual rent), and the owner's consequent tax liability. Later, they also became the basis for lists of electors.

Early valuation rolls

From the seventeenth century, the Commissioners of Supply (see p. 63) were responsible for compiling property valuations for the landward (i.e. non-burgh) areas of Scotland on a county-by-county basis. Not all of these have survived, but those which have are mainly in the National Archives of Scotland (NAS) among the records of the Exchequer.

The earliest record of this type is from the 1640s. Sometimes the information is not all that illuminating to genealogists as, for example, when burgh taxes were paid in one lump sum with the individual contributors not listed. A few of the 'stent rolls', as they were called (a contraction of 'extent', meaning 'value'), may be held locally in burgh or county collections among the Commissioners of Supply records. Glasgow, for instance, has one roll from 1697, then about 1,000 from 1802 for individual wards. The picture is obviously incomplete. Rolls from the seventeenth and early eighteenth centuries usually listed the name of the estate and not the name of the owner. The estates of large landowners may be subdivided into smaller estates. A useful source of information is Timperley's book with its snapshot of Scottish land ownership in 1770 (see Further Reading, p. 63).

There is also a series of early valuation rolls from 1796 for nine counties in the records of the Inland Revenue at NAS (Ref. IRS/4). These may indicate relationships of legatees, reason for inheritance of property, names of executors, lawyers and clerks etc.

The 1854 Lands Valuation (Scotland) Act

The 1854 Act established a recognisably modern system of assessment, based on the concept of 'annual value' – either the actual annual rent (if let at a real economic value rather than a 'peppercorn' rent) or an estimate by the assessor as to the sum for which the property might fetch if let from year to year, net of the cost of repairs and other expenses. Allied to these are the valuations of the Assessor of Railways and Canals (known as the Assessor of Public Undertakings from 1934), and those of public utilities, such as water or town gas companies. Churches, schools, charitable premises and crown properties, including prisons, military establishments and post offices, plus certain other properties, were exempt from assessment. The 1854 Act required that one copy of each roll was to be sent to the Keeper of the Records, so the National Archives of Scotland (NAS) has a complete set of the rolls for the whole country from 1855 up to 1989, the date of enactment of the Abolition of Domestic Rates Etc. (Scotland) Act 1987.

The electoral franchise originally depended on a property qualification, so valuation rolls were also the basis of electoral registers and therefore contained useful information such as adult names. Soon, extra information was incorporated including the amount of any ground annual (annual charges on the land) or feu duty. The Scottish valuation rolls are much more complete and contain more information than their English equivalent, the Rate Books.

Compiling the rolls

The 1854 Act established Assessors' offices in each county and royal burgh, which remained until the abolition of counties and burghs in 1975. The rolls record a description of the property, what sort of property it was (e.g. dwelling house, farm building, shop etc.), the name of the owner, the tenant (if let) and other occupants (if sub-let) and the occupation of most of the tenants and occupiers. County rolls were organised by civil parishes. From the early twentieth century, burgh rolls were organised by municipal wards.

Tenancies usually ran from the 'removal day' or 'flitting term', 28 May each year. The word 'flit', still used in Scotland for moving house, has overtones of escaping with unpaid rent still due, and indeed this was often the case. Not only were poorer families more mobile, following the Head of Household with each change of job, they would have far fewer possessions, making it easier to leave the area, sometimes with unpaid bills with local shops and suppliers. Once the 'shift' had settled down the new rolls would be compiled.

In the case of a city like Glasgow, a team of surveyors would each take a part of the previous roll and go around noting changes in ownership or tenancy and valuing any new or substantially changed properties, although the vast majority of entries would be the same from year to year. There was also a printed form to be completed by every owner or factor (the owner's or landlord's agent) and returned, after which the two sets of information would be evaluated and compared, and discrepancies looked into. By 25 August every owner and occupier received a notice of the relevant finalised entry or entries and could appeal up to 8 September to a committee of the town council, sitting as a Valuation Appeal Court. This was a rather breathless procedure as the determinations of the court (and appeals to the Court of Session in Edinburgh) had to be heard by 30 September when the roll was sent to be printed. Meanwhile, the actual annual rates payable would be calculated. This was often a complex set of calculations as there could be as many as twenty or more separate municipal rates, to pay for sewage, harbour construction, parks, libraries, reservoirs, prisons and the like. By agreement, some rates were paid by the owner, some by the occupier or tenant, or these were shared.

Tracing individuals through valuation rolls

There is no question that the geographical organisation of valuation rolls does make for frustration. They require a bit more spadework than a simple look-up. For one thing, they tend to be organised by street address rather than by name of occupier, which may mean searching the record for an entire town or area. In the large cities, the records are arranged by parish (up to 1909 in Glasgow and 1895 in Edinburgh), and later by electoral ward. The 1975 Local Government (Scotland) Act abolished county and burgh assessors, and the new Regional Assessors had a different format of valuation roll to implement, where each region was subdivided by local government districts, and then electoral wards.

Another caveat is that only properties valued at over £4 may list all occupiers; those of lower value give only the Head of Household.

Finally, remember that street names and their numbers may have changed over time. This is especially the case in large and expanding towns and cities, and more so when there were successive boundary changes. There was no need, for example, to worry about identical street names in Partick, Springhill and Govan (all in Glasgow) when these were more or less independent, but it became obvious later that there could be confusion and occasional renamings took place, particularly around the 1930s. This can be frustrating if working from a modern street atlas, but Glasgow Archives' street indices often have notations indicating changes of name or ward number, and there is a modern card index of name changes. Fortunately, there are usually finding aids. A large-scale Ordnance Survey map will help; so will Street Indexes, such as the ones compiled to accompany censuses, or Glasgow's 1875–6 Street Index which helpfully identifies the parish. There may also be local telephone, trade and address directories. Glasgow has a computerised Valuation Roll Index for the years 1832, 1861, 1881 and 1911 which includes some 350,000 individuals, but at the time of writing it is not available on the Internet.

Edinburgh's records are at the Edinburgh Central Library and Glasgow's at the Mitchell Library. Most other local areas have some valuation rolls, but often not before about 1880. The complete sets are at the National Archives of Scotland (NAS), along with Inland Revenue records from 1911–12, when every property in Britain was re-assessed. The idea, later dropped, was to have the basis for a new Land Tax.

ADAM, JAMES	GROCER	161104 SAUCHIEHALL ST, 352	895
ADAM, JAMES	MOULDER	213205 CORN ST, 8	865
ADAM, JAMES	STOREKEEPER	220102 JAMIESON LANE, 2	905
ADAM, JOHN	CALENDERER	170714 GEORGE ST, 116	862
ADAM, JOHN	CALENDERER	170714 RICHARD ST, 33	904
ADAM, JOHN	DESIGNER	030716 DUNCHATTAN ST, 11	914
ADAM, JOHN	GREEN GROCER	160701 NORFOLK ST, 52/50	942
ADAM, JOHN	LABOURER	220601 DRYGATE ST, 97	851
ADAM, JOHN	MALE WITH NO OCCUPATION GIVEN	999995 CAMDEN ST, 12	933
ADAM, JOHN	MALE WITH NO OCCUPATION GIVEN	999995 SOUTH COBURG ST, 43	942
ADAM, JOHN	MASON	110103 GROVE ST, 9	864
ADAM, JOHN	MOULDER	213205 CLYDE ST, 57	901
ADAM, JOHN	PORTER	060507 GREENSIDE LANE, 14	935
ADAM, JOHN	RAILWAY SERVANT	060105 MAITLAND ST, 20	896
ADAM, JOHN	UPHOLSTER	110703 MILTON ST, 14	896
ADAM, JOHN	WAREHOUSEMAN	060401 DALE ST, 72	944
ADAM, JOHN SENI R	BLEACHER	170709 TOWNMILL RD, 400	851
ADAM, JOSEPH	FLESHER	160401 ST VINCENT ST, 473	904
ADAM, M	CAP MAKER	180104 ARGYLE ST, 278	891
ADAM, MISS	UNMARRIED WOMAN	260301 BURNBANK TERR, 2	923
ADAM, MISS	UNMARRIED WOMAN	260301 DUNCHATTAN ST, 18	914
ADAM, MRS	MARRIED WOMAN	260201 CASTLE ST, 222	851
ADAM, MRS	MARRIED WOMAN	260201 CHURCH PLACE, 4	865
ADAM, MRS	MARRIED WOMAN	260201 CUMBERLAND ST, 104	934
ADAM, MRS	MARRIED WOMAN	260201 GREEN ST, 17	925
ADAM, MRS	MARRIED WOMAN	260201 GREENHEAD ST, 21/5	883
ADAM, MRS	MARRIED WOMAN	260201 HOLYROOD CRESC, 12	923

An example of the Valuation Roll Index, in this case from Glasgow, 1861. The index numbers can be used to track down the original entries.

COMMISSIONERS OF SUPPLY.

*Adam, W. P., of Blair Adam
Aitken, Jas., of St Margaret Stone
Alexander, Jas., of Balmule
Allan, John, of Halcroft
Beveridge, W., of Bonnyton
Birnie, M., of Over Inzivar
Colville, Andrew, of Barnhill
Colville, Alex., of Hillside
*Dalgleish, Jas., of West Grange
Dalgleish, John J., of Dalbeath
Douglas, John, of Wester Lochend
Duff, J. Grant, of Balbougie
Flockhart, D. E., Craigduckie
Halkett, Sir P. A. of Pitfirrane

Henderson, G. W. M., of Fordell
*Hopetoun, John, Earl of
*Hunt, J. A., of Pittencrieff
Inglis, Wm., of Temple Hall
*Moubray, W. H., of Otterstone
*Newton, R. P., of Castland Hill
*Oliphant, G., of Over Kinneddar
*Rolland, Adam, of Gask
*Sligo, A. V. Smith, of Inzievar
*Spowart, T., of Broom Head
*Stenhouse, J., of North Fod
Telfor, D., of Balgonar
Wardlaw, A. L., of Stevenson's Beath
Young, Harry, of Cleish

Convener—J. W. Melville, Benarty. Clerk—W. Patrick, Cupar.
Treasurer— G. H. Pagan, Cupar.

Those marked * are Justices of the Peace. The Resident Chief Magistrates in Royal Burghs are also Justices of the Peace.

A list of the Commissioners of Supply for Dunfermline and West Fife, 1871.

I. CRAWFORD VALUATION, 1875-76.

Subject.	Proprietor.	Occupier.	Rent.		
Farm, Up. How-cleuch	Wm. Bertram of Kerswell, Carnwath	John Paterson	£314	18	0
Sheep-f., Cramp	Ditto	Robt. Paterson	320	0	0
Shootings	Ditto	Allan Home	15	0	0
Tollhouse, Glengeith	Big. and P. Road T.	Ten. under £4	6	10	0
Farm, Kirkhope	Duke of Buccleuch	J. T. Milligan, Hayfield, Thornhill	608	15	0
„ Whitecamp	„	Richd. Vassey, Far., Morningside	530	0	0
Ho. and garden	Robt. Baird, shepherd	...	4	0	0
Manse	Minister	...	30	0	0
Land	„	...	16	0	0
Ho. Crawford	Thos. Cranstoun, labourer	...	2	10	0
Ho. Crawford inn	Hrs. of A. Cranstoun, innkeeper	...	14	0	0
Ho. and gar., C.	Wm. Carmichael, labourer	3 ten. under £4	4	15	0
	„	Empty	1	15	0
Man. Ho. land, and shootings, Newton	Mrs Louisa Catterson	J. A. Callender, Braemain Villa, Morningside, Edinburgh	145	0	0
Woods	Ditto	Mrs L. Catterson	5	0	0
F., Over Fingland	Ditto	Wm. Rae, Gateslick, Thornhill	300	0	0
F., Shortcleuch	Ditto	Alex. Paterson, Carmacoup, Douglas	300	0	0

A page from the Valuation Roll of Crawfordjohn, Lanarkshire, taken from God's Treasure-House in Scotland, the Revd J. Moir Porteous (Minister at Wanlockhead), 1876. Image courtesy of James Bell, http://www.crawford-john.org.uk

With increasing digitisation of records, name searches for individuals will become easier and more possible from remote locations. Glasgow's Valuation Rolls for 1913–14 can be searched (by street or neighbourhood) at www.theglasgowstory.com/valindex.php. There is also a useful set of Ward maps.

Commissioners of Supply

The Commissioners were established in each county in 1667, originally to collect 'cess' (land tax) for the Crown but later were effectively the local government. They were in many ways a hangover from the feudal days, and composed mainly of the larger landowners of the county. The commissioners carried on after the Act of Union (1707) and in 1718 also became responsible, along with Justices of the Peace, for bridges and roads and (from 1832) for raising 'rogue money' for keeping the peace. They often appointed constables until the Police (Scotland) Act 1857 required them to establish a county police force (except for Police Burghs). Their powers remained until county councils were established by the Local Government (Scotland) Act 1889, but they still met annually to appoint members to a Standing Committee, responsible for the county constabulary; the other members were nominated by the county council and it was chaired by the sheriff. In truth, their days were over, but the Commissioners of Supply were not finally abolished until the Local Government (Scotland) Act 1929.

Further reading

Timperely, Loretta R., *A Directory of Land Ownership in Scotland*, (c. 1770).

POLL TAX AND HEARTH TAX

These were two rather clever ideas, dreamed up – or rather, reinvented – to pay for the ruinous wars which underpinned the 'glorious revolution' of William III (r. 1689–1702) and his Stuart wife and co-ruler, Mary (who died in 1694). The difference is that a poll tax is a capitation, based and levied on an individual. A hearth tax, by contrast, is levied on the 'hearth', essentially per house regardless of who lived there.

The poll tax was first imposed in England during the financial crisis at the end of the reign of Edward III (1377), when everyone in the kingdom, except mendicants and minors under 14, had to pay one groat (fourpence) per head. This 'tallage of groats' was regressive – it hit the poor more than the rich – and failed to raise as much as expected. So, there were graduated poll taxes in 1379 and 1380 in which the common herd (older than sixteen) paid a groat as before, and the scale rose up to barons (who paid three marks[1]), earls, bishops and abbots (six marks) and viscounts and royal dukes (ten marks). This was effectively an income tax, and again failed to solve the fiscal issues. The poll tax of 1380 had a narrower banding – fourpence to twenty shillings (one pound) – and had a built-in safety net by which the better-off should help the less fortunate; instead it had the unintended consequence of leading to the great Peasants' Revolt of 1381. Whatever its intentions, it was seen as the poor bailing out the rich. That finished it off as a taxation method for almost three centuries, and ultimately brought down Margaret Thatcher in the 1990s for many of the same reasons.

Hearth tax has an equally chequered career. It was an idea of Charles V of France, and just as the poll tax led to dissent in England, the taxes Charles levied to support the wars against

---

[1] One mark (in Scotland, merk) was two-thirds of a pound, or thirteen shillings and fourpence, 67p in today's terms. Note also that a Pound Scots varied in its value in relation to the English Pound Sterling.

the English disaffected the French peasantry. On his deathbed (fearing God's view of the iniquitous hearth tax, perhaps) he announced its abolition. The government, realising the disastrous effects on the country's finances, refused to bring down any other taxes, and so the Maillotin revolt happened in 1382.

William and Mary faced a similar situation to the English and French monarchs of the fourteenth century. Also, they knew that one of the most valuable lessons learned by both sides in the English Civil War of 1642–6 and 1648–9, was the unreliability of voluntary contributions. The days of melting down plate and ornaments to pay for armies were over. Parliament had also abolished feudal tenures and dues in England, so poll tax and hearth tax were back on the scene.

Hearth tax in Scotland 1691–5

There had been hearth taxes in England from 1662 to 1688, levied twice a year at Lady Day and Michaelmas, one shilling a time per hearth of evey householder whose property was worth more than 20s annually, and who paid rates and poor rates to the local church. The hearth tax returns and assessments which survive are from the period 1662–74 and although the tax continued until 1688, only the assessments for 1662–6 and 1669–74 ended up with the Exchequer. At other times it was licenced out to private collectors who paid a fixed sum for the privilege and kept the rest. Just as unpopular with the lower classes as they had been 300 years before, they had the virtue of being easily accounted. This tax was thought rather simple to collect, as hearths do not move about the way people do, and houses cannot hide from the tax collector. William abolished English hearth tax, so increasing his popularity at the beginning of his reign, but he had no such scruples in Scotland, and at various times from 1691–5 the Scottish parliament levied 14 shillings Scots on every hearth in the land, affecting landowner and tenant alike. Each hearth in a house attracted its own levy, which would seem to be progressive – richer families had more fireplaces – but required internal inspection. Counting chimneys from the outside would have been easier. The money was to pay for the army, and the only exemptions were the poor living on parish charity and in hospitals. The tax proved difficult to collect in practice, especially in remote communities and, of course, the Highlands, where there was probably little enthusiasm for paying towards an army to fight off the Jacobites, whether they were sympathisers or not. Finally, in August 1694 a proclamation required all hearth tax lists to be sent in within two months.

At first sight, these lists would seem to be excellent sources for genealogists, but there are problems. They are arranged by county and parish, and some give names of the owners or occupiers, and the number and names of those exempt by reason of poverty. However, some lists – those for the county of Inverness, for example – only provide the total number of hearths under the name of the heritor (p. 55), but do list the individual poor. Others – the Glasgow parishes are an example – list only the total number of hearths and the monies collected. The accuracy of many of the lists has also been called into question.

Not all have survived – Orkney and Caithness parishes are completely missing – and some are in collections of private papers such as the Leven and Melville Muniments (parishes in Dumfriesshire, Fife, Edinburgh and Shetland) and the Cromartie Muniments (certain parishes in Ross-shire).

The repository for these is the NAS, where they can be found referenced as E69, GD26 (Leven and Melville) and GD305 (Cromartie). However, a number of Family History Societies have extracted the relevant lists for their localities and offer these for sale as printed booklets or on the Internet. For instance, there is a good description of the 1691 Ayrshire hearth tax at www.maybole.org/history/archives. These records are valuable in that almost everyone had at least one hearth – tenants as well as landowners – but be aware that records have not survived for all of Scotland.

Poll tax, 1694–9

Another 'good' idea which did not quite work was the poll tax, imposed in Scotland around the same time as hearth taxes. If the hearth taxes were to pay for the armed forces, the poll taxes of 1694, 1695 and 1698 (twice) were meant to settle the arrears and debts of the army and navy. This was means- and rank-tested starting at 6 shillings Scots with the poor and minors under sixteen exempt. Again, collection proved complicated and the records are acknowledged to be incomplete. Those that exist are arranged by county and parish, but the information is variable – some give names of the Head of Household as well as children and servants.

As with hearth tax lists, these are available for consultation at NAS under Ref. E70 (which also lists some printed versions) and there are local extracts from some Family History Societies. Also like hearth tax, the surviving records are not Scotland-wide and, although they cover just about everyone, the information given is limited.

Other tax records

The eighteenth century post-Union (1707) was a veritable ferment of taxation, which means fertile ground for genealogists. There is a list below, but bear in mind that even though certain taxes would appear to apply to all households or householders (such as commutation tax, inhabited house tax, window tax and consolidated assessed tax), in reality they were only paid by the well-off and thus do not provide complete lists of residents in any given area. Some were levied for specific purposes, such as the additional property taxes to pay for the war with France from 1793. Some were frankly ridiculous – dog tax and clock tax shine out. These records are at the NAS, mostly under Ref. E326 or 327, although some are in other series. They are organised by county and parish or by royal burgh.

Table 12. Notice how almost all of these taxes were replaced by Income Tax in 1799.

Tax	Dates	Description	NAS Refs
Window Tax	1747/8–98	Gives names of householders in houses with seven or more windows or a rent of over £5 a year.	E326/1
Male Servants Tax	1777–98	Certain categories of manservants, with the names of servants, their masters or mistresses given and sometimes the servants' duties. Bachelor householders paid double.	E326/5
Inhabited House Tax	1778–98	Gives names of householders and annual value of houses.	E326/3
Commutation Tax	1784–98	Similar conditions to window tax, in commutation for excise duties on tea.	E326/2
Cart Tax	1785–98	Gives names of owners of carts with two to four wheels.	E326/7
Carriage Tax	1785–98	Gives names of owners of carriages with two or four wheels.	E326/8
Horse Tax	1785–98	Gives names of owners of carriage and saddle horses.	E326/9
Female Servants Tax	1785–92	Gives names of masters or mistresses, names of servants and in some records their duties.	E326/6

Shop Tax	1785–9	Gives names of retail shopkeepers (but not usually the nature of the business) where the annual rent exceeds £5. Not comprehensive.	E326/4
Income Tax	1799–1802	Gives names of individuals with annual incomes of £60 or more from property, profession, trade or office. Very incomplete (two fire-damaged volumes) covering counties A–L, Perthshire and West Lothian. See below for Midlothian. This was replaced in 1803 by an income-based property tax (below).	E326/14
Farm Horse Tax	1797–8	This is the most useful of the 'minor' taxes as it gives the names of owners of (and numbers of) horses and mules, and is therefore a list of tenant farmers and tradesmen. It carried on as Consolidated Schedules of Assessed Taxes (below).	E326/10
Dog Tax	1797–8	Gives names of owners and the number of dogs owned.	E326/11
Clock and Watch Tax	1797–8	Gives names of owners of clocks and gold, silver or metal watches, and the number owned. One for the horologists.	E326/12
Aid and Contribution Tax	1797–8	The only lists which survive are for Peebles-shire. This was an 'additional' tax for one year only on those already assessed to pay duties on houses and was replaced by income tax in 1799.	E326/13
Consolidated Schedules of Assessed Taxes	1798–9	Names of householders, value of houses, number of windows, male servants, carriages, horses and dogs. Counties: Aberdeenshire–Midlothian, West Lothian; also burghs.	E326/15
Midlothian Tax Records	1735–1812	These are the working documents of the tax office, which included Edinburgh, and contain land tax collection records 1735–1803; income tax assessments 1799–1801; property taxes 1803–12 (below); small house duty collections 1803–12; militia and reserve army deficiency assessments 1805; payment ledgers to militia wives and families 1803–15.	E327
Midlothian Income Tax Records	1803–12	This replaced income tax (above) and was unusual in being a property tax assessed on income for all sources. It gives occupations and offices held.	E327

Further reading

Gibson, Jeremy: *The Hearth Tax, other later Stuart Tax Lists, and the Association Oath Rolls*, Federation of Family History Societies.

ELECTORAL REGISTERS

Nowadays, we rather take voting for granted. To an extent, it's hard to avoid. But for a considerable period of Scotland's history, and until quite recently, the franchise was restricted to certain classes of people (see the list on p. 67). When the vote did become more widespread, it was necessary to have lists of those who could vote. That meant names, usually addresses and sometimes even ages and occupations, all of which are beloved of genealogists. The reason was that the eligibility criteria had to be recorded. Some records even give the name of the representative voted for by each individual – so much for the secret ballot!

The study of who could vote and when that happened justifies a book all to itself (and the book by Gibson and Rogers is just that, although it is light on Scottish detail) but in simple terms it happened this way:

Before 1832 – hardly anyone. Representatives of the counties were elected by freeholders (owners of land or other heritable property in the county above a certain value)

1832 (Reform Act passed)[2] to 1867 – owners, tenants and occupiers (male) of land and houses

1868 – male 'prosperous lodgers' – those paying rent of over £10 annually

1882 – unmarried females and married women not living in family with their husbands, if proprietors and tenants, could vote in burgh council elections

1889 – females as above could vote in county council elections

1918 – males over 21, females over 30

1929 – almost everyone over 21, except lords and lunatics

The effect of the 1832 Act in Scotland was that most of the counties continued to be represented by one member, but the six small counties which previously had elected their MP in alternate parliaments, joined in with all the others. In the process, Clackmannanshire and Kinross-shire became a single constituency, Buteshire and Caithness-shire gained separate MPs and the new county constituencies of Elginshire and Nairnshire and Ross and Cromarty were formed. Glasgow and Edinburgh each had two MPs, Aberdeen, Dundee, Greenock, Paisley and Perth one each and the remaining burghs combined into eighteen districts, each electing one MP but with individual votes being added up among the burghs in the relevant constituency. Before there had been a sort of electoral college system whereby representatives from each burgh met to elect the MP. There were some boundary changes, so a burgh for parliamentary election purposes might not be co-terminus with the burgh boundaries or other purposes. But the main change in Scotland was that the proportion of electors in the population changed from 1 in 125 to 1 in 8.

The registers

There are different forms of electoral registers (also called voters' rolls) during these various periods. There will be local elections separate from parliamentary elections, and burgh registers may not be held with counties. Burghs were separate parliamentary constituencies from the counties and some burghs were grouped together as one constituency. For large towns and cities they will be organised by electoral ward. County registers are arranged by parish. Information provided (from 1832 to 1918) will include (by address) name; street number; occupation; whether owner, tenant or boarder, property entitling the individual to vote (because someone may not be living at the address by which he is made eligible). Female voters will be in supplementary registers. Voters' rolls are also useful in that they give the descriptions of wards and districts, with street names.

---

[2] The Reform Act was not a single act, but a series of related statutes, passed by Westminster in 1832: Representation of the People Act; Parliamentary Boundaries Act; Representation of the People (Scotland) Act; Corporate Property (Elections) Act; Representation of the People (Ireland) Act; Parliamentary Boundaries (Ireland) Act.

In 1832 it was possible, and indeed common, for those with qualifications in different constituencies to register and vote in all of them, so an individual might appear on more than one roll, not all of which reflected an actual address.

Sadly, not all registers have survived. By no means are all of them in the NAS (some are, particularly for the period 1832–70 and the rolls of freeholders pre-1832, see below), and many are held in local archives or libraries or at sheriff courts (burgh registers). Some are manuscript and some printed. In some cases, they have been microfilmed. Very few indeed are available on computerised indexes or on the Internet.

Table 13. The NAS has the above registers of electors.

Burghs:		Counties:	
Culross	1832–51	Caithness-shire	1832–60
Dunbar	1832–60	Clackmannanshire and Kinross-shire	1832–62
Dunfermline	1868	Cromarty	1832–3
Earlsferry	1902–4	Hawick district, Roxburghshire	1832–46
Falkirk	1840–65	Inverness-shire	1832–72
Hamilton	1864–5	Kirkcudbrightshire	1832–62
Lauder	1832–61	Linlithgowshire	1837
Newburgh	1833–70	Nairnshire	1847–73
Newport	1899–1900	Peeblesshire	1832–61
North Berwick	1832–1915	Selkirkshire	1832–61
Perth	1876–7, 1892–3	Stirlingshire	1832–62
Stirling	1868	Wigtownshire	1832–61

Further reading

Gibson, Jeremy and Rogers, Colin, *Electoral Registers Since 1832*, Federation of Family History Societies.

BURGESS ROLLS

The history of the Burgess Rolls is as old as that of the burghs themselves. In order to work in a burgh, it was necessary to join a guild of the Incorporated Trades, and this required a Burgess Ticket as a freeman of the burgh. The Edinburgh Burgess Roll, for example, can be traced back as far as 1406. The guilds were effectively medieval trade unions, but also took on some civic responsibilities such as keeping public order, serving with or providing men for the army and payment of crown taxes. Burgesses paid a fee to be admitted, although in early times this was not cash but 'spices and wine' as a treat for the others. The Burgess system was abandoned as late as 1975 when burghs disappeared but most of the guilds, although still in existence, had little function except for charitable activities.

The relationship between the burgh and the guilds was often a complex one. At its simplest, a tradesman, craftsmen or merchant became a Burgess and Guild Brother (abbreviated 'B. and G.B.' in many records). A Royal Burgh was a vassal of the Crown and so a burgess had some responsibility for helping to guard the burgh, serving with the King's or Queen's army when called, paying royal taxes etc. Often burgess records show that a man possessed a corselet, hagbut or other weapon. In return, a freeman could expect the right to work in the burgh, protection from the 'unfree' (both in terms of trade competition and personal safety). The burgesses were, or composed a large part of, the Burgh Council and elected from among their ranks those who ran the burgh. This was especially the case in Stirling, where the guild was exceptionally strong.

REGISTER OF PERSONS ENTITLED TO VOTE IN THE

ELECTION OF A MEMBER OF PARLIAMEN|

FOR THE BURGH OF PERTH,

1914-1915.

FIRST WARD.

§ Disqualified as a Municipal Elector.

NO.	CHRISTIAN NAME AND SURNAME OF EACH VOTER AT FULL LENGTH.	PLACE OF ABODE	OCCUPATION.	NATURE OF QUALIFICATION.	STREET, LANE, OR OTHER PLACE WHERE PROPERTY IS SITUATED.
1	William Abernethy,	19 Unity place,	messenger,	occupant of house,	19 Unity place, Scott street.
2	Charles Adams,	110 South street,	fruiterer,	occupant of house,	110 South street.
3	William Adam,	Woodhead, Guildtown,	fruit merchant,	tenant of shop,	92 South street.
4	Owen Agnew,	67 South street,	scavenger,	occupant of house,	67 South street.
5	Thomas Agnew,	67 South street,	painter,	tenant of shop and store,	67-69 South street.
6	David A. Ainslie,	22 St. John street,	clerk,	lodger,	22 St. John street.
7	Alexander Airth,	20 St. Johnstoun's buildings,	porter,	occupant of house,	20 St. Johnstoun's buildings, Charles st.
8	George Alexander,	Wilson street,	clothier,	proprietor of shop,	198 High street.
9	John Alexander,	17 Princes street,	tailor's cutter,	occupant of house,	17 Princes street.
10	Thomas Alexander,	14 Watergate,	police officer,	occupant of house,	14 Watergate.
11	William Alexander,	142 South street,	labourer,	occupant of house,	142 South street.
12	James G. T. Allan,	26 St. Johnstoun's buildings,	postman,	occupant of house,	2 St. Johnstoun's buildings, Charles st.
13	Robert Allan,	21 King street,	plasterer,	occupant of house,	21 King street.
14	Robert Allan,	198 South street,	dyer's cleaner,	occupant of house,	198 South street.
15	Simon Allan,	147 South street,	iron turner,	occupant of house,	147 South street.
16	Thomas Allan,	89 Canal street,	barman,	occupant of house,	89 Canal street.
17	Alexander W. Anderson,	4 King Edward street,	joiner,	lodger,	4 King Edward street.
18	David Anderson,	91 South street,	lodging-house keeper,	occupant of house,	91 South street.
19	James Anderson,	70 South street,	fireman,	occupant of house,	70 South street.
20	John Anderson,	206 South street,	reel maker,	occupant of house,	206 South street.
21	John Anderson,	41 Canal street,	engine driver,	occupant of house,	41 Canal street.
22	Joseph Anderson,	34 Rose crescent,	sports outfitter,	proprietor of shop,	15 St. John street.
23	Matthew S. Anderson,	8 Kincarrathie crescent,	china merchant,	tenant of shop,	29 St. John street.

Part of the voters' roll for Perth, 1914. Reproduced courtesy of Perth & Kinross Archives.

The merchant guild initially would have included all burgesses, whether merchants or craftsmen. A guild brother was governed by the laws of the guild, framed by the same people, usually, who administered the burgh. In many burghs the merchant and craft guilds fell out and separated over time and each guild kept separate records. There are remnants of the burgess and guild systems in many towns and cities to this day. The tradition of appointing important or influential individuals as burgesses 'gratis' (free) continues in the tradition of conferring 'freedom' of the town or city on a visiting dignitary – a wholly honorary thing. In some places – Stirling is a good example – the guild still exists and performs charitable works. The symbol of the Stirling guildry is a sort of reversed 4 and it can be seen all over the town. One charming hangover of this is that at their meetings the guild members are served with pies whose crusts are decorated with this symbol. The idea was to take it home to prove to a sceptical wife that the husband had indeed been at a Guildry meeting rather than away misbehaving elsewhere.

The Rolls were originally lists of the admitted burgesses who could vote in local elections, initially just by surname, then often arranged by surname within an electoral ward and later more like modern electoral registers – according to house number, street, and ward. After voting reforms in 1884, property requirements were similar to those for entry in Burgess Rolls, so Burgess Rolls and electoral registers not only became virtually the same thing, but looked similar.

There are Burgess Rolls in the libraries or archives of most ancient burghs, and in the NAS. While they may give no more than a name and a trade or guild, they may also provide an address and the name of a father. Since trades were passed on within families, complete lines of relationship can be established.

The earliest entries are in old script and in Latin, with many contractions and abbreviations. Some have made their way into print thanks to the Scottish Records Society and local FHSs. Some are available for download from the Internet (see, for example, The Roll of Edinburgh Burgesses and Guild-brethren 1406–1841 and others at www.scotsfind.org).

Often, someone will be listed according to trade, as in 'Freeman Burgess Barber' or 'Member of the Incorporation of Taylors of Edinburgh'. Watch out also for a tendency to double up surnames when, for example, two brothers are listed, as in, 'prentice to William and James Dods', meaning the Dod brothers.

> **Eason (AEsone)**, James, B., s. to James AE., taileor in Edr., p. to James Walker, skinner, B. 31 Jan. 1694
>
> **Eason**, Thomas, B., mt., by r. of w. Bessie, dr. to umq. Wm. Bowie, skynner, B. 5 Dec. 1655
>
> **Eason**, Capt. Nicholas, commander of H.M. ship 'Chester', B. and G., gratis, by act of C. 7 Nov. 1715
>
> **Eason**, Wm., tanner, B. (admitted first as an unfreeman for payment of 100 merk and then, on production of his discharged indentures, and his master's burgess ticket, as p. to Peter Cowan, paying £5 and 24 shilings in place of the 100 merk already mentioned) 24 Sept. 1742
>
> **Eason**, John, weaver, B., in r. of fr. Adam E., weaver, B. 21 Jan. 1778

Extracts of Eason surnames from the Roll of Edinburgh Burgesses and Guild-brethren. For abbreviations and unfamiliar terms, see chapter 16. Notice that women had the right to pass on their fathers' memberships to their husbands, and widows their husbands' membership to their sons. Those acquiring a burgess ticket by right of inheritance or marriage generally paid a lower fee than those rising from an apprenticeship, and the highest fee was paid by an 'unfreeman' – an outsider who wished to live and work in the burgh.

POOR LAW

The traditions of poor relief in England and Scotland are quite different. In England and Wales, this was originally the province of the local parish, with Acts of 1597 and 1601 ordering the election of an Overseer of the Poor, responsible to the Parish Vestry and the local Justices of the Peace, with tax-raising powers. There were also charities for relief, often administered on the behalf of these and the parish by feoffees (trustees). The Act of Settlement (1662) formalised this and sought to define the responsibilities of the parishes. The resulting system was not wholly satisfactory and demands on local funds increased as the population grew, so various reports and commissions led to the Poor Law Amendment Act (1834) which established Poor Law Unions (of parishes) each run by a board of elected 'guardians'. This system, with its Dickensian workhouses and other familiar props, carried on right up to the reforms of the Liberal Government from 1906 to 1914, which provided what we would recognise as social services (including old age pensions and national insurance) without the stigma that the Poor Law brought about.

Scotland had a different system, based on a voluntary 'giving'. There had been a Poor Law since 1579 (unaltered at the 1707 Act of Union) which, frankly, started out as a set of measures to suppress 'vagaboundis and strang beggaris' (vagabonds and strange beggars). However, it became the practice that the poor should be provided for and that those entitled to relief were essentially the aged and infirm.

The responsible parochial authorities were inevitably the Kirk Session and the heritors. Although the 1579 Act enabled parishes to levy a poor rate, this hardly ever happened and the funds came from church collections (the 'poor box'), seat letting charges, charitable donations and so on. This system was probably fine for rural societies, and where the Kirk held sway, but increasing urbanisation and increasing secession from the established Kirk ate away at its influence.

There were legal assessments introduced in some of the larger burghs in the 1830s but many parishes refused to grant allowances at all. Where granted, the general criteria were:

- over 70
- disabled and insane (and so unable to work)
- children orphaned or destitute

The Poor Relief system from 1845 to 1930

This situation led to Scotland's own Royal Commission in 1843, from the report of which followed the Poor Law Act (Scotland) of 1845, providing an allowance for all those entitled. There was a central Board of Supervision in Edinburgh, but administration continued to be parochial.

A network of poorhouses was established, which differed from English workhouses in minor ways. And not all the poor went to poorhouses – those that did were said to have 'indoor relief', while 'outdoor relief' was one single payment or small weekly payments of cash, or sometimes in the form of clothes, school fees or medicines, given to those not in the poorhouse.

The parochial boards which administered Poor Relief and built poorhouses even took on the registration of births, marriages and deaths, until they were abolished in 1894 and replaced by elected parish councils. Up until the depression of the 1920s there had been a rule that unemployment alone was not an entitlement to Poor Relief. The Poor Law Emergency Powers (Scotland) Act 1921 dealt with that issue, and the parishes then kept separate records of 'ordinary' applications from the 'able-bodied'. There were other inconsistencies in this system. Not only did the amount of relief vary from one area to another, the responsible parish was in theory the parish of birth, or where the individual concerned had been 'settled' for the past seven years, and often paupers were transported back to their home town, or one parish asked another to contribute to the upkeep of a 'stray', sometimes looking to the law to resolve where the responsibility lay.

Poor Law records

In the main, records after 1845 contain far more individual information such as names and ages. The information can be extremely rich and can include: date and hour of application; name, residence and country of birth; date of inspector's visit to applicant; condition (married/single etc.); age; occupation; religion; weekly earnings; disabilities; names and ages of dependants; names of children not dependant; previous applications and their results; disposal (i.e. how settled); grounds of refusal (if refused).

The records of most parochial boards, heritors and parish councils in Scotland have passed to local authorities. Many are now in local authority archives or library services and some at the NAS, particularly some parishes in East Lothian, Midlothian and, unaccountably, Wigtownshire. The local availability is variable – those of Aberdeenshire, Ayrshire, Dumfriesshire and Fife are worth consulting, but the records of others have not survived well (for example, Lanarkshire and Renfrewshire, now largely encompassed by Glasgow, and those of Aberdeen city, Dundee and Edinburgh). Glasgow itself is an honourable exception (see below).

What may be less than crystal clear to researchers are the separate but overlapping responsibilities of Kirk Sessions, parochial boards and heritors, which mean that records are sometimes mixed together – Kirk Session minutes catalogued and archived with heritors' records and vice versa. Consult them all.

Poor Law on computerised indexes

A good example of a database index is that carried out for almost 350,000 people from the Glasgow City, Barony and Govan parishes from 1851 to 1910, which can be consulted on computer at the Glasgow City Archives in the Mitchell Library. There are also indexes for Lanarkshire, Renfrewshire and Dunbartonshire for 1855 to 1900. These records are particularly interesting because of the huge influx of Highlanders and the Irish into Glasgow and the West of Scotland at that time. Once a name is found, the original record books can be consulted. A logical extension of this would be to put the index on the Internet, and to digitise the books themselves and make the images available.

Table 15. Examples of output from the Glasgow City Archives Poor Law index. The reference numbers allow the researcher to consult the actual record in bound volumes.

Poor Law Glasgow

Name2	Name1	Name3	DOB	Born in	Applied	Age	Ref.	
ANDERSON	Janet	Durie	1804	Maryhill	1862	58		
BAIN	Annabelle	Durie	1815	Glasgow	1886	71	D-HEW	15/4/4 p 1264
BAIN	Isabella	Durie	1815	Glasgow	1868	53		
DURIE	Agnes	Durie	1816	Kilmacolm	1882	66	D-HEW	10/3/66 p 268
DURIE	Agnes	Black	1816	Kilmacolm	1874	58	D-HEW	16/16/50 p 21
DURIE	Ann	Crum	1874	Glasgow	1910	36	D-HEW	17/666 p 124455
DURIE	Archibald		1883	Anderston	1909	26	D-HEW	17/653 p 118025
KILPATRICK	Ann	Durie	1848	Glasgow	1913	65		16/13/285 p 42635

Poor Law Lanarkshire

Name2	Name1	Name3	DOB	Born in	Parish	Stated age	No.	Vol.
DURIE	Alexander		1863	Shotts	Shotts	21	1632	CO1/54/38
DURIE	Alexander		1864	Shotts	Shotts	21	618	CO1/54/32
DURIE	Bernard		1849	Bothwell	Hamilton	44	2468	CO1/43/21
DURIE	Fanny	Cowan	1844	Govan	Cadder	26	115	CO1/24/21
DURIE	Fanny	Cowan	1844	Govan	Cadder	27	290	CO1/24/20
DURIE	James		1867		Cadder	11	29	CO1/24/27
DURIE	James		1869	Cadder	Cadder	9	440	CO1/24/20
DURIE	Jemima	(Athya)	1857	Glasgow	Cambusnethan	29	106	CO1/26/66
DURIE	Robert		1868	Cadder	Cadder	10	441	CO1/24/20
DURIE	Robert		1869		Cadder	9	30	CO1/24/27

By contrast, the Edinburgh Poor Law records survived well into the 1970s but were destroyed specifically because an historical researcher wanted to examine them closely. Apparently the concept of poverty was one the Edinburgh Council officers couldn't countenance with any comfort.

Other sources

A number of crafts and trades guilds and similar bodies had a fund to help poor members, or established schools, hospitals and other institutions. Their minute books may include named donations to the poor.

There were also special Highlands Destitution Boards set up after 1846 in response to poverty after the potato crop failure that year. From then until 1852 the Boards gave meals or money in return for work. The registers are in the NAS (Ref. HD) and in most cases give the names (and occasionally the ages) of individuals and families in receipt of this relief.

Further reading

Cage, R., *The Scottish Poor Law 1745–1845*, Scottish Academic Press, (1981).

There are examples of Poor Relief Register entries at www.scan.org.uk/researchrtools/poorrelief.htm.

The Kirkcaldy Kirk Session minutes for 1630–53 are available as a downloadable file from: www.scotsfind.org/kirkcaldy_access/kirkcaldie.pdf.

5

Trades, Craft, Professions and Offices

Examining census and BMD records, you may see abbreviations or occupations which at first make no sense. That is either because the trade has since disappeared, or the usage is local. There is a list of occupations and their typical abbreviations in chapter 16.

While censuses etc. give occupations, it is sometimes fruitful to look at lists of employees, tradesmen and so on to check if individuals appear.

PROFESSIONS

Clergy

There are many printed lists of clergymen for the different denominations. The most important of these, if only numerically, is the *Fasti Ecclesiae Scoticanae* (the succession of Scottish ministers in the Church of Scotland from the Reformation). This multi-volume work, found in most large libraries, gives details of the ministers in the Church of Scotland from 1560 and includes useful biographical, genealogical and other information, plus details of the parish itself. The *Fasti*, published every so often since 1866, is arranged chronologically and by parish. The latest edition by Revd Hew Scott, published in Edinburgh from 1915 to 1928 (7 volumes) covers the period up to then, with four recent volumes taking it up to 1999. Volumes I and II are available online thanks to David Walker at his Scottish Ministers web pages (www.dwalker.pwp.blueyonder.co.uk/Map.htm). The entire volumes can be downloaded as PDFs from The Internet Archive (www.archive.org).

POLMONT

[Disjoined from Falkirk, and erected by the Commissioners of Teinds, 22 July 1724.]

1733 – PATRICK BENNET, born 1705, son of Andrew B., min. of Muiravonside; licen. by Presb. of Linlithgow 7th July 1731; called 1st Sept. 1732; ord. 21st March 1733; died 12th April 1783. He marr. 22nd Dec. 1752, Margaret Henderson, who died at Dundas, 11th Oct. 1800, and had issue-Andrew, born 19th Sept. 1754, died 28th Sept. 1769; George, born 11th Oct. 1755; Lilias, born 4th March 1757 (marr. David Clark); Elizabeth, born 21st Aug. 1758, died 16th Dec. 1760; William, min. of Duddingston; and Margaret, Elizabeth, Patrick, John, who all died in childhood. [Dalmeny Sess. Reg.]

Example of an entry in *Fasti Ecclesiae Scoticanae*

Other publications of this type include:

Bertie, David M. (ed), *Scottish Episcopal Clergy 1689–2000*, Edinburgh (2000).

Burleigh, J.H.S., *A Church History of Scotland*, OUP (1960).

Couper, William J., *The Reformed Presbyterian Church in Scotland, Its Congregations, Ministers and Students,* Edinburgh (1925).

Ewing, Revd William (ed), *Annals of the Free Church of Scotland*, 2 vols, Edinburgh (1914).

Goldie, Frederick, *A Short History of the Episcopal Church in Scotland from the Restoration to the Present Time*, (1952).

Lamb, John (ed), *The Fasti of the United Free Church of Scotland 1900–1929*, Edinburgh (1956).

Lawson, John P., *History of the Scottish Episcopal Church from the Revolution to the Present Time*, Edinburgh (1843)

MacGregor, Malcolm B., *Sources and Literature of Scottish Church History*, McCallum (1934).

McNaughton, Revd Dr William D., *The Scottish Congregational Ministry 1794–1993*, Glasgow: Congregational Union of Scotland (1993).

Roman Catholic Priests 1732–1878, The Innes Review, vols 17, 34, 40, Scottish Catholic Historical Association.

Small, Revd Robert, *History of the Congregations of the United Presbyterian Church from 1733 to 1900*, 2 vols, Edinburgh (1904).

Should it be necessary to contact a particular congregation, church, parish or presbytery, a good place to start is Kirkweb (www.kirkweb.org/home.htm), a wesite of resources for ministers, elders and members of the Church of Scotland.

The United Free Church of Scotland has a *Fasti* laid out in the same way as the Kirk's covering the period 1900–29.

Anyone interested in Catholic clergy should contact the Scottish Catholic Archives in Edinburgh (www.catholic-heritage.net/sca) which has a manuscript collection mainly dating from before 1878, plus the records of the Dioceses of Argyll and the Isles; Dunkeld; St Andrews and Edinburgh; Galloway and Motherwell; the Scots Colleges at home (Blairs, Scalan and Aquhorties) and abroad (Paris, Douai, Madrid and Rome). They will not undertake family history research, but they do try to answer queries. There is also the Catholic Family History Society (www.catholic-history.org.uk/cfhs). The Catholic Record Society (www.catholic-history.org.uk/crs) specifically states that it does not help with genealogical enquiries.

Schoolteachers

Before 1872, when the Education (Scotland) Act made education compulsory in Scotland, teachers in burgh schools were appointed by the Burgh Council. They will be recorded in council minutes. In non-burghal parishes, the heritors and minister of the parish nominated a schoolmaster for interview by the presbytery. Often, the schoolmaster was also the Kirk Session clerk. Appointments of parish schoolmasters will therefore be recorded in Heritors' or Kirk Session records (p. 63) and their confirmations in the Presbytery Minute Books. The Scottish History Society (4th Series, vol 2, Miscellany X) has reprinted lists of schoolmasters appearing in a Parliamentary Commission of 1690 for a number of parishes.

The Free Church of Scotland, which broke away in 1843, also founded its own schools with the teachers appointed by the church deacons. Deacons' Court minutes (rather than the Session minutes) record their appointments. These are available at the NAS.

The Highlands and Islands had particular educational needs, which were met from three sources – the government itself, a charitable gentleman named James Dick and the Society in Scotland for Propagating Christian Knowledge (SSPCK). The upshot is that the poor educational provision led to better recording by the schoolteachers sent to sort it out, than in less troublesome parts of Scotland. There are government records for 1840 to 1863, with the names of schoolmasters at the NAS (Ref E224). The SSPCK records have an alphabetical list of the schoolmasters (NAS Ref GD95) but it may be simpler to consult a copy of *SSPCK Schoolmasters 1709–1872*, edited by A.S. Cowper (Scottish Record Society, 1997). Then there was Mr James Dick, whose will set up the Dick Bequest Trust to assist schoolmasters in the non-burghal parishes of Aberdeen, Banff and Moray. The Trust's records, from 1832, are at the NAS (Ref. DG1/4).

The Educational Institute of Scotland (EIS, the main teachers' trade union) began in 1847 and its records are deposited in the NAS; they name its members but also include earlier records of teachers in Glasgow (1794–1836), Roxburgh (1811–40) and Jedburgh (1824–72).

After 1872, all teachers (and pupil-teachers) will be listed in School Board minute books. These are mainly kept in local archives or libraries, with a few at the NAS. Teacher training colleges may also have lists of graduates.

Lastly, do not neglect the school itself, which may have records going back far enough, or know where they are. There may also be a history written about a particular school, which will be with the school or in the local library. Bear in mind, too, that school records may well contain class lists, admissions records and log books for pupils from 1872. There are collections of Leaving Certificates at the NAS from 1908, but with a 75-year closure period, so they can only be consulted back to the 1930s.

Doctors and other medical professions

Remember that a doctor practising in Scotland may have qualified elsewhere, and the reverse is also the case. Until quite recently, Scotland had five university medical schools – St. Andrews (which no longer teaches Medicine), Edinburgh, Aberdeen, Glasgow and John Anderson's University (which had a medical school from 1799–1947 and is now incorporated into the University of Strathclyde). However, not everyone who qualified as a medical practitioner would necessarily have graduated from one of these. A case in point is doctor, missionary and explorer David Livingstone, who studied at Anderson's College, furthered his studies in London, and returned to Glasgow to qualify, taking the examinations of the Royal College of Physicians and Surgeons, because the fees were lower than those at the universities. Others may have taken a qualification with another Royal College, or from a university or other body in England or elsewhere, such as becoming a Licentiate of the Apothecaries of Cork.

For information before 1858, contact the Royal College of Physicians and Surgeons of Glasgow (from 1785), the Royal College of Surgeons of Edinburgh (from 1770) or the Royal College of Physicians of Edinburgh. In the case of the RCP Edinburgh, all licentiates had to have studied at a university. In general, universities are likely to have more details on the individuals concerned (See Universities and University Graduates, p. 76).

The Medical Register, the official list of registered practitioners in Britain maintained by the General Medical Council, has been published annually since 1859. Scottish doctors were listed in *The Medical Directory for Scotland* (1852–60), *The London and Provincial Medical Directory* (1861–9) followed by *The Medical Directory* (1870 onwards). The latter has more detailed entries with a summary of the doctors' careers, qualifications, posts, published papers and books etc.

The British Medical Association Library in London has most of these as well as membership lists of Royal Colleges and other professional associations, and will take biographical and genealogical enquiries. Contact the library staff if this would be useful (www.bma.org. uk). Another avenue is to contact the library of the Wellcome Institute for the History and Understanding of Medicine, also in London (www.wellcome.ac.uk/library). Doctors will also be listed (usually under Physicians and Surgeons or Apothecaries) in local and trade directories.

Nurses' registers from 1885 to 1930 are at the NAS. There were published annual registers for nurses (from 1921), chemists, pharmacists and apothecaries (from 1869), dentists (from 1879) and midwives (from 1917) but these are not generally accessible, except perhaps at specialist libraries such as the Royal College of Surgeons of Edinburgh, university libraries or the archives of professional bodies such as the Pharmaceutical Society.

Records of health boards started, in many cases, in the eighteenth century and are mainly unindexed, although some are catalogued. There are large collections at Aberdeen Royal Infirmary, Crichton Royal Hospital, Dumfries, Edinburgh University Library (with a special subsite at www.lhsa.lib.ed.ac.uk) and Glasgow University Archives. Local archives and libraries may have records of the local hospitals and health boards. These may also contain details of patients.

Lawyers

Advocates are court lawyers, the equivalent of barristers, and the Faculty of Advocates is the Bar in Scotland. Apart from local street and trade directories, the best source for names is Sir Francis J. Grant's *The Faculty of Advocates in Scotland 1532–1943 with Genealogical Notes*, (Edinburgh: Scottish Record Society, 1944) with the name of the advocate and his father, the date of his birth, death and admission to the faculty, address and details of marriages.

Solicitors in Scotland were called Writers and many, but not all, were Writers to the Signet. These are listed in *The Register of the Society of Writers to the Signet* (1983) from the 1600s to the 1980s. Details include date of birth, father's name, name of spouse and date of marriage and name of apprentice-master. Also consult *The History of the Society of Advocates in Aberdeen* (Henderson, 1912) with details of members from 1549 to 1911 (but note that, despite the name, these are solicitors, not advocates), and *Index Juridicus: The Scottish Law List 1846 to 1961* (Edinburgh: A & C Black).

MOWBRAY, JOHN, OF HARWOOD   30 November 1792
    Apprentice to William Campbell of Crawfordton.—Second son of Robert Mowbray, Merchant in Edinburgh. *Born* 1768. *Married* (1) 7 April 1801, Elizabeth (*died* 1 November 1804), daughter of John Scougall, Merchant in Leith ; and (2) 26 June 1807, Patricia Hodge (*died* 14 December 1852) of Awalls. *Died* 19 September 1838.

MOWBRAY, JOHN THOMSON, LL.D.   8 March 1832
    Apprentice to John Mowbray.—Son of Robert Mowbray, Merchant in Leith. *Born* 12 May 1808. Treasurer, 1882. Author of *An Analysis of the Conveyancing (Scotland) Act*, 1874, and other legal works. *Died* 17 April 1892, unmarried.

An extract from the listing of The Signet Library, reproduced with permission.

Universities and university graduates

The four 'older' universities in Scotland have matriculation lists (those who entered the university) and lists of graduates. In earlier times, when most students were aiming for the clergy and were expected to be unmarried, the students may be listed as 'Bachelors' (gaining a B.A. degree after two years) and graduates, (with an M.A. degree after four years), as 'Masters'.

Some of these lists are printed in book form and others are available for web browsing, although the information in them is variable, sometimes being no more than a name and the date of entry of graduation. St Andrews has matriculations from 1747–1897 although other published lists exist (e.g. *Early Records of the University of St Andrews*, published by the Scottish History Society). Glasgow has published matriculation lists from 1728–58 and graduation lists from 1727–1897. Aberdeen's lists cover 1593–1860. Edinburgh only published lists of graduates in certain disciplines. Anderson's University is now part of the University of Strathclyde in Glasgow, where the records are held.

Businesses

Many businesses have had their records deposited in local or other archives and some will have lists of employees, directors and shareholders, including wage books. Good places to start are the National Register of Archives for Scotland at the NAS (www.nas.gov.uk/nras); Glasgow University Archives Business Records Centre (www.archives.gla.ac.uk) and local archives. The Business Records Centre has particular collections dedicated to the Scottish

Brewing Archive (with records of the brewing industry in Scotland), the Greater Glasgow NHS Board Archive (dating back to the late eighteenth century), the Business Archives Council of Scotland, materials relating to Clyde shipbuilding and an index of bankruptcies from about 1745–1914 (although the original records are held at the NAS).

Some banks have consolidated the archives of all their constituent banks and associated businesses, two good examples being the Bank of Scotland (www.hbosplc.com/abouthbos/history/group_archives.asp) with records from 1695, and the Royal Bank of Scotland (www.rbs.com/about01.asp?id=ABOUT_US) from the 1660s.

INDUSTRIES

Coal mining

As mining was one of the major employers in the nineteenth and early twentieth centuries, there is a great deal of information in the records of mining companies. This will mainly be no more than a name, grade of work and pay, but in the absence of a census record, it may tie a person or a family (since women and children were employed too) to a particular locality. All mineworkers lived more or less on top of the pit, often in villages constructed specially to house them. This can be a help in tracing someone who disappeared from a locality, as they may have moved to find mine work elsewhere. Early on, the mines were in private hands and the records may be in private archives (or perhaps donated to the NAS or a county archive), or in a large archive such as Glasgow's Business Records Centre. Those mines which became part of the National Coal Board when nationalisation took place in 1947 may have their records collected, along with other NCB material, at the NAS, some of which dates back to the 1700s. Some Family History Societies have collected names of local miners in their publications.

Railways

There were a great many railway companies in Scotland, which gradually merged, were swallowed up or just disappeared. Tracking down their records can be a nightmare, but as ever the NAS is a good place to start. The most complete are those of the North British Railway Company. These records may give a worker's date of birth, job and location (not an address as such, but a good indication).

Working out which railway companies existed and became part of others is a genealogical puzzle in itself, but help is at hand: *British Railways: Pre-grouping Atlas and Gazetteer* (1997) lists and describes the companies before 1923, and *Was Your Grandfather a Railwayman?* (Richards, 2002) is also a great help. Ewan Crawford's diligent work on www.railscot.co.uk is well worth consulting – it also shows the routes of older railways using linked, clickable maps, which can be a help in tracking down how people may have got from A to B via X, Y and Z in the nineteenth century.

SERVICE PERSONNEL

Almost all official records for the armed services are held at The National Archives (TNA) in Kew, London. There is really no option but to visit, request a search, or try to find digitised records via their website (www.nationalarchives.gov.uk). On the positive side, they do have many resources online, including World War I Medal Cards (essentially a record of service) searchable by name and downloadable as PDFs. These are six to a sheet, by surname, so it is possible to discover an unknown relative or ancestor by one of those happy accidents which pepper genealogical research.

Medal cards are also available on Ancestry's website, thanks to a deal with the Western Front Association. These have the advantage over TNA website records of having both sides of the card imaged – sometimes there is a correspondence address or other information on the back.

The Medal Cards records are remarkably complete – approximately 90% of those who fought in the British Army in the First World War – and have the added benefit of including all ranks, whereas most services' sources list officers and warrant officers only. However, they are not great quality and also take some practice to interpret (See Fig. 21). It is worth concentrating on one, as what seems like sparse information actually contains a wealth of detail. In the case of my grandfather's service record, all that we knew was that he had joined the Household Cavalry (the family joke was that he had lied about his height) and spent some of the war breaking horses shipped over from Argentina to France. The Medal Card tells a more complete picture, most of which was new information.

The First World War Medal Card of the author's grandfather, David Durie. Courtesy of The National Archives.

Table 16.

Name	Corps	Rank	Regiment No.
DURIE,	5th Dragoon Guards	Private	12079
David	Machine Gun Corps	Private	41089
	Royal Canadian Regiment	Private	12079
Medal	Roll	Page	Remarks
Victory (X)	CMG/102B	57	
British	do	do	
Star (15)	MGC/2C	Y	
Theatre of War served in	1		
Date of entry therein	18 5 15		

The 'Roll' entry is to the Army Medal Office references of the original medal rolls for each medal. The Theatre of War first served in is 1 (Western Europe) and the date he went there; often this is left blank, usually indicating that the soldier was sent to France in 1916 or after. 'Remarks' might have included (but not in this case) a commission date, if commissioned from the ranks; date of death; whether taken prisoner of war; discharge date; and other details.

1914/15 Star (*left*)

Authorised in 1918, the 1914/15 Star was awarded to those individuals who saw service in France and Flanders from 23 November 1914 to 31 December 1915, and to those individuals who saw service in any other operational theatre from 5 August 1914 to 31 December 1915.

British War Medal (*middle*)

The British War Medal 1914–1920, authorised in 1919, was awarded to eligible service personnel and civilians alike. Qualification for the award varied slightly according to service. The basic requirement for army personnel and civilians was that they either entered a theatre of war, or rendered approved service overseas between 5 August 1914 and 11 November 1918. Service in Russia in 1919 and 1920 also qualified for the award.

Victory Medal (*right*)

The Victory Medal 1914–1919 was also authorised in 1919 and was awarded to all eligible personnel who served on the establishment of a unit in an operational theatre.

From this and other information (see below), it is possible to piece together the following:

– Private David Durie received the service medals given to everyone in the 1914–18 war, in his case the Victory Medal, the British Star and the 1914/15 Star
– When he joined up on 18 May 1915, at seventeen, he was originally in the 5th Dragoon Guards, more properly called the 5th Battalion (Princess Charlotte of Wales') Dragoon Guards, mustered in August 1914 at Aldershot. They were part of the 1st Cavalry Brigade, 1st Cavalry Division (The Cavalry Division was renamed the 1st Cavalry Division in September 1914). This was one of the first divisions to move to France, and remained on the Western Front throughout the war. It took part in most of the major actions where cavalry were used as a mounted mobile force, and also many others where the troops were dismounted and effectively served as infantry. Their battle honours were: Mons, Le Cateau, Retreat from Mons, Marne 1914, Aisne 1914, La Bassée 1914, Messines 1914, Armentières 1914, Ypres 1914–15, Frezenberg, Bellewaarde, Somme 1916–18, Flers-Courcelette, Arras 1917, Scarpe 1917, Cambrai 1917–18, St Quentin, Rosières, Amiens, Albert 1918, Hindenburg Line, St Quentin Canal, Beaurevoir, Pursuit to Mons, France and Flanders 1914–18
– The 1st Cavalry Brigade Machine Gun Squadron was formed on 28 February 1916 and he is recorded as being with the Machine Gun Corps
– Later, he was with the Royal Canadian Regiment, possibly as a machine gunner/instructor

Most of this information came from the wonderfully informative www.regiments.org and from the sources listed elsewhere in this chapter. The details of the medals are taken from www.nationalarchives.gov.uk/documentsonline/medals.asp.

Other records for the Armed Forces
The National Archives website has excellent information guides (start with 359) which summarise the records held there and elsewhere, but a few others are worth mentioning.

Army
British Army WWI Service Records, 1914–1920 are available at Ancestry (licenced from TNA), although they are in no sense complete. Many of the 'burnt records' were lost or damaged during enemy action in the Second World War. They cover non-commissioned officers and other ranks and include not only the expected name, age, birthplace, occupation, marital status, and regiment number but other useful details such as height, hair colour and some detail of the service career, including misbehaviour.

Ancestry (via TNA) also has the British Army WWI Pension Records 1914–1920. These are essentially the service records of non-commissioned officers and other ranks who claimed disability pensions for service in the First World War after discharge, and payments to widows.

The Army List (an official publication) was first published in 1740 and regularly from 1754, with officers indexed by name from 1766 and arranged by regiment.

Hart's Army List is a multi-annual publication covering the period 1839–1915, and some volumes will be available in larger libraries. Certain years are available on CD-ROM, and they are starting to become available as PDF downloads at Google Books (books.google.co.uk).

Remember also that the East India Company had its own armed forces up to 1857, and produced an *East India Register and Army List*. It also contains lists of civil servants, chaplains and judges and others, including a list of stockholders at the time. The 1819, 1845, 1857 and possibly other editions are available at Google Books.

Navy

National Archives records include:

- Royal Naval seamen (www.nationalarchives.gov.uk/documentsonline/royal-navy-service.asp): non-officers in the Royal Navy 1873–1923.
- Second World War merchant seamen's medals (www.nationalarchives.gov.uk/documentsonline/seamens-medals.asp).
- *Steel's Navy List* (1782–1817), the official annual *Navy List* (from 1814) and the *New Navy List* (1839–55) cover officers; *The Naval Biographical Dictionary* by W.R. O'Byrne (1849, but covering lieutenants and rank above active or retired in 1846) has more information including the officer's father.

The National Archives also has ships' muster lists (including information covering Scotland from 1707–1878) with the place of birth and often the age of ratings and officers, but only if the name of the ship is known. From 1853 it is possible to trace any seaman by name in the Continuous Service Engagement Books (1853–72) and the Registers of Seamen's Services (1873–95) which also has date and place of birth and service details.

Ancestry has a database of Royal Naval Division Casualties of The Great War, 1914–1924, listing name, service branch and unit, date and cause of death, service history, and burial information.

Royal Air Force

Apart from records at The National Archive, for officers serving in the RAF (formed in 1918 from the Royal Flying Corps and Royal Naval Air Service) there is the *Air Force List*, published from 1919. In many cases, the records of soldiers who transferred from the army to the RFC or RAF will be among army service records.

Militia and yeomanry

As these are local forces, their records will be with sheriff court and county records, or in the private papers of local landowners, in some cases deposited at the NAS, which also has some Ministry of Defence records including lists of Territorial and Auxiliary Forces Association members and Volunteer Forces. The largest collections are from the Napoleonic times when the whole country felt imminently threatened by invasion. Privy Council papers (NAS Ref. PC15/15) contain the registers of the East Lothian Militia 1680–3 and although there is little of immediate genealogical relevance (family connections can, however, be inferred from similar surnames), there are often ages and sometimes heights of the militiamen recruited. A nationality is often given in terms of Scottish, English, Irish or Foreign.

London Gazette

Service personnel commissioned, promoted, posted or awarded a medal or other honour are 'gazetteed' – that is, listed in the *London Gazette*. Larger libraries may have printed copies of the *Gazette*, but the entire historical archive is being digitised, and the two World Wars plus twentieth-century Honours and Awards are available online. Search the archive at www.gazettes-online.co.uk/index.asp for a name. This will produce a PDF of the page in question. Various legal notices, including insolvencies, were required by law to be published in the *London Gazette* (or its Edinburgh and Belfast counterparts) and so can also be a useful source of information on companies, individual bankruptcies and property purchases.

ROYAL HORSE ARTILLERY
Glamorgan; Private John Hubert Elliot Lawson
from Inns of Court Officers Training Corps,
to be Second Lieutenant. Dated 19th August, 1915.
ROYAL FIELD ARTILLERY.
1st Highland Brigade; Lieutenant John R. Cooper
to be temporary Captain. Dated 1st June. 1915.
Extract 8248 from the Supplement to the *London Gazette*, 18 August, 1915.

Scottish armed services

The National War Museum of Scotland at Edinburgh Castle holds records concerning the history of Scottish service personnel from the seventeenth to the twentieth century, including regimental order books, private diaries, the papers of some regiments including the Royal Scots Greys and information on some local militia and fencibles (www.nms.ac.uk/warmuseumhomepage.aspx). This covers all service personnel who were of Scottish origin, not just those in Scottish regiments.

There are also excellent records in many of the Regimental museums around Scotland, including:

Argyll and Sutherland Highlanders, Stirling (www.argylls.co.uk)
Ayrshire Yeomanry, Alloway-by-Ayr
The Black Watch, Perth (www.theblackwatch.co.uk)
The Cameronians (Scottish Rifles) collection at Low Park, Hamilton (www.southlanarkshire.gov.uk)
Fife and Forfar Yeomanry, Cupar (www.army.mod.uk/qoy/c-squadron)
Gordon Highlanders, Aberdeen (www.gordonhighlanders.com)
The Highlanders Regimental Museum and Queen's Own Highlanders, Fort George, Inverness
Royal Highland Fusiliers, Glasgow (www.rhf.org.uk)
Royal Scots Dragoon Guards, Edinburgh (www.scotsdg.org.uk)
Royal Scots, Edinburgh (www.theroyalscots.co.uk)

Muster Rolls for the Scottish Army, in the Exchequer records at the NAS (Ref. E100), date from the 1640s and unfortunately are organised by regiment. One way to cut down the search of literally thousands of rolls is to guess the name of the local landowner or Clan Chief and check if he were a colonel of a regiment. The rolls give names and residences of both officers and men, their ranks and a muster date, but nothing explicitly genealogical unless there is a run of similar surnames. In certain parts of the country, notably the Highlands, this might not indicate a familial link as much as fealty to a chief.

Details of the Commonwealth War Graves Commission are given on p. 303.

Merchant seamen

These records are rather different, as they are in effect commercial. Agreements between masters and crew were made compulsory in 1835 and crew lists for Scottish vessels survive in the NAS and Glasgow City Archives, as well as the National Archives (Kew) and the National Maritime Museum in London. These agreements give the name, age and place of birth of crew members, but usually the name of the ship or the home port is needed before any search is possible. Fortunately, they are being digitised and transcribed, but slowly. A worthy example is Bob Sanders and the Cardiff crew agreements at his maritime history website (www.angelfire.com/de/BobSanders/CREWIN.html).

For a list of trades and occupations, their common abbreviations and Latin equivalents, see chapter 16.

OLD FACES, OLD PLACES,

AND

OLD STORIES OF STIRLING.

By WILLIAM DRYSDALE.

STIRLING:
ENEAS MACKAY, 43 MURRAY PLACE.
1898.

LIST OF SUBSCRIBERS.

Adam, Robert, Royal Gardens.
Aitken, James, Whins of Milton.
Aitken, John, Rockvale Mills.
Alexander, William, 15 Park Place.
Allan, William, 1 James Street.
Anderson, George, Beechgrove, Bridge of Allan.
Anderson, Mrs, 11 Princes Street.
Andrew, Dr, Doune.

Bain, William, 30 Barnton Street.
Bald, William, Edinburgh.
Barker, Daniel, Craigview.
Barrett, F. T., for Mitchell Library, Glasgow.
Baxendine, Andrew, Bookseller, Edinburgh.
Begbie, George, 26 Port Street.
Beith, Gilbert, 15 Belhaven Terrace, Glasgow.
Beith, Robert D., 32 Hartington Place, Edinburgh.
Bennie, Andrew, District Bank, Manchester.
Borland, Mrs, 82 Baker Street.
Boss, W. G., Edinburgh.
Boswell, William, Albert Place.
Bowie, Thomas, Broom Cottage, Alloa.
Bowie, William, 17 Cowane Street.
Bridges, James, Registrar, Perth.
Brown, A. Harvie, Larbert.
Brown, Andrew, Dollar.
Brown, James, Windsor Place.
Brown, John, Murray Place.
Brown, J. T., Gibraltar House, Edinburgh.
Brown, William, 2 Arcade.
Buchanan, Andrew C., Whitehouse.
Buchanan, John, 7 Broad Street.
Buchanan, Treasurer Andrew, 9 Baker Street.
Burden, John, Troy, U.S.A.

Cairns, Robert, Union Bank.

An example of the Subscribers List for a book, some with occupations and addresses. The book itself has interesting biographical material.

Clubs, societies and subscriptions

If an occupation, profession or interest is known, it can be worth checking the records of relevant organisations. Many of these will be in the NAS, but societies themselves may have kept early records (See, for example, the Writers to the Signet, p. 76). These may be no more than a roll of members, sometimes with an address or at least a town or village, and a date, but may also indicate a father's name. If the minutes of clubs are available, they may have useful insights – if someone died, applied for relief, or took office within the society, it may be noted.

Also, people subscribed to books which, essentially, they paid for up front so that the author or publisher could afford to produce the volume. Second-hand bookshops are as good a source of these as any, but many libraries have them tucked away.

6

Courts and the Scottish Legal System

Scots law

Scottish law (Scots law) is different from the law of England and Wales; always has been and still is today. Scotland has had some form of parliament since the twelfth century and was a completely separate country up until 1603, when James VI of Scotland also became James I of England (The Union of the Crowns) and maintained its own laws and parliament. At the Union of the Parliaments in 1707 under Queen Anne, last of the Stuart monarchs, the parliaments of Scotland (in Edinburgh) and of England and Wales (in Westminster) were united in Westminster, but separate Scottish acts were passed. This was the situation until 1999, when the Scottish parliament was reopened after almost 300 years. It deals with 'devolved' matters such as education, health and prisons, while issues with a UK-wide or international impact, such as certain taxes or defence, are 'reserved' to Westminster. Technically, Scotland, England and Wales make up Great Britain, and the United Kingdom includes Northern Ireland. However, unlike Wales or Northern Ireland, Scotland is a nation-state.

The Scottish legal system

Although it shares *some* institutions with England, such as the House of Lords (when sitting as a court), the Scottish legal system is different in its character and its institutions, including the courts. In its origins, Scots law had feudal law (dealing with land and immoveable property and their inheritance), Roman law (for moveable property) and canon law (for ecclesiastical matters). Later, there was statute or enacted law.

Statute law comes from a body with legislative powers, such as Royal proclamations or orders, acts of parliament (either the old Scots parliament, the UK parliament or the new, devolved Scottish parliament), European Community Treaties or European legislation when adopted into local laws, local authority by-laws etc.

Common law derives its authority from judgment in the courts and is based on the Scots legal tradition. It relies on precedent and was initially derived from Roman law (as codified under the Emperor Justinian), canon law (the law of the church), the writings and considerations of eminent legal scholars such as Lord Stair, Erskine and Bell, Hume, and Alison (the 'institutional writers') and from feudal land tenure.

Both common and statute law have equal authority and often deal with the same subjects, but enacted law can override common law.

Scottish lawyers are either solicitors (in older times called 'Writers') who deal with clients, or advocates (equivalent to English barristers) who argue cases 'at the bar', i.e. in court. Recently, some solicitors – called solicitor-advocates – have been able to argue cases before a judge. Judges may be appointed either from the ranks of solicitors or advocates.

The Not Proven verdict

A particular and much-cherished feature of Scots criminal law is the possibility of one of three verdicts – 'guilty', 'not guilty' and 'not proven', the latter being controversial for 300 years. In 1827 Sir Walter Scott, who was a lawyer and a sheriff as well as an author, described it as 'that bastard verdict, not proven'. It means that the judge or jury feel that there is a case, but the prosecution has not made it well enough. The original verdicts in Scots law were 'culpable and convict' or 'cleanse'. The terms 'guilty' and 'not guilty' were introduced by Oliver Cromwell during the Usurpation (1653–8), when English judges were imposed on Scotland. After the Restoration of the Monarchy with Charles II (1660), Scottish judges reverted to pronouncing whether the facts in an indictment were 'proven' or 'not proven'. The verdict of 'not guilty' was reintroduced in 1723.

COURTS

The main reason for genealogists to search out court records is for criminal or civil cases, or for wills. Chapter 9 deals with wills and testaments in greater detail, but here the structure and succession of the courts is considered.

There are two strands of the Scottish courts – criminal (which governs the relationship between the individual and the state) and civil (relationships between individuals).

- The criminal courts are, in ascending order of authority: The District Court, the Sheriff Court, and the High Court of Justiciary.
- The civil courts are, in ascending order of authority: The Sheriff Court, the Court of Session, and the House of Lords (in London).
- There are also specialist courts dealing with, for instance, employment matters, land, criminal offences against children and Heraldry (the Court of the Lord Lyon).
- Previously, from the Reformation (1560s) until roughly the 1860s there were commissariot courts, which took over the executry functions of the bishops' dioceses, and had identical boundaries.
- There were Barony Courts up until 1747.
- There was also the Privy Council, sitting as a court.

While a decision of a higher court is binding on a lower court, the High Court of Judiciary (criminal) and the House of Lords (civil) are not bound by their own decisions, nor is a decision of an English court binding upon a Scottish court, except that the House of Lords sitting as an English court will be persuasive in a similar Scottish case. Scottish judges may sit in both criminal and civil courts, although some are considered to specialise in particular areas.

Privy Council and the High Court of Justiciary

In the early days the highest court was the Privy Council, which heard cases concerning the more serious crimes (including witchcraft[1] and sedition) up to its abolition in 1708. After that the High Court of Justiciary took on that function.

The records of these courts contain not only the details of convicted criminals, but may also have information on addresses, family members, relationship to witnesses and so on. They also make for fascinating reading concerning the social conditions of the day. Mainly, Privy Council cases concerned the rich and landed, but High Court cases did not, so they are a good source of information on ordinary citizens, unlike so many records.

---

[1] There is an online database of Scottish witchcraft cases by Edinburgh University at www.arts.ed.ac. uk/witches/index.html.

Privy Council cases have been printed and indexed for 1545–1691, published in thirty-five volumes. The latter few years (1692–1708), are not indexed, but the original case records and minute books are at General Register House, Edinburgh (NAS Ref. PC).

High Court of Justiciary

The High Court (established 1672) became, and is still, the supreme criminal court in Scotland, with exclusive jurisdiction over serious crimes (murder, treason, heresy, counterfeiting, rape and other sexual offences and crimes likely to lead to transportation). The High Court is also a court of appeal from criminal proceedings in the Sheriff or other lower courts. Trial records before 1800 are at General Register House, later ones at West Register House and those less than seventy-five years old restricted, with court. If looking for case files themselves, they tend to be in three separate categories:

– Processes or precognitions (also known as 'small papers', 'case papers' or 'sitting papers') – the documents presented in the court including the indictment (charges against the accused), depositions (witness statements, evidence, statements by the accused etc.), confessions, other relevant information on the crime and the accused and also the jurors and witnesses. Also consult the Lord Advocate's Department (NAS Ref. AD14–15);
– Minute books – the summaries of the trial proceedings in court (for cases tried in Edinburgh from 1576 and circuit cases from 1655). Not all cases come to trial from precognition;
– Book of Adjournal – the official account including indictments, verdict and sentence, if any (cases in Edinburgh, cases from 1576 and circuit cases from 1890) plus some trial transcripts from 1888 onwards (NAS Ref. JC36), details of which will shortly be added to our electronic catalogue.

Documents for the period 1800–55 are relatively easy to find, but for earlier years there may be a fair amount of digging to do in old file boxes. Case papers from 1840 onwards are catalogued and searchable at www.nas.gov.uk/catalogues, and those from 1801–39 are being added. Anyone interested in the details of the trials themselves should consult the Further Reading on p. 89.

Court of Session

The Court of Session (established in 1532) looked after non-criminal cases, except for certain offences against property such as arson. There are some minute books, some of these printed and indexed, and Session records are slowly appearing online. Divorces before 1900 – a rich source of family history information – are sadly among the slowest to appear. There is a card index at West Register House. Sometimes further paper was produced after a case, for instance, to check if a court decision had been enforced or followed – settlement of debts would be one example. These appear in the Diligence Registers which have minute books and in some cases indexes. Hornings (a legal hangover from the days of being 'put to the horn') are where the court instructs someone to pay or carry out some duty. If this fails, inhibitions prevent someone selling goods or property until debts are settled and Apprisings (adjudications) are where the court hands over a debtor's property to a creditor.

Commissary Courts

Wills are a different matter, discussed in Chapter 9. Before the Reformation (c. 1560), bishops could confirm testaments submitted to them by parish priests and administer the estates of the intestate deceased. In February 1564, after a period of some confusion, the first Commissary Court was established in Edinburgh by letters patent, followed by a further twenty-one, these taking over the duties of the ecclesiastical courts.

The 'commissariots' (the districts in the jurisdiction of Commissary Courts) were administered by officials called 'commissars'. Their geographical boundaries were the same as those of the pre-Reformation church courts, more or less the medieval sees (dioceses) with no reference or relationship to the historic county boundaries. For instance, property in the county of Perth could be dealt with by Dunblane, Dunkeld or St Andrews Commissary Courts; property in Fife by St Andrews or Edinburgh. Beware cases where the county of death has the same name as a Commissary Court.

The Edinburgh Commissary Court was the principal one, which heard appeals from the local courts, could confirm testaments of those with moveable property in more than one commissariot, deal with the property of Scots dying furth of the realm (outside Scotland), and of foreigners who had assets in Scotland. They were abolished by the Commissary Courts (Scotland) Act of 1823 to be replaced by Sheriff Courts, but did not disappear overnight.

Sheriff Courts

Sheriff Courts date back to the twelfth century but had real force from 1 January 1824 when the Commissary Courts (for land and inheritance matters) were wound down. The Sheriff Courts took over responsibility for the confirmation of testaments with some overlap (the Edinburgh Commissary Court remained until 1836). Therefore, check testamentary records and registers of both Commissary Courts and Sheriff Courts from 1823 to the 1830s.

Just to confuse matters further, when a Sheriff Court was exercising its powers of executry it used the term 'commissary'. The Commissary Office of Edinburgh Sheriff Court took over the role of confirming executry of Scots who died abroad leaving moveable property in Scotland. Between 1858 and 1900 non-Scottish courts will have fuller versions of such wills.

However, Sheriff Courts dealt with all sorts of other matters, civil and criminal, some of which would be appealed to the higher Court of Session or High Court. There were 'solemn' trials (involving a sheriff and jury) and 'summary' trials (heard by the sheriff alone). Sheriff Courts may also hold records for other administrative procedures – certificates and licences, roups (bankrupt auctions) and sequestrations, small debts, deeds, aliment (dealing with the support of illegitimate children), fairs and markets and the like – as well as thefts, assaults, minor nuisances, accident enquiries and juvenile cases. The state of these records and their cataloguing is variable in terms of quality and extent (sometimes civil and criminal cases are held separately, and sometimes, like in earlier periods, together) but for post-1824 matters, always check the local Sheriff Court. The records themselves may be in the local County Archive or at West Register House (NAS Ref. SC) if the records are over twenty-five years old. This is not the case for the Sheriff Courts of Lerwick (held by Shetland Archives) or Kirkwall (Orkney Archives).

Burgh (burghal) Courts

These were the equivalent of Sheriff Courts for minor offences committed within Royal Burghs and their records will be at General Register House, (NAS Ref. B, unindexed) or in local archives.

Justices of the Peace Courts

The Justices of the Peace Courts (NAS Ref. JP) also considered minor offences and the records are either held locally or at West Register House, unindexed.

Other courts

The Admiralty Court (NAS Ref. AC) was concerned with crimes committed on the high seas (smuggling, piracy etc.) and also crimes committed in harbours. The records start from 1557 and include criminal trial from 1705 to the court's closure in 1830, (NAS Ref. AC16) at West Register House.

Franchise Courts

These were local courts where a local landowner held criminal and civil jurisdiction from the Crown for the relevant area. There were four categories depending on the nature of the landholding:

- regality courts
- barony courts
- stewartry courts
- bailiery courts

See pp. 130–33 for more details. All of these, except barony courts, were abolished in 1747, and the barony, whose powers were effectively curtailed, fell away, too. The records are mostly at General Register House (NAS Ref. RH11) and some have been digitised (not yet available online, but in the NAS search rooms). They may also be part of private collections, or in Burgh and Sheriff Court records.

Covenanters

The Registers of the Privy Council (NAS Ref. PC) and the High Court of Justiciary (Ref. JC) plus a special collection (Ref. JC39) deal with Covenanters and can be consulted at the NAS. Privy Council records have names of Covenanters (and others) sent to North America in the seevnteenth century. Most of these are in the third series, vols VI–X for 1678–85. High Court papers have, in particular, records of actions against Covenanters, 1679–88, with lists of those accused, depositions of the prisoners and witnesses and other material (Ref. JC39).

Jacobites

The trials were held in London and so the records are at TNA in Kew; some High Court of Justiciary records include material on Jacobite treason trials in 1748 and 1749 (NAS Ref. JC7).

Transportation

The details of prisoners sentenced to be transported can be found along with the registers for the prisons local to the courts where they received sentencing (NAS Ref. HH). Transportation was actually from England so TNA, Kew, has records within files for the Home Office (transportation registers, 1787–1870) with microfilm copies under RH4/160/1-7 at West Register House. The registers run chronologically according to the date of departure of the relevant ship, with a list of convicts by name, place of transportation and length of sentence. There are also some transportation records for 1653–1853 within the High Court files at NAS (Ref. JC41).

Prisons and prisoners

The Scottish Office Home and Health Department records at West Register House (NAS Ref. HH) have prison registers (Ref. HH21) which give details on trials and sentences, place of birth, age, height, occupation and religion and in some later instances, photographs. Digital versions are on computers accessed in the search rooms. There are also some prison registers in Sheriff Court records (Ref. SC) for Angus (1805–27); Ayr (1860–3); Fort William (1893–1936); Jedburgh (1839–93); Kirkcudbright (1791–1811); Selkirk (1828–40); Stirling (1822–9). Some entries from the Tolbooth warding and liberation books of Edinburgh 1657–1816 (NAS Ref. HH11) are published in Fairley's *Book of the Old Edinburgh Club*.

Further reading

Pitcairn's Criminal Trials in Scotland, 1498–1624, Bannatyne Club (1829–31).

Selected Justiciary Cases, 1624–1650, Stair Society (1953, 1972 and 1974).

Records of the Proceedings of the Justiciary Court, Edinburgh, 1661–1678, Scottish History Society (1905).

Roughhead, William, *Notable Scottish Trials*, William Hodge & Co., Edinburgh (1905 onwards), see www.edinburghclub.org.uk.

Fairley, J. (ed), *Book of the Old Edinburgh Club.*

A List of Persons Concerned in the Rebellion, Scottish History Society (1890).

Dobson, D., *Directory of Scots Banished to the American Plantations*, Genealogical Publishing Company (1983).

Seton, B.G. and Arnot, J.G. (eds), *The Prisoners of the '45'*, Scottish History Society (1928–9).

Legal terms, Scotland's People – www.scotlandspeople.gov.uk/content/help/index.aspx?r=551&431

Counties & Commissariots List – www.scotlandspeople.gov.uk/content/help/index.aspx?r=551&572

Courts Map – www.scotlandspeople.gov.uk/content/help/index.aspx?r=551&636)

Scottish Counties, Scottish Archives Network (SCAN) www.scan.org.uk

7

Charters

The Registers

Three excellent sources of family and historical information are:

  – Registers of the Privy Council of Scotland (1545–1689)
  – Register of the Great Seal of Scotland (Registrum Magni Sigilii Regum Scottorum, 1306–1546) or Reg. Mag. Sig.
  – Register of the Privy Seal of Scotland (Registrum Secreti Sigilli Regum Scotorum, 1488–1584) or Reg Sec. Sig.

These are not consulted as much as they might be, because they are considered 'difficult'. Certainly, they tend to be in Old Scots or Latin up to a certain date, but they are rather formulaic and even without understanding much of the matter to hand, names, dates and land details are usually easily understood.

Before looking at the records themselves, it is worth considering the bodies which produced them.

The Privy Council of Scotland

The job of the Privy Council of Scotland was to advise the King, as with the equivalent body in England (which continues to the present in an altered form). The Privy Council of Scotland existed from the thirteenth century (although there are few records from that time), flowered in the late fifteenth, and came to its full powers during the minority of various monarchs, when it effectively ruled Scotland along with the Regent. It found a new role after 1603 – when James VI left Scotland to more or less rule itself while he went to be James I of England – and lasted until its abolition on 1 May 1708, after the Union of 1707. The Privy Council developed from the King's Council (Curia Regis), which was the body of royal officers and advisers to the sovereign.

In some ways the Privy Council was more important than parliament, as its registers show. It dealt with administrative, economic and social matters as well as the political aspects of government, including the administration of justice, regulation of trade and shipping, overseas travel (with a form of passports), took oaths of allegiance, dealt with beggars, witches, recusants, Jacobites, Covenanters and outlaws. It is mostly the records of its judicial function which have survived.

In February 1490, according to the parliamentary record of that time, parliament elected six barons (landowners), eight royal officers, two bishops and an abbot or prior, to form a council for the 'ostensioun and forthputting of the King's authorite in the administracioun of justice'. These Lords of Secret Council, together with the Lords of Session and the Lords Auditors of Exchequer, were part of the larger body, the Lords of Council. After 1532 the judicial aspects were handled by the new College of Justice (later the Court of Session) and from 1545 it kept a separate register.

James VI told the English parliament that he governed Scotland with his pen, by which he meant that he sent written instructions to his Privy Council who carried them out. He instituted this form of government which was carried on by Charles I, interrupted by the Covenanters (who set up their own governing body from 1638 to 1641) and the occupation of Scotland by Cromwell. The register has gaps corresponding to these periods of inactivity. Charles II set up a Privy Council in London to direct government in Edinburgh after his Restoration in 1660, and James VII carried it on. Although this Privy Council survived the Revolution of 1688–9, it only lasted one year past the 1707 Act of Union.

Lord President of the Privy Council

The Lord President was counted one of the Great Officers of State in Scotland. Initially, the Lord Chancellor was its President *ex officio*. (The Lord Chancellor of Scotland was another of the Great Officers of State. The office existed from at least the 1120s, and from the fifteenth century it was normally an earl or a bishop). From 1610 the President of the College took the seat in the Chancellor's absence, and from 1619 there was an additional President of the Privy Council, the two presidencies separated in 1626 by Charles I. Charles II made the Lord President of the Council one of the King's chief officers in 1661. The Lord President was assisted by the Keeper of the Privy Seal (used to impress the king's stamp in wax, rather than have him sign every document); the Keeper was also a Great Officer of State.

The Chancery and the Great Seal

From the twelfth century, the Chancery was the office which issued written documents in the name of the monarch. These included not only Acts (brieves or brief warrants relating to judicial and administrative matters) but also charters, grants of lands and titles, letters patent conferring nobilities, dignities and offices, naturalisations and legitimisations (of children, so they could inherit), remissions (pardons), charters of incorporation, patents (until 1853) and licences to operate a mint or print money. To indicate the sovereign's authority under which these were granted, they bore the Great Seal, kept by the Chancellor as head of the Chancery and his Keeper of the Great Seal (only a slightly lesser title). Later, the Chancellor and Keeper also passed documents under 'Quarter Seal' (in fact, the top half of the Great Seal) and the Prince's Seal.

The Quarter Seal, first used in the reign of James I, was impressed on precepts (orders) to Crown officers to give sasine of lands after retours, and of landed property belonging to or fallen to the Crown as the *ultimus haeres* (ultimate heir). The Prince's Seal was reserved for grants of land in the Stewartry (principality) mainly in the Lothians, Ayrshire and Renfrewshire.

Passing the seals

There was a complex hierarchy of checks and stages that charters went through before finally being authorised, the whole process known as 'passing the seals'. First, there was a 'signature' – a warrant to drawing up the charter under the royal 'sign manual' (hence 'signature') and typically written in Scots. The Signet Office issued a precept (in Latin) which ordered the Keeper of the Privy Seal (See below) to issue another precept under that seal authorising the issue of the charter under the Great Seal. One reason why this unwieldy procedure was used may relate to the fact that a fee was payable at every stage, and the money was needed because there were a lot of clerks and officials to pay at every stage. If that seems like circular logic and an excuse to keep lawyers, officers of state and copying clerks in jobs, that may be as much explanation as is needed. In the late 1600s it became possible for some grants to go directly from the signature to the Great Seal, and the entire exercise finally collapsed in 1847.

After 1707 and the Act of Union there was only one Great Seal for the whole of Britain (and later the United Kingdom) but a new seal was used in Scotland for 'private rights'. From 1999 the First Minister of Scotland is the Keeper, and the Keeper of the Registers of Scotland is deputed to have custody of the Great Seal, the Quarter Seal, the Prince's Seal and the cachet (a stamp bearing the royal sign manual).

Great Seal registers

The early charters and charter rolls are mainly lost, not least because Edward I burnt or removed many before 1300 or so, and the earliest surviving roll comes from the reign of Robert Bruce after 1315. Only in 1424 did the registers start as volumes. Apart from the Cromwellian period, the charters are in Latin right up to 1847. Fortunately, hardly ever does any genealogist or family historian need to look at the original registers, as fully indexed abridgements are published for charters from 1306–1668 (indexes are in Latin until 1651) in the volumes universally known as Reg. Mag. Sig. or RMS.

Apart from the documents in the NAS (Table 17), many libraries have volume copies of Reg. Mag. Sig. and they are available for sale printed, on CD or by download from MEMSO (see Further Reading, p. 96).

Table 17. The references for Great Seal materials at the NAS.

NAS reference	Description
C1-3	Register of the Great Seal of Scotland 1315–current (1300s to 1668 published in 11 volumes) with indexes of people, places and offices at the end of each volume
C2	Charters in the Register of the Great Seal 1668–1919
C2, C3, also C7, C19, PS2, SP4	Remissions 1668–1906
C3	Charters in the Paper Register 1668–1852
C3, also in C16, C38	Commissions 1668–1955
C4	Register of Confirmations and Resignations 1858–68
C4, C5, also C16, C17	Charters in the Principality Register 1716–1913
C5	Register of Crown Writs 1869–74
C6	Indexes 1582–1919 (superseded by Reg. Mag. Sig.)
C7	Great Seal Warrants (1st series) 1663–1794, 1807–current
C10	Draft Great Seal Warrants 1732–1886
C11	Draft Great Seal Warrants (Paper Register) 1738–1902
C13	Warrants of Crown Writs 1869–74
C14	Quarter Seal Record 1751–61, 1831 onwards (contents per volume from 1831)
C14–C15	Quarter Seal records, 1652 onwards
C15	Quarter Seal Warrants 1652–8, 1662 onwards (but incomplete before 1775)
C16	Prince's Seal Registers 1620–1819 (many missing)
C17	Prince's Seal Warrants 1717–1874 (many missing)
C18	Draft Prince's Seal Warrants 1739–1819 (many missing)

The Privy Seal

Originally the king's own personal seal, probably from the time of Alexander III (after 1272), the privatum sigillum or privy seal came into customary use during the reign of Robert Bruce (1306–29), mainly for everyday and minor matters, and to instruct the Chancellor to issue charters under the Great Seal (See Passing the seals, p. 91). The earliest records in the Register of the Privy Council are from 1488, and by then the whole intricate edifice of the use of the signet, cachet and sign manual was in place. Obviously, there was no use of the Privy Seal during the Cromwellian years, as there was no king. The last use of the Privy Seal of Scotland was in 1898.

There were two procedures for grants under the Privy Seal, largely to do with authenticating that the original warrant or order was genuine. When there was a warrant under the sign manual ('per signaturam'), the Privy Seal was sufficient power on its own to grant leases of Crown lands, pensions, respites, moveable property which had fallen to the Crown (by reason of *ultimus haeres*, escheat, suicide or straightforward confiscation) plus appointments and presentations to minor offices, benefices, university chairs and the like, travel warrants and various licences (such as permission to print). These are mainly in Scots or later in English.

A charter passed after a warrant was issued under the signet (*per signetum*) had to pass the Great Seal. This mostly concerned charters, remissions (pardons), and legitimisations, and Latin was used.

Obviously, there should be a correspondence between an entry of a precept in the Privy Seal Register (*Registrum Secreti Sigilli Regum Scotorum*, abbreviated as Reg. Sec. Sig. or RSS) with one later on in the Great Seal Register, but not all are there. Be aware also that the documents and their abridgements in the register are ordered by the date of sealing, which was sometimes months or even several years after the issue of the original warrant, even if the grant was backdated. For this reason, it is worth checking indexes of warrants as well as the registers' indexes.

The records

All of these are available in the Historical Search Room, General Register House, Edinburgh.

Table 18. The references for Privy Seal materials at the NAS.

NAS reference	Description
PS1	Register of the Privy Seal, old series 1488–1651 (1488–1584 also published in 8 volumes) indexed by people, place and office, plus a subject index in vol. 8
PS1	Presentations to Benefices under Privy Seal 1567–1600, people and places
PS2	Register of the Privy Seal, new series (Latin) 1661–1788, 1795–1810, some indexed (also PS7)
PS3	Register of the Privy Seal, new series (English) 1661–1898, some indexed. Gap 1789–95 (also PS7)
PS3 (also PS13)	Privy Seal English Record 1660–1782, people and offices
PS4	Register of Precepts of Remissions under the Great Seal 1611–22
PS5	Register of Precepts for Charters under the Great Seal to Baronets of Nova Scotia 1625–38
PS6	Minute Books 1499–1745 (also PS7)
PS7	Various indexes 1499–1811:
	Index to apprisings and offices, 1499–1651
	Latin Register, index of persons, 1661–1705
	Minute book for Latin Register, 1744–73
	Minute book for English Register, 1745–1811
PS8	Responde Books (fees payable) 1752–91, 1795–1847
PS9	Account Books of Privy Seal fees 1763–97, 1808–98
PS10–13	Warrants for the English and Latin Registers 1571–1898
PS14	Not used
PS15	Registers of Precepts for Charters to Baronets of Nova Scotia 1627–37
PS16	Miscellaneous papers c. 1600–1898

1586. At Edinburgh, 13 Jan.
A Lettre of Gift maid to JOHNNE BRISBANE and his assignais, ane or maa,—of all the gudis movable and unmovable that pertenit to Donald Brisbane, his brudir, and now pertening and may pertene to the kingis hienes as eschaet, throu the being of the said Donald fugitive fra his lawis and at his horne for the slauchter of umquhil Robert Noble: With command to the schiref of Dunbertane to mak the said Johnne be answerit of the said eschet guddis, etc.   Subscripta per dominum Regem. vs.   iii. 145.

1587. At Strivelin, 22 Jan.
A Lettre maid to JAMES, ABBOT OF DUNFERMLIN, thesaurare, and his assignais, ane or maa,—of the gift of the warde, releif and nonentres of the landis and barony of Dury, liand in the schirefdome of Fyff, and of all utheris the landis, rentis, and possessiouns, with tenentis, tenandriis, and service of fre tenentis, togidder with the malis, proffitis and dewiteis of the sammin, with thair pertinentis, quharesumevir thai be within the realme,—quhilkis pertenit to umquhil Johne of Dury of that ilk, and now pertening to the king and being in his handis be resone of ward be the deces of the said umquhil Johne . . .; and als of the mariage of Robert Dury, sone and aire to the said umquhil Johne, quhilk failzeand the mariage of the aire or airis male or femel succedand to the said umquhil Johnis heretage, etc.   Per Signaturam subscriptam per Regem. Gratis.   iii. 152.

of Raith, knicht, and James Kirkcaldy of the Grange, fra all passing on inquestis, etc., apoun actionis criminale for thair lifetymes, etc. Subscripta per Regem.
vi. 49 et vii. 52.

3572. Apud Edinburgh, 11 Dec.
Preceptum Legitimationis ANDREE STRATOUN, bastardi, filii naturalis David Stratoun burgensis de Dunde, etc. Per Signetum.   vi. 69 et vii. 78.

3573. At Edinburgh, 12 Dec.
Ane Respitt maid to ALEXANDER MURE and four utheris personis, for thair tresonable remaning and byding fra the oist and army of Sulway in contrar the kingis lettres, proclamationes, etc. Per Signaturam manu Regis, etc.
vi. 60 et vii. 65.

3574. At Edinburgh, 13 Dec.
Ane Lettre to HENRY KEMPT his airis and assignais,—of gift of all males and proffittis of the landis of Ottirstoun with the pertinentis, liand within the schirefdome of Fiffe, of all termes bigane that thai have been in our soverane lordis handis throw nonentre of the richtuis air thairto and ay and quhill the richtuis air or airis thairof recover the samin . . .; with power . . . to occupy the saidis landis with his awne gudis or to set thaim to tenentis . . . Per Signaturam manibus Regis et thesaurarii subscriptam.   vi. 42 et vii. 42.

Extracts of the sort of abridgements found in the printed versions of Reg. Sec. Sig. and Reg. Mag. Sig. Notice the sort of matters dealt with – precepts of naturalisation and legitimisations, criminal law, land transfer confirmations etc. Notice that they are listed (top of the page) by calendar year and regnal year. For explanations of the terms used, consult Chapter 16.

However, these and many other printed volumes of early charters are available digitised at MEMSO (Medieval and Early Modern Sources Online). There are many English records here, too. It is a subscription service but can be accessed for free (and complete volumes downloaded) by anyone with an Athens password, which most University students and staff will have (log on at www.tannerritchie.com/memso.php).

Genealogical information in Great Seal and Privy Seal Registers

Not everyone will have ancestors who appear in these records, as they mostly concern individuals who had some direct dealings with the sovereign or Officers of the Crown.

183. 9th June 1481.] Instrument of Sasine following on a precept from King James the Third (dated at Edinburgh, 19th May 1481), for infefting HENRY PITCARNE as heir of his father, George Pitcarne, of a fifth part with a thirtieth part of the lands of Colernie, in the sheriffdom of Fife. The precept is addressed to the baron of the barony of Ballinbreich, and sasine is given by John Scot, serjeant and bailie of George, Earl of Rothes, 9th June 1481, on the west side of the principal messuage of the lands. Witnesses, John Oliphant of Kelle, Walter Oliphant, John Mallwing, Thomas Dischington, John Lesle, John Dure, and George Fyff; John Symsone, A.M., of St. Andrews diocese, by imperial authority notary public. [1833, Box 47.

374. 21st February 1529.] Charter by William Lummysden of Ardree, selling and alienating to DAVID PITCARNE of Forthir-Ramsay, and ELIZABETH DURIE, his spouse, in conjunct fee, and their heirs, etc., the whole two parts of his lands of Forthir-Ramsay, in the sheriffdom of Fife and barony of Ardree: To be held from the granter of the king and his successors, in fee and heritage for the service of ward and relief. At Forthir-Ramsay, 21st February 1528-9. Witnesses, Robert White in Benethyl, John Cokburn of Newton, Adam Lummysden, Sir David Bangall and Sir George Bunat, chaplains, Thomas Paige and Thomas Maknevyn, laymen, and Sir Alexander Gaw, notary public. Signed by the granter. [2648, Box 68.

377. 23rd April 1529.] Instrument of Sasine following on and narrating a precept dated at Craill, 27th March 1529, by William Lumsden of Ardre, baron of that barony, for infefting DAVID PITCAIRN of Forthir, and ELIZABETH DURIE, his spouse, in the two part of the granter's lands of Forthir-Ramsay, in the barony of Ardre and shire of Fife. Sasine given, 23rd April 1529. Witnesses, James Pitcairn, Thomas Paige, John Edward, and Thomas Millar. Thomas Ferye, of St. Andrews diocese, by apostolic authority notary. Witnesses to precept, Adam Lumsden, Thomas Maknevin, and others. See No. 374. [923, Box 26.

384. 4th February 1532.] Charter by William Lummysden of Ardree, selling and alienating in favour of DAVID PITCAIRN of Forthir-Ramsay, and ELIZABETH DURE, his spouse, their heirs, etc., the third part [cf. also No. 374 *supra*] of the granter's lands of Forthir-Ramsay, in the sheriffdom of Fife and barony of Ardree: To be held of the king for ward, relief, and other due services. Signed by the granter, 'Wylȝem Lūysd of Ardre wᵗ my hand.' [Seal gone.] At Forthir-Ramsay, 4th February 1531-2. Witnesses, John Cogburne [Cockburn] of Newton, A . . . Paige, William Terwat, John Lawsoun, and Sir John Findlaw, presbyter, with Sir Thomas Walterstoun (?), presbyter and notary public. [2003, Box 51.

Abridgements of a linked series of land transfers from Laing Charters.

However, due to the ready availability of the printed and indexed registers (and indexes of later records not yet printed or digitised) they are worth using for early surname or place name hunting.

Other charters

There are other printed indexes to and abridgements of various charters, royal and court documents and the like. One of the best known is the widely available Laing Charters, a calendar of documents held by the University of Edinburgh and covering the years 854 to 1837. The abridgements and indexes are in English.

Parliamentary records

Best of all, the entire proceedings of the Scottish Parliament from the first surviving act of 1235 to the Union 1707 are now available in a fully searchable online database thanks to ten years' diligent work by the School of History at the University of St Andrews. The website (www.rps.ac.uk) offers parallel translations of original Latin, French and Scots text into modern English with standardisation of place names and personal names and direct links from the modern translation to the original manuscript record.

This is not just dry-as-dust lists of acts and minutes – there is real genealogical information in here. For example, the successful 1567 Summons of Reduction concerning 'the wife and bairns of the late George Gordon, 4th Earl of Huntly', is a complaint at the forfeiture of the late Earl's lands because of his 'crimes of lese-majesty' – conspiracy against and laying hands on Mary Queen of Scots' person at Aberdeen and the slaughter of various lords of council and session, even though he was Roman Catholic – and praying to be restored to 'their ancient honour, fame and dignity and be able to possess and enjoy offices, honours and dignities'. It lists all the 4th Earl's children. Another example is the *Ratification in favour of William Scott and his brethren* (1641) which gives a genealogy spanning generations and continents. Ancestor-hunters and those researching families back to their origins can find the first mentions of a name and, if lucky, the attachment of the name to land and the name of a parent, wife or son.

Further reading

The following series will be available at large libraries and also, in many cases, on CD-ROM from commercial publishers:

Registers of the Privy Council of Scotland (1545–1689), edited between 1877 and 1970 by John Hill Burton, David Masson, Peter Hume Brown and Henry Macleod Paton.

Register of the Great Seal of Scotland / Registrum Magni Sigilii Regum Scottorum 1306–1546, 11 volumes edited by J. Maitland Thomson and J. Balfour Paul, Edinburgh: Scottish Record Society (1984) in Latin

Register of the Privy Seal of Scotland / Registrum Secreti Sigilli Regum Scotorum 1488–1584, 8 volumes edited by M. Livingstone et al., Edinburgh: H.M. General Register House/Her Majesty's Stationery Office (1908–82)

Calendar of the Laing Charters, edited by Revd John A. Andrews, University of Edinburgh (1899)

The Scottish Record Society (www.scottishrecordsociety.org) has published a number of lists, indexes, abridgements and transcripts of records.

The Scottish History Society (www.scottishhistorysociety.org) publishes longer editions of historical documents.

MEMSO (Medieval and Early Modern Sources Online). Many early document sources in printed form are accessible as searchable PDFs from www.tannerritchie.com/memso.php.

RPS. Records of the Parliaments of Scotland to 1707, available as searchable lists from www.rps.ac.uk.

8

Local Records

Scottish 'County' records

Scotland isn't as simple as 'thirty-three counties, thirty-three records centres'. For one thing, there are no counties any more, ever since the last-but-one reorganisation of regional government in 1974. Then there was a further reorganisation in which Regions disappeared. (What is it with politicians that they think the answer to everything is to change the maps?) There are now, since 1995, thirty-two Scottish unitary local authorities (ULAs), with the added complication that the Scottish Executive has governmental powers. For simplicity's sake, genealogists continue to talk about 'County' archives, recognising that this is a convenient fiction.

For various historical reasons there is not a one-to-one mapping of ULAs to archives. The functions of some of the smaller administrative units became subsumed within Regions, which no longer exist. For example, the records of Renfrewshire etc. are now and forever bundled with Glasgow, and Banffshire with Aberdeenshire. Others, though, retained some form of record independence: Clackmannanshire (which used to be Britain's smallest county with Britain's longest county name) is a ULA with its own archives. Also, some have delegated censuses etc. to a local library, or a dedicated Family History Centre, as in the Borders with the building of the Heritage Hub (Scottish Borders Archive and Local History Centre) in Hawick (www.scotborders.gov.uk/council/specialinterest/heartofhawick).

The map on p. 98 shows the 'historical' counties (pre-1974) and Table 19 on p. 104 has the list of archives, by 'historical' county. Some historical designations (e.g. Glasgow, Lanarkshire or Edinburgh, Midlothian) have had no real administrative validity for a long time. They have significance in that older census and BMD records will be tagged by county and then parish. For the purposes of census data pre-1911 these county designations are appropriate, but they lose all meaning in more recent BMD records, for example. This can lead to database problems where a record of, say, Barony will come under Lanark in earlier records but Glasgow in later ones. It makes searching difficult and in some cases downright misleading.

THE HISTORICAL COUNTIES AND BURGHS OF SCOTLAND, ENGLAND, WALES AND IRELAND

Genealogists are used to seeing British census data, vital records, civil registrations and other information given in terms of County and (in Scotland) Burgh. But Britain has had no counties, nor Scotland any burghs, since 1975. It's important to know, therefore, how present-day administrative areas fit with the older system, and more importantly, where the records are now held. In the process, we can have some fun with the history of how Scotland, England and Wales were organised and managed. Americans will recognise concepts like 'County' and 'Sheriff', which they adopted from the Scottish tradition.

The punchline is this – although counties no longer exist as administrative units of local government in the United Kingdom, the equivalent areas roughly correspond to the old

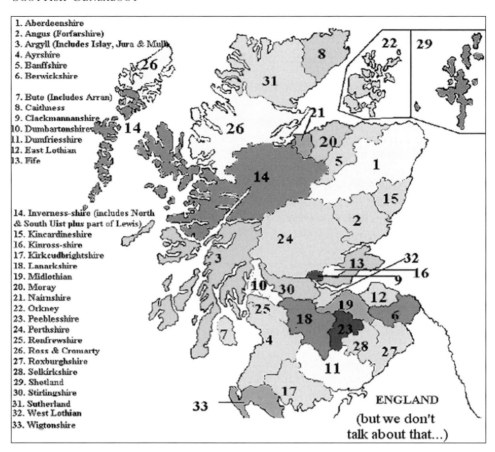

1. Aberdeenshire
2. Angus (Forfarshire)
3. Argyll (Includes Islay, Jura & Mull)
4. Ayrshire
5. Banffshire
6. Berwickshire

7. Bute (Includes Arran)
8. Caithness
9. Clackmannanshire
10. Dumbartonshire
11. Dumfriesshire
12. East Lothian
13. Fife

14. Inverness-shire (includes North & South Uist plus part of Lewis)
15. Kincardineshire
16. Kinross-shire
17. Kirkcudbrightshire
18. Lanarkshire
19. Midlothian
20. Moray
21. Nairnshire
22. Orkney
23. Peeblesshire
24. Perthshire
25. Renfrewshire
26. Ross & Cromarty
27. Roxburghshire
28. Selkirkshire
29. Shetland
30. Stirlingshire
31. Sutherland
32. West Lothian
33. Wigtonshire

ENGLAND
(but we don't talk about that...)

The 'historical' counties of Scotland pre-1974.

historical counties, despite two major rearrangements in the 1970s and 1990s. These are sometimes known as the 'Ceremonial Counties' or 'Postal Counties'. But how did all this come about?

The monarchy

Scotland has a sovereign, who is simultaneously the sovereign of England, a situation which began when King James VI of Scotland also became James I of England in 1603, and was further entrenched at the Union of the Parliaments in 1707. At present, the sovereign is Queen Elizabeth II – there are those who claim that the present queen should properly be called Queen Elizabeth I of Britain and Scotland, and Queen Elizabeth II of England, but this was cleared up by the 1953 Royal Style and Titles Act 1 & 2 Eliz. 2 c.9. A number of postboxes bearing the EIIR cypher were vandalised so Scottish postboxes now only bear the crown of Scotland to prevent any further mischief. In Scotland, Her Majesty is known as 'Queen of Scots'.

At the Union of Parliaments under Queen Anne (the last Stuart monarch), when Great Britain and later the United Kingdom were formed, Scotland retained control over its laws, courts, church, education, medical system, banks, censuses, civil registration and other activities. Since 1999 Scotland has had its own parliament in Edinburgh, and largely runs its own affairs. Matters which affect the whole of the United Kingdom, or have an international dimension like defence, international relations, economic policy, taxation and so on, are 'reserved powers', dealt with by the UK parliament in Westminster. However, most of Scotland's administration was laid down before 1603 and much of it remained in place until well into the twentieth century.

Counties and Burghs

First, some definitions: A county is the same as a shire, as in Renfrewshire in Scotland (which is the county around Renfrew); likewise Oxfordshire in England. But the two words have different origins. It's strange that Britain had counties at all, as it traditionally meant the realm of a Count, as in many European countries, but Britain has no Counts. It does, however, have Dukes, Marquises, Earls, Viscounts and Barons (which aren't the same in Scotland). But Earl equals Count, and an Earl's wife is a Countess.

A Shire was the area around a fortified castle, administered by a sheriff – an Anglo-Saxon official whose main job was to raise taxes. This defended place usually became the shire town. In Scotland, a Burgh, sometimes called a 'Schire' in old documents, is a town with special legal status, as we will see. And a city is a large town with a special charter (in England it also has to have a cathedral).

Modern counties are therefore an amalgam of the medieval county (the land ruled by a noble) and the shire (an administrative unit), with the most prominent settlement becoming the county town, which may or may not be a Burgh (Scotland) or Borough (England).

Still with me? It's about to get more complicated.

How it all started

During Anglo-Saxon times, and when the Danes were in charge, England was run by four great jarls (earls) with taxes raised on the king's behalf by a sheriff, looking after a shire. Scotland had been a semi-unified country since the 850s, but in practice large swathes of the Highlands and Islands were still under the control of great mormaers (equivalent to earls or jarls) who more or less paid attention to the king in the Lowlands, but not much and not always. Wales had a series of warrior-princes. Ireland was still tribal, under a complex system of kings and a high king, whose position was largely ceremonial and federal. From the time of Brian Boru's rule (about AD 1000) up to the Norman takeover in 1171, the high king was anybody who could take the Hill of Tara and hold it until pushed off. American readers will recognise the echo of this situation in the children's game King of the Hill.

The Normans never conquered Scotland, as they did England in 1066 and Ireland soon after, but there was considerable Norman influence over Scottish Lowland society, as the rulers of both countries intermarried and the nobles became exposed to each other's ways. The characteristic attribute of the Anglo-Norman structure was the feudal system of land-holding. The political and military needs of medieval society were such that the monarch had to control the whole country – difficult at a distance – and also had to be sure of armed men when necessary. This became a social and economic system supported by law.

The main relationship in the feudal system was that between superior (lord) and vassal (tenant). The king ultimately owned all land but granted out parts of it 'in knight fief' – meaning that armed and mounted fighting men could be provided when necessary, paid for out of the proceeds of the land. A fief could also be an office of the Crown, a right to hunt or fish, collect wood and so on. In turn, such a superior could give over part of his land or fief to a vassal, who then owed a duty of homage and fealty plus certain services. These could be military, ceremonial (e.g. being a standard bearer), practical (such as supplying bread, flour, crops etc.) or monetary. In exchange, the superior guaranteed protection to the vassal. The provision of land was confirmed by a charter in writing. These charters are a great source for early genealogy, as they mention land holders and give names of witnesses.

Land-holding by a vassal from a superior was a life interest only and not necessarily passed down. The superior needed to know that the land was held by loyal and capable men, and if the duty was military the Crown had the right to repossess the land if the heir in possession was a child or a female. However, an heir could negotiate to avoid this aspect of the tenure by redeeming the conditions by, say, paying money or goods instead. But the Crown retained an interest in the land. Later, when the development of longbow and artillery rather took away the point of mounted knights-in-armour, new forms of tenure emerged, particularly blench tenure (where no feu duty was paid at all) and feu farm or feu-ferme tenure.

As well as being the ultimate land-holder, the king was also the fount of justice. Just as the land was parcelled out, so was local administration and the justiciary courts, so the feudal system also became a decentralised government. While this worked well in England, Scotland was different. The kings, based in the Lowlands, had a shaky grip on the northern parts of the country, where powerful earls were themselves kings in all but name, as they had been under the old Celtic system. In effect, Scotland was divided into separate principalities called 'regalities'. The growing influence of Anglo-Norman ideas at the court of Malcolm III (Malcolm Canmore), from the mid-eleventh century onwards, came about because of the years he spent in exile at the English court of Edward the Confessor, and his marriage to Margaret, sister of an Anglo-Saxon claimant to the English throne. Four of Malcolm's sons became King of Scotland after his death in 1093 and the last, David I ('David the Saint'), who married an English princess, the grand-niece of William the Conqueror, strongly promoted the feudal system. Many later famous families came to Scotland during David's reign, notably Bruce, Huntingdon, Lindsay and Somerville, and they brought their Anglo-Norman ideas with them. David was also Earl of Northumberland and Huntingdon and Prince of Cumbria. At the death of England's Henry I, David pushed the Scottish border the furthest south it had ever been, or would ever be again. He also set the scene for the later Stewart dynasty by appointing Walter FitzAllan the first hereditary Steward of Scotland. But most importantly, he thoroughly reorganised the government and justice systems, as well as the Church and the burghs. He spent the end of his life gardening and planting apple orchards, leaving a large and prosperous Scotland to his eldest grandson Malcolm IV in 1153.

Barons, baronies and baronets

This is an area of great potential confusion. In England a baron is a peer of the realm, meaning a lord. Baron is the lowest rank of the peerage and, until recently, entitled the holder to sit in the House of Lords. In Scotland, it's different. A baron was a 'Great Man' who held lands directly of the king by a grant *in liberam baroniam* ('in free barony'), so barons were therefore large landowners. They could levy taxes and tolls for goods taken through their lands or sold on them. In exchange for the right to do this, the baronies helped manage the kingdom. The king's control was exercised locally through barony and regality courts, so a barony became an administrative unit, and baronial duties included maintaining public justice, with the powers of fossa and furca, (the pit and the gallows), by which women were drowned and men hung – literally the power of life and death. Some great barons had a 'holding in regality', meaning that the king gave so much power to a baron that it excluded the rights of the king's officers (with the exception of trials for treason against the king's person).

But a Scottish baron is not a noble, although individual barons may also have had other noble titles. For that reason, in Scotland they are 'Baron of Such-and-such', as opposed to a noble, 'Baron So-and-so'. One person could hold several, or many, baronies, and occasionally you will see these for sale on Internet sites. The barony does not necessarily carry with it any lands, houses or money, and has no real duties or rights any more. The '*caput*' of the barony may be (and usually is) no more than a pocket-handkerchief-sized piece of land or just a piece of legal paper. But a barony can be inherited, transferred or sold. The holder is not entitled to call himself 'Lord Such-and-such' although his wife will be addressed as 'Lady Such-and-such', which may account for their changing hands at $100,000 and upwards. Anyone turning up in, say, Inversneckie, waving a certificate declaring him to be Baron of Inversneckie, and expecting to get as much as a cup of coffee on the house, is in for a disappointment.

A baronetcy is different again – it's a kind of hereditary knighthood dreamed up by King James VI and I in 1611, partly to raise money for wars (it was an early 'cash for honours' system) and partly to encourage settlement and development in the province of Ulster in Northern Ireland. It was rather clever in that it did not depend on giving a seat in the House of Lords. Somewhat different were the Scottish baronetcies of Nova Scotia instituted in 1625 by King Charles I in an attempt to encourage settlement in the colony (but few even went to see their lands and by then Nova Scotia was in French hands anyway).

Since the Union of 1707, all baronetcies are of the United Kingdom. Queen Victoria used baronetcies to honour the deserving middle classes without giving them grand peerages.

Baronets are titled, for example, Sir Hufton Tufton Bart. or Bt. and his wife would have the courtesy title Lady Tufton. A female baronet would be Dame Hilda Bracket Bt. They are not in any sense nobles, nor necessarily, land-holding; it is just an honour. Margaret Thatcher became a Baroness (a peerage) in her own right, but her husband Dennis was granted a baronetcy, now inherited by his son, which explains why he is Sir Mark Thatcher Bt. although he did nothing to deserve it except belong to the right family. Baroness Thatcher's title is a life peerage and will die with her, so Sir Mark will not become a baron (Lord Thatcher). While Prime Minister, she rewarded her retiring Deputy, William Whitelaw, with a Viscountcy, which is hereditary. Rather cleverly, the succession was limited to his heirs male, and as he had only daughters, the title died with him.

Burghs

In time towns became more important than baronies. David I granted many charters establishing burghs, as did his successors. The burgh was a centre of administration and also had trade privileges such as the right to hold a market or fair. The real power of a burgh was its ability to levy tolls and taxes, but it also had to keep the peace within its confines. Many Scottish towns still have a tollbooth, or at least a street called Tollgate, Tollboth Wynd or similar. Soon, burgh courts emerged to deal with petty crime and civil matters – the tollbooth was also the prison – and the Dean of Guild Courts (composed of merchants and other guildsmen) also evolved to look after what we would now call building regulations, public safety and policing. The *curia quatour burgorum*, or Court of Four Burghs, represented the interests of Edinburgh, Berwick, Roxburgh and Stirling (or, when Berwick and Roxburgh were in English hands, as happened from time to time, Linlithgow and Lanark). This was a kind of supreme civil and commercial court, and could resolve any question, judicial or legislative, relating to the Scottish burghs, and heard appeals in these matters. The *leges quatour burgorum*, (Laws of the Four Burghs, and based on an English model), became the authoritative burgh law. Burghs (in Scotland) and boroughs (in England) still had some administrative meaning until recently, as we will see.

For a long time, the Convention of Royal Burghs was just about the most important body in Scotland apart from parliament itself, and almost constituted a second chamber. The burghs more or less financed the Crown and when they grew from forty-six in 1560 to fifty-eight in 1640 and sixty-seven by 1700, each was represented in parliament by one commissioner (two for Edinburgh). Because the commissioners met about three times a year in the Convention of Royal Burghs, they were able to decide a common policy for upcoming meetings of the 'estates' (parliament) and could swing the agenda.

Shires and sheriffs

Whereas a county is properly the land controlled by a count (or earl), a shire is the land controlled from a castle. Such an area needs administering and, building on another Anglo-Saxon model, David I also established the office of sheriff (originally shire-rieve) in Scotland. The function of the sheriff was to administer the local area, to represent royal judicial power and to carry out other military and financial functions, with civil and criminal jurisdictions. In time, the office became hereditary. Scotland still has sheriffs (essentially local judges) and it is easy to see how this evolved into the American concept of the local lawman for a county. England has a high sheriff for each ceremonial county, whose role is largely ceremonial.

The modern age

As the power and responsibilities of large landowners and nobles fell away, it was replaced with civil administration. By the twentieth century, most of the UK's local government had become organised in two broad tiers, each with its own responsibilities – the County Councils and, below them, an admixture of city, burgh or borough, metropolitan district, urban district and rural district councils. However, some of the larger cities and towns had a single layer of local government and were designated a 'County Borough' or a 'County of itself', or in Scotland, a 'County of a City'. Scotland also had Royal Burghs as administrative units.

Most County Council boundaries were the same as those of the geographical counties, but those with larger land areas or populations were subdivided – in England, Yorkshire had three 'Ridings' (meaning a 'thirding'), North, East and West; there was East and West Sussex; and Lincolnshire and Suffolk were similarly divided. London was also different, as it consisted of two cities (the City of London, the square mile around the Bank of England and the financial district, and the City of Westminster, where parliament is) plus a number of boroughs, all of which were properly in counties. For example, Richmond was in Surrey, Islington in Middlesex and Ilford in Essex. In 1899 the County of London was forged from the city plus parts of the surrounding counties of Middlesex, Kent and Surrey, and their boroughs.

In 1965 the long-used but unofficial concept of Greater London became official, with the formation of the Greater London Council, taking in London, Westminster and the area covered by the former counties of London and Middlesex together with parts of Essex, Kent, Surrey and Hertfordshire, including three former County Boroughs (Croydon, West Ham and East Ham). The tier below this, which had consisted of a rather unwieldy eighty-two borough, metropolitan and urban district councils, was reorganised into thirty-two London boroughs and the City of London.

All change in the 1970s

There was a similar situation in Northern Ireland, but on 1 October 1973 the seventy-three councils (the six counties of Antrim, Armagh, County Down, Fermanagh, County Londonderry or Derry and Tyrone, two single-tier county boroughs, plus ten boroughs, twenty-four urban districts and thirty-one rural districts), became twenty-six single-tier District Councils. For administrative purposes at least, the six historic counties were gone.

(Be aware that everything to do with Northern Ireland is loaded with political meaning, including what it gets called. Unionists and Loyalists in the North itself often refer to it by the inaccurate term 'Ulster' or 'The Province', both a reference to the centuries-old Four Provinces, of which Ulster was one, but included the six counties plus another three now in the Republic. Nationalists, Republicans and even some official bodies in the Republic avoid using 'Northern Ireland' on the grounds that this implies acceptance of the political divide of 1921, and instead call it 'the Six Counties' or 'the Occupied Six Counties', and refer to the Republic as 'the Twenty-Six Counties', or else refer to it as 'the North of Ireland' or 'the North', ignoring the fact that the most northerly part of Ireland, in County Donegal, is in the Republic.)

Six months later, 1 April 1974, England and Wales were reorganised. Apart from Greater London, the two-tier system was extended with the abolition of County Boroughs, the County Councils reduced from fifty-eight to fifty-three (six of which, around the larger cities, became Metropolitan County Councils) and the 1,250 local councils replaced by 369 District Councils. Several historic counties disappeared, such as Rutland, and most had major boundary changes, to the fury of local inhabitants. One month later, it was Scotland's turn. Over 400 councils, including thirty-four historic counties, were replaced by nine Regions, fifty-three District Councils and three single-tier authorities covering some of the islands. Also lost were the Royal Burghs, many of which had stretched back 600 years or more.

On 31 March 1986 the government, jealous and suspicious of the power, popularity and political colour of the Greater London Council and the six Metropolitan County Councils, abolished these. The London boroughs and the Metropolitan District Councils gained a status similar to the pre-1974 county boroughs, but the counties as administrative units were gone.

All change again in the 1990s

Frankly, none of this worked. People had a long-standing loyalty to their historic areas, which any family historian will recognise as pride of place, and resented being told that their county no longer existed, or that suddenly they lived in a different county because of a boundary change. In Scotland, almost everyone hated the regions – Strathclyde was too big, nobody felt any warmth towards a region called 'Central' and there was a yearning for the old names. Only Fife was relatively unscathed. Properly known as The Kingdom of Fife (although it has not had a king since Pictish times) it has remained more or less the same size and shape throughout recorded history. It may be the longest-standing recognisable geopolitical entity in Europe, apart from some islands.

There have been subsequent changes to all of Wales and Scotland and most of England, some of which simply reversed the reorganisations of 1974–5. In Wales the eight counties and thirty-seven district councils were abolished in 1996 to be replaced by twenty-two new unitary authorities called either Counties or County Boroughs. At the same time in Scotland the nine unpopular regions, the three island authorities and the fifty-three second-tier districts, were replaced by thirty-two unitary authorities, known by the unlovely term 'Council Areas'. Counties and burghs have gone forever. In England there were various changes with some areas being unaffected but others moving over in a phased manner, between 1995 and 1998. Four of the 1974 County Councils were abolished and the rest turned into a number of unitary authorities plus the two-tier county and district structure. This reinvented a number of the old county and county borough names, but the boundaries are different in almost all cases. Frankly, it's a mess. More recently, the reality of Greater London was again recognised and it now has a unified government under a mayor.

Genealogist's guide

That was all a bit complicated. The bottom line is, apart from twenty years or so in the twentieth century, you will recognise most historic counties in the names of the current administrative units, although some individual towns, villages and parishes may have 'moved'. Some counties have disappeared forever, particularly in Scotland and in South Wales; the old Glamorgan is now ten or so units.

The real question is, to find information on someone who lived in 1881 in, say, Roxburghshire (Scotland) or Huntingdonshire (England) or Montgomeryshire (Wales) or County Fermanagh (Northern Ireland), where would you now look? These tables and maps are intended to

Table 19

Scotland					
Historic County	**CCC**	**Administration until 1975**	**Region 1975–96**	**CCC**	**Unitary Authorities post-1996**
Aberdeenshire	ABD	Aberdeenshire	Grampian	GMP	Aberdeenshire (U)
		Aberdeen (C)			Aberdeen City (U)
Angus (Forfarshire)	ANS	Angus	Tayside	TAY	Angus (U)
		Dundee (C)			Dundee City (U)
Argyllshire (including the islands Islay, Jura and Mull)	ARL	Argyllshire	Strathclyde	STD	Argyll and Bute (U)
			Highland 1	HLD	
Ayrshire	AYR	Ayrshire	Strathclyde 2	STD	East Ayrshire (U)
					North Ayrshire (U)
					South Ayrshire (U)
Banffshire	BAN	Banffshire	Grampian	GMP	Moray (U)
Berwickshire	BEW	Berwickshire	Borders	BOR	The Scottish Borders (U)
Bute (includes Arran)	BUT	Bute	Strathclyde	STD	Argyll and Bute (U)
Caithness	CAI	Caithness	Highland	HLD	Highland (U)
Clackmannanshire	CLK	Clackmannanshire	Central	CEN	Clackmannanshire (U)
Dunbartonshire 5	DNB	Dunbartonshire	Strathclyde	STD	East Dunbartonshire (U)
					West Dunbartonshire (U)
Dumfriesshire	DFS	Dumfriesshire	Dumfries and Galloway	DGY	Dumfries and Galloway (U)
East Lothian	ELN	East Lothian	Lothian	LTN	East Lothian (U)
Fife	FIF	Fife	Fife	FIF	Fife (U)
Inverness-shire (includes North Uist, South Uist, Skye and part of Lewis)	INV	Inverness-shire	Highland	HLD	Highland (U)
			Western Isles	WIS	Western Isles (U) 3
Kincardineshire	KCD	Kincardineshire	Grampian	GMP	Aberdeenshire (U)
Kinross-shire	KRS	Kinross-shire	Tayside	TAY	Perth and Kinross (U)
Kirkcudbrightshire	KKD	Kirkcudbrightshire	Dumfries and Galloway	DGY	Dumfries and Galloway (U)
Lanarkshire	LKS	Lanarkshire	Strathclyde	STD	North Lanarkshire (U)
					South Lanarkshire (U)
		Glasgow (C)			City of Glasgow (U)
Midlothian	MLN	Midlothian	Lothian	LTN	Midlothian (U)
		Edinburgh (C)	Borders	BOR	City of Edinburgh (U)
Moray	MOR	Moray	Grampian	GMP	Moray (U)
			Highland	HLD	
Nairnshire	NAI	Nairnshire	Highland	HLD	Highland (U)
Orkney	OKI	Orkney	Orkney	OKI	Orkney Islands (U)
Peeblesshire	PEE	Peeblesshire	Borders	BOR	The Scottish Borders (U)
Perthshire	PER	Perthshire	Tayside	TAY	Perth and Kinross (U)
			Central	CEN	
Renfrewshire	RFW	Renfrewshire	Strathclyde	STD	Renfrewshire (U)
					East Renfrewshire (U)
					Inverclyde (U)
Ross and Cromarty (includes part of Lewis)	ROC	Ross and Cromarty	Highland	HLD	Highland (U)
			Western Isles 3	WIS	Western Isles (U)
Roxburghshire	ROX	Roxburghshire	Borders	BOR	The Scottish Borders (U)
Selkirkshire	SEL	Selkirkshire	Borders	BOR	The Scottish Borders (U)
Shetland	SHI	Shetland	Shetland	SHI	Shetland Islands (U)
Stirlingshire	STI	Stirlingshire	Central	CEN	Stirling (U)
			Strathclyde	STD	Falkirk (U)
Sutherland	SUT	Sutherland	Highland	HLD	Highland (U)
West Lothian	WLN	West Lothian	Lothian	LTN	West Lothian (U)
			Central	CEN	
Wigtownshire	WIG	Wigtownshire	Dumfries and Galloway	DGY	Dumfries and Galloway (U)

help track down the likely current repositories of information. But be careful – check the neighbouring places too! To tie down a particular place, try the online parish locator covering the whole of the UK (but not Ireland) at Genuki (www.genuki.org.uk/big/churchdb).

Some of the old abbreviations for English counties may cause confusion. Oxford is Oxon, from the Latin name Oxonia; Shropshire is Salop, from the earlier name Sloppsberrie; Hampshire is still known as Hants, from the old name Hantshaving, and the same goes for Northants (Northamptonshire).

Notes

1. Highland Region included Skye.
2. Strathclyde region included Arran, Bute, Islay, Jura and Mull.
3. Western Isles included Lewis, North Uist and South Uist.
4. Watch the spelling here – the town of Dumbarton is in Dunbartonshire.
5. CCC = the Chapman County Code; C = County of a City; U = Unitary Authority

Table 20

English counties			
pre-1974 (40)	**CCC**	**1974–96 (46)**	**post-1998 (47)**
Because of boundary changes, these do not necessarily correspond one-to-one			
Bedfordshire (Beds)	BDF	Bedfordshire	Bedfordshire Luton (U) 1
Berkshire (Berks)	BRK	Berkshire	Bracknell Forest (U) West Berkshire (U) Reading (U) Slough (U) Windsor and Maidenhead (U) Wokingham (U)
Buckinghamshire (Bucks)	BKM	Buckinghamshire	Buckinghamshire Milton Keynes (U)
Cambridgeshire (Cambs) – including Isle of Ely	CAM	Cambridgeshire	Cambridgeshire Peterborough (U)
Cheshire (Ches)	CHS	Cheshire	Cheshire Halton (U) Warrington (U)
Cornwall (Corn) including Scilly Isles	CON	Cornwall	Cornwall
Cumberland (Cumb)	CUL	Cumbria	Cumbria
Derbyshire	DBY	Derbyshire	Derbyshire Derby City (U)
Devon	DEV	Devon	Devon Plymouth (U) Torbay (U)
Dorset	DOR	Dorset	Dorset Bournemouth (U) Poole (U)
Durham	DUR	Durham	County Durham Darlington (U)
		Cleveland	Hartlepool (U) Middlesbrough (U) Redcar and Cleveland (U) Stockton-on-Tees (U)
		Tyne and Wear	Newcastle-upon-Tyne (MD) North Tyneside (MD) South Tyneside (MD) Gateshead (MD) Sunderland (MD)
Essex	ESS	Essex	Essex Southend (U) Thurrock (U)
Gloucestershire (Glos)	GLS	Gloucestershire	Gloucestershire

Hampshire (Hants)	HAM	Hampshire	Hampshire Portsmouth (U) Southampton (U)
		Isle of Wight (IOW)	Isle of Wight (U)
Herefordshire	HEF	Hereford and Worcester	Worcestershire Herefordshire (U)
Hertfordshire (Herts)	HRT	Hertfordshire	Hertfordshire
Huntingdonshire (Hunts)	HUN	(Now part of Cambridgeshire)	(Now part of Cambridgeshire)
Kent	KEN	Kent	Kent The Medway Towns (U)
Lancashire (Lancs)	LAN	Lancashire	Lancashire Blackburn with Darwen (U) Blackpool (U)
		Greater Manchester	Greater Manchester 2
		Merseyside	Wirral (MD) Sefton (MD) Liverpool (MD) Knowsley (MD) St Helens (MD)
Leicestershire (Leics)	LEI	Leicestershire	Leicestershire Leicester City (U) Rutland (U)
Lincolnshire (Lincs) – including Holland, Kesteven, Lindsey	LIN	Lincolnshire	Lincolnshire
London	LND	Greater London	Greater London 3
Middlesex	MDX		
Norfolk	NFK	Norfolk	Norfolk
Northamptonshire (Northants) – including Soke of Peterborough	NTH	Northamptonshire	Northamptonshire
Northumberland (Northumb)	NBL	Northumberland	Northumberland
Nottinghamshire (Notts)	NTT	Nottinghamshire	Nottinghamshire Nottingham City (U)
Oxfordshire (Oxon)	OXF	Oxfordshire	Oxfordshire
Rutland	RUT		Rutland
Shropshire (Salop)	SAL	Shropshire	Shropshire The Wrekin (U)
Somerset (Som)	SOM	Somerset	Somerset
		Avon	Bristol (U) North Somerset (U) Bath and NE Somerset (U) South Gloucestershire (U)
Staffordshire (Staffs)	STS	Staffordshire	Staffordshire Stoke on Trent (U)
Suffolk (East & West)	SFK	Suffolk	Suffolk

Surrey	SRY	Surrey	Surrey
Sussex	SSX	East Sussex	East Sussex Brighton and Hove (U)
		West Sussex	West Sussex
Warwickshire (War)	WAR	Warwickshire	Warwickshire
		West Midlands	West Midlands
Westmorland	WES	(Now part of Cumbria)	(Now part of Cumbria)
Wiltshire (Wilts)	WIL	Wiltshire	Wiltshire Swindon (U)
Worcestershire (Worcs)	WOR	Hereford and Worcester	Worcestershire (Worcs)
Yorkshire (Yorks) – East Riding, North Riding, West Riding	YKS	North Yorkshire	North Yorkshire York (U)
		South Yorkshire	Barnsley (MD) Doncaster (MD) Rotherham (MD) Sheffield (MD)
		West Yorkshire	Calderdale (MD) Bradford (MD) Leeds (MD) Wakefield (MD) Kirklees (MD)
		Humberside	East Riding of Yorkshire (U) City of Kingston upon Hull (U) North Lincolnshire (U) North East Lincolnshire (U)

1. Abbreviations: (MD) = Metropolitan District; (U) = Unitary Authority

2. Greater Manchester consists of: Wigan (M); Bolton (M); Bury (M); Rochdale (M); Oldham (M); Tameside (M); Stockport (M); Manchester (M); Salford (M); Trafford (M)

3. Greater London consists of: Barking and Dagenham; Barnet; Bexley; Brent; Bromley; Camden; Corporation of London; Croydon; Ealing; Enfield; Greenwich; Hackney; Hammersmith and Fulham; Haringey; Harrow; Havering; Hillingdon; Hounslow; Islington; Kensington and Chelsea; Kingston-upon-Thames; Lambeth; Lewisham; Merton; Newham; Redbridge; Richmond-upon-Thames; Southwark; Sutton; Tower Hamlets; Waltham Forest; Wandsworth; Westminster

Table 21

Wales: Counties and Unitary Authorities			Unitary Authorities
pre-1974 (13)	**CCC**	**1974–1996 (8)**	**post-1996 (22)**
Anglesey	AGY	Gwynedd	Anglesey
Brecon	BRE	Powys, Gwent, Mid Glamorgan	Powys
Caernarvonshire	CAE	Gwynedd	Aberconwy and Colwyn
			Gwynedd
			Conwy
Cardiganshire	CGN	Dyfed	Ceredigion
Carmarthenshire	CMN	Dyfed	Carmarthenshire
Denbighshire	DEN	Clwyd, Gwynedd	Denbighshire
(parts of Denbigh and Flint became)			Wrexham
Flintshire	FLN	Clwyd	Flintshire
Glamorgan	GLA	Mid Glamorgan	Merthyr Tydfil
			Bridgend
			Rhondda Cynon Taff
		South Glamorgan	Vale of Glamorgan
			Cardiff
		West Glamorgan	Swansea
			Neath Port Talbot
Merionethshire	MER	Gwynedd, Clwyd	Gwynedd
Monmouthshire	MON	Gwent, Mid Glamorgan, South Glamorgan	Monmouthshire
			Caerphilly
			Blaenau Gwent
			Newport
			Torfaen
Montgomeryshire	MGY	Powys	Powys
Pembrokeshire	PEM	Dyfed	Pembrokeshire
Radnor	RAD	Powys	Powys

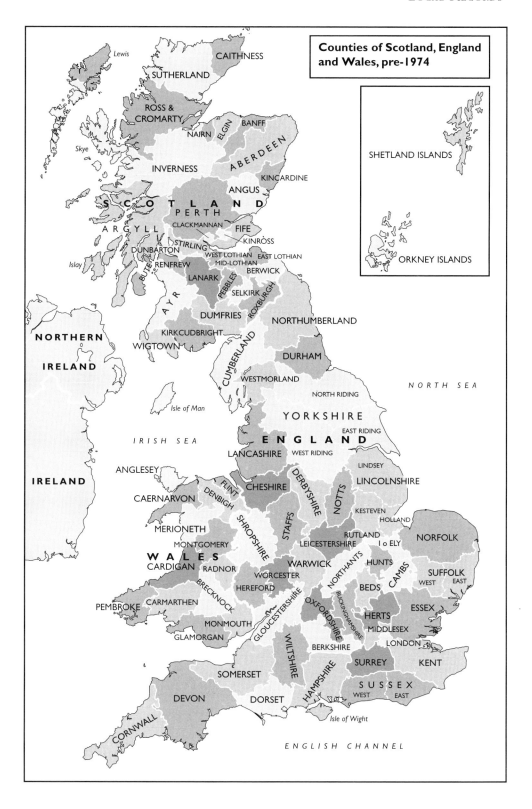

Counties of Scotland, England and Wales, pre-1974

Regions of Scotland, Counties of England and Wales, 1974–96

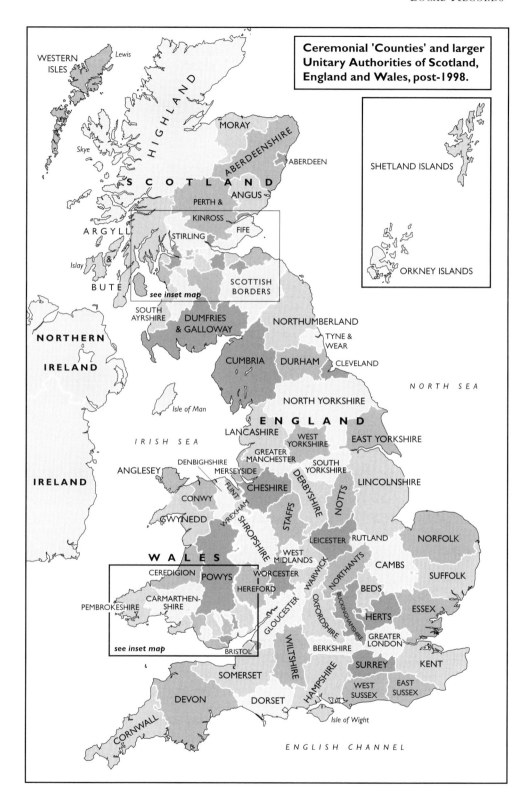

Ceremonial 'Counties' and larger Unitary Authorities of Scotland, England and Wales, post-1998.

The smaller counties of Scotland and Wales

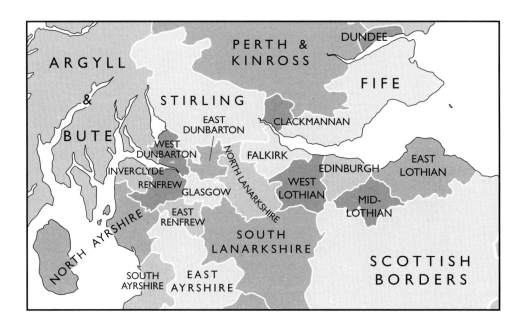

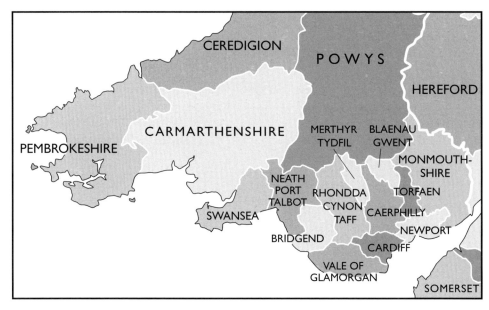

9

Scottish Wills and Testaments

Scottish testamentary documents can be disappointing for genealogists as they are often devoid of names of any relatives, or details on property or possessions. To understand why this is so, it is necessary to explore the nature of inheritance in Scotland.

Strictly speaking, inheritance is managed by a testament. A will is one particular clause of a testamentary document. Up until quite recently (1868), only moveable property could be included in a Scottish testament. The laws of inheritance were such that:

- there was a difference between immoveable or heritable property and moveable property (money, tools, furniture, animals etc.)
- the eldest son inherited everything heritable (immoveable property, land and buildings)
- all other children had an equal share of moveables, regardless of primogeniture
- the law of primogeniture still applied to heritage from 1868 until 1964
- heritage (heritable property) could be bequeathed after 1868 but from the early 1800s it is increasingly common to find dispositions, settlements, trust dispositions and settlements, etc. recorded by the Commissary Courts and including instructions about heritable property

Heritable property (immoveable) consisted of land and buildings as well as any minerals and mining rights, and passed to the eldest son (or daughter if there was no son) by the law of primogeniture. Land and houses were included. The important sources for land and property information are under Charters (chapter 7), retours of services of heirs and sasines (chapter 10). See also Courts (chapter 6).

Moveable property was anything that could be picked up (clothes, household and personal goods, money, jewellery, investments, bank accounts, tools and machinery, animals, crops, books, papers and so on). It is referred to in testaments as 'goods, gear, sums of money and debts'. This could be divided into three parts at most:

- the widow's part: *jus relictae*
- the bairns' part: *legitim* (all children, not including the eldest, having an equal share)
- the deid's part (in other words, the dead person could dispose of it according to his or her wish)

If a man was survived by a wife and children, one-third went to the widow, one-third was divided equally among the children (or all to an only child), and the remaining third disposed according to any instructions the deceased gave in a will. The widow's and bairns' parts were automatically vested in the wife and children without any need for these parts to be given up by the executor to the Commissary Court for confirmation. However, the deid's part required the court's confirmation if not stipulated in a will. In the absence of any disposition this share was taken up by the deceased's next of kin by confirmation. In the absence of a surviving wife or children, the next nearest of kin were deemed to be his surviving brothers and sisters and the estate would be distributed equally between them.

However, where there was 'heritage', it went to the eldest son, and he was automatically barred from receiving a share of the *legitim* but did inherit the heirship moveables (the best of the furniture, farming animals and implements, etc.) so that the house and land were not an empty inheritance.

If there was no surviving wife the moveables were divided into two equal parts, one half to the children and the other to any persons named in the deceased's will.

If survived by a widow and no children the division was in two halves – the widow's part and the deid's part (if a will existed).

If no surviving wife or children the whole of the moveables were the deid's part, bequeathed as per any will, a pre-existing marriage contract, bonds of provision for children of a marriage etc.

The moveable estate of a widow was divided into two parts, *legitim* and the deid's part.

On death, an executor was appointed to dispose of moveable property. The executor may have been named in a will, or if not, appointed by a court. If there was no will, the deceased was intestate. Either way, the executor had to report to the court about the disposition of assets. The record of this process would either be:

- if the deceased left a will: a testament testamentar
- if the deceased left no will: a testament dative

Where wills exist, these records are a rich source of genealogical information as they give the names of heirs, friends, relatives etc. Most people did not leave a will (in a testament testamentar), however, and most had very little to dispose of, and in this case there was absolutely no need to name the eldest son, the widow/widower or any other children.

Making sure it happened

To settle affairs before death, it was possible to draw up a testament giving instructions about the disposal of possessions, naming an executor to administer the estate and so on. However, the executor had to be confirmed by a court and a document was drawn up (by the court) for this purpose.

Testament testamentar – this was where the deceased died testate (left a will). It typically had four sections:

- an introductory clause
- an inventory of moveable estate (money, household goods, furniture, animals, crops, tools and other personal possessions
- a copy of the deceased's will (or 'legacie'), with his or her wishes as to disposal of the estate and naming an executor (usually close family). If a copy of the will is not included, there will be a reference to where it was recorded (most likely in the court's Registers of Deeds).
- a confirmation clause (the equivalent of English probate)

If the deceased had died intestate (no will) a testament dative was drawn up by the court and served to appoint and confirm an executor on the court's behalf. It had three parts:

- introductory clause
- inventory of possessions
- confirmation clause

The executor might be a family member, but if there was considerable debt, the court might appoint a creditor as executor. If so, the testament would include a list of the debts and would allow their discharge to be authorised. This is the equivalent of English 'letters of administration'.

Inventory

This is a list of all the moveable property belonging to the deceased at the time of death, as well as money owed (to creditors) and due (from debtors). Sometimes it only gives a short, total valuation, but in some testaments it can be detailed, with every item listed and valued. Where items were sold at a roup (auction) the inventory will have a 'roup roll' itemising each lot, the amounts paid and in some cases with the buyers' names.

Remember…

1. An eldest son would inherit all immoveable property (land, buildings) but if he was not to receive any moveable property, his name might not appear in any will or testament.
2. Before the 1560s wills were Church records.
3. After 1564 Commissary Courts were established, and their records are indexed. There were twenty-two Commissary Courts, but the Edinburgh Court had jurisdiction over all Scotland and those dying abroad. So check Edinburgh and local court records.
4. Sheriff Courts took over these duties from 1823.
5. From 1868 individuals could pass on heritable property (including land and buildings) by a will. The elaborate procedures of testaments and services of heirs fell away.
6. In early testaments there will be no references to land and buildings.
7. There was no legal requirement to make a will and few did. There was also no legal requirement to use a court procedure and in most cases the deceased's affairs were settled without a testament, and so there is no legal trace today.
8. On the other hand, it sometimes became necessary for a court to to be involved years after the death, for example, in the event of a dispute, and so a will or testament may exist but recorded at a later date.
9. Much to the despair of genealogists, the eldest son may not be named in a testament, as he would inherit the immoveables rather than the moveables. Likewise, a wife, who would automatically get the widow's part, may not be mentioned.

The courts

Up to 1823 testaments were recorded in the local Commissary Court which had jurisdiction over the deceased's parish. Commissariots bear more relation to the pre-Reformation medieval dioceses (St Andrews, Edinburgh etc.) than county boundaries. The Edinburgh Commissary Court was superior and could confirm testaments where the deceased had moveable property in more than one commissariot, across commissariot boundaries and where a Scot had died 'abroad' (including England).

From 1 January 1824 Commissary Courts ceased to exist and Sheriff Courts took over confirmation of testaments (but there is some overlap during the hand-over). See chapter 6 for more detail on the court system.

...a further two pages of Inventory...

The testament dative and inventory of George Durie Lord Rutherford, 1759.

Getting to know testaments

Truly it is said: anything is easier to read if you know what it says. The knowledge of the form of a document, the typical or fomulaic phrases and the vocabulary used is called the diplomatic of the document.

Table 22. If necessary, consult Dates and Numbers (pp. 255–7), Money (p. 181), Weights and Measures (p. 197), Latin (p. 254) and Abbreviations (p. 291).

Typical diplomatic	Taken from the Testament Dative and Inventory of George Durie Lord Rutherford, 1759. (Fig. 30.)
deceased and date	Testament umqll [umquhile = deceased] George Lord Rutherford
introductory clause	The Testament Dative and Inventory of the goods, gear & Debts of George Lord Rutherford within the parish of Burntisland and Sherriffdom of Fyffe the time of his decease which was upon the eighteenth day of June the last by past. Faithfully made and given up by Margaret Lady Rutherford relict of the said Defunct and Executrix Dative qua Relict Deceased to him after due citation by publick edicts By decreet of the Commissariot of St Andrews dated the 29th day of August 1759 years
inventory clause	There was pertaining and belonging to the said Defunct the time of his decease foresaid and which the Exec[utri]x gives up for confirmation. The particular moveables underwritten Estimate and valued as follows viz. Imp[rimi]s In the Dyning Room of the Defuncts house a small marbly table at v ss [5 shillings] one eight day clock at 1 lb x ss [£1 10s] Two small round tea tables v ss Eight Chairs and four Elbow Do. old vij ss vi d [7s 6d] a Chimney tongs, poker & fire shovell vi s a looking glass v ss five old family pictures gilded pictures but much torn and Dam[age]d v ss Eight other pictures of Different kinds plain framed ii ss… … Summa Inventarij is L lb viij ss i d [£50 8/1] Sterling which in Scots money is viHiv lb & vij ss [£604 16s] Salvo Justo Calculo
will or legacie clause	[None in this Testament Dative]
confirmation clause	The before written Testament is Confirmed upon the 29th of August 1759 years and David Lord Rutherford is become Cautioner for the Exec[utri]x

Common words and phrases

Get to know and recognise the words and phrases you will find in each clause, regardless of careless writing or abbreviations. Examples are:

Table 23. Note that 'cautioner' is pronounced 'cay-shunner' and is the person giving a bond or surety that the disposition of the effects will happen as confirmed.

cautioner	decreet	imprimis = first	summa inventarij
citation	defunct	inventory	testament
Commissariot	estimate and valued	moveables	testamentar
confirmed	executor/executrix	parish	the time of his decease
dated	faithfully made and given up by	pertaining and belonging to	umqll (umquhile = deceased)
dative	foresaid	relict	underwritten
deceased	goods, gear & debts	Sherriffdom	viz (videlicet) = namely

Transfer of heritage (land and buildings)

Before 1868, wills could only transfer moveable property. Land and buildings could be inherited by the separate process of retours of services of heirs or by a Trust Disposition and Settlement ('deed of settlement'), below. From 1868 to 1964 both moveable and heritable property could be transferred by a will. Check both testament records and retours. From 1964, most property was inherited through wills.

Trust dispositions and settlements

The trust disposition let an individual specify the transfer of landed property to his named heirs. In effect, the ownership of the property was transferred to a group of named trustees by a deed of trust disposition. The granter retained certain powers and retained more or less complete use of and control over the property. Normally the deed was recorded only after the death of the granter and often included a settlement of succession to the granter's moveables. As these documents did not have to be registered to have validity, and could be registered in a number of places, they can be hard to track down. A major landowner would probably use the register of deeds of the Court of Session in Edinburgh and most others would record the disposition in the register of deeds of the local Commissary Court (up to 1809), the local Sheriff Court or the appropriate Royal Burgh.

After 1868 inheritance was by conventional will.

Unclaimed estates and chancery

England has a chancery system where unclaimed estates can be held until claimed. There is no Scottish chancery system of that type. If the beneficiary of a will could not be found, the property was reported to the king (or queen) and the Lord Treasurer's Remembrancer (nowadays, the Crown Office) and known as *bona vacantia*. Property would be sold off and the cash held until a claimant appeared.

If an individual died intestate and without known heirs, the property fell to the Crown as *ultimus haeres* ('the last heir'), advertised, and sold. After a decent interval it became 'the Crown's share'. There are records of *bona vacantia* and *ultimus haeres* in the series of Exchequer records at the NAS, and are dealt with by the Crown Office in Edinburgh. We might speculate that those who claim to be the heirs of unclaimed fortunes left in chancery or its equivalent should be termed 'chancers'.

Finding testaments

All testaments and inventories (except Orkney and Shetland) are with the NAS and some 600,000 have been indexed and digitised. They can be downloaded from Scotland's People for £5 ($10). A search of the index is free, after registration (www.scotlandspeople.gov.uk). Bear in mind that there is no way of knowing whether the document relates to the correct person until it has been paid for and read (there are at least four John Smiths with testaments registered at the Edinburgh Commissary Court between 1740 and 1750). Remember to check for both testaments and inventories, as a will is likely to give names of family members whereas an inventory might only name the executor and possibly the relict. Another nicety to the Scotland's People index search is that the will and inventory might not be registered under identical names – Margaret Durie in one but Mgt. Dury in the other, or alternate spellings of Mowbray and Moubray, for example. There may also be an Eik (pronounced 'eek') which is an addition, amendment or codicil to a previous testament.

If searching on the computers at the ScotlandsPeople Centre it is free to view the document (although you will have paid for the half-day or day to be there) so they can be read before purchasing the print-out.

Older testaments

The handwriting is usually fairly easy to interpret back to about 1700, but before that date it requires practice. This is covered in Chapter 13. However, the structure of the earlier wills is the same and similar phrases crop up.

10

Land

Before examining land records, it is necessary to understand something of inheritance (chapter 9), and also the feudal system in Scotland (chapter 11). Remember also that the vast majority of Scotland's inhabitants were tenants rather than landowners or houseowners until well after the 1950s, and that 100 years before that most were agricultural tenants, millworkers, miners and so on. Clearly, land and property ownership records will only be genealogically useful for tracking and identifying property owners rather than tenants or workers. However, after 1858 it was possible, but not necessary, to register long leases on properties, so renters might well appear in the Register of Sasines (below).

Inheritance and property under the feudal system

Scotland had a feudal system until the Abolition of Feudal Tenure (Scotland) Act 2000, which came into force in 2004. In theory, all land belonged to the Crown, which passed ownership to immediate vassals ('subject superiors' or 'Crown tenants'), who in turn could pass on ownership to their tenants and vassals.

Originally this was a system of military duty in return for land granted, but later the service aspect was replaced by payment of tithes (teinds) of produce or money. For instance, the Crown could grant lands to an abbot, bishop, baron or some other worthy person, who could then dispose of it in parcels to others. This was one way of ensuring that abbeys, churches and other lands were maintained and worked, and that money and produce flowed upwards. But it also meant that when a vassal died, it was not automatic that the property would be passed to an heir. It depended on the nature of the grant of land, and on proving inheritance.

The important sources for land and property information are charters, valuation rolls, electoral registers and hearth tax records (all dealt with in other chapters), plus wills and testaments (Chapter 9) but also retours of services of heirs, sasines and estate records. Briefly, transfer of ownership (or, properly, vassalage) was by means of sasines. Inheritance was by 'service of heirs' rather than any form of will, until 1868.

Heritable immoveable property and retours of services of heirs

Under the old feudal laws, when a vassal died, his heir had to prove the right to inherit. In the case of a subject superior (a vassal directly of the Crown), a jury of local landowners convened to hear pleas and decide who was the rightful heir. Their findings were sent as a retour (return) to the Royal Chancery to confirm inheritance. If approved, the Chancery would serve the individual as heir and the process could start to give full title to the property. Retours are especially important before 1868, as up until then it was not possible to leave heritable property in a will (see p. 113 for an explanation). For family history purposes, they often help illuminate generational connections, such as when someone left land to a grandson, cousin or nephew.

Special retours dealt with lands of subject superiors, and unambiguously described the property. They are recorded in the records of the Chancery.

When it concerned their own vassals, subject superiors used a simpler system, confirming a right to inherit by a precept of *clare constat*, essentially authorising the grant of title to the heir. There is no central register of these, but they are within many collections of family papers at the NAS and elsewhere. However, a vassal may have had to prove to a subject superior the right to inherit, possibly because there was a dispute or because the superior did not know the heir personally, or was refusing to grant title for some reason. Vassals could use the Chancery to get a jury's opinion on the claim and use this, if beneficial, to get the superior's consent or to require him to consent. The returns are called general retours and do not give any detail about the property itself, merely the people involved in the transfer.

General retours are recorded in the records of the Chancery (NAS Ref. C22 and C28). However, these were indexed and calendared by the wholly wonderful Thomas Thomson in 1811 to 1816, in two series – 1544–1699 (mostly in Latin except for 1652–9, but all with English indexes) and 1700–1859. The first series consisted of two volumes of printed summaries, *Inquisitionum ad Capellam Regis Retornatarum Abbreviatio* and a third volume index, arranged by county, names (*Index nominum*) and places (*Index locarum*). Usually the printed Thomson abridgement is all the information needed. Two CD-ROMs are available from the Scottish Genealogy Society.

UNDERSTANDING A RETOUR

A retour begins with the date of the inquest, the names of the jury, the name of the deceased, the lands concerned (if a special retour), and the name of the legitimate heir. The Extent (worth) of the land was sometimes given in Old Extent (A.E.) and New Extent (N.E.), reflecting the change in value of the Scottish Pound, or in merk. There are also lists of valuations of land and enquiries into matters Tutory (looking after minors) and Curatory (looking after the infirm etc.).

(18)   **Dec. 9. 1640.**
ARCHIBALDUS STIRLING, *hæres* Archibaldi Stirling burgensis de Stirling, *patris*,—in annuo redditu 640*m.* de terris dominicalibus de Menstrie ;—terris de Westertoun et Middiltoun de Menstrie, in parochia de Logie ;—et de terris de Westertoun de Tulliecultrie, infra parochiam de Tulliecultrie :—E. 512*m.*—annuo redditu 508*m.* de prænominatis terris et baronia de Menstrie, extendentibus ad 20 libratas terrarum antiqui extentus, in parochia de Logie, et de firmis, &c. dictarum terrarum et baroniæ de Menstrie.—E. 406*m.* 5*s.* 4*d.*   xvi. 135.

(30)   **Oct. 6. 1654.**
ALEXANDER BRUCE, *heir* of Hendrie Bruce son to Sir Robert Bruce of Clakmanan knight, *his father*,—in ane annuelrent of 200*m.* furth of the barroney and lands of Clackmanan ;—ane uther annuelrent of 200*m.* furth of the said lands.   xxiii. 72.

The abridgements of two special retours from Clackmannanshire in the 1600s, one abridgement in Latin, one in Scots. The end references (xvi. 135 etc.) are to the actual retours.

> **Translation**
> ARCHIBALD SIRLING, heir to Archibald Stirling Burgess of Stirling, his father, – in annual rent 640 merk of the demesne lands of Menstrie; the lands of Westerton and Middleton of Menstrie in the parish of Logie; and of the lands of Westerton of Tillicoutry, under the parish of Tillicoutry: – Extent 512 merk – annual rent 508 merk of the aforesaid lands and barony of Menstrie, extending to 20 Pounds [Scots] of land of Old Extent, in the parish of Logie, and of the forms etc. of the said lands and barony of Menstrie – Extent 420 merk 5s 4d.

(50)   Oct. 16. 1600.
STEPHANUS LAW, *hæres* Alexandri Law notarii ac incolæ
burgi de Edinburgh, *patris*.   ii. 67.

(51)   Oct. 18. 1600.
MAGISTER GEORGIUS BONYMAN, *hæres* Georgii Bony-
man mercatoris ac burgensis de Edinburgh, *patris*.   ii. 64.

(52)   Oct. 31. 1600.
JOANNES GORDOUN, *hæres* Domini Joannis Gordoun de
Petlurg militis, *patris*.   ii. 61.

(53)   Nov. 8. 1600.
MAGISTER JACOBUS DURHAME de Duntarvie, *hæres* Ca-
pitanei Alexandri Durhame de Houschgour in Denmark, *filii
patrui*.   ii. 79.

The abridgements of some general retours from the 1600s.

---

(50) STEPHEN LAW, heir to Alexander Law notary and resident of the town of
Edinburgh, his father.

(51) MASTER GEORGE BONYMAN, heir to George Bonyman merchant and
burgess of Edinburgh, his father.

(52) JOHN GORDON, heir to Sir John Gordon of Petlurg, knight, his father.

(53) MASTER JAMES DURHAM of Duntarvie, heir to Captain Alexander Durham
of Houschgour in Denmark, his father's son (i.e. his brother).

Note that Dominus when followed by *militis* = Sir (a knight) and Magister signifies a
graduate (M.A.).

---

(38)   Oct. 4. 1603.
MAGISTER THOMAS GAIRDYNE de Blairtone, *patruus*
WALTERI, GILBERTI, MARIÆ, MARGARETÆ et ISA-
BELLÆ GAIRDYNIS, liberorum legitimorum quondam Magistri
Gilberti Gairdyne de Boithis,—*propinquior agnatus*, id est con-
sanguineus ex parte patris dictis liberis quondam Magistri Gilberti
sui fratris germani.   iii. 54.

A retour of Tutory (care of minors).

MASTER THOMAS GAIRDYNE of Blairton, uncle of Walter, Gilbert, Mary,
Margaret and Isabella Gairdyne, free legitimate [children] of the deceased Master
Gilbert Gairdyne of Boithis, – nearest relation by blood on father's side of the said
children of the deceased Master Gilbert his brother-german [full brother].

TAILZIE

An heir might be served as 'heir of tailzie', meaning that the property was 'entailed' – essentially, its further transfer was restricted to, say the male line, for subsequent generations. This prevented the property going outwith the family and could, for instance, require the heir of tailzie to take the surname of the entailer. Thus, an outsider marrying a sole heir daughter would take the daughter's family name.

RETOURS FOR COUNTIES AND BURGHS FROM 1700

From 1700–1859 the printed Indexes to the Services of Heirs in Scotland are arranged as a decennial section, after which they became annual. From the name of the heir in the index it is possible to find the heir's designation, details about the ancestor (sometimes with the death date), the type of heir, the names of lands (if a special retour) and the retour date. Original records before 15 November 1847 have the NAS reference prefix C22, and after that, C28.

DON'T BE CONFUSED BY DATES

There was no time limit for recording a retour, unlike with sasines, so do not expect to equate the retour date with the death date; it could sometimes take years. Some heirs only bothered to get a retour later if, for example, the inheritance was challenged or if they wanted to sell the property and required evidence of clear title.

Register of Sasines and Notary Public Records

Before 1617 property transfers were recorded by the notary public. The word sasine is related to seize – a landholder was seized of land, which implies physical holding, and indeed this is what happened. On a sale and purchase, the two parties would call out the notary public to witness the new owner physically hold a token piece of the land (usually a stone or a clod of earth) and the notary would write an instrument of sasine (seizing) in a protocol book. Some of these still exist.

This system eventually evolved into the Register of Sasines, after 1617, although there was an early and incomplete attempt at a register from 1599–1609 and they are fairly complete from about 1660. Held at General Register House, Edinburgh, the Register is a large series of records as it recorded every change in ownership of property in Scotland until 6 April 1981 when it was gradually replaced by Registration of Title, county by county, (held by Registers of Scotland in Edinburgh). This means that the Scottish sasine register is one of the oldest continuous records of land transfers in Europe.

The sasine register indexes are organised by location and date. Details of purchase, sale or handing-down will, in theory, be recorded, with dates and names of the parties, and the land referred to. These are being digitised and will be available online, starting with the most recent and working back. Manual searches in the Register of Sasines at General Register House will be necessary for some time to come.

Another useful aspect to the sasine register is the recording of secured debts, such as mortgages. This was intended to prevent fraud, such as property being used as security for multiple loans. This information can tell the genealogist about financial relationships between landowners, merchants, lenders etc., but needs time, patience and a good supply of pencils.

The register is public and while the NAS charges for consulting the register for legal reasons, there is no charge when doing so for family history or historical purposes. The various sasine registers, not all indexed, are:

– Secretary's Register: 1599–1609, incomplete, by counties
– General register: 1617–1720 and 1781–1868 for all of Scotland, except the three Lothians, and for properties that were over county boundaries

– Royal Burgh registers: there are sixty-six, some indexed from about 1809 (Glasgow, Aberdeen and Dundee pre-1809 kept locally)
– County registers: 1617–1780, 1781–1868 and 1869 onwards

Although the General Register is indexed from 1617 to 1735 the indexes to sasines are incomplete before 1781. For instance, there are no indexes to Clackmannan, Peebles, Renfrew, Roxburgh, Selkirk, Stirling or Wigtown. On the plus side, many of the existing indexes are published and available in libraries although there are hardly any published indexes for burgh registers until the 1900s when they became amalgamated with the county registers – those that do exist are manuscript or (later) typescript and are only available at the NAS. Otherwise, use the Minute Books – compiled daily by the clerks writing the sasines into the register and so in chronological order, with a short summary of each and the date of registration from which you can find the full document in the register.

From 1781 the indexes are good and there are printed abridgements for every record, arranged in county volumes and covering both general and individual registers. The index identifies people and/or properties, which leads to the abridgement, and so to the original document if needed (usually the abridgement is enough). There is a full set of abridgements at the NAS (General Register House, Edinburgh) and some local authority archives have local sets. Check the Scottish Archive Network (SCAN) website for details.

There are also search sheets for property in Scotland from 1876, giving the volume and page numbers of all the sasines and deeds for a building or piece of land. These cost a modest amount of money and are a useful starting point and short cut.

Instrument of sasine

The instument is the legal document which records the transfer of ownership of land or a building by sale or inheritance. It was (and still is) legally required to record a sasine or equivalent title deed within a few days of it being drawn up. However, if a person was already resident in the inherited property with undisputed possession (say, a sole son on his father's death) there would be no need to incur the cost of having a sasine executed, unless possession was later disputed, or if the property were to be sold.

The basic structure is: date, principal parties, type of transaction, land concerned, exact time and names of witnesses. Sasines before the early twentieth century are usually handwritten.

Apr 1 1808. Matthew Hay, sometime changekeeper in Haggs of Bankier and William Hay his Son, seised in liferent and fee respectively Feb 27 1808:– in 1 rood of lands of Haggs of north Garngrew, par. Denny;– on feu con, between the said … and William Cuthill of Banknock, May 17 1799, and Mary Thomson spouse of the said Matthew Hay seised, *eod die*, in liferent of the said subject, *propris manibus* of him for himself, and as attorney for the said William Hay.

June 26th 1835. Janet Forsyth, relict of George Wilson in Carmacoup, Catherine Forsyth, relict of William Milligan in Knowe, Jean Forsyth, relict of John Paterson in Fleshclose, Mary Forsyth, spouse of Thomas Reid in Waterymeetings – and William Ireland, jun., residing in Kirkcudbright as Heirs Portioners to John Forsyth of Troloss, their brother and uncle respectively.

Examples of sasine abridgements. For explanations of abbreviations, Latin etc. see chapter 16.

If the original writing looks cramped, it's because in the early years clerks had to buy the blank sasine volumes themselves and so tried to get as much on each page as they could.

Estate papers and lands grants

Private records of estates are obviously a source of information concerning the estate holders themselves, but may also contain details of estate workers. A search of the NAS Online Public Access Catalogue (OPAC, at www.dswebhosting.info/NAS) by name of estate, barony, parish or county, or by a personal name, will produce a list of references to relevant documents, if any. The reference produced may not contain any names of interest, but will indicate whether, and under what reference, such estate papers exist. The reference number itself can be followed to show other documents in that collection. Some private estate papers may also be in local archives.

Registers of deeds

Deeds include legal agreements, contracts and other writs created between parties taking some common action. To register a deed, the presenting party paid a court clerk to copy the original document (called a warrant) into the register. The parties involved each received a certified extract. Only the warrant had the original signatures of the parties. In some cases the clerk made a brief note of the registration in a minute book, which can serve as an index. If the relevant register has disappeared or is unreadable, the minute book reference, extract or original warrant may survive.

Examples of such deeds would be bonds, dispositions and settlements (a form of will), marriage contracts, wills and codicils, tacks (lease agreements), apprenticeship indentures, factories (the appointment of factors), business contracts and so on, some of which will pertain to lands, and other business agreements. The main register of deeds with the Court of Session (also known as the Books of Council and Session) has an index of the names of the parties concerned and where it exists. However, deeds could also be registered with Sheriff Courts, burghs, hereditary jurisdictions (such as baronies, up to 1748), Commissary Courts (up to 1809) and some local courts (up to 1748), but all of these are kept, if they exist, by the NAS, and not all are indexed.

The **NATIONAL ARCHIVES** *of* **SCOTLAND**   **NAS** Catalogue

Home	Sort Fields	Search	Help	What's Not On

Record: 1 of 13   Forward 1 record   Forward 10 records   Last record

RefNo	Title	Date
GD26	Papers of the Leslie family, Earls of Leven and Melville	1200-1853
GD26/3	Writs for Sheriffdoms of Fife, Perth, Miscellaneous, Tacks of Teinds, Inventories of Writs	1446-1899

CountryCode	GB
RepCode	234
RefNo	GD26/3/162
Repository	National Archives of Scotland
Title	Extract Contract of Wadset whereby James Boswell of Lochgellie [Lochgelly] and David Boswell of Cragincate [Craigencat], his brother, and cautioners, dispone to John Durie, portioner of Overgrange of Kynghorne [Kinghorn] Wester, and Christian Rutherfurde [Rutherford], his spouse, and annualrent of 1100 merks from lands and barony of Balgonie, under reversion of 11000 merks. Registered in B. of C., 10 April, 1632.
Date	29/5/1630
AccessStatus	Open

Click on the RefNo to see other items in this Collection

One result of a search in the NAS OPAC for Overgrange. It contains links to the main collections which contain the document cited.

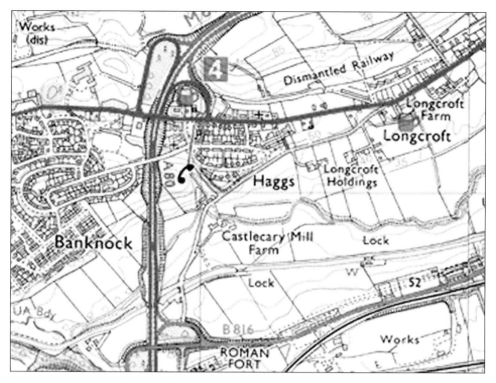

The present–day map of Haggs, Falkirk. (Wikipedia, Ref. NS791791)

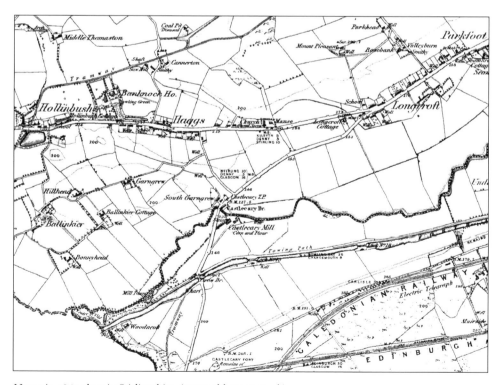

Haggs in 1865, then in Stirlingshire. (www.old-maps.co.uk)

Using maps

A good source for old maps is the Ordnance Survey and Landmark's, www.old-maps. co.uk, which mostly deal with the nineteenth century. Another is www.british-history.ac.uk. It is not always possible to identify a place from older documents, or from a description, because the name may have changed, or was not recorded at the time the map was drawn, so a map can help. Use the more modern Ordnance Survey maps to search for places (www. getamap.ordnancesurvey.co.uk/getamap/frames.htm) then correlate it with an older map.

For example, one of the sasine abridgements on p. 123 refers to 'lands of Haggs of north Garngrew, par. [parish of] Denny'. A Google search for Haggs produced a Wikipedia reference containing the grid reference NS791791, which produced the present-day map shown below. A search for Haggs in Old Maps led to the 1865 one shown in Fig. 36. The two can easily be compared and farms such as Garngrew identified.

Other ways to track down the locations of older place names are the *Gazetteer for Scotland* (www.geo.ed.ac.uk/scotgaz) which may also have lots of useful historical information. Haggs appears within the context of Denny. Remember that boundaries have changed over time, so the place in question may be in what seems to be a neighbouring county. Haggs was then in Stirlingshire, but is now part of Falkirk.

Further reading

Inheriting Land and Buildings, (National Archives of Scotland guides) www.nas.gov.uk/guides/inheriting.asp.

Senior-Milne, Graham, *Farewell to Feudalism*, The Scottish Genealogist (September 2004). www.scotsgenealogy.com/online/farewell_to_feudalism.htm.

Young, Margaret D., *Land Registers and Valuation Rolls as Sources for Genealogy*, The Scottish Genealogist (September 1986) www.scotsgenealogy.com/online/land_registers.htm.

11

Feudal Land Tenure and Baronies, and Titles

The feudal system probably originates from the courts of the Franks (in Germany, France and the Low Countries) in the eighth century, in the time of Charles Martel, grandfather of Charlemagne. It was introduced to England by the Normans in 1066 and adopted almost a century later in a slightly different form in Scotland, which was never subject to Norman rule but was certainly open to Norman influence, especially where good ideas were concerned. Feudalism derived from two earlier Roman concepts, benefice or usufruct (in Latin, *beneficium* and *usufructus*) and vassalage. (The word 'vassal' probably derives from an old Celtic word 'gwas' meaning 'young man', and with a similar meaning in modern Welsh. But 'knight' also derives from a word meaning a young, untried man – 'knecht' in Germanic.) The two principles, benefice or usufruct and vassalage, were related but not necessarily intertwined. Someone could be given benefice or usufruct (for example, granted land) and a vassal would agree with a superior that the two would mutually aid each other – the superior offering protection and the vassal providing men-at-arms, for instance. In time, the two became one. (Benefice is a non-heritable living, for example, granted to a churchman for his tenure in post, whereas usufruct can be inherited.) The sovereign was the ultimate superior (*ultimus haeres*, or ultimate heir) and owned all the land. With land came responsibility, and also jurisdiction. Therefore, all legal authority and all responsibility for upholding the law rested with the Crown. However, the Crown could give subjects the usufruct of land, in return for some service (the reddendo, see below). These subject superiors, who were direct vassals of the Crown, could in turn parcel out land to *their* vassals, and they could do likewise (to an extent); so there was a hierarchy in which someone could be vassal to a superior (ultimately the sovereign), but superior to his vassals, who themselves would be superiors to *their* vassals.

By the eleventh and twelfth centuries, the system had developed so that it became virtually the same as ownership. Vassals were in no sense slaves – they could marry, hire workers, acquire and dispose of property and pass on inheritances without the permission of the superior – but there was a reciprocal duty from one to the other, and the conditions of vassalage imposed certain restrictions on the vassal. But ultimately, feudalism precludes personal ownership of land, and even the Crown held, say, Scotland, as a vassal of God. Putting the hands together in the attitude of prayer is a reflection of the feudal act of a vassal doing homage to a superior.

The system of feudal land tenure was partially reformed in Scotland in 1974 and formally done away with by the Abolition of Feudal Tenure etc. (Scotland) Act 2000, fully enacted from 28 November 2004. To this day, England and Wales are feudal, in the sense that all land belongs to the Crown and everyone holding land is a vassal, although there is no further feudal division of land.

The feudal system emerged in Scotland almost full-blown in the reign of David I (1124–53) but never penetrated to Scandinavia. This explains why, even now, the Orkney and Shetland Islands, which belonged to Norway until 1469, have vestiges of an older, non-feudal land law – allodial or udal law (see p. 128).

The level of landholding below the Crown was the earldom and the manor (in England) or barony (in Scotland), more of which later. But essentially the Crown handed out large parcels of land in exchange for an expectation that the individuals concerned would rule, administer, dispense justice and generally look after that land in the sovereign's stead. Earldoms (in early times) and Scottish baronies differ from other titles in that they are territorial – based on land rather than being personal awards (as with duke, marquess, viscount and, later, baronet).

English feudal baronies

Up to 1290 in England, there was Feudal Barony by Tenure but the statute of *Quia Emptores* prohibited land from being subject to a feudal grant, and to being transferred without the feudal superior's permission, so breaking the link between title and landholding.

Allodial tenure

The alternative to feudal land tenure was allodial (also called odal or udal) tenure. This means full ownership, and while it could not be applied to land (except that the Crown might be said to have allodial tenure over the whole of, say, Scotland) it did apply to personal goods (moveables). However, there is some udal land in Orkney and Shetland, and in the rest of Scotland the Church was allowed to own allodially its kirks and kirkyards. The present-day situation is confusing, with some kirks, manses and glebes held feudally of the Crown, but kirkyards remaining allodial.

Registering landholding

All land titles appear in the sasine register or the land register of Scotland (see chapter 10). However, because the Crown is ultimately 'seised' of all land in Scotland (as a vassal of God alone), the Crown cannot be 'infeft' of land, and so all Crown landholdings would not be recorded. The implication is that where no register title can be found to a piece of land, it belongs to the Crown (a doctrine called 'abiding supreme allodial sasine'). Likewise, when land falls vacant by the death of a vassal without heirs, and there is no other superior, the land reverts to the Crown but there may be no trace of this in the registers. Occasionally, speculative foreigners turn up at registers of Scotland looking for 'unclaimed land'. There is no such thing. Searching for lands in the sasine register and the land register is discussed in Chapter 10.

Feudal duties and responsibilities

The single most important thing to bear in mind about the feudal system of land tenure is this: no one owned land, but had the use and benefit of it, and the right to pass it on to heirs, as if it were truly owned, but according to a set of agreed principles.

Dominium

In an attempt to marry two legal underpinnings of the Scottish system – Roman law, in which individual ownership was central, and feudal law in which land ownership could not exist – it was necessary to invent a new concept: dominium.

The compromise was that land was said to be in multiple ownership, with the Crown having *dominium eminens*, and the rights to land split between the *dominium directum* (right to direct), belonging to the superior, and *dominium utile* (right of use) which belonged to the vassal. The use of these terms gets confused at times, but the convention is that any superior, even if he himself is a vassal, has *dominium directum* and the ultimate vassal at the bottom of the chain has *dominium utile*, but obviously mid-superiors also have *dominium utile*. This is further confused by the usage *dominium plenum* (full ownership) when, for example, a vassal acquires the superiority over his land, or one *dominium* is merged with another. But in the main, a superior who has *dominimum directum* grants *dominium utile* to a vassal, and the two terms are sufficient.

Feus

A vassal owes the superior 'fealty' (literally faithfulness, from the Latin *fidelitas*) and also 'homage' (from *homo*, man, as the vassal was the superior's 'man'). They are linked but different. Homage was a deeper obligation and included fealty, and was signified by the vassal putting his hands together between the hands of the superior, indicating the relationship of protection.

The superior could expect certain things back for granting *dominium utile*. The land was 'feued', the vassal was 'infeft' and the vassal owed a 'fee' or 'feu duty' or 'fief' to the superior, and was a feuar (meaning the same as 'vassal' but without its overtones of servitude). Obviously, all of these words have the same derivation. The feu was originally one of four types:

- ward: essentially military service, the provision of a specified number of mounted knights, armed men etc., abolished in the time of George II by the Tenures Abolition Act of 1746
- blenche-ferme: the original 'peppercorn' rent, where the payment was nominal (one peppercorn, a silver penny, an apple, a horseshoe, a mirror for larks) and often only if asked for
- alms: the vassal said prayers or paid for church services for the superior, often where land had been given *in collegiam* (not to any one person) to build a church
- feu-ferme: some form of physical payment, either produce or money

In time, the need for military service passed away (or the government disliked the idea of large landowners being able to raise an army, especially in Scotland), prayers became less of an issue and single peppercorns were unprofitable, so the feu became the predominant form of payment. (More on this below.)

The end of feudalism

To be frank, strict feudalism started to decline in the late 1300s, but its traces can be seen in the legal practices of land transfer right up to present day. However, James VI and I brought the landed nobles to heel during his reign (1567–1625) and the link between land and service was abolished in Scotland by two Acts, both the result of Jacobite uprisings – the Clan Act of 1715 and the Tenures Abolition Act of 1746.

A later law, the Heritable Jurisdictions Act 1747, removed the powers of life and death and other criminal jurisdictions from the Baron Courts and the owners received compensation.

In the 1970s, legislation made it possible for the voluntary or compulsory redemption of feu duty by a one-off payment, and in 2004 all feudal tenure disappeared from Scotland altogether. In strict legal terms, under Section 63(1) of the Act, a Scottish barony that was a 'prescriptive barony by tenure' is now not attached to the land and is 'incorporeal feudal hereditament', but the dignity of Baron is preserved. Such titles can be freely transferred and so a Scottish barony is the only genuine, prescriptive, degree of title capable of being bought and sold in the UK.

THE FEUDAL BARONIES OF SCOTLAND, REGALITY, BARONY AND JURISDICTION

In the marvellous *1066 and All That*, authors Sellers and Yateman send up various aspects of British history with a schoolboy's confused understanding, and give the duties of a baron as:

- to be armed to the teeth
- to extract from the Villein saccage and soccage, tollage and tallage, pillage and ullage, and, in extreme cases, all other banorial amenities such as umbrage and porrage
- to hasten the king's death, deposition, insanity, etc., and make quite sure that there were always at least three false claimants to the throne

– to resent the Attitude of the Church. (The barons were secretly jealous of the Church, which they accused of encroaching on their rites)

– to keep up the Middle Ages

Notice the deliberate misspellings 'banorial' and 'rites' and the complete confusion terms such as soccage, ullage, pillage and porrage. What Sellers and Yateman were caricaturing was the quaint view of now-irrelevant feudal practices, but their description, like all good satire, is not too far off the mark. However, it was written from an English perspective. Scottish baronies were, and are, a far more serious matter.

Territorial and personal titles

In early medieval Scotland the titles of earl and baron were the only nobilities. The other ranks appeared later – the grant of an earldom as a personal title in 1358 (Douglas), duke (1398), marquess (1599), viscount (1606) and later the lesser rank of baronet (not a peerage, but a form of hereditary knighthood invented by James VI and I to raise money). Earldoms and baronies were territorial titles – linked to land – as opposed to personal titles. The land itself was 'erected into' an earldom or a barony by a charter under the Great Seal and then that earldom or barony was granted to some person using a formula like *the lands and barony of Hauch to be held of the King in liberam baroniam*. This made sense in a society where wealth, power, military capability and administration depended on land ownership, so a mere title in itself would have been meaningless. Someone became an earl or a baron by virtue of being granted the physical earldom or barony (a fief of the Crown that also conferred nobility). In strict terms, a barony or earldom is not a parcel of land, but jurisdiction over an area of land. The important point here is that the lands and the barony went together but were two separate legal entities. The logical consequence of that is, that where the land is disposed of, the new title-holder (normally the heir but could be by purchase) the title goes with it. Scottish feudal baronies can be, and are, sold. It happened less frequently with earldoms.

The original earldoms were seven in number, corresponding to the ancient kingdoms, and each earl was in effect a prince or a minor king in his lands. With time, and as land available to parcel out became sparse, personal earldoms were created – a cheap form of patronage, as an empty title costs nothing. Such nobles were designated 'of' somewhere, as is still the case, but the name has no significance other than the desire of the ennobled person to assert a relationship. The Duke of Fife does not own Fife; and Lord Mackay of Clashfern – the Scottish mathematician and advocate who was Lord Chancellor under Margaret Thatcher from 1987–97 – had no special rights in Clashfern.

Barony

Where land was held in *liberam baroniam* (in free barony) the holder was a territorial baron (barony by tenure or *baro minor*), but not necessarily a baron with a peerage (barony by writ or *baro major*). The distinction is most important in Scotland, where the vast majority of barons were not peers – they did not sit in the House of Lords alongside dukes, earls, marquesses and viscounts. They were and are referred to as Baron of Such-and-such whereas a titled baron would be Baron So-and-so. Of course, a particular person could be both, holding a peerage as a baron but also being baron of certain lands. Barons had considerable jurisdiction over the baronies (discussed below) and the barony was the effective social and judicial unit of Scotland for a long time.

The barony is the equivalent of the manor and a baron a lord of the manor in England. But if the land was the barony, so to speak, how could the land be divided up and sub-feued? The legal fiction was that the barony attached to the *caput* (Latin meaning 'head'), originally the 'moot-hill' or place where the Barony Court was held, or the castle or manor house itself, but later a notional piece of land, a standing stone, a tree etc. (The *caput* of Scotland, for example, was the moot-hill at Scone where kings were crowned on the Stone of Destiny.) The barony was legally attached to the *caput* so the baron could dispose of the lands but retain the *caput*, or the feudal superiority over the *caput*, and so retain the barony and the jurisdiction. Land was 'partible' (capable of being divided and 'alienated') but the *caput*, the baronial jurisdiction, the title of baron and any heraldic additaments (such as the baron's chapeau on the coat of arms) were 'impartible' (could not be legally divided or separated from each other). In general, if the *caput* was sold or inherited the barony went with it unless specifically reserved. In the course of time, many baronies have shrunk to just the *caput* which could be a handkerchief-sized piece of ground or a particular stone, and since 2004 need have no physical presence at all.

With the Abolition of Feudal Tenure Act in Scotland in 2004 baronies became personal titles no longer attached to land, like present-day peerages. As such, sales of feudal baronies no longer have to be recorded as property transactions in the Register of Sasines.

In theory, being a superior conferred and imposed certain duties, including jurisdiction over the vassal's lands. In practice this was only the case when the superior held the land in regality or in barony. It could be neither. No Scottish feudal baronies have been created since 1800. But unlike personal titles, feudal baronies cannot be extinguished; they exist forever, for someone to claim if they can prove entitlement.

For more on this fascinating subject see Sir Malcolm Innes of Edingight, 'The Baronage of Scotland: The History of the Law of Succession and the Law of Arms in Relation Thereto', *The Scottish Genealogist*, June 2000.

Regality

The distinction between regality and barony is potentially confusing. A regality is very similar to a barony, but usually had greater jurisdiction and was not held heritably by one person, but by the office. For example, Dunfermline Abbey (and therefore its abbot, as the commendator and usufructuar) held the regality of Dunfermline. In practice, though, the extent of any powers would be spelled out in detail in the relevant grant.

Thus, regalities were super baronies held in *liberam regalitatem*. They had even greater jurisdictional powers and privileges and were equivalent to the English Palatine Counties (Durham, Lancashire and Cheshire) or Palatinates in Europe. A lordship of a regality had almost the power of the Crown, including total criminal jurisdiction (including the Four Pleas of the Crown – murder, rape, arson and robbery – but excluding treason or other offences against the sovereign's person) and could have their own chanceries and mints. Officers of the Crown, including the justiciars of the north and south and sheriffs, had no authority in a regality and appeals again the decisions of regality courts in civil matters could only be heard by parliament. Land in regality was a major source of wealth and power, so such grants were usually made only to members of the royal family and leading nobles, as with the earldoms of Atholl, March, Moray and Strathearn, the lordships of Badenoch, Carrick, Garioch and Renfrew, the lands of the Earls of Angus and Douglas and Douglas of Dalkeith and some baronies. However, a regality was usually erected over one existing earldom or a number of existing baronies held by one person, so there was little difference in the practical administration of justice or day-to-day affairs. Regality jurisdiction went out with the Heritable Jurisdictions Act in 1747 (although lords of regality retained the restricted baronial jurisdiction), but the title 'Lord of Regality' survived.

Stewartry

In addition, there were stewartries. This was a Crown property administered by an appointed or hereditary steward, rather than a sheriff. Examples were The Mearns (from the Gaelic word for stewartry) Strathearn and Menteith and Orkney and Shetland. Later, these became county

Sheriff Courts, although the stewartry of Kirkcudbright retained the name, and approximately the same area of Dumfries and Galloway is still referred to that way. Stewartry courts had extensive jurisdiction, abolished by the Heritable Jurisdictions (Scotland) Act of 1746 which took effect from 25 March 1748.

Bailieries

These were instituted by feudal lords or the Crown; for example, Ayrshire originally was in four districts of Cuninghame, Kyle Stewart, King's Kyle and Carrick, each with its own bailiery court and religious centre – Cuninghame's bailiery court was at Irvine and Kilwinning Abbey was granted to the Tyronensian Order of monks.

Military service

Originally, the feudal earldoms and baronies were held of the Crown by military service, requiring a specified number of knights for a defined period (normally forty days) when requested. The earls and barons sub-feued part of their lands to these knights, held of them by knights' service (knights' fees), and the knights might in turn sub-feu parts of these lands to other vassals, as husbandmen (tenant farmers) and so on in a hierarchy down to the final vassals, who might have serfs and others to work the land. (A knight's fee would be about a square mile or a few hundred acres.) Therefore, a whole network of people would have an interest in the earldom or barony land, with the tenants-in-chief, who owed feus to the Crown, having nobility conferred on them. Their feus were military (or some other honourable service) while the 'ignoble' at the bottom of the chain paid their feus in money, produce or labour. None of this depended on the number of people in the hierarchy – a tenant farmer ploughing a field on land directly held by the Crown (a 'royal demesne') was every bit a direct vassal of the Crown as an earl.

Courts and jurisdiction

Criminal and civil jurisdiction was also hierarchical. Tenants-in-chief of the Crown (earls and barons) had the right and duty to attend the *Curia Regis* (King's Court) of which they were considered the 'peers' (Latin *pares* meaning equal in rank); and this gradually evolved into a parliament. Feudal superiors were also obliged to hold courts for their immediate vassals, which as well as being courts of law were a local parliament or council but limited in geography and powers. The Barony Court mainly occupied itself with the regular administration of the estate but could ordain local laws (like present-day by-laws) regulating the vassals' behaviour and relationships. At its highest, the Barony Court had the right of 'pit and gallows' (the exercise of trial and capital punishment by hanging for men and drowning for women) and could appoint Baron Baillies (bailiffs), Baron Sergeands (effectively police officers), a Dempster ('doom-sayer', who pronounces sentences, and therefore a sort of judge) and other officers with what we would now recognise as legal authority and police powers.

The baron had the rights of private jurisdiction as any landholding feudal superior but also had public jurisdiction as a baron, delegated from the Crown. In reality, serious cases in the Barony Court were overseen by the local sheriff and the baron was not in any sense judge and jury. The baron's immediate vassals were the peers of his court (which is the origin of everyone's right to be tried by a jury of his or her peers). The baron saw that justice was administered according to the proper procedure and he was legally in the same position as his vassals – a litigant. However, the barony retained any fines in recompense for the administrative costs.

Much of this had passed away by the 1500s but was still sufficiently operative in the Highlands of Scotland for the Hanoverian government to blunt the local power of clan chiefs after the 1745 Jacobite Rebellion by the Heritable Jurisdictions Act of 1747, which restricted baronial jurisdiction. It is unclear, after the abolition of the Scottish feudal system in 2004, whether barons may still hold private courts and what their jurisdictions would be.

Parliament and the 'Thrie Estaites'

Originally the landed earls and barons and the senior churchmen constituted a parliament. The earliest mention in Scottish records is 1235, but by 1326 this was composed of the 'three estates' (landed nobility, senior clergy and burgh commissioners, representing the commoners) the phrase itself first used around 1357. In fact, this parliament was a body which ratified decisions of a variety of committees, the most important being the Lords of the Articles – a sort of inner cabinet – whose membership was managed by the sovereign, ensuring a high degree of direct royal control.

Parliament met wherever the sovereign decreed, and had no fixed home until 1632 when Charles I ordered the building of a fixed site for parliament and the courts in Edinburgh. Parliament House, adjacent to St Giles' Cathedral on the Royal Mile, was first used by the Estates in 1641 and is still the site of the law courts.

Feudal barons were technically competent to sit in parliament as part of the nobility but, by Acts passed in 1428 and 1587, they could send two representatives from each sheriffdom. Before 1587 Scottish barons had the right to attend parliament. Not many did – imagine the expense – although in the Reformation parliament of 1560 more than 100 feudal barons attended in person. The Act of Relief of 1587 gave the barons in each shire the right to elect two representatives each year to attend on their behalf, known then as Commissioners and later as Lords of Parliament. By 1627, the Barons lost their right to sit in parliament by negative prescription. There is at least one 'baron' today (Dr Nelson Ying from Florida, who purchased the Barony of Balquhain) who feels he may have a right to sit in the new Scottish parliament.

Later, '40 shilling freeholders', and eventually everyone, had universal suffrage. The Scottish parliament went through many other changes – the gradual replacement of the barons by nobles with personal titles, the assertion of its own authority in the last half of the sixteenth century, the removal of bishops and their reinstatement, opposition to Cromwell's changes, direct elections and finally the merger with Westminster in 1707 and devolution in 1999. There is more detail on this at www.scottish.parliament.uk.

Baronies today

As Baronies had less and less practical use – baronial jurisdiction all but disappearing in 1747 and parliamentary attendance no longer an issue – many feudal titles were simply forgotten. They did not disappear – only an Act of Parliament or an edict of the Crown could extinguish a barony – and are probably acquired unknown to the purchaser of, say, an estate or a castle. As few as 150 out of the likely total of 1,500 or more are recorded as having arms with baronial additaments by the Lord Lyon, and most of these are with the original family or a landed aristocrat. But every so often one is bought and sold, usually for ridiculous amounts considering it is merely a title and not even a noble one. With the changes effected in 2004 it is likely that their value will now dwindle to almost nothing.

Tracing a barony

Some 400 baronies existed in 1405 and most of those later created date from then until the seventeenth century, when a considerable number were erected. (See *Atlas of Scottish History to 1707.*)

Refer to the Retours of Services of Heirs (available on CD from the Scottish Genealogy Society), the Register of the Great Seal and the Register of Sasines. If the original charter is lost an official extract can be obtained from the Register of the Great Seal, which has the same legal status as the original charter.

Usage and heraldry of a Scottish barony

The barony is not a peerage, but is a noble title or 'dignity' of below-peerage rank. The owner of the Scottish barony Inversneckie, may use his existing name and add the title, as in 'Iain MacSwine, Baron of Inversneckie' and be addressed as 'Inversneckie' or take the territorial designation as part of his surname, 'Iain MacSwine of Inversneckie, Baron of Inversneckie'. A married couple are 'The Baron and Baroness of Inversneckie', 'Inversneckie and Lady Inversneckie' or 'The Baron and Lady Inversneckie'. Notice the baron is NEVER 'Baron Inversneckie'. In most formal situations, a Scottish baron and baroness are styled 'The Much Honoured'.

Baronial heraldry

A Scottish feudal baron's arms bear a steel tilting helm garnished with gold, the baronial chapeau (cap of estate) and the baronial mantle which is blazoned as 'Gules doubled silk Argent, fur-edged miniver and collared in ermine, fastened on the right shoulder by five spherical buttons Or'. This indicates a red (Gules) cape with a white (Argent) lining, with furs as indicated and five gold (Or) buttons.

Chapeau

It was the case until recently that when new arms are granted, or a matriculation of existing arms includes a barony, the armiger may add a chapeau (cap of maintenance) to the armorial achievement directly above the shield and below the helmet. This is blazoned as 'gules doubled ermine' for barons in possession of the *caput* of the barony, and a *chapeau azure* is considered appropriate for the heirs of ancient baronial families who are no longer owners of the estates themselves. The chapeau can be used on stationery or to ensign the circlet of a crest badge. However, the new Lord Lyon (appointed in 2008) may take the view that acquiring a barony title does not mean that the baronial additament of a chapeau will be added to arms. Any such decision will likely be appealed to the Court of Session.

Feudo–baronial mantle

The robe of estate is a particularly Scottish heraldic additament, blazoned as 'gules doubled silk argent, fur-edged of miniver and collared in ermine fastened on the right shoulder by five spherical buttons'. It can be pavilioned, draped behind the complete achievement or the shield alone and tied open with cords and tassels.

Helmet
The helmet of a baron is a feudal steel helm garnished in gold affronté, and occasionally garnished with one or three grilles.

Supporters
These are now usually reserved for the older baronies (chartered before 1587) and those which have been in continuous ownership of one family. In England, by contrast, supporters are reserved for the peerage. Occasionally a compartment was granted, representing territories, with or without supporters, but even in 1637 this was contentious.

Barons of Dundas, Halton, Polmais, &, v. Lord Lyon, June, 1673

(Brown's Supplement to Morrison's Dictionary of Decisions, Court of Session (Scotland) 1622–1780, iii. 6)

1673. June. Sundry BARONS, &c. against The LORD LYON.
… a process some Barons and Gentlemen had intended against my Lord Lyon, to hear and see it found and declared that he had done wrong in refusing to give them forth their coats of arms with supporters, whereof they and their predecessors had been in possession past all memory, and never quarrelled till now; and, therefore, that he might be decerned to immatriculate them so in his register, and give them forth an extract; conform, as is provided by the late Act of Parliament in 1672. The Lyon's reason is, because, by an express letter of his Majesty's, none under the dignity of a Lord must use supporters. (He grants them now to some who were in possession of them of old.) But the gentlemen answer, that Lords at the beginning, having been only Barons, and in regard of the considerable interest they had in their respective shires, being commissionate from the small barons and freeholders to represent them in parliament, they, because of that credit, got first the denomination of Lords, without any patent or creation; and, upon the matter, were nothing but Barons: and so what is due to them is also due to the other, they originally not differing from the rest by any essential or superior step of dignity. So Craig, pages 78 and 79.
—REPLIED, Whatever was their rise, the other Barons have clearly acknowledged a distinction now; in so far as they have renounced their privilege of coming to parliaments by the 113 Act in 1587; and the distinction being made, and their privileges renounced, by the small Barons in the parliament 1427.
—DUPLIED, that act is introduced in their favours, and nowise debars them; but allenarly dispenses with their absence, and the penalty they incurred thereby, &c. The Gentlemen found on the Interdictum uti possidetis: the Lyon says, it is but vetustas erroris, and a usurpation.

Notes: Duplied indicated a rejoinder; *Interdictum Uti Possidetis* gives relief to an owner of moveable property in actual possession, provided he had not obtained the possession against another party (i.e. no one else was deprived of it); by *vetustas erroris*, Lyon meant to indicate that it was an error of old.

Further reading

For much, much more on this, and a long argument as to the current legal status of baronies, see:

An article by Graham Senior-Milne, 41st Baron of Mordington at www.gmilne.demon.co.uk/Baronies.htm.

A 1945 article by Innes of Learney, a previous Lord Lyon, in *Proceedings of the Society of Antiquaries of Scotland*, vol. 79 available at www.prestoungrange.org/core-files/archive/university_press/proceedings.pdf.

An example of the proceedings of a modern-day (2004) Barony Court at www.prestoungrange.org/core-files/archive/trinity_session/14_protection_of_dignity_of_baron.pdf.

Gretton G., *The Law of Property in Scotland*, pp. 31–100, Reid, Kenneth G.C. (ed), Butterworth's Edinburgh: Law Society of Scotland (1996).

McNeill, P.G.B. and MacQueen, H.L. (eds), *Atlas of Scottish History to 1707*, University of Edinburgh (1996).

Retours of Services of Heirs available on CD from the Scottish Genealogy Society, www.scotsgenealogy.com.

Abolition of Feudal Tenure etc. (Scotland) Act 2000, www.hmso.gov.uk/legislation/scotland/acts2000/20000005.htm.

Report on Abolition of the Feudal System, www.scotland.gov.uk/deleted/library/documents-w10/afs1-00.htm.

The Scottish Baronage Registry, www.baronyregistry.com.

Burke's Peerage, www.burkes-peerage.net/sites/peerageandgentry/sitepages/home.asp.

Baronial heraldry

The Heraldry Society of Scotland, www.heraldry-scotland.co.uk.

The Court of the Lord Lyon, www.lyon-court.com.

College of Arms, www.college-of-arms.gov.uk.

12

Church and Religious Records

In a sense, all registrations pre-1855 are Church records, as there was no civil system on the scale of the Statutory Registers. Old parish registers (OPRs) are dealt with in Chapter 3 and Kirk Session records – with their valuable insights into the social life of the parish, not to mention the Session's views on matters such as drunkenness, adultery, illegitimacy and witchcraft. Records concerning clergy themselves are considered in chapter 5. But here we will deal with the records of churches other than the established Kirk.

NONCONFORMISTS

This is a general title applied to anyone not normally observant within the Church of Scotland. Although most Scots were, especially when it was dangerous or at least uncomfortable not to be, there were many variants of 'nonconformity'. This would include the Episcopalian Church and the Catholic Church – both of which claimed to have been there first – as well as the many Protestant sects which sprang up during the secessions of the 1700s, the Disruption of 1843 and after. The main result of the Disruption was the formation of the Free Church of Scotland and later the United Presbyterian Church of Scotland, but there were other denominations too. Gradually, most of these fell away or merged, and some reunited with the Kirk. These records are fairly scattered, but many are in the NAS. They contain the expected, including baptisms, marriages and burials, but also lists of members and minute books.

Other than that, a number of Family History Societies have produced printed or online lists of nonconformists in their local areas. There are also many useful publications entitled *My Family Were (Baptists, Quakers etc.)*, also available through FHS sources.

The records of the Roman Catholic Church in the NAS are photocopies of pre-1855 baptism, marriage and death registers, mostly from the nineteenth century but a small number before that, even to the early 1700s. The originals (or other copies) are either with parish priests or with the diocese or archdiocese. The Archdiocese of Glasgow, for example, has registers for some Glasgow and nearby parishes. Various Catholic archives and societies are given on p. 138. However, from 1700–14 Church of Scotland ministers kept lists of Catholics within the parishes and reported them to the General Assembly of the Church of Scotland.

Many of the records of the Episcopal Church of Scotland (the established church from 1603–38 and the 1660s) are still with the local priest or the diocese, but the NAS has some originals and microfilm copies. However, there has been a survey of known Episcopal Church records and the results can be found on the National Register of Archives for Scotland (NRAS) website.

Baptist, Congregational, Methodist, Quaker and Unitarian records are mostly in the NAS, or in an archive in the area where they exist, but Glasgow City Archives has a large collection for the West of Scotland (except for the Congregational Church records, which are from all over the country). In every case, it is worth contacting the headquarters of each church in Scotland (except for Baptist records, where the individual church is the first port of call).

NAS collections referred to above are in General Register House, Edinburgh (mainly Ref. CH), and they are restricted access, which requires a signed form.

A search on the NRAS website (start at www.nas.gov.uk/nras/register.asp) will produce information such as:

NRAS2702   Scottish Episcopal Church: Diocese of Edinburgh   eighteenth century–twentieth century

From this, it is possible to search for NRAS2702 and see what the holdings actually are. But be aware that access is not open and general, as is the case with OPRs and civil records.

Recusants

Not a denomination as such, but recusant lists are a valuable source for genealogists. In theory, recusants were anyone who did not belong to the established church, but were mainly Catholics. 'Recusancy' was the term for non-compliance with the established form or religion. Recusants were early on subject to criminal penalties and later to civil penalties, the inability to take certain offices or occupations and general discrimination. There was a 'Test' of faith so written that almost anyone asked to take it would be bound to fail. Laws passed under James VI and I and Charles I mainly targeted Roman Catholic recusants, most of which were not repealed until the time of George IV, although they had ceased to be enforced by then. Recusants also included Protestant dissenters, although after the restoration of Charles II these were what came to be known as nonconformist.

The genealogical importance of this was that various people drew up lists of recusants within the local parish, burgh or court area. In 1634 there was a Royal Commission warranting specified persons 'to search out and punish all recusants or their resetters' (meaning those who harboured them). The best source is Privy Council records, as this court dealt with recusancy, but local archives may have records too.

Useful Websites for Non-Conformist, Catholic and Jewish Records

Church of Scotland Kirkweb, www.kirkweb.org/home.htm
Strict Baptist Historical Society, www.strictbaptisthistory.org.uk
Catholic Central Library, www.catholiclibrary.dernon.co.uk
Catholic Record Society, www.catholic-history.org.uk/crs
Scottish Catholic Archives, www.catholic-heritage.net/sca
Catholic Family History Society, www.catholic-history.org.uk/cfhs
Jewish Consolidated Surname Index, www.avotaynu.corn/csi (some 2 million names from 30 datasources)
Jewish Genealogical Society of Great Britain, www.ort.org/jgsgb

13

Palaeography

There will come a time in every genealogist's research life when an apparently unreadable document rears its head. In fact, it is often not as difficult as it seems, especially since most documents are written in a rather formulaic way.

The majority of documents that family history researchers will deal with will be testaments (loosely called wills) which are normally in English or old Scots; only a few examples from the 1500s are in Latin. If you do come across a Latin document, it would be useful to read Chapter 9 before embarking on this one.

Hands

There are a number of forms of handwriting which genealogists will come across when researching older documents. In rough chronological order these are:

Book hands – usually fairly readable, found in books before the widespread availability of print and produced in scriptoria.

Court hands – for business and literary purposes, some quite stylised and individual to particular offices or professions such as Chancery hand or Exchequer hand. They survived alongside Secretary hand.

Chancery hand – the official style used in the Royal Chancery at Westminster, which continued to be used for the enrolment of Acts of Parliament until 1836.

Italic hand – created in Italy around 1400, popular from the early 1500s and a major influence on Secretary hand.

Secretary hand – a development of the Court hands of the early sixteenth century and in general use for almost 200 years. It met the growing need for a universally intelligible script as the amount of business, legal and personal correspondence increased after the Renaissance. Another reason for its spread, strangely, was the introduction of printing at the end of the fifteenth century. There was less work for the medieval penman and the scriptoria, so they taught writing to the growing middle classes.

Round hand – gradually this overtook Secretary hand from the 1650s onwards, producing the Italic hand we use today.

They would all be easy to read except for:

- – unusual (i.e. non-modern) letters
- – idiosyncratic writing flourishes
- – abbreviations
- – unfamiliar words

Start by looking at a document which is easy to read (Testament of George Durie, Lord Rutherford, 1759, p. 116) and familiarise yourself with its structure, contents and vocabulary. We can use the diplomatic of this document to understand older ones, in less familiar hands.

The testament of David Durie of that ilk of Scotscraig dated 1601. See pp. 146–7 for transcripts

1. Get to know some letters

Some letters are very similar to modern versions:
a, b, d, f, i/j, l, m, n, o, p, t, u/v/w, z

Some are very different:
c, e, g, h, k, q ,r, s, x, y

Some are particular to this time:
yogh ('gh'), thorn (hard 'th')

a	b	c	d	e	f	g	h	i/j	k	l	ll	m	n

n	o	p	q	r	s	t	u/v	w	x	y	z	yogh	thorn

2. Start by identifying typical words and phrases, the most common letters, letters most similar to ours and letters not similar to ours.

From his name, we can see some letter shapes.
David Durie
xxiiij februarij 1601
(24 February)
Notice the final i written as a j and the two variants of D

3. Identify words already known

David Durie
Find -

ye (the)

yat (that)

Find formulaic words:
testament
testamentar
dative
inventar
guid gere,
sowmis (sums) of money and
dettis (debts)

4. The most common letters are:

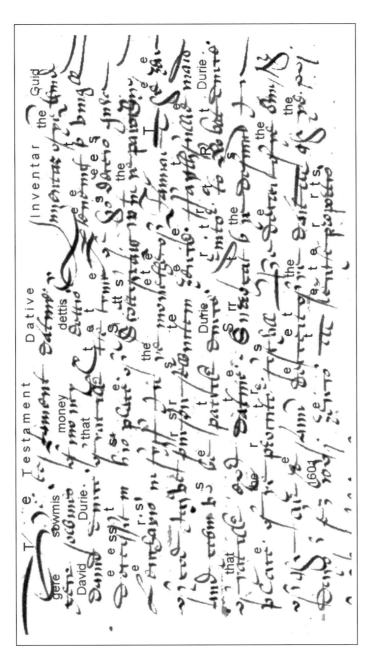

Next: a, b, d, f, i/j

5. Some letters are very similar to modern versions

a	
b	
d	
f	
i/j	

Next: l, m, n, o, p, u/v, w, z

Next: c, g, h, k, q, x, y, &, yogh (gh), thorn (th)

l	m	n	o	p	u/v	w		z

6. Some letters are very different to our modern versions

7. Be careful with these letters and numbers

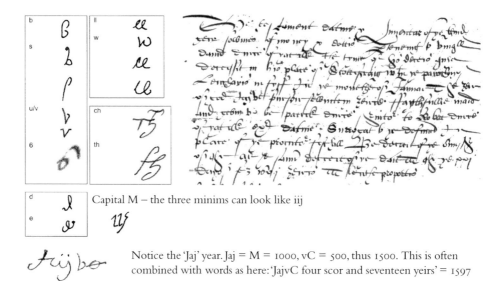

b	ß	ll	ℓℓ
s	Ꝝ	w	ʍ
	ſ	ce	ce
u/v	ʋ		ce
	v	ch	T
6	ꝺ	th	ſs

| d | ł |
| e | ℯ |

Capital M – the three minims can look like iij

ℳ

Aiijᵇᵒ

Notice the 'Jaj' year. Jaj = M = 1000, vC = 500, thus 1500. This is often combined with words as here: 'JajvC four scor and seventeen yeirs' = 1597

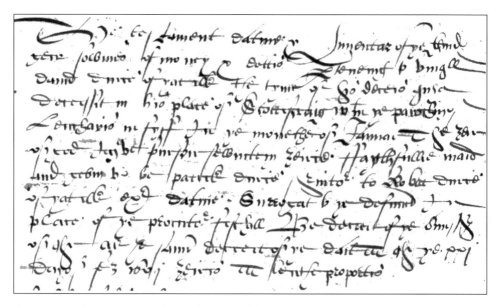

On p. 140 is the testament of David Durie of that Ilk of Scotscraig, who died in 1601. It is written in fairly typical Scottish Secretary hand, and here we'll concentrate on the first two paragraphs. (For unfamiliar words and abbreviations, consult the Glossaries in chapter 16.)

Translation of above document:

The testament Dative and Inventar of the Guid gere, sowmis of money & Dettis p[er]teneing to umquhile David Durie of that ilk the tyme of his deceis quha Deceissit in his place of Scottiscraig wit[hi]n the parochin of Leucharis in fyf In the monethe of Januar The yeir of god MvC four scor seventeen yeire (1597). Faythfullie maid and given up be Patrick Durie heritor to Robert Durie of that ilk ex[ecuto]r Dative & surrogat to the Defunct In place of the procu[ra]tor fischall Be Decrei of the Commis[ariot] of Edinburgh the said Decreit of the Dait of the xxi Day of f(ebruar)y 1601 yeiris At lenthe proportis.

8. Now transcribe this paragraph (without looking at the transcription below):

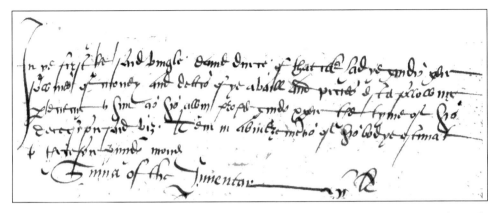

In the first the said umquhile David Durie of that ilk had the guidis gere sowmis of money & dettis of the availl and prices e[n]t[ere]d following p[er]teneing to him as his awn proper gudis & gere the tyme of his deceis forsaid viz. Item in abuilyements of his bodye estimat threescore punds mone

    Suma of the Inventar Lx lib

['Abuilyements' (various spellings) are the personal possessions – clothes, money, etc. – on the deceased's person at death. In total, he was worth 60 pounds Scots (= £12 Sterling) in terms of his moveables.]

For palaeography exercises, tutorials and information:

    www.nas.gov.uk/learning/publications.asp
    www.scottishhandwriting.com
    www.nationalarchives.gov.uk/palaeography
    medievalwriting.50megs.com
    www.geocities.com/CollegePark/Library/2036/paleo.htm
    www.ualberta.ca/~sreimer/ms-course/course/pal-hist.htm

For legal and land terms, consult the Scotland's People website: www.scotlandspeople.gov.uk/content/help/index.aspx?r=551&431. For Scots words more generally, see the Scottish Language Dictionaries website at www.scotsdictionaries.org.uk. Images of wills and testaments from 1513–1901 are available on this site: www.scottishdocuments.com and www.scotlandspeople.gov.uk.

Further reading

Gouldesbrough, Peter, *Formulary of Old Scots Legal Documents*, Edinburgh: Stair Society (1985).

Hector, L.C., *The Handwriting of English Documents*, reprint of 2nd edn, Dorking, Surrey: Kohler and Coombes (1980). Originally published in 1966.

Johnson, Charles and Jenkinson, Hilary, *English Court Hand AD 1066 to 1500: illustrated chiefly from the public records*, New York: F. Ungar Publishing Co. (1967), 2 vols. Originally published in 1915.

Rosie, Alison, *Scottish Handwriting 1500–1700: A self-help pack*, Scottish Records Association and the National Archives of Scotland.

Simpson, Grant G., *Scottish Handwriting, 1150–1650: an introduction to the reading of documents*, new edn, East Linton Tuckwell Press (1998).

14

DNA Testing and Genealogy

The field which has come to be known as Genetic Genealogy adds DNA testing to traditional genealogical sources research. Strangely, it has very little to do with genes.

Up until now, we have relied in the main on a number of sources of family information:

- civil and ecclesiastical records such as censuses, BMD registers
- legal records: testaments, tax assessments, poor law, court records
- personal records: wills (which are also legal, of course), military lists and so on
- published records: biographies, newspaper items (such as BMD announcements, obituaries and news stories), membership lists, occupational lists and the like
- private records: family archives, company records etc.

All of these suffer from the same difficulties and problems:

- they are usually paper, which the ravages of time and human error can damage or destroy
- they are almost bound to be incomplete
- they may well be wrong, for a variety of reasons
- they can't readily be gone back over and re-analysed for more information

For example, we have all seen our own names misspelt or wrongly printed. If the records in question have been transcribed and secondarily published (as with lists of gravestone inscriptions, for example) or added to a database (like census information), there is another layer of potential error. And, of course, not everyone gives correct or complete details in the first place.

To take the most obvious example – your father may think he is your father but your mother, who certainly knows she's your mother, may know that your father isn't your father. Every record confirms that these are your parents. But what if they aren't?

Equally, what if you were adopted and know nothing of your original descent, and have no paper trail to help you find out? Or what if there is some mystery or confusion over your family's origins – an ancestry abroad of which the details are now lost; a change of surname for any number of reasons; a second marriage or less regular relationship not properly accounted for?

No amount of paper records will help if no such record exists, or if the records are just plain wrong. What is needed is something objective that can tie you to your biological parents, and through them, to all of your ancestral lines. Wouldn't it be wonderful, in fact, if we were all born with some sort of 'ancestral barcode' passed on from parent to child.

Fortunately, we have exactly that. It's our DNA. Unfortunately, anyone who fondly imagines that sending off a DNA test kit will immediately solve a genealogical problem and prove that Harry is Joanne's third cousin once removed, is in for a severe disappointment. It's a lot more complicated that that. But DNA testing is changing the face of genealogy, so every genealogist ought to know what the results mean, and how they are derived from the tests available.

Molecular biology for the faint-at-heart

We are about to step off the cliff here and plunge into the very forefront of human biochemistry and statistical population genetics. But we'll take it slowly and try not to panic.

You are built from one sperm, gratefully provided by your biological father, and one egg, kindly supplied by your biological mother. The human female is born with about 400 eggs which she will release, one by one, on an almost-monthly basis from puberty to the menopause. If one egg gets fertilised, it has a good chance of becoming an embryo which will develop into a foetus and then a new-born baby, the whole process taking about 270 days (nine months). The human male, on the other hand, makes something like 1,500 sperm every second from puberty until death and if only one of these reaches an egg and fertilises it, his part in the process is more or less over, aside from building the doll's house or buying the train set. Knowing that should explain a lot about human behaviour.

So when someone says that you have your father's nose or your mother's eyes, they mean you have inherited certain physical characteristics from your parents. But what exactly have you inherited? Most cells in the body have a cell nucleus (human red blood cells, for instance, don't, but other species do).[1] This nucleus contains chromosomes (literally, 'coloured bodies', because they can be stained with chemical dyes to make them visible under a microscope) and chromosomes are long strands of DNA (deoxyribonucleic acid) wound up with specialised proteins.

Humans have twenty-three pairs of chromosomes in each normally nucleated cell (we'll see why 'pairs' are important in a moment) and when a cell divides, each chromosome unwinds so it can be copied.[2] All cells have the same DNA, but different parts of it are expressed in different cell types, so a muscle cell has the same DNA as a brain cell, but not all of it is turned on in each case. Once a cell becomes a muscle or brain cell, it is fixed in that pattern. Cells with the potential to become many different types of tissue are called stem cells.

DNA is a very simple molecule, although it is very long. To cram forty-six sets of DNA into each cell, it is highly curled and folded, but if unwound the DNA in each chromosome would be six feet long. Multiply that by the trillions of cells in your body, and you have enough DNA to stretch about 12 million miles. If you did unwind the DNA you would see (but not with the naked eye) that it is a double-stranded helix – a bit like a twisted ladder. Each strand is a chain of quite simple chemicals called bases of only four types, known as A, T, C and G, each joined to a sugar (deoxyribose) with a phosphate. The sugar phosphates are the thread of the necklace and the bases hang from each sugar like beads. What's more, A on one strand always pairs with T on the other, and the same for C and G. So if one strand has the base sequence AACTTACCTGG, it is paired with TTGAATGGACC:

---

[1] Red blood cells, which carry oxygen and carbon dioxide around the body, are the only human cells without a nucleus. They cannot divide and replicate, but are produced from stem cells in the bone marrow – about 2,300 every second – and are destroyed in the spleen and liver after four to six months. Birds, on the other hand, have nucleated red blood cells, as did the dinosaurs they evolved from, and the reptiles (lizards etc.) and amphibians (frogs, newts and the like). Mammals' red blood cells start out with a nucleus but lose it when they mature. Other human blood cells – white cells, for instance, which help with infections and wound healing – do have a nucleus, so you can get DNA from human blood.

[2] The amount of DNA and the number of chromosomes isn't all that crucial, although it's always the same number in each species. For example, chimpanzees and all other great apes have twenty-four pairs while the horse has thirty-two pairs. For the record, the Congo eel salamander has more DNA in each cell than any other vertebrate.

AACTTACCTGG
TTGAATGGACC

Only one of these strands (called the 'sense' strand) contains the information to make proteins. The 'antisense' strand is its alter-ego. But when the strands separate so that the DNA can be copied, each strand is the template for its opposite number. AACTT … attracts the bases TTGAA … and TTGAA … attracts the bases AACTT … So, barring accidents, you end up with two DNA double-strands which are each an exact copy of the original double strand. Once replicated, the whole DNA winds up into a chromosome again and each copy passes on to one of the two cells made when the original cell divides.

However, you have two copies of each chromosome (twenty-three pairs, remember). You inherited one of each pair from your father and one from your mother. So every nucleated cell has a copy of your father's DNA, and a copy of your mother's. Well, not all cells, because there are two important exceptions – sperm and eggs. Coming back to chromosomes for a moment, in the case of twenty-two of these, one of the pair looks just like its pair twin. These are called the twenty-two 'autosomes'. But in the case of the sex chromosome, one of the pair (Y) is a stunted version of the other (X). Males have YX and females XX in all of their body cells. That's what makes us male or female.[3] But when an egg is made, only one of the X chromosomes ends up in each egg. Likewise, each sperm gets either the Y or the X chromosome. If a Y sperm fertilises the egg, it's a boy (YX); if the sperm has an X chromosome it meets another X chromosome in the egg and makes a girl (XX).

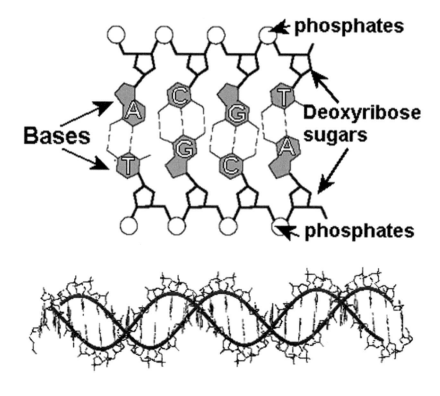

---

[3] Birds, as usual, are different. Female birds have XY chromosomes and the males are XX.

So, we can say with absolute confidence that the Y chromosome in a man's sperm must have come from his father, and the X from his mother. That would tend to suggest that we could determine a father from the child's Y and the mother from the child's X. But it doesn't happen that way. In the egg, the single X could have come from the woman's father or mother. What's more, chromosome pairs undergo a sort of crossover shuffling of genes called recombination, so it is not as simple as two X chromosomes (in a girl), one from each maternal grandparent. But the X and Y in a male do not crossover, so while a baby boy's X chromosome will have genes that came from its mother's mother and its mother's father, the Y chromosome genes are only from the father (and all direct male ancestors before him).

Think of it this way:

If a couple has four children, the chances are (on average) they will have two boys and two girls. The two girls will have their father's X chromosome and the other X chromosome from the mother (which will have genes from both of her parents). The boys will have their father's Y chromosome and an X chromosome from the mother, again with genes from either of the maternal grandparents (like their sisters). The two X chromosomes in these girls will also shuffle their genes.

This means that a Y chromosome in a boy has been inherited all the way down the paternal line and can, in theory, be traced back through that line, father to grandfather to great-grandfather etc. That will also be the case for male cousins, uncles etc. in the same paternal line – they will have the same Y chromosome. So even a distant third cousin four times removed or a great-great-great-uncle (if descended from a common male ancestor) will share the Y chromosome. But the individual genes on an X chromosome, in a boy or a girl, could have come from any of the vast tree that is the maternal ancestry, male or female. This suggests that Y chromosomes are very useful for tracing the surname heritage, but the X chromosome isn't. Fortunately, there is another way to explore the female line – mitochondrial DNA (mtDNA) as we'll see later.

DNA again

If DNA is so simple – only made of four chemicals – why does it produce the myriad of proteins in our bodies, and how can it be used as a barcode? Well, think about a computer program – as far as your computer is concerned, every instruction is just a string of 0s and 1s, but these could be anything from a word processing program to the instructions for getting a spacecraft to Mars. It depends on the precise order and pattern of the 0s and 1s. The same is true of our everyday numbering system – we only have ten digits (0 to 9) but we can make any number we like and 12345 isn't the same as 135420.

So it is with DNA. The order of A, T, C and G along the 'sense' strand of the chromosome determines the protein that part of the DNA instructs to be made. The details don't matter for our purposes, but essentially every three base-pairs get interpreted by the cell's protein manufacturing machinery as equivalent to one of twenty or so amino acids.[4] The machinery 'knits' these amino acids into a particular protein sequence, using the DNA as the 'knitting pattern' and depending on the exact base sequence, the protein could be the one that makes your hair blonde or the one that makes your eyes blue, or any one of thousands of other proteins whose actions you can't see but which nevertheless are part of you – the proteins in your muscles, bones, blood etc. Susceptibility to allergies, the ability to run fast and hereditary

---

[4] There is a bit more to it than that: the DNA is copied into a slightly different chemical strand called ribonucleic acid (RNA) and it is the RNA which the protein-making system 'reads' as its instructions. But the principle is the same – the information started off in the DNA.

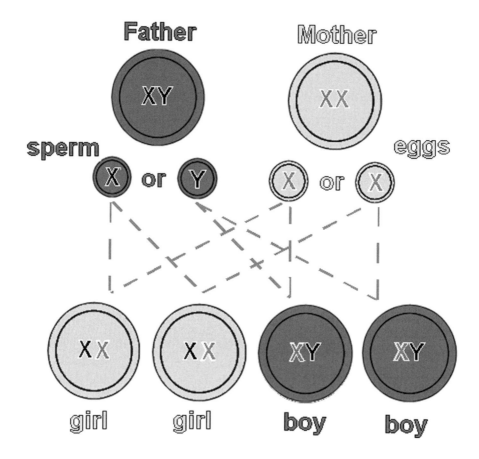

diseases like Huntington's Chorea can be passed down the generations just as eye or hair colour, because the DNA instructions are inherited.

Each bit of DNA which has the instructions for one protein – plus some instructions at either end, a bit like the 'cast-on' and 'cast-off' instructions in a knitting pattern – is called a gene. Genes make proteins. Proteins make you. The human genome (all the DNA in one cell) is perhaps 30,000 to 40,000 genes 'coding' for that number of proteins. If you wrote that out as … AATCGGTAACC … etc., it would fill more than 2,000 books like this one. But when DNA is analysed for genealogical purposes it is usually the DNA which DOESN'T make up genes!

Genetic genealogy isn't about genes

Remember that what we're looking for is not any particular gene, but evidence that DNA has been inherited from a particular line of a family tree, and we don't use genes for that. Surprisingly, only some 2% of the DNA contains genes, in the sense that it codes for proteins. The rest is a sort of packing material with a variety of functions from helping the chromosome curl up in a certain way, to no function at all. Biologists have given this the unflattering title 'junk DNA', but it is far from junk where genealogists are concerned. It varies from person to person, just as genes do, and it comprises 98% of your DNA. This is where DNA-testing laboratories look when doing genetic studies by analysing STRs (see opposite).

More big words

There are three main types of analysis in genealogical DNA studies:

1. DNA sequencing
2. Single Nucleotide Polymorphisms (SNPs, pronounced 'snips')
3. Short Tandem Repeat (STRs)

DNA sequencing is determining the actual order of ATCG bases in a particular area of DNA, and is used mainly in female line investigations, as we'll see later.

SNPs

Single Nucleotide Polymorphism (SNP) is the technical term for occasions where one base-pair in DNA has changed. This is one mechanism of mutation. It does say above that Y and X chromosomes are inherited unchanged down generations, but sometimes mistakes creep in, because of exposure to radiation or certain chemicals for example, or perhaps because the DNA replication mechanism has had a hiccup for some reason. This is called a mutation. There are mechanisms in the cell to repair such errors, but they don't always get caught.

The result is a polymorphism (meaning literally 'different shapes') as even closely related individuals may have a different 'shape' to that particular bit of DNA. Obviously, this mutation changes the protein coded for by that gene. Sometimes a mutation is lethal and the organism does not survive, or doesn't develop in the first place. But they can be a good thing, too – if there were no mutations there would be no evolution, as this depends on improved proteins being passed down and making fitter offspring. Without mutation and evolution, we would all still be some form of pond slime.

The mutation has to affect the cells which make sperm and eggs otherwise it can't be hereditary – you don't inherit your ancestor's muscle cells, after all, just the DNA in sperm and eggs, which contains the information to make muscle. In genealogical testing, the laboratories look for a single base-pair change – a Single Nucleotide Polymorphism. If you are reading this book you can assume you have had many generations of ancestors and any mutation they had wasn't lethal. But you will have the inherited polymorphisms. These mutations happen quite infrequently, so the polymorphisms are relatively rare and are useful for placing an individual within a deep ancestral cluster known as a haplogroup. It may tell the genealogist very little about recent ancestry, but it can give valuable information about ancestral origins thousands of years ago and can therefore indicate ethnic origin, continental migration etc. The sequence – AATCGGA – at a certain place in a chromosome may be very common in Scandinavians while Chinese might have – AGTCGGA – for example.

SNPs are given a letter code (for the laboratory or research team that discovered the particular SNP) and a number (for the order in which it was first found). For example, M151 is the 151st SNP recorded by group M. As we'll see, SNP testing can be carried out on Y chromosome DNA, autosomal DNA and mtDNA.

STRs

Short Tandem Repeat (STR) analysis is more useful for recent ancestry research, especially in Y chromosome analysis. Within 'junk' DNA there are short sequences that repeat themselves, usually 2–5 bases long. For example a TGATA sequence might be repeated several times (– TGATATGATATGATA –). Every individual has STR segments at certain loci (locations) on the chromosome but one individual may vary from another in the number of times the

STR segment repeats. For example, at a particular locus on the chromosome, one individual may have ten –TGATA– STRs and another individual only seven. Alternative sequences at a particular locus are called alleles (pronounced AL-eels), in this case alleles ten and seven. The collection of alleles for an individual at specific loci (also called markers)[5] make up that person's unique DNA profile, called the haplotype. These profiles or haplotypes can help determine relatedness and paternity. The loci or markers are usually notated as DYS (DNA Y chromosome Segment) followed by a number, for example DYS284, meaning on the Y chromosome (DYS) at position 284.

In actuality Y chromosome DNA markers are defined areas which are known to vary from one individual to another, flanked by two 'static' regions (the same in all or most males). The static regions are molecular mileposts that allow the variable region to be measured accurately. For example:

Variable region

CCGTAATACGGAATAAGGCTTTAGGCGCATACATACCGTTACCCTTA

Static		Regions

At most loci commonly tested, the flanking static regions are found in only one place in the DNA. However, there are some multi-copy markers (including DYS385, DYS459, DYS464 and YCAII) found in more than one locus on the Y chromosome, and will return more than one value.

How DNA is tested

So, we'll need a sample of your sperm, or one of your eggs, right? Fortunately not. Remember that every cell in the body contains all the DNA used by all cells, so any cell will do. Most commonly cells from inside the cheek are used, because they come away easily (it happens all the time as you chew and swallow) and that's easier than taking blood or cutting off an ear. Some DNA collection procedures use a cotton swab on a stick to scrape away buccal cells. Others provide a mouthwash and ask the sampler to swirl it around inside the mouth for 45 seconds or so. The swab method is quicker and possibly more reliable. The sample is stabilised in a small vial of preserving fluid (in the case of the mouthwash it's the same thing) and posted to the laboratory. Samples may be stored for short periods in the fridge. The sample tube is usually bar-coded at the lab for easy tracking. Typically, the tester will also ask for genealogical information such as a four-generation pedigree chart.

The DNA is extracted and purified from the cheek cells on the swab or in the mouthwash, but obviously it will be a tiny amount. Fortunately, there is a technique called amplification which uses the polymerase chain reaction (PCR) method to make many millions of copies of the DNA sequences of interest very quickly and by an automated process. Mostly, it's done by simple, programmable robots.

The DNA is then analysed – either it is sequenced, an SNP is looked for or STRs identified. The data is reviewed, entered into a database and – if this was the agreement – sent back to the sampled individual or the sampler. The sampled individual may have signed up to a

---

[5] Strictly speaking, the *marker* is what is tested and the locus is where the marker is found on the chromosome, but the terms are often used interchangeably.

surname or geographic project and will be able to log in to an appropriate website, check results against others', look for potentially related individuals etc.

There is usually an option to have the DNA destroyed after testing, or stored for possible further analysis as new tests come along in the future. Usually this is time-limited (twenty years is common).

How genealogists use the test results

The main chromosomal analyses of interest to genealogists are Y chromosome, mitochondrial, and autosomal.

Y chromosome STR testing is currently the most widely applied to genealogy. We have seen that the Y chromosome is passed (usually) unchanged from father to son down the generations and is shared by all paternally related males. In most western cultures it will follow the surname. In short, direct paternal descendents of a common ancestor will have the same Y chromosome, or very similar, just as they will share a surname or a close variant. However, there can be problems (see below).

Depending on the testing laboratory (and the fee paid) the analysis will typically report somewhere between twelve and sixty-seven different values (alleles) on specific loci of the Y chromosome. There are over 100 marker tests available, and more coming all the time. These loci have been chosen to provide the best specificity, but tend not to be standardised between laboratories. Therefore, the more loci the better, especially when comparing results from different labs or stored in various databases.

Results from STR testing give the personal haplotype which can be matched to a standard haplogroup. SNP results indicate the haplogroup.

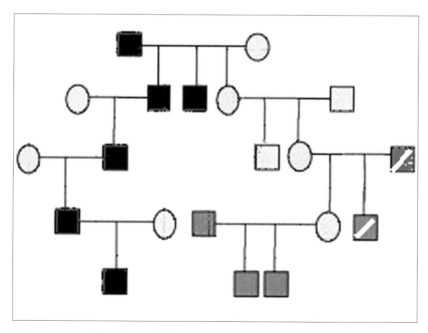

Y chromosomes follow the male line

A typical (but invented) result for a twelve-marker STR test is shown in the table below:

Haplogroup				DYS No.									
Q	DYS390 I	DYS19/394	DYS385a	DYS 385b	DYS 388	DYS 389 II	DYS 390	DYS 391	DYS 392	DYS 438	DYS 439	DYS19/394	Ancestor No. 1005
ID No. 1234	12	16	24	13	9	20	16	10	8	15	29	15	

The DYS No. is the actual marker name. The ID No. identifies the sampled participant (and may link to an email address, or more information such as a name and address, if the individual has allowed that) and the final number at the right gives the participant's oldest known ancestor (which may link to that person's vital data, or a pedigree chart). The lowest row is the allele (the number of repeats) at the specified marker.

A twelve marker STR test is usually not sufficient to give conclusive matches for common surnames and at least a twenty-five marker test should be considered. STR results may also indicate the most likely haplogroup but this will be confirmed by testing for the SNPs typical of that haplogroup.

Haplogroups

These are the 'superfamilies' of haplotypes which can indicate large genetic populations and often the geographic location or origin of an ethnic group. If everyone stayed exactly where they were born, then a Y chromosome mutation, when it occurred, would be fixed to that location. However, humans move around and always have done. There were at least two large migrations from Africa starting 170,000 years ago, right across Europe and Asia and eventually over to present-day Alaska and down the Americas. The males in these populations carried their Y chromosomes with them and therefore some indication of the place of origin of any mutations.

The first hunter-gatherers arrived in Europe before the last Ice Age (about 40,000 years ago – the Aurignacian culture) and there were two later migrations into Europe, the last some 8,000 years ago, who brought agriculture with them. Of course, there were more migrations over time and populations intermarried, so one particular country or area today will not contain males all in the same haplogroup. However, from the specific SNP mutations we can construct a family tree of Y haplogroups.

SNP mutation(s) used to identify haplogroup (not complete)	Haplogroup (years ago)	Origin and current distribution
M91	A = 'Y-Adam'	East Africa, Ethiopian Jews, Southern Africa (Khoisan, inc. Bushmen)
M60	B	Sub-Saharan Africa
M168 M130	C (60,000)	Australia and nearby, Siberia, North America (originated in India or the South Asian coast)

M168 M174	D (50,000)	Tibet, Japan (in particular the Ainu), Andaman Islands
M168 M96	E (50,000)	Africa, Middle East, Mediterranean ('out of Africa')
M168 M96 M33	E1	Mali
M168 M2 M75	E2	North Africa, Middle East, Mediterranean
M168 M96 M2	E3a (25,000)	Africa
M168 M2 M35	E3b (22,000)	North Africa, Middle East, Mediterranean
M168 M89 P14, M213	F★ (45,000)	South India
M168 M89 M201	G (30,000)	Caucasus, Anatolia
M168 M89 M52	H (20–30,000)	India, Roma ('Gypsies')
M168 M89 M170	I (20,000)	Europe (most commonly in Scandinavia, Sardinia, Croatia, Bosnia), Middle East
M168 M89 12f2.1	J (10–15,000)	Middle East, Morocco, Italy
M168 M89 12f2.1	J★ (all of J except J1, J2)	
M168 M89 12f2.1	J1	Levant, Bedou, Palestinian Arabs, Cohens (Jewish priestly tribe)
M168 M89 12f2.1 M172	J2	Levant and Anatolia (Sephardic Jews, Ashkenazy Jews, Muslim Kurds, Central Turks, Georgians, Lebanese)
M168 M9	K (40,000)	New Guinea, Australia (ancient link between Eurasia and parts of Oceania)
M168 M9 M70 M353 M387	K1	Melanesia
M168 M9 M70 M184 M193 M272	K2	Africa, Asia, Middle East
M168 M9 M20	L (30,000)	South Asia, India, Pakistan
M168 M9 M4	M (10,000)	South-east Asia (Melanesia, Indonesia, Micronesia, New Guinea)
M168 M9 LLY22g	N	Siberia, Russia, Northern Scandinavia, Finland
M168 M9 M175	O (35,000)	East and South-east Asia, South Pacific
M168 M9 M122	O3	Central Asia, East Asia, South-east Asia
M168 M45	P (35–40,000)	West Eurasia, North Eurasia, Americas
M168 M45 M242	Q (15–20,000)	Siberia, Americas
M168 M45 M3	Q3 (15,000)	Representative of Native Americans
M168 M45 M207	R (30–35,000)	Representative of Europeans and Western Eurasians
M168 M45 M173	R1	Europe, West Asia
M168 M45 M173 SRY1532	R1a	Central Asia, North India, Central Europe, Eastern Europe
M168 M45 M173 M343	R1b	Western Europe
M168 M45 M173 M124	R2	South Asia, Central Asia, Iran, Caucasus, some Roma

What does all this mean?

By itself, it means very little. It's rather like being the first person to own a telephone: who can you call? These results must be compared with results from other individuals tested, and the more test records there are, the more information we can build from it. In the same way, having a telephone starts to make sense when lots of other people have telephones. Even then, a match can only indicate that two people share a common ancestor, not who the ancestor was.

Even the haplogroup on its own is not very revealing. It becomes useful when linked to an individual's specific haplotype, from STR marker tests. Depending on how many markers were tested, the number of matches can be used to generate a probability of how long ago this common ancestor lived. It should be obvious that the likelihood of getting meaningful results depends on having a lot of individuals' results in the database.

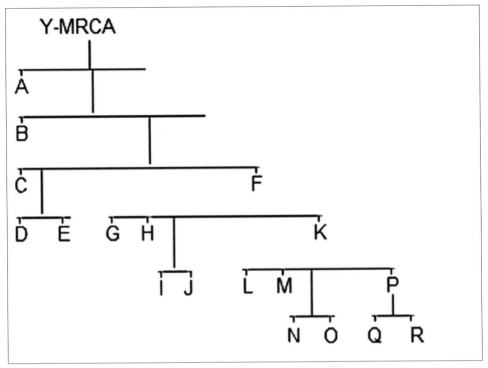

A 'family tree' of haplogroups

TMRCA – Time to Most Recent Common Ancestor

The Y chromosome is passed from father to son, usually an exact copy, so the markers of a son, father, grandfather, paternal uncle, paternal cousin etc. should be identical. However, we know that there are mutations on rare occasions. These are either an insertion (an additional repeat added to a marker) or a deletion (one less repeated STR). Mutations are random – they could arise in a son, but not his father – so it is possible for distant cousins to have exact matches in all the Y chromosome markers tested, while two brothers (even identical twins) might not have exact matches, if one carries a mutation. There is a science of randomness, and it's called statistics. We can use statistical techniques to find the probability of the Time to Most Recent Common Ancestor (TMRCA). This isn't straightforward – you would have to know the rate of mutation and the actual number of mutations – and in general there is just not enough data to be accurate about either of these, so we have to make certain assumptions based on what we do know. Such mathematics is beyond the scope of this book, but Dr Bruce Walsh's Time to Most Recent Common Ancestry Calculator has most of the details: http:// nitro.biosci.arizona.edu/ftdna/TMRCA.html. His paper on the subject is at www.genetics. org/cgi/reprint/158/2/897.pdf, or for a non-pdf version see www.genetics.org/cgi/content/ full/158/2/897.

For now, let's just accept some commonly used numbers:

Rate of Mutation = 0.002.
This means that any given marker has a 0.2% chance of mutating each generation, and you would expect any marker (on average) to change once in 500 generations. This is probably too many, and will give a longer TMRCA. But let's be conservative.

Number of mutations:

Counting any change in a marker (insertion or deletion) as a single mutation and scoring each marker as a match or a non-match, we get an estimate of single mutations. This may be an underestimate, and will similarly underestimate the TMRCA.

With any luck, the overestimate and underestimate will balance each other out.

These assumptions allow a statistician to set up an equation which shows the probability (the chance) that, given a certain number of markers and matches, the TMRCA would be a certain number of generations.

So, if two males submit for a thirty-seven marker test and find they have thirty-five matches, does this mean there is a 35/37 (95%) chance they are related? Sadly, no. It only means that they could be 50% sure they had a MRCA within the last nineteen generations and 90% sure they had a MRCA within thirty-seven generations. Their lines could have diverged anywhere from 400 to 1,000 years ago. Hardly a good reason for a family party.

So how do we get and use these probabilities? Based on these assumptions we can derive a cumulative probability table like the one below. This gives the number of generations corresponding to the 50%, 90% and 95% probability levels for various numbers of matches. For example, with a complete match of twelve markers there is a 50% chance that the MRCA was within fourteen generations. You could be 90% sure the MRCA was within forty-eight generations. However, two mismatches (10/12) and there is a 50% chance the MCRA was within sixty-one generations. Increase the number of markers tested, and even with one mismatch two individuals could be 50% sure they had a MCRA within the last twelve generations and, if they had no mismatches, they could be 90% certain there was a MCRA within sixteen generations or so.

		Probability of TMRCA		
Markers	**Matches**	50%	90%	95%
12	12	14	48	62
12	11	37	85	103
12	10	61	122	144
21	21	8	27	36
21	20	20	47	58
21	19	33	67	79
25	25	7	23	30
25	24	17	40	48
25	23	28	56	66
37	37	5	16	20
37	36	12	27	33
37	35	19	37	44

This assumes a mutation rate of 0.002. Newer research indicates it may be as high as 0.003 or even 0.005. Higher mutation rates reduce the TMRCA. For example, for a 90% probability at thirty-seven matches in thirty-seven markers, we get this:

			Probability of TMRCA		
Mutation rate	Markers	Matches	50%	90%	95%
0.002	37	37	5	16	20
0.003	37	37	3	11	14
0.0048	37	37	2	7	8
0.002	37	35	19	37	43
0.003	37	35	12	25	29
0.0048	37	35	8	15	18

If the mutation rate for these thirty-seven markers really is 0.0048, the 90% probability for a match of thirty-five out of thirty-seven is fifteen generations rather than thirty-seven.

Yes, it is complicated. And in case anyone is under the impression that these numbers were worked out by hand, they were derived using B.G. Galbraith's MCRA Chart program, freely available at www.clangalbraith.org/DNATesting/MRCA.htm. The equations used are based on Bruce Walsh's work. The Clan Galbraith site itself has test results and good information on how these can be used in a one-surname context. There is another, simpler calculator, written by Ann Turner, at http://members.aol.com/dnacousins/MRCA.exe.

There are ways to make the assumptions more accurate. More data on the actual number of matches and a better estimate of the mutation rate will come as more and more people have their DNA tested. Also, the mutation rate figure used is averaged over several markers, and the calculation doesn't take into account that different markers might mutate at different rates.

An example of how different average mutation rates affect the TMRCA at 50% probability:

Mutation rate	Matches	Mismatches	Median No. of Generations
0.0020	25	0	7
0.0020	25	1	17
0.0020	25	2	28
0.0030	25	0	5
0.0030	25	1	11
0.0030	25	2	19
0.0040	25	0	4
0.0040	25	1	8
0.0040	25	2	14
0.0050	25	0	3
0.0050	25	1	7
0.0050	25	2	11

As more genetic data is accumulated and a more precise estimate of mutation rate obtained, more accurate TMRCA values will emerge. But notice that doubling the assumed mutation rate more or less halves the TMRCA.

The table below turns the figures on their heads and shows the likelihood (percentage probability) that for a certain number of matches to twenty-four or thirty-seven markers tested, the MRCA will have lived within four to forty generations (about 100 to 1,000 years).

Markers	Matches	Generations (approximate years)					
		4	8	12	16	20	40
		(100)	(200)	(300)	(400)	(500)	(1,000)
25	25	33%	55%	70%	80%	87%	98%
25	24	6%	18%	33%	46%	58%	90%
25	23	1%	4%	11%	20%	30%	75%
37	37	45%	70%	80%	91%	95%	99.7%
373	36	12%	32%	52%	68%	79%	98%
37	35	2%	11%	25%	40%	55%	93%
(Mutation rate = 0.002)							

What is a mutational non-match?

We are simply assuming that a match is no mutations and a non-match is one mutation. It could be that two individuals each have a mutation in the identical place and so end up the same, even though that's really two mutations. In one, A mutates to C and in the other T mutates to C, at exactly the same place – but it's so unlikely, we discount it. Also, a non-match could be due to two mutations in one of the individuals, or even a mutation in both individuals, which are both really two mutations. An insertion mutation followed by a deletion mutation in the same individual's DNA is two mutations, but it looks the same as no mutations at all. But for the most part, statisticians use what they call the 'infinite alleles' assumption, which comes down to 'keep it simple' – assume a non-match is one mutation.

Another major problem is this: Suppose there are 100 markers available for testing, and two individuals choose to test at twenty-five of them. They get a 25/25 match. So they assume they are highly related. Then some bright spark analyses the other seventy-five possible markers and finds no matches at all. They are about as unrelated as bees and bananas, but by chance they picked the exact few markers that do match. From this, it's clear that the more markers tested, the more reliable the results. However, cost and time limit the number each of us can do. Testing twenty-five markers is considered a reasonable compromise on cost and forty or so is better.

Generation times

All of the TMRCA results given here are in terms of generations. To translate these into years we would have to assume the average number of years in a human generation. The usual values given are from fifteen to twenty-five years, but remember this varies with geography and local or religious custom.

Problems

Clearly, the more markers tested, the fewer the number of generations to TMRCA. However, as the number of marker tests available increases, the more every individual should test for, in order to be sure of the result. This means increasing cost and complexity. On the other hand, tests are getting quicker and cheaper and there is a point where more tests will not reduce the TMCRA by much.

Y chromosome analysis can only verify current genealogy; it will not establish a direct multi-paternal relationship in the absence of other records. If the MCRA (sometimes called the Patriarch) of a line is known, a Y chromosome test could help establish whether someone is likely to be a descendant and within how many generations. This can be useful if, say, a branch of the family has emigrated and the name has changed.

Any female interruptions to the paternal line will make the surname link meaningless, and the relationship of individuals who are not related after the interruption will not be established this way.

Here are two examples from the Durie family:

John Durie's granddaughter Janet (b. 1540) was the sole heir to his eldest son, Robert (d. 1554). She was well-off, landed and single. King James V decided that it would be suitable if she married Henry Kemp, one of his favourites and Master of the Bedchamber. In order to preserve the Durie inheritance, Henry changed his name to Durie. However, male

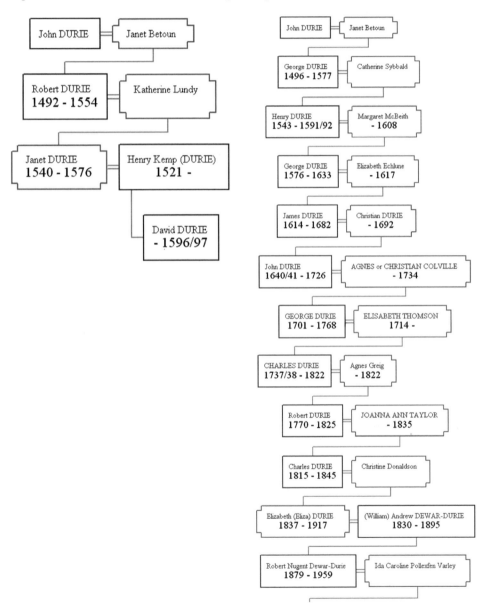

descendants down that line will now have the Kemp Y chromosome, even though they are, legally, the descendants and heirs of John Durie.

Similarly, the direct line of male heirs from John Durie through Robert's brother, George, descends to Charles Durie (1815–45) who died leaving a daughter, Eliza, in possession of his estate of Cragluscar. She married Dr Andrew Dewar, who changed his name on marriage to Dewar-Durie. Males descended from that marriage have the Dewar Y chromosome.

So today's Duries in either of these lines, although they are indeed distant cousins separated by about twenty generations, have no likelihood of finding John and their common ancestor from a Y chromosome test.

A living descendant of the Janet Durie/Henry Kemp marriage has the haplotype I1a2b1 and a living descendant of the Eliza Durie/Andrew Dewar marriage has the haplotype R1b1. This does NOT mean they aren't related – their other chromosomes are inherited in part from John Durie – but their Y chromosomes have come from two different sources, presumably the Kemp and Dewar lines respectively.

Mitochondrial DNA (mtDNA)

This test can provide information about the direct maternal line. The DNA used has nothing to do with the chromosomes in the cell nucleus or the X chromosome.

Cells contain tiny power units called mitochondria, which produce most of the energy each cell depends on. They also have their own DNA. This is because, about 1.5 billion years back in evolution, they started out as free-living bacteria-like organisms which developed a symbiotic relationship with larger one-celled creatures and in return gave up their ability to live independently. But they retained a small piece of circular DNA, containing some genes the mitochondria need.

Mitochondria exist in eggs and sperm, but only those from the eggs passed on from a mother to her children, whether male or female. However, only her daughters will pass the mtDNA on to the next generation in their eggs. So, a brother and sister of the same mother have the same mtDNA as their mother, their mother's mother, their mother's mother's mother, and so back along the maternal line. The sister's children will have the same mtDNA, but the brother's children will have his wife's mtDNA.

Each of us carries an almost exact copy of our mother's mtDNA so it is a valuable investigative tool for determining if individuals share a direct maternal line. Just like Y chromosome SNPs mtDNA haplogrouping can also indicate someone's deep ancestral roots – for example, Scandinavian, Asian or Native American ancestry. This is not genealogically valuable in the traditional sense.

mtDNA analysis

The small circular strand of DNA in mitochondria contains only some 16,500 bases and so is quite easy to sequence in total, compared with the billions of bases in chromosomal DNA. There are thirty-seven genes coded for by mtDNA. About 80% of mitochondrial DNA is 'genetic' (contains genes which instruct for proteins), as opposed to the 2% in chromosomal DNA. However, the main areas of interest are the hypervariable regions of the D-loop of mtDNA, which has certain characteristics useful for genetic genealogy. There are two long stretches of poly-C (repeated Cs) in two hypervariable regions. HVRI is from 16001–16569 with the poly-C region at 16184–16193 and HVRII is from 073–577 with poly-C at 303–315. The poly-C regions usually have a T somewhere in the middle. Often there is insertion or deletion of one or more Cs down the generations – after all, this DNA doesn't do much, so who's counting? – and the T can be changed to a C. So, such 'structural heteroplasmies', if found in a number of individuals, can be evidence of maternal kinship. On the other hand,

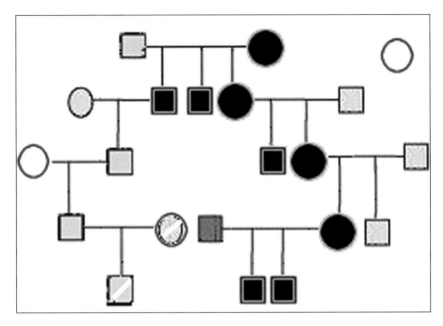

mtDNA follows the female line into males and females

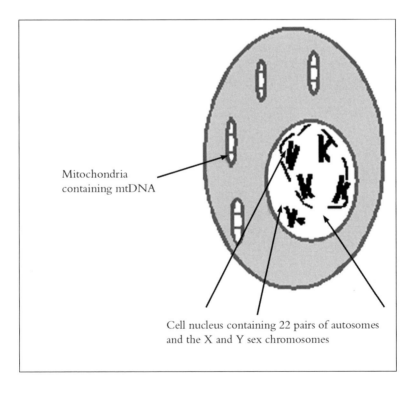

Mitochondria
containing mtDNA

Cell nucleus containing 22 pairs of autosomes
and the X and Y sex chromosomes

if there is not absolute concordance within poly-C regions, this is not strong evidence against the maternal kinship of any two people.

Individual sequence results can help identify genealogically significant family links within the last 1,000 years and in particular it is a good way of excluding someone from a maternal line as well as identifying maternal cousins etc.

Haplogroups

Haplogroups, stabilised tens of thousands of years ago, correspond to some early human migrations and can be linked back to geographical locations, as with Y chromosome halplogroups. Bryan Sykes used this finding in his best-selling, if somewhat fanciful, book *The Seven Daughters of Eve*, the main premise of which is that about 95% of individuals of European origin can trace their maternal line to one of seven women who lived in Europe between 10,000 and 45,000 years ago. One such haplogroup is H – Sykes called the matriarch Helena – and because her descendants were the most successful in reproductive terms, some 30–40% of people of European origin (including those who have migrated to other parts of the globe) share her H haplogroup. Anyone who also shows up as H has, in theory, hundreds of millions of maternal cousins and far-cousins back through time. This is about as helpful to standard genealogy as knowing that practically everyone of recent English descent is related in some way to King Edward I – interesting, but rarely relevant.

Haplogroups so far identified have been given the letter codes: A, B, C, D, E, F, G, H, HV, I, J, K, L1, L2, L3, M, N, Q, R, T, U, V, W, X, and Z. These are themselves in an evolutionary relationship or family tree.

H is the protypical European haplogroup and it can be further tested for sub-haplogroups H1–H15 by looking for SNPs at (respectively) 7028, 3010, 4769, 951, 750, 6776, 14365, 4336, 3915, 6869, 4793, 13101, 3591, 14470, 13759, 3936, 2259, 11377 and 6253.

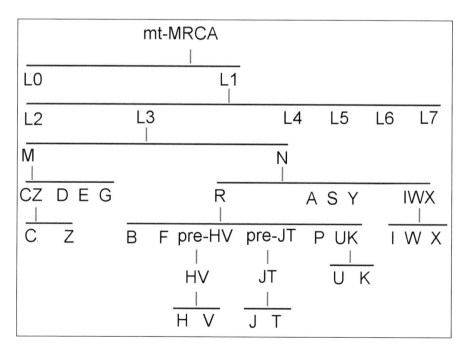

In general terms, we can think of the origins of mtDNA haplogroups as follows:

Europe: H, V
Northern Europe: T, U, X
Southern Europe: J, K
Near East: J, N
Africa: L, L1, L2, L3, L3*
Asia: A, B, F, M (composed of C, D, E, and G)
Native American: A, B, C, D, and less commonly X

National Geographic has a fascinating multimedia presentation on migration of mtDNA haplogroups at https://www3.nationalgeographic.com/genographic/atlas.html?card=mm004.

Sub-haplotypes and sub-haplogroups

Haplogroups are being refined all the time. U can now be sub-classified into many subclades such as U5a1a, which arose in Europe less than 20,000 years ago, and is mostly found in north-western and north-central Europe. Knowing this level of detail should help tie down relationships more precisely.

mtDNA sequencing

The entire mtDNA sequence is compared to the revised Cambridge Reference Sequence (rCRS), the first human mitochondrial genome to be sequenced, and published in 1981. For interest's sake, part of the hypervariable regions (HVRs) are as follows, with start and end numbers shown and the poly-C regions highlighted:

| 301 | aa**CCCCCCCT CCCCC**gcttc tggccacagc acttaaacac atctctgcca aaccccaaaa | 360 |
| 16141 | cttgaccac ctgtagtaca taaaaaccca atccacatca aaa**CCCCCTC CCC**atgctta | 16200 |

There is more information and a complete mtDNA sequence at www.mitomap.org.

So, complete sequencing of mtDNA is a possibility. But is it a good idea? One downside is that this can cost up to £200 ($400) at current prices, so the chances of many people having a complete sequence performed, and thus the chances of making any comparisons, are low. The other is that mtDNA is linked to some medical conditions, including certain muscle myopathies, and possibly also diabetes, cardiovascular disease, stroke, some cancers, osteoporosis, Alzheimer's disease, Parkinson's disease, and many others. Mutations in mtDNA are thought to play a part in the aging process itself. Does someone really want to know all this, and have their children know it, and publish it for the world to see? Already some insurance companies are looking into the possibility of using mtDNA results as a way to exclude high-risk customers, so why make it easier for them? A genealogist cannot play genetic counsellor, so other professional help may be warranted in some cases.

Heteroplasmy

Not all of the mtDNA taken from one individual will be identical. Mutations in mtDNA happen about ten times more frequently than in nuclear DNA, so there is a high variation between mitochondria, not only between individuals, but even within the same person or between close relatives. Two people chosen randomly for mtDNA testing may have fifty or more differences. So when mtDNA is extracted from a number of cells and analysed together, some positions will give a double result. For example, if the first character in the above sequence were T in some mitochondria and A in others, this would be reported as a T/A structural heteroplasmy. It is fairly common.

Interpreting mtDNA results

Some people do mtDNA testing rather expecting to receive a print-out which says: 'Your great-grandmother came from Peebles and your ancestry is three-quarters Scottish with a bit of Viking thrown in.' If only it were that simple.

What comes back is something like:

ID No.	Most Distant Ancestor	Haplo	HVR1	HVR2	
62903	Michael Dysart b. 1821, Perth, Scotland	H	080A, 161C, 448T		272G, 311A, 315G

This invented example shows the variations from the rCRS – A at position 16080, C at 16161, T at 16448 in HVR1 (notice that the first two digits – 16 – are often left out for simplicity's sake) and in HVR2 a G at 272, A at 311 and G at 315. The sample has been equated with haplogroup H and the sampled individual has supplied the details of the most distant ancestor known.

However, there are some instances where mtDNA testing can help genealogical research.

– Rare mtDNA. Even if an individual is in haplogroup H, the mtDNA may have some additional mutations that will pare down the number of exact matches. Finding a match with someone else in an mtDNA database may throw up a family relationship unsuspected beforehand.
– If you have a particular genealogical puzzle involving the female side, it may be possible to use mtDNA to solve it. One of the author's clients knew that her grandmother had married twice and had had children by both husbands. One daughter (the client's mother), appeared after the death of Husband 1 but rather too soon after the marriage to Husband 2. So whose child was she? Because the relatives of both husbands lived in the same village to this day, some strategic mtDNA testing of six females (and some rather careful diplomacy) found the answer. She was the child of neither! There were hints of mid-European ancestry, and Polish soldiers had been billeted in the village during the Second World War. Granny was some gal.
– DNA degrades. John Brown's body lies a-moulderin' in the grave, and his DNA is a-moulderin' with it. The chances of getting a sufficient amount of unfragmented DNA from Y to track down the Brown boys to the present day, are not high. But mtDNA is different – it is less fragile that the Y chromosome and there is lots more of it, so the chances of finding enough to reconstruct the original are greater. This procedure is regularly used to identify bodies (murder victims, people in mass graves, the remains of service personnel found abroad etc.) and track down living maternal kin.

Autosomal DNA testing

There are the twenty-two pairs of 'autosomes' in each nucleus, as well as the sex chromosomes X and Y. Autosomal DNA testing is essentially a scan for SNPs through all twenty-two chromosomes to verify or establish nuclear family relationships. Unlike Y or mtDNA analysis there are no gender restrictions, and a certain relationship can be tested for directly, e.g. grandparent, cousin, parent or sibling (but only two generations back). The main reason for this is recombination – the genes on each chromosome of a pair swap over and shuffle, so the complete chromosome, for example, from a mother or a father, is not passed on and each offspring, except identical twins, will have a different mix.

The most common use of autosomal testing is paternity but extended family testing is also possible. It can also be used to identify ethnic background to some extent, although this is controversial. In this case it produces a 'genetic percentage' of markers thought typical of certain ethnicities in an individual. One company defines four ethnic groups:

Native American (migration from Asia to the Americas)
European (includes Middle East, South Asia, India, Pakistan and Sri Lanka)
East Asian (Japan, China, Mongolia, Korea, South-east Asia, Pacific Islands)
African (Sub-Saharan Africa e.g. Nigeria and Congo)

Another company takes this further to a likelihood score of origin in each of twenty-three regions, based on the frequency of the profile within major areas. It does not depend on a system of presumed ethnic classification, like the STR test described above.

Alaskan (Inuit)
Athabaskan (Western North America)
North-east Amerindian
Salishan (American Pacific North-west)
South Amerindian
Mestizo ('mixed', Native American with European and African)
Arabian
Asia Minor (East Mediterranean and Anatolia)
North African
North Indian
South Indian
Sub-Saharan African

Eastern European (Slavic speaking area)
Basque
Finno-Ugrian (Uralic speaking region of North-eastern Europe, including Finns)
Mediterranean (Romance language region)
North-west European (Celtic and Germanic speaking areas)
Australian (Aboriginal)
Chinese
Japanese
Polynesian
South-east Asian (including the Malay Archipelago)
Tibetan (Himalayas and Tibetan Plateau)

What's in genetic genealogy for the genealogist?
The three most commonly asked questions at 'Ask The Genealogist' sessions are:

Do you have to dig up dead people?
Will I have to give blood?
Can you tell me if my ancestors really did come over with the Normans?

The answers, of course, are no, no, and no. DNA testing works best when it is carried out among people who already know or suspect they share an ancestry, but are not sure exactly who their most recent common ancestor was. It is even better at excluding people from family trees – demonstrating that the Vermont McSneckies and the Kentucky McSneckies have not been closely related to each other or to the Inversneckie McSneckies back in Scotland for at least ten, twenty, thirty etc. generations. It can also help to resolve surname-variant disputes, such as: Are the McSneckies and the MacSnuckies related?

Most genetic genealogy at present is restricted to the immediate nuclear family (back to grandparents) and the direct paternal and maternal lines. But hardly ever will it indicate an exact generation of divergence from a common ancestor, or who that common ancestor was. A Y chromosome may help determine if two people are descendents of a common male ancestor (Patriarch), but it can be difficult to tease apart the lines of brothers without testing more loci.

Ethnicity and race

Forgive an old biologist for going on here, but the term 'race' has no application in humans. This is not a political stance, but a scientific one. There is one human species and any number of ethnic groups, language groups, tribes and the like, but no races. The strict biological definition of a race is genetic differences between populations within subspecies of a species, where the average difference between the populations is greater than the average difference within the population. There are different races of snails, lilies, bacteria and many other life forms, but this is simply not the case with humans. There are no human subspecies (since the Neanderthals died out) and humans are, in a genetic sense, all virtually the same. In fact, DNA testing would not work the way it does if we were all more different. (See *Genes, Peoples and Languages* by L.L. Cavalli-Sforza for more on this subject.) Genetically, two ethnic Chinese people might be more different from each other than a particular Chinese person is from a particular Swede. That's why we talk in terms of ethnicity, language groups, cultural groups, place of origin etc. No respectable genealogist should ever be heard to utter the words 'white race', 'racially Asiatic', 'of the African race' and so on. It is not good biology, and not good science.

Scottish Genes?

Are we justified, then, in looking for DNA markers or test results which would pin someone to being of Scottish ancestry? Let's start by considering some population groups where such a question does have some scientific meaning.

European maternal clan testing

There are said to be seven, eight or twelve European maternal 'clans' based on mtDNA haplotype testing, taken from Brian Sykes's book *The Seven Daughters of Eve*. These are the original seven of Sykes – X, U (excluding K), J, T, K, H, V) – plus M, I and W, but others suggest H, J, K, N1, T, U4, U5, V, X and W. Remember that the original carriers of these mutations (sometimes called 'clan mothers') did not all live at the same time, and some are descendents of earlier ones, but that they all shared a common ancestor, 'Mitochondrial Eve'.

European SNP subgroup testing

This has identified four large groupings:

NOR – Northern European or Irish
MED – South-eastern European (Greek or Turkish)
MIDEAS – Middle Eastern
SA – South Asian (Indian)

Hindu and Buddhist testing

There is a thirty-seven marker Y test which claims to place individuals within one of the forty-nine gotras (a gotra is a clan or family claiming descent from a common ancestor, usually an ancient guru or sage). This matters, because there can be no marriage between individuals of the same gotra and historical gotra genealogies were drawn up before engagements and marriages, and even business partnerships.

African ancestry

Many ancestral African Americans were enslaved and their names and tribal or national affiliations erased or forgotten, so surname, census and property searches and other traditional means offer little to the researcher. Y-DNA and mtDNA testing has therefore become very popular, although it has shown that almost one-third of African American males have European Y chromosome haplogroup markers, and yet more than 70% of enslaved Africans were Bantu. Mitochondrial haplotype testing has identified some 300 tribal groupings, though it is uncertain how much reality these have.

Native American ancestry

An mtDNA haplogroup test for mutations in HVRs 1 and 2 may show up one of the five recognised Native American haplogroups (A, B, C, D or X), suggesting that that person has some Native American ancestry. It has not proved easy, though, to find tribe-specific haplotypes. As a result, mtDNA haplotyping is not accepted as evidence for admission to a tribal group. Only genealogical linking back to recorded census data is considered evidence for enrolment.

Cohanim ancestry

The Cohanim (or Kohanim) are the patrilineal priestly line of Judaism, and many (though not all) have the surname Cohen. The Bible has Aaron, brother of Moses, as the Cohanim ancestor, so the hunt is on for the 'Y-chromosomal Aaron', to go with the 'Y-Adam' and the 'mitochondrial Eve'. This whole field started when a Canadian doctor found that the vast majority of Jewish male Cohens had approximately the same set of markers, suggesting a lineal descent from a founder priest, who might as well be Aaron. The set of markers used to determine Cohanim ancestry is known as the Cohen Modal Haplotype. It comes in two flavours – 6 marker (CMH-6) and 12 marker (CMH-12).

6-marker Cohen Modal Haplotype (CMH-6)	12-marker Cohen Modal Haplotype (CMH-12)
DYS19 = 14	CMH-6 plus
DYS388 = 16	DYS426 = 11
DYS390 = 23	DYS439 = 12
DYS391 = 10	DYS385a = 13
DYS392 = 11	DYS385b =15
DYS393 = 12	DYS389-1 = 13
(Haplogroup J)	DYS389-2 = 30

However, the same haplotyping turns up in Italians, non-Jewish Arab and Kurdish populations which suggests that these markers belong to a common ancestral group that precedes all the others. It shows up with high prevalence in Cohanim Jews because they have not intermarried to the same extent.

It will come as no surprise that a number of DNA-testing companies market specific kits for African, Native American, Jewish and other ancestries.

Is there a Scottish haplotype?

To a large extent, the question is meaningless. It's not as if Scotland contains a genetically homogeneous population, and probably never did. From the first re-colonisation after the ice melted, and the North Sea was formed, some 10,000 to 12,000 years ago, Scotland has always been visited by seafarers and by those who came the old-fashioned way, up through England. When the Romans arrived in the first century they found the North full of (presumably Celtic) Picts, and the South an admixture of the British tribes they classified together as the Caledonii – Damnonii, Venicones, Matae, Novantae, Selgovae and others. The Romans never gained any real foothold in Scotland and hardly intermingled, as far as we can tell. By the time they left, the Picts were well established in the central and eastern parts and the Angles had started their incursions into what we would now call the Lothians and Borders areas. From the fifth century onwards, there were waves of Scotii (the original 'Scots') from Dal Riata, Ireland into Dalriada (modern Angus) and Norwegian Vikings were all over Orkney, Shetland, Ross and Cromarty, Sutherland, Caithness and parts of the west coast. From around 840, when Kenneth MacAlpin started to forge the united nation called Alba, at least the Scots, Picts and Britons were intermarrying, while Danes were arriving from Northumbria into the south-east. The Normans who arrived some 200 years later made no great impact on Scotland in population terms – like the Romans, they failed to gain any sort of foothold – but noble and landed families from both sides of the border, including the Anglo-Norman royal families, started to marry into each other. The next 1,000 years is relatively stable in terms of migration to Scotland, and is also the period when surnames became stabilised. That is, except in the nineteenth and early twentieth centuries when various peoples from the Baltic states (often lumped together popularly as 'Poles', but often Lithuanians and Latvians), as well as Italians and middle-European Jews, arrived to hew coal and join in the vast manufacturing enterprise that was Glasgow.

So, the chances of finding some archetypal 'Scottish' genetic barcode is remote. The thing to remember is that individuals in different haplogroups have no common ancestor for thousands of years back. That said, the Y-haplogroup (or rather sub-clade) R1b and its own sub-clades (R1b1, R1b1c etc.) are said to be more predominant in Scotland and Ireland than elsewhere in Britain, especially in the Western Isles, Angus and up the Great Glen. Given the many Scots who have migrated to England, and back-migrated to Ulster, it is not surprising that it also turns up with high prevalance in those regions. The east of Scotland also has R1a, called the 'Celtic haplogroup' as it is prevalent in Scandinavia and Iceland but arose in Central Eurasia, and haplogroup I (predominantly Scandinvian). For more details see John McEwan's excellent and informative website and in particular www.geocities.com/mcewanjc/scotsr1b.htm.

This has led to back-calculations of various likely modal haplotypes such as:

The haplogroup characterised by DYS 390, 391, 392 = 24, 10, 13 is known in the DNA genealogical community at large as the Scots Modal Haplotype. The single marker difference (15/16 at DYS 456) is highlighted.

As for mtDNA, haplogroup H and to a lesser extent U predominate. This is no surprise, as H is a mainly European haplogroup associated with an expansion and migration of the human population beginning about 20,000 years ago, as the ice started to recede. Perhaps 40% of all European mitochondrial lineages are haplogroup H.

There are, of course, sub-clades of H. H1 (about 13,000 years old) is the most common branch (30%) of H and thus about 14% of all Europeans, but 46% of the maternal lines in Iberia. H3, the other major sub-clade of H, which emerged 10,000 years ago, is also at its highest prevalence in Iberia (and Sardinia) but not to any great extent in the Near East.

There is a problem in all this, however. Assigning a place of origin to a lineage depends on the person being analysed knowing the details. In one Campbell project only about three-quarters of the participants have any reliable documentary evidence that their genetic ancestors came from either Scotland or Ireland. Most have genealogical evidence that stretches back to the 1700s at best. Given the constant flow of people back and forth between Ireland and Scotland, it is often not possible to say where the 'origin' of the family is located. Attempts to solve this problem typically rely on analysing DNA from a Clan or Family Chief, or someone whose family can be shown to be in the same place for centuries. Then other DNA samples of the same or similar surname can be compared with these.

Dal Riata R1b Modal Haplotype

Marker	Value
438	12
442	12
CDY b	38
CDY a	37
570	17
576	18
607	15
456	**15**
YCA IIb	24
YCA IIa	19
H4	12
460	11
464d	17
464c	17
464b	15
464a	15
449	30
448	19
437	15
447	25
454	11
455	11
459b	10
459a	9
458	18
389-2	30
392	13
389-1	13
439	12
388	12
426	12
385b	14
385a	11
391	10
19	14
390	24
393	13

Scots R1b Modal Haplotype

Marker	Value
438	12
442	12
CDY b	38
CDY a	37
570	17
576	18
607	15
456	**16**
YCA IIb	24
YCA IIa	19
H4	12
460	11
464d	17
464c	17
464b	15
464a	15
449	30
448	19
437	15
447	25
454	11
455	11
459b	10
459a	9
458	18
389-2	30
392	13
389-1	13
439	12
388	12
426	12
385b	14
385a	11
391	10
19	14
390	24
393	13

Table 24. Y chromosome DYS marker tests used by Relative Genetics and FamilyTree DNA.

RG	RG	RG	FT	FT	FT	FT
18	26	43	8	15	22	67
			195	195	195	195
385a	385a	385a	385a	385a	385a	385a
385b	385b	385b	385b	385b	385b	385b
388	388	388	385	386	387	388
389 I	389 I	389 I	389i	389i	389i	389i
389 II	389 II	389 II	389ii	389ii	389ii	389ii
390	390	390	390	390	390	390
391	391	391	391	391	391	391
392	392	392	392	392	392	392
	393	393	393	393	393	393
19/394	19/394	19/394				425
426	426	426	426	426	426	426
	437	437		437	437	437
438	438	438			438	438
439	439	439	439	439	439	439
		441				441
		442			442	442
		444				444
		445				445
		446				446
447	447	447		447	447	447
448		448		448	448	448
		449		449	449	449
		452				452
	454	454		454	454	454
	455	455		455	455	455
		456			456	456
		458		456	457	458
		459a		459a	459a	459a
		459b		459b	459b	459b
460	460	460			460	460
	461	461				461
	462	462				462
		463				463
		464a		464a	464a	464a
		464b		464b	464b	464b
		464c		464c	464c	464c
		464d		464d	464d	464d
					570	570
					576	576
					607	607
	635	635			CDYa	CDYa
					CDYb	CDYb
	Y-GATA-A10	Y-GATA-A10			GATA A10	GATA A10
					GATA C4	GATA C4
Y-GATA-H4★	Y-GATA-H4★	Y-GATA-H4★			GATA H4	GATA H4
	GGAAT1B07	GGAAT1B07			GAT1 B07	GAT1 B07
YCAII a	YCAII a	YCAII a			YCA IIa	YCA IIa
YCAII b	YCAII b	YCAII b			YCA IIb	YCA IIb

This is the sort of information found on databases:

Result	Matches	DY5385	DY5388	DY5389I	DY5389II	DY5390	DY5391	DY5392	DY5393	DY5394/19	DY5426	DY5437	DY5438	DY5439	DY5441	DY5442	DY5444	DY5445	DY5446	DY5447	DY5448	DY5449	DY5452	DY5454	DY5455	DY5456	DY5458	DY5459	DY5460	DY5461	DY5462	DY5463	DY5464	GGAATB07	YCAII	YGATAA10	YGATAC4	YGATAH4
1	18/18	11 14	12	13	29 29	24	10	13	13	14	12	15	12	12	13	12	12	12	13	25	19	29	11	11	11	15	17	9 10	11	12	11	22	15 15 17 17	10	19 23	13	23	12
2	13/ 13																																					

BROWN [USA-KS], BROWN [USA-NA], BROWN [USA-CT]

POWELL [USA-KY], POWELL [USA-TX], POWELL [USA]: 2 gen

Pedigree for Match #1

	Gen 1	Gen 2	Gen 3	Gen 4
			Frank BROWN	John BROWN
			b. 19 Jul 1855 Berlin, Nebraska, USA	b. 21 Jul 1820 Pawphuket, Kentucky, USA
		PROTECTED		Eliza GRAHAM
				b. 24 Sept 1821 Lynchem County, Kentucky, USA
			Harriett Josephine POWELL	Lewis POWELL
			b. 1 May 1853 Houston, Texas, USA	b. 2 Feb 1826 Houston, Texas, USA
	PROTECTED			Clarissa FISHER
				b. 4 Sep 1827 Eastbrook, Pennsylvania, USA

Match of 18/18 Markers	Generations	Years
Most Likely TMRCA	1	31

Further reading

There is vastly more on this subject at these websites:

International Society of Genetic Genealogy (http://isogg.org)

This was the first organisation founded to promote the use of DNA testing in genealogy. It has links to many genetic genealogy tools and information resources.

Contexo.Info (www.contexo.info/DNA_Basics)

An education website about the basics of molecular genetics and biology.

Time to Most Recent Common Ancestry Calculator by Bruce Walsh (http://nitro.biosci.arizona.edu/ftdna/TMRCA.html)

How to use genetic markers on the Y chromosome to estimate the TMRCA, and the various models used. Mathematically, quite heavy going.

The National Human Genome Research Institute (www.genome.gov/glossary.cfm)

The NHGRI created the Talking Glossary of Genetic Terms to help those with little scientific background understand the terms and concepts used in this field.

Primer on Molecular Genetics (www.ornl.gov/hgmis/publicat/primer/toc.html)

This primer is also available as a PDF version at (www.ornl.gov/hgmis/publicat/primer/primer.pdf)

Why Y? The Y Chromosome in the Study of Human Evolution, Migration and Prehistory (www.ucl.ac.uk/tcga/ScienceSpectra-pages/SciSpect-14-98.html)

Neil Bradman and Mark Thomas of The Centre for Genetic Anthropology at University College London explain how modern genetic analysis of the Y chromosome can help explore human history.

Genetics & Genealogy: Y Chromosome DNA and the Y Line (http://genealogy.about.com/library/authors/ucroderick1e.htm)

Thomas H. Roderick at the Center for Human Genetics discusses the Y chromosome as a genealogists' tool.

Short Tandem Repeat DNA Internet DataBase (www.cstl.nist.gov/div831/strbase/index.htm)

There is no single place where all the information on STR tests and testing systems is brought together, so this website tries to do just that.

GENEALOGY-DNA-L (http://lists.rootsweb.com/index/other/Miscellaneous/GENEALOGY-DNA.html)

A mailing list for anyone wishing to share results of DNA testing in genealogical research.

The ABCs of mtDNA (http://blogs.ancestry.com/circle/?p=479&o_iid=23557&o_lid=23557&o_it=23560)

Excellent introductory explanation by Megan Smolenyak Smolenyak

Chromosome STR haplogroup predictor from Whit Athey (https://home.comcast.net/~whitathey/hapest/hapest.htm)

Guide to the Main DNA Sources of the Counties of the British Isles by John Eckersley and Katherine Borges (www.isogg.org/britishcodnasources.htm)

Scotland DNA Project (www.ourfamilyorigins.com/scotland/dna.htm)

British Isles DNA Project (http://britishislesdna.com)

15

Clans, Families, Crests and Tartans

This book is not the place for a long discussion on the vexed subject of clans and families, and the tartans and other symbols they may or may not wear. Nor is there space for a disquisition on heraldry that the subject merits. However, the following brief descriptions might help avoid confusion and settle a few arguments.

Not every Scotsman has a clan

The clan system was peculiar to the Highlands, although similar tactics were adopted by the grand Borders families. It is generally accepted that 'clan' refers to the Highlands and 'family' to the Lowlands, although this is not universally respected. The Bruces, for example, refer to themselves as a Family, although their American association uses the term Clan.

Clan-based surnames

There is a popular misconception that anyone bearing a clan surname is descended from the appropriate clan chief. The point of a clan was to hold territory and defend it from other clans. This obviously depended on having as many followers as possible and, in turn, being in a large and powerful clan was an advantage to the individual, particularly when the Highlands were at their most lawless.

There were other reasons to adopt a clan name other than just protection: for food and shelter, to demonstrate solidarity, to gain favour with the Chief or Laird, to associate with a powerful neighbour, or just because there was little or no choice in the matter.

Not all members of a clan used the clan name. Clan Gregor was proscribed in 1603 and many MacGregors adopted other surnames and, after the proscription was lifted in 1774, many did not revert to MacGregor. The infamous Rob Roy MacGregor (cattle thief, blackmailer, murderer and spy for the English) spent most of his adult life known as Campbell. So there may be Ramsays, Stewarts etc. who are in fact descended from MacGregors.

Some clans' lands were feudally held – e.g. the Gordons were granted lands by Robert Bruce, then gained more territory, becoming the Lords of Badenoch. They increased their clan by offering a 'bow' o' meal' to anyone who would adopt the name. This implies nothing about genetic heritage.

Tartan and Highland dress

The tartan we see today bears little relation to the original. The plaid cloth ('plaid' being the garment, not a pattern) was a simple woven fabric, coloured with natural dyes. It was fairly plain, with a practical purpose. The earliest evidence of the distinctive design is a small scrap of multi-coloured fabric, found buried in a clay jar in the north of Scotland, dating from the third century AD. Other early references to Highland dress tell of the Scots using broad lengths of brightly coloured checkered or cross-striped cloth, called 'Heland tertane'. These were wrapped around the body, over the shoulders and belted at the waist. In Gaelic, this *feleadh mor* (pronounced like 'filamore'), or 'big wrap', served as a sturdy blanket by night for sleeping on the heather and was wrapped, tucked and folded by day into the garment recognisable as Highland dress. There was also a smaller version, the *feleadh beag* (philabeg) or 'little kilt', the modern version of which was probably first designed to replace the ancient plaid by an English garment manufacturer called Thomas Rawlinson, for Ian MacDonnell, chief of the MacDonnell's of Glengarry in the 1720s, This was soon worn throughout the Highlands. The plaid became a separate wrap and was secured with a brooch over the left shoulder and was often worn over a regimental or dress jacket, or with the slim tartan trousers (breachan trews).

The idea of a tartan being specific to a clan or locality, and used as a means of family differentiation is a modern one with no real historical basis. This was invented out of Victorian romanticisation of the Celts and the Highlanders and lives on in the 'shortbread-tin' image of Scotland (see below).

The proscription of the Highland dress

For thirty-six years following the disasters of the Jacobite rebellion and the defeat at Culloden, Highland men and boys were forbidden, on pain of death, to wear the tartan. However, it could still be worn by Scots regiments – a clever move on the Hanoverian's part, which linked the 'Government' or Black Watch tartan with loyal fighting spirit – and by lowland gentry who remained obedient to the English crown.

> That from and after the First Day of August 1747, no man or boy within that part of Great Britain called Scotland, other than such as shall be employed as Officers and Soldiers of His Majesty's Forces, shall on any pretext whatsoever, wear or put on the clothes, commonly called Highland clothes (that is to say) the Plaid, Philabeg, or little kilt, Trowes, Shoulder-Belts, or any part whatever of what peculiarly belongs to the Highland Garb; and that no tartan or party-coloured plaid or stuff shall be used for Great coats or upper coats, and if any such person shall presume after the first said day of August, to wear or put on the aforesaid garments or any part of them, every person so offending . . . shall be liable to be transported to any of His Majesty's plantations beyond the seas, there to remain for the space of seven years.

The above Act of Proscription (1747) made wearing the tartan punishable by seven years transportation. It was repealed in 1782, but for almost two generations the tartan, pipes etc. were not a normal part of life in Scotland. Notice the exemption for soldiers. The proclamation, issued in Gaelic and English, was as follows:

> Listen Men. This is bringing before all the Sons of the Gael, the King and Parliament of Britain have forever abolished the act against the Highland Dress; which came down to the Clans from the beginning of the world to the year 1746. This must bring great joy to every Highland Heart. You are no longer bound down to the unmanly dress of the Lowlander. This is declaring to every Man, young and old, simple and gentle, that they may after this put on and wear the Truis, the Little Kilt, the Coat, and the Striped Hose, as also the Belted Plaid, without fear of the Law of the Realm or the spite of the enemies.

Notice the assumption there that clans had had their individual tartans 'from the beginning of the world'. This was already part of the mythology. In fact, the link between clans and tartans in most cases began some forty years later than 1782.

How did this happen? As usual, it was money and opportunism. The State Visit to Edinburgh of George IV in August 1822, was the first by a reigning monarch for over 200 years. Stage-managed by Sir Walter Scott and his son-in-law, it attracted the Clan Chiefs, bedecked in 'historical' finery, which then kicked off a tartan frenzy. The Borders and Lowland weavers cashed in to meet the demand. Many Highland Clan Chiefs had no idea whatsoever about an 'ancient tartan' and so picked one they liked from the pattern-books of cloth manufacturers in Edinburgh and Bannockburn, who were weaving hard-wearing checked cloth mostly for the American and Canadian markets. Thus, many 'ancient' tartans were worn in the New World before they ever became associated with a clan. The Highland Society of London conspired in the 'ancient clan tartans' myth which was spurred on by the brothers Allen, a pair of Welsh rogues going under the invented name of Sobieski Stuart, who published the two books *Vestiarium Scoticum* and *The Costume of the Clans* in the 1840s, claiming their derivation from ancient manuscripts, which no one else ever managed to find. It was all nonsense, as was their claim to be descended from Bonnie Prince Charlie.

New, brighter patterns were developed and the manufacturers encouraged customers to have their 'own' tartan, and Scots were recruited to the army by forming Highland regiments each with their own identifying tartans. By the end of the eighteenth century the first of many 'tartan revivals' was well under way.

Today anyone can create a tartan provided it is not a direct copy of any existing pattern. There are around 100 recognised Clan and Family names, but about 2,000 named tartans and now there is an official Keeper of Tartans (a function of the Keeper of the National Archives), with a Register of Tartans but no regulatory powers as such. Bodies with impressive-sounding titles such as The Scottish Tartans Authority and Scottish Tartans World Register are commercial organisations with no official standing, although they do valuable work in educating the world about tartans.

Tartans are not just for clans or families

Districts, societies, corporations, military services, foreign countries, provinces and regions of Canada and the Royal Family have the only group of tartans restricted for ordinary wear.

In practice, any man may wear a tartan he feels akin to, but should really wear a tartan allied to his clan, family, sept or district, and women should wear the tartan of their husband. If the husband has no tartan, or the lady is unmarried, she should take her father's tartan. But these rules are more honoured in the breach than the observance.

Heraldry

This book does not deal with heraldry, but the most contentious issue in the whole subject can be dealt with very simply: there is NO such thing as a 'family coat of arms' in Scotland. Arms are the individual, heritable property of one person and must be granted by the Lord Lyon King of Arms (www.lyon-court.com). Almost any 'worthy and virtuous person' of Scottish descent can apply for a new grant of arms, or re-matriculate arms of a direct ancestor. New arms will reflect those of a previous armiger (someone who has arms) of the same name. But this does not mean that anyone can simply adopt arms of their surname. To do so in Scotland is illegal, and anyone who has stained glass windows, dinner services, silver cutlery or anything else made carrying arms they do not legally possess, may find the lot confiscated and a fine imposed.

A coat of arms consists of at least a shield, helmet, wreath and mantling, and may also have a crest and a motto. Certain classes of people and organisations may also be granted supporters (the figures or animals to each side of the shield).

The crest however has a special place in Scottish genealogy and family history.

Crests

The crest is the device adornment above the helmet and within the wreath. Originally it was an additional aid to the identification of a knight and also helped ward off sword-blows to the

Family Member

The chief's crest and motto in a buckled strap; can be worn by anyone who has allegiance to the chief.

Armiger

A single eagle feather behind the chief's crest and motto in a circlet.

Chieftain

Two eagle feathers behind the chief's crest and motto in a circlet.

Chief

Three eagle feathers behind the chief's crest and motto in a circlet.

Crest badges, based on the crest and motto of the chief. Members of the British Peerage may wear the appropriate coronet above the circlet or strap, if they choose.

head. These are reflected in the clan or family badge worn by a chief and anyone who swears fealty to that chief. Therefore, they have, since the nineteenth century, been worn as cap badges, kilt pins, plaid brooches and the like. Before this, Highland clans used specific plants worn in the bonnet or hung from a pole or spear – examples are rosemary for Bruce, myrtle for Campbell, broom for Home. Now, the plant can be stuck behind the cap badge.

Crest badges may be worn by any member of a clan or family, although strictly speaking the crest is the personal property of the chief. They usually consist of the chief's personal crest surrounded by a strap and buckle and the chief's motto or slogan.

Where a clan or family does not have a chief recognised by the Lord Lyon King of Arms, family members may wear the crest badge of the last known chief. In some other cases, clan and family members wear a crest badge based on that of a prominent clan or family member who was never recognised as a chief. They sometimes show one clan or family's relationship to another by having near-identical crests and mottoes – all the clans in the great Clan Chattan confederation, for example.

While a clan or family member wears the chief's crest and motto in a strap-and-buckle (symbolising allegiance) the chief himself or herself, chieftains of significant branches and any armiger of that name have a simple circlet and motto with a number of eagle feathers behind.

Crest badges are by nature metal and are NEVER coloured, despite the lurid renditions seen on many clan and family websites. Married women wear the crest badge of their husband's name, unmarried women that of their father's name.

Chiefs of Name and Arms

Chiefs of clans and families have a real position in Scotland. The Lord Lyon must recognise the Chief of Name and Arms. Lyon is not concerned with clans and families as such. The Standing Council of Scottish Chiefs of Clans and Families looks after the interests of the chiefs, but not the various clan and family associations, societies and groupings (www.clanchiefs.org).

The Standing Council also approves and licences certain manufacturers to make and sell crest badges.

16

Resources

DEGREES OF KINSHIP

How related are you?

Confused over whether two individuals are second cousins or first cousins once removed? Use the chart on p.182 to determine the relationship between them.

1. Determine the ancestor which the two people share.
2. Starting with the shared ancestor, find the relationship of person 1 (P1) across the top row.
3. Again starting with the shared ancestor, find the relationship to person 2 (P2) down the left column.
4. Find the box where the P1 column and the P2 row coincide. This is their relationship.

Examples:

1. P1 and P2 share a great-grandfather. P1 is a great-grandchild; P2 is a great-grandchild; P1 and P2 are second cousins.
2. The grandfather of P1 is the uncle of P2; therefore the great-grandfather of P1 is the grandfather of P2; they are first cousins once removed.
3. P1 is the child of the shared ancestor; P2 is the great-grandchild; P1 is the great-aunt or uncle of P2, who is a great-niece or nephew.

Note:

This excludes direct ancestry (for instance, if the grandfather of P1 is the great-grandfather of P2, they could be father (or mother) and child. It only works for blood relations – not for uncles and aunts by marriage.

BRITISH MONEY AND COINAGE

When you see the term 'Five Pounds' in an old Scottish document, what does that really mean? And what coins were used? The answer depends on the year the document was written, and whether the currency is expressed in pounds sterling or pounds Scots.

L.S.D.

Britain (and Scotland even more so) had a confusing system of currency in earlier times. It was based on pounds, shillings and pence identified by their Latin names *Libri, solidi, denarii*, hence L.S.D. and the pound symbol (£, standing for L, *Libri*). In documents and writings as late as the Victorian times, values in pounds may be expressed as 5 l rather than £5.

The origin of the old monetary system is in weights of silver – 20 (troy) pennyweights of silver = 1 oz, 12oz = 1 pound. (A pound, symbol lb, is 454 grammes). The French livre and Italian lira were also a pound of silver at some point in their histories.

SHARED ANCESTOR	Child	Grandchild	Great-Grandchild	Gt-Gt-Grandchild	Gt-Gt-Gt-Grandchild	Gt-Gt-Gt-Gt-Grandchild
Child	Sibling	Niece/Nephew	Great-Niece/Nephew	Great-Great-Niece/Nephew	Gt-Gt-Gt-Niece/Nephew	Gt-Gt-Gt-Gt-Niece/Nephew
Grandchild	Aunt/Uncle	First Cousin	First Cousin Once Removed	First Cousin Twice Removed	First Cousin 3 x Removed	First Cousin 4 x Removed
Great-Grandchild	Great-Aunt/Uncle	First Cousin Once Removed	Second Cousin	Second Cousin Once Removed	Second Cousin Twice Removed	Second Cousin 3 x Removed
Gt-Gt-Grandchild	Gt-Gt-Aunt/Uncle	First Cousin Twice Removed	Second Cousin Once Removed	Third Cousin	Third Cousin Once Removed	Third Cousin Twice Removed
Gt-Gt-Gt-Grandchild	Gt-Gt-Gt-Aunt/Uncle	First Cousin 3 x Removed	Second Cousin Twice Removed	Third Cousin Once Removed	Fourth Cousin	Fourth Cousin Once Removed
Gt-Gt-Gt-Gt-Grandchild	Gt-Gt-Gt-Gt-Aunt/Uncle	First Cousin 4 x Removed	Second Cousin 3 x Removed	Third Cousin Twice Removed	Fourth Cousin Once Removed	Fifth Cousin

In Britain the basis of currency was (and is) the pound sterling, meaning the fixed, authorised national value. 'Sterling' applied to any silver coin of fine quality in previous centuries, and is often said to derive from Stirling in Scotland, near where the finest silver was found (in the Ochill hills), but this is doubtful. Thus, there were in theory 240 pennies in each pound weight of silver, but they coined 252 pennies to the pound to turn a profit for the royal treasury.

Although coins originally had an intrinsic value (they actually contained an amount of silver or gold equivalent to the value) they eventually became tokens of baser metal, valueless in themselves but signifying a value guaranteed by the Crown. This was largely a recognition of the gradual debasement of intrinsic value as practically all monarchs realised they could adulterate pure precious metals with cheaper alternatives. Eventually it became clear that this token – of no real value in itself – didn't even need to be metal, and banknotes were born. Bear in mind, too, that when someone said 'half-a-pound', they may have meant literally that – coins were often cut up and notes torn in half to provide smaller values.

Pre-decimalisation (1971)

Some British people still talk about 'the old money', by which they mean the system of L.S.D. abolished in 1971. There were 240d. (pennies) to a pound, 12d. to a shilling and thus 20s. in a pound. Amounts were written as (for example) £5 10s. 6d. or £5 10/6. There was the added complication of half-pennies and farthings, and the convention that £1 1s. (21s., today £1.05p) is called a guinea, although there has been no coin of that value issued since 1813 (made of high-quality Guinea gold and therefore worth more than the £1 value sovereign). The crown was not a coin in circulation since 1937, but the half-crown was. (Americans who find this quaint or puzzling should remember that they call 25 cents 'two bits' although there is no coin equal to one 'bit' – a reference to the peso or 'piece of eight' into which a dollar could be divided.)

Values	Coins (nineteenth and twentieth centuries up to 1971)	Notes (nineteenth and twentieth centuries)	Equivalences (ignoring inflation)	
			Pre-1971	**Post-1971**
4 Farthings = 1 Penny (1 *d*) 12 Pence = 1 Shilling	Farthing	10 shillings		
(1s or 1/-) 2 Shillings = 1 Florin	Half-penny	1 pound	*c.* 2½*d.*	1p
(2s or 2/-) 2 Shillings and 6 Pence = 1 Half-crown (2s. 6d. or 2/6)	Penny Threepenny bit Sixpence	5 pounds etc.	*c.* 5*d.* 1s. 2s. 6d.	2p. 5p 12½*d.*
5 Shillings = 1 Crown	Shilling		5s.	25p
20 Shillings = 1 Pound (sovereign)	Florin (2s.)		10s.	50p
(£1 or L1) 21 Shillings = 1 Guinea	Half-crown (2s. 6d.)		10s. 6d.	55p

You will also find references to the shilling as a 'bob' (2 shillings = 2 bob, 10 shillings = 10 bob) and occasionally to a 'dollar' (meaning 5 shillings) and half-a-dollar (2s. 6d, half-crown), but this was a jokey reference to American servicemen failing to come to terms with the British currency during the Second World War, when the exchange rate was around $4 to £1. However (it will come as a surprise to most British people), there was a silver dollar in use from 1895–1934 specifically for trade with the East, and Scotland had the dollar in the time of Mary, Queen of Scots, derived (as is the American version) from the Thaler or Joachimsthaler of central Europe. The Scots Dollar (or Ryal) was silver and worth 30s. Scots, 6s. English. Charles II had a different value dollar worth 4 merk, or £2 16s. Scots, 4s. 8d. English (See What was Scots money worth? on p. 186).

In Scotland, the sixpence was often called a bawbee, and earlier there were additional coins such as the groat (initially 6d. or 1s. but latterly a silver 4d. piece), which survived in Britain as a whole until 1855 (see the table opposite).

Currency today (since 1971)

This system prevailed up to 15 February 1971 (Decimal day) when Britain swept away the denominations it had obtained over 1,200 years. There was also a change to pronunciation, as words like ha'penny, penny ha'penny, tuppence and thruppence disappeared to be replaced with 'two pee', 'three pee', etc.

The modern British monetary system is relatively straightforward. The basic unit is still the pound sterling (£ or GBP). There are 100 pennies (p) to the pound, and coins are issued in denominations of 1p and 2p (copper-plated steel); 5p, 10p, 20p and 50p (cupro-nickel); and £1 and £2 (nickel-brass). There are £5 coins issued for commemorative or ceremonial purposes. Real gold sovereigns (£1) and half-sovereigns (50p) are still available, but not in general circulation. A 22 carat gold bullion sovereign is worth about £100.

Notes are slightly more confusing. The Bank of England issues £5, £10, £20 and £50 notes. However, three clearing banks in Scotland – the Bank of Scotland, the Royal Bank of Scotland and the Clydesdale Bank – also issue their own notes up to £100 (the Royal Bank of Scotland alone issues a £1 note, now unknown in England) as do various banks in Northern Ireland. These are all sterling, and are identical in value, despite the problems some Scottish and Northern Irish tourists have changing them abroad. The Republic of Ireland now uses the euro, in common with many other European Union countries, but not all (such as the UK).

Incidentally, Scottish banknotes are not legal tender in Scotland (they are promissory notes) but then, neither are English notes legal tender in Scotland. It hardly matters, as the definition of 'legal tender' has nothing to do with what notes or coins are used for monetary transactions (in shops, for instance) but only to payments a debtor can make into a court in a form which allows the debtor not to be further pursued for the debt. Any form of payment that two parties agree to exchange makes for a valid transaction. You could pay in light bulbs or lemons if someone agreed to take them.

Other sterling currencies

Sterling banknotes are also issued by British dependencies outside the UK: the Isle of Man; Jersey; Guernsey; Gibraltar; Saint Helena; and the Falkland Islands. These are all for local use, but are exchangeable at par with the pound sterling and circulate freely alongside English, Scottish and Northern Irish notes.

Coinage pre-decimalisation

Originally coins had an intrinsic value (they actually contained an amount of silver or gold equivalent to the value) but eventually became tokens of baser metal, valueless in themselves but signifying a value guaranteed by the Crown. Banknotes are not included in the table, and only the most important coins are given.

Coin	Value	Dates	Composition	
farthing	¼d.	1279–1672	silver	
		1672–1860	copper	
		1860–1956	bronze	
halfpenny	½d.	1280–1672	silver	
		1672–1859	copper	
		1860–1970	bronze	
penny	1d.	eighth cen.–1797	silver	
		1257	gold	
		1797–1860	copper	
		1860–1970	bronze	
threepence	3d.	1551–1944	silver	
		1937–1970	nickel-brass, 12 sided	
groat	4d.	1279–1662, 1838–55	silver	
groat (Scots)	6d.	1406–37	silver (Scotland)	
groat (Scots)	12d.	1437–88	silver (Scotland)	
bawbee (Scots)	6d. Scots	1538–1697	silver	
sixpence	6d.	1551–1920	silver	
		1920–46	half silver	
		1947–67	cupro-nickel	
shilling	1s.	1504–1919	silver	
		1920–46	half silver	
		1947–66	cupro-nickel, still legal tender value 5p	
florin	2s.	1344, 1526–1625	gold, value: 6s. not 2s.	
		1849–1919	silver	
		1920–46	half silver	
		1947–67	cupro-nickel, still legal tender value 10p	
demi-lion	2s. 6d.	1390–1406	gold (Scotland)	
half-crown	2s. 6d.	1470–1551	gold	
		1551–1850, 1874–1919	silver	
		1927–37	half silver	
		1947–67	cupro-nickel	
half-noble	40d.	1344–1634	gold	
double florin	4s.	1887–90	silver	
half demy	4s. 6d.	1406–37	gold (Scotland)	(never popular
crown	5s.	1526–51	gold	in general
		1551–1902	silver	use, and often
		1927 37	half silver	commemorative)
		1951, 1953, 1960,	cupro-nickel	
		1965, 1981	(commemorative)	
half lion	5s. Scots	1437–60	gold (Scotland)	
half lion	6s. 8d. Scots	1488–1513	gold	
lion	5s.	1390–1406	gold (Scotland)	
quarter guinea	5s.	1718, 1762	gold	
dollar	$1	1895–1934	silver (for trade with the East)	
noble	80d.	1344–1634	gold	
demy	9s.	1406–37	gold (Scotland)	
third guinea	6s. 8d.	1797	gold	

lion	10s. Scots	1437–60	gold (Scotland)
lion	13s. 4d. Scots	1488–1513	gold
half sovereign	10s.	1831–1915, 1980–now	gold
half guinea	10s. 6d.	1625–1760	gold
merk (mark)	160d. = 13s. 4d.	till the eighteenth century	
merk (thistle	13s. 4d.	1580–1660	silver (there were also ½, 2 and 4 merk coins half dollar)
unicorn (Scots)	18s. Scots	1460–1513	gold (Scotland)
	20s. Scots	1513–42	gold (Scotland)
	22s. Scots	1526–67	gold (Scotland)
sovereign	£1	1489–1660, 1831–1925, 1957–now	gold
	20s.	1642	silver
		1660–85	gold
pound	£1	1914–83	note
guinea	21s.	1663–1799, 1813	gold, fixed at 21/- in 1717
two pound	£2	1831, 1887, 1893, 1902, 1911, 1937, 1980, 1982–3	gold
two guineas	£2 2s.	1625–1760	gold
five pound	£5	1839, 1887, 1893, 1902, 1911, 1937, 1980–1982, 1984–5, 1990	gold
five guineas	£5 5s.	1625–1760	gold

Scottish coinage

David II groat, 1329–71.

The first coins were silver pennies issued by King David I (David the Saint) in 1136. These were crude in manufacture, as were the contemporary English ones. Until 1373 Scottish coins were exchanged freely in England and had the same values. In fact, Scottish silver from near Stirling (do not confuse with 'sterling' silver) was the best quality, and the standard for centuries and during the reign of David II (1329–71), and English coins were modeled on the Scottish. Scots money initially had denominations similar to the prevailing English coins, but the Stuart kings' close links with France produced an assortment of denominations, many based on French equivalents and reflecting French influence in design. The lion and demi-lion of Robert II are examples. This trend reached its peak, especially in gold coinage, during the reigns of Mary, Queen of Scots (1542–67) and James VI and I (1567–1625).

James III groat, 1460–88.

However, in 1403, rising bullion prices had led to a reduction in weight, by about a third, of all Scottish coins, gold and silver. Under James I (1406–37) the discrepancy between Scottish coins and English coins increased and for the first time Scottish silver coins were debased. But James I also increased the weight of gold coins. This led to considerable confusion over coinage. The groat, originally worth 4 pence, was revalued at 6 pence and later 12 pence, and eventually they were the 'light groat' and 'heavy groat'. The silver penny and halfpenny were debased by the addition of copper, a mixture known as billon. In James III's time (1460–88) the exchange rate was 4:1. A half-groat issued in 1485 is said to have borne the first real coin portrait of a monarch to be seen north of the Alps.

In the reign of James IV (1488–1513) the silver penny was worth three billon (cupro-silver) pennies and there were strange coins like the plack (4d.) and half-plack (2d.).

In sixteenth-century Europe there was a general silver coin and its imitators: crown, daler, dollar, écu, écu á la couronne (crown), kroner, peso, piastre, seudo, tallero, thaler (taler). The American dollar ($) has its origin in the thaler and the Spanish dollar – there were eight pesos to a dollar, hence 'pieces of eight'.

The pound Scots

Mary, Queen of Scots crown, 1559.

The pound Scots ('pund') was a definition made necessary when James VI of Scotland became James I of England in 1603, so as to be able to exchange Scots money with English. Equivalent values are given in the table from that date. In 1560, 5 pounds Scots equalled 1 pound sterling. When James VI succeeded to the throne of England the exchange rate was fixed at 12 pound Scots to 1 pound sterling (English) making the 'pund' worth 1s. 8d. sterling; and 1s. Scots was the same as 1d. English, reflecting the relative prosperities of the two nations.

(If you think that's bad, consider that in the fourteenth century the pound and the Italian lira were equivalent, but in March 2002 there were over 2,500 lira to the pound. Now, of course, the lira no longer exists and has been replaced by the euro, as have the deutchmark, franc and other European currencies, but not the pound sterling.)

Charles I simplified this somewhat. Then in 1682, during the reign of Charles II, several of the Scottish mint officials were convicted of corruption and the mint closed. James VII and II reopened it in 1686. During William and Mary's time (1689–94) the Scottish mint struck currency equivalent to English coins, but still based on a relative value of 12:1 (e.g. the 60 shillings piece was equivalent to the English crown, or 5 shillings).

The merk

Land was often valued in merks with a value of 160*d.* = 13*s.* 4*d.* or ⅔ of a pound, originally a mark of pure silver (20 silver pennies). There were also, which many people find surprising, coins such as dollars, ryals, ducats, testoons, pistoles and unicorns at various times.

After the Union under Queen Anne in 1707, the Edinburgh mint for a time produced crowns, half-crowns, shillings and sixpences marked with a letter E. At this point the monetary and weights and measures systems for the whole of Britain were unified and the pound Scots went away. However, even in documents as late as 1800 (especially inventories) values are often given both in Sterling and Pounds Scots.

Above: James VI sword dollar or ryal (worth 30s.). *Below:* Balance half merk (worth 6s. 8d. or about 17p, 35 cents), both 1590s.

What was Scots Money Worth?

This is a vexed question, and depends on the date.

The relative values of Scots and English currency varied from monarch to monarch, and was as susceptible to political vagaries as to the intrinsic value of the coin in silver or gold. A rule of thumb, though not absolute, is:

– Scottish and English currencies were unified when Scotland adopted the English pound at the Union of 1707
– However, some people still thought in terms of the pound Scots, set at 12:1 from 1603 when James VI became James I of England. Thus, 1 pound Scots = 20*d.* (1*s.* 8*d.*)
– During the reign of Mary, Queen of Scots and James VI (from 1560–1603) the exchange rate was 5:1
– From 1460–1560, the exchange rate was 4:1
– Before this, the currencies were equivalent
– Scotland also had the mark or merk (⅔ of a pound Scots or 13*s.* 4*d.* Scots)

So, in a document from 1650, 30 merks = 20 pounds Scots = £1 13s. 4d. English. But in a document from 1600, 30 merks = 20 pound Scots = £4 English.

Frankly, this is all so confusing that it is worth giving a table of coinage values for each Scottish monarch:

Table 26. Coinage for each Scottish monarch.

Monarch and reign	Coin	Value	Composition (% silver)	English equivalent value
JAMES I				
1406–37	Demy	9s.	Gold	9s.
	Half Demy	4s. 6d.	Gold	4s. 6d.
	Groat	6d.	Silver	6d.
	Penny	1d.	Billon	1d.
	Halfpenny	1s. 2d.	Billon	1s. 2d.
JAMES II				
1437–60	Lion	10s.	Gold	10s.
	Demi-Lion	5s.	Gold	5s.
	Groat	12d.	Silver	12d.
	Half Groat	6d.	Silver	6d.
	Penny	1d.	Billon	1d.
JAMES III		Exchange rate 4:1 from 1460		
1460–88	Rider	23s.	Gold	
	Half Rider	11s. 6d.	Gold	
	Quarter Rider	5s. 9d.	Gold	
	Unicorn	18s.	Gold	
	Light issue			
	Groat	12d.	Silver	
	Half Groat	6d.	Silver	
	Groat	6d.	Billon (70%)	
	Half Groat	3d.	Billon (70%)	
	Heavy Issue			
	Groat	12d.	Silver	
	Half Groat	7d.	Silver	
	Penny	3d.	Silver	
	Plack	4d.	Billon (50%)	
	Half Plack	2d.	Billon (50%)	
	Penny	1d.	Billon (50%)	
	Halfpenny	1s. 2d.	Billon (base)	
	Farthing	1s. 4d.	Copper or brass	
JAMES IV				
1488–1513	Unicorn	18s.	Gold	
	Half Unicorn	9s.	Gold	
	Lion	13s. 4d.	Gold	
	Demi-Lion	6s. 8d.	Gold	

	Heavy issue			
	Groat	14*d*.	Silver	
	Half Groat	7*d*.	Silver	
	Light Issue			
	Groat	12*d*.	Silver	
	Half Groat	6*d*.	Silver	
	Penny	3*d*.	Silver	
	Plack	4*d*.	Billon (25%)	
	Half Plack	2*d*.	Billon (25%)	
	Penny	1*d*.	Billon (25%)	
JAMES V				
1513–39	Unicorn	£1 = 20*s*. then 22*s*.	Gold	
	Half Unicorn	10*s*. then 11*s*.	Gold	
	Crown	20*s*.	Gold	
	Groat	18*d*.	Silver	
	Third Groat	6*d*.	Silver	
	Plack	4*d*.	Billon (25%)	
1538–42	Ducat	40*s*.	Gold	
	Two-thirds Ducat	26*s*. 8*d*.	Gold	
	Third Ducat	13*s*. 4*d*.	Gold	
	Bawbee	6*d*.	Billon (25%)	
	Half Bawbee	3*d*.	Billon (25%)	
Mary, Queen of Scots		Exchange rate 5:1 from 1560		
1542–67	Ryal or Ducat	60*s*.	Gold	
	Half Ryal/Half Ducat	30*s*.	Gold	
	(Double Unicorn)	44*s*.	Gold	
	(Unicorn)	22*s*.	Gold	
	Crown	20*s*. then 22*s*. 10*d*.	Gold	
	Crown	20*s*.	Gold	= 4*s*.
	Dollar (Ryal)	30*s*.	Silver	= 6*s*.
	Two-thirds Dollar	20*s*.	Silver	= 4*s*.
	Third Dollar	10*s*.	Silver	= 2*s*.
	Testoon	4*s*. then 5*s*.	Silver	= 1*s*.
	Half Testoon	2*s*. 6*d*.	Silver	
	Groat (Nonsunt)	12*d*.	Billon (50%)	
	Bawbee	6*d*.	Billon (25%)	
	Plack	4*d*.	Billon (25%)	
	Half Bawbee	3*d*.	Billon (25%)	
	Lion	1½*d*.	Billon (10%)	
	Penny	1*d*.	Billon (25%)	
JAMES VI				
1567–1603	Twenty	£20 (400*s*.)	Gold	= 80*s*.

	Ducat	£4 (80s.)	Gold	= 16s.
	Thistle Crown	48s.	Gold	
	Thistle Noble	11 merk (146s. 8d.)	Gold	= 10s. approx.
	Sword & sceptre	£6	Gold	= £1 4s.
	Half Sword & Sceptre	£3	Gold	
	Rider	£5 (100s.)	Gold	= £1
	Half Rider	50s.	Gold	= 10s.
	Lion Noble	75s.	Gold	= 15s.
	Two-thirds Lion	50s.	Gold	= 10s.
	Third Lion	25s.	Gold	= 5s.
	Forty Shillings	40s.	Silver	= 8s.
	Sword Dollar (Ryal)	30s. later 36s. 9d.	Silver	= 6s. or 7s.
	Thirty Shillings	30s.	Silver	= 6s.
	Two-thirds Ryal	£1 = 20s. later 24s. 6d.	Silver	= 4s. or 5s.
	Twenty Shillings	20s.	Silver	= 4s.
	Sixteen Shillings	16s.	Silver	
	Third Ryal	10s. (later 12s. 3d.)	Silver	= 2s.
	Ten shillings	10s.	Silver	= 2s.
	Eight shillings	8s.	Silver	
	Five shillings	5s.	Silver	= 1s.
	Four shillings	4s.	Silver	
	Thirty pence	2s. 6d.	Silver	= 6d.
	Two Shillings	2s.	Silver	= 5d.
	Two Merk	26s. 8d.	Silver	
	Merk	13s. 4d.	Silver	= approx 30d. (Half Crown)
	Half Merk	6s. 8d.	Silver	
	Quarter Merk	3s. 4d.	Silver	
	Eighth Merk	1s. 8d.	Silver	
	Groat	8d.	Billon	
	Plack	2d.	Billon (25%)	
	Two pence (Hardhead or Turner)	2d.	Billon (4%)	
	Penny	1d.	Copper	
JAMES VI & I		Exchange rate 12:1 from 1603		
1603–25	Unit	£12	Gold	= £1
	Half Unit/Crown	£6	Gold	= 10s.
	Quarter Unit	£3	Gold	= Crown (5s.)
	Half Crown	30s.	Gold	= Half Crown (2s. 6d.)
	Sixty Shillings	60s.	Silver	= Crown (5s.)

	Thirty Shillings	30s.	Silver	= Half Crown (2s. 6d.)
	Twelve Shillings	12s.	Silver	= 1s.
	Six shillings	6s.	Silver	= 6d.
	Two Shillings	2s.	Silver	= 2d.
	Shilling	1s.	Silver	= 1d.
CHARLES I				
1625–36	Unit	£12	Gold	= £1
	Double Crown	£6	Gold	= 10s.
	Crown	£3	Gold	= Crown (5s.)
	Half Crown	30s.	Gold	= Half Crown
(1633 only)	Angel	10s.	Gold	= 10d.
	Sixty Shillings	£3 = 60s.	Silver	= Crown (5s.)
	Thirty Shillings	30s.	Silver	= Half Crown (2s. 6d.)
	Twelve Shillings	12s.	Silver	= 1s.
	Six Shillings	6s.	Silver	= 6d.
	Two Shillings	2s.	Silver	= 2d.
	Twelve Pence	1s.	Silver	= Penny
	Half Groat (Turner or Bodle)	2d.	Copper	
	Penny	1d.	Copper	
1632–39	Half Groat (Turner or Bodle)	2d.	Copper	
	Penny	1d.	Copper	
1636–42	Unit	£12	Gold	= £1
	Double Crown	£6	Gold	= 10s.
	Crown	£3	Gold	= Crown (5s.)
	Half Crown	30s.	Gold	= Half Crown (2s. 6d.)
	Sixty Shillings	60s.	Silver	= Crown (5s.)
	Thirty Shillings	30s.	Silver	= Half Crown (2s. 6d.)
	Twelve Shillings	12s.	Silver	= 1s.
	Six Shillings	6s.	Silver	= 6d.
	Three Shillings	3s.	Silver	= 3d.
	Two Shillings	2s.	Silver	= 2d.
	Twelved	1s.	Silver	= 1d.
	Half Merk	6s. 8d.	Silver	
	Quarter Merk	3s. 4d. (40d.)	Silver	
	Eighth Merk	1s. 8d. (20d.)	Silver	
CIVIL WAR				
1642–50	Half Groat (Turner or Bodle)	2d.	Copper	
OLIVER CROMWELL/CHARLES II				
1650–86	Four Merk (Dollar)	53s. 4d. 56s. in 1681	Silver	
	Merk	13s. 4d. 14s. in 1681	Silver	

	Half Merk	6s. 8d. 7s. in 1681	Silver	
	Quarter Merk	3s. 4d. 3s. 6d. in 1681	Silver	
	Bawbee	6d.	Copper	
	Turner or Bodle	2d.	Copper	
JAMES VII & II				
1686–8	Ten Shillings	10s.	Silver	
WILLIAM & MARY				
1689–94	Sixty Shillings	£3 = 60s.	Silver	
	Forty shillings	£2 = 40s.	Silver	
	Twenty Shillings	£1 = 20s.	Silver	
	Ten Shillings	10s.	Silver	
	Five Shillings	5s.	Silver	
	Bawbee	6d.	Copper	
	Turner or Bodle	2d.	Copper	
WILLIAM III				
1694–1702	Pistole	£12	Gold	
	Half Pistole	£6	Gold	
	Sixty Shillings	60s.	Silver	
	Forty shillings	40s.	Silver	
	Twenty Shillings	20s.	Silver	
	Ten Shillings	10s.	Silver	
	Five Shillings	5s.	Silver	
	Bawbee	6d.	Copper	
	Turner or Bodle	2d.	Copper	
ANNE				
prior to 1707	Ten Shillings	10s.	Silver	
	Five Shillings	5s.	Silver	
1707 onwards	*Currencies equivalent throughout Britain*			

And if you think money was confusing, wait until we get to Weights and Measures!

RELATIVE VALUES

Table 27.

Year	Relative value
1500	1
1510	1
1520	1
1530	1
1540	1
1550	2
1560	3
1570	2
1580	3
1590	3
1600	4
1610	3
1620	3
1630	4
1640	4
1650	6
1660	5
1670	4
1680	4
1690	3
1700	4
1710	4
1720	4
1730	4
1740	4
1750	4
1760	4
1770	5
1780	5
1790	5
1800	10
1810	9
1820	8
1830	7
1840	7
1850	6
1860	7
1870	7
1880	7
1890	6
1900	6
1910	7
1920	17
1930	11
1940	13
1950	20
1960	30
1970	45
1980	163
1990	307
2000	415

Ask any three economists how to calculate the relative value of money between any two dates and you'll get at least five answers. Perhaps the most useful is purchasing power for basic commodities like bread, a day's hire, meat and so on. This is fraught with historical, interpretative and economic difficulties, but as a rough guide, the table here gives an estimate of purchasing power relative to 1 in the year 1500, drawn from a number of sources.

This year was chosen because there was relatively little inflation before that — prices and the value of money remained fairly stable — but started to rise after.

To use it, divide the relative value from one year by another. For example:

–£100 in 1700 would be worth about 100 × (415 ÷ 4) which = about £10,750 in 2000.

–£25,000 in 2000 would be equivalent in 1850 to 25,000 × (6 ÷ 415) = about £370.

Notice the periods of high inflation around 1800, 1920 and since 1970. For more discussion on the different vales to calculate value and worth, and a handy calculator, consult:

Economic History Net (http://eh.net/hmit)

Current Value of Old Money (www.ex.ac.uk/~RDavies/arian/current/howmuch.html)

Consumer Price Inflation Since 1750 (www.statistics.gov.uk/cci/article.asp?ID=726)

OLD SCOTS WEIGHTS AND MEASURES

Scotland will doubtless one day see sense and give up the inch, foot, yard and mile in favour of the more logical metric system, just as it previously dropped the pound Scots, the ell, the reel, the boll, the chopin, the firlot and the lippie.

Scottish measurements fell into line with the English (Imperial) measures in 1707, although Scots merchants had to use both for purposes of trade. Earlier references may be to the 'old' measures.

Weight	
In Scots Troy weight 1 pound was slightly heavier than a pound avoirdupois (about 496 *vs* 454 grams). But weights varied between towns. Local weights were called Tron weights, from the place where measures were taken to assess tolls, duties, etc., although the Tron units were also standardised to a degree. Many towns still have a 'Tron' (Trongate in Glasgow, the Tron Kirk in Edinburgh etc.). The ounce (oz) Troy was equal to 478.309 Imperial Troy grains (31.1 grams) whereas the oz Tron was 641.6337 Imperial Troy grains (41.72 grams).	16 drops (or draps) = 1 ounce 16 ounces = 1 pound (496 grams) 16 pounds = 1 stone (almost 8kg) This is more logical than the English (Imperial) 14 pounds per stone
Length and area	
Scots inches, feet, chains and miles were slightly longer than the Imperial equivalents (perhaps because Scotsmen had bigger feet than Henry VIII). The ell was 42 Scots inches but 37 Imperial inches and was supposed to measure the distance between the end of the nose and the fingertips. Hence all those Scottish merchants with short arms! There is a pervasive myth that the Scots mile was defined by the real distance from the gate of Edinburgh Castle to the gate at Holyrood House, making Edinburgh's 'Royal Mile' exactly a Scots mile long.	12 inches = 1 foot 3½ feet = 1 ell 6 ells = 1 fall (or fa) 4 falls = 1 chain 10 chains = 1 furlong 8 furlongs = 1 mile = 80 chains (1976.52 Imperial yards, 5929.56 Imperial feet)
Square measure	
The ell was also a square measure used for cloth, slightly larger than an Imperial square yard and slightly smaller than a square metre.	36 sq. ells = 1 sq. fall 40 sq. falls = 1 rood 4 roods = 1 acre (1,257 Imperial acres) 12–13 acres = 1 oxgang (literally 'where the ox can go') 8 oxgangs = 1 ploughgate, about 100 acres 4 ploughgates = 1 davach, roughly 400 acres, 162 hectares or ⅝ of a square mile
Dry measure	
The basic measure was the firlot, equal to about 36 litres of wheat, peas, beans and meal, or about 53 litres of barley, oats and malt. A smaller unit, the lippie or forpet, was 1/16th of a firlot and thus around 2.25 or 3.3 litres. It was equivalent to the Imperial (English) half-gallon or 4 pints. Prices were usually expressed by the boll (4 firlots or 2 Imperial gallons). There was also the leispund, lesh pund or lispund, a weight equal to 18 pounds Scots; used mainly for butter, wool and oil. Its value is often different in, say, Shetland from other parts of Scotland.	4 lippies or 4 forpets = 1 peck 16 lippies = 4 pecks = 1 firlot (2214.3 cubic inches or 8 Imperial gallons for wheat etc., 3230.3 cu. in. or 11.65 Imp. gall. for barley etc.) 64 lippies = 16 pecks = 4 firlots = 1 boll 16 firlots = 4 bolls = 1 quarter (equivalent to an English bushel) 64 firlots = 16 bolls = 4 quarters = 1 chalder 31 Scots pints = 1 barley firlot

Liquid Measure

The Scots pint was equal to about 2¾ Imperial pints (1.56 litres), later standardised at 104.2034 cubic inches, or 3.01 Imperial pints (1.7 litres). Thus the Scots gallon was 3 Imperial gallons (13.7 litres) and a barrel equivalent to about 41 litres. (Remember that a US gallon is 0.833 of Imperial (UK) gallons.)

The gill is an interesting unit, as it is still used in whisky measures today. The standard measure of a glass of spirits in England is 1/6th of a gill, whereas in Scotland it is 1/5th (the 'nip') or in the better pubs, 1/4 of a gill. There are therefore 80 nips in an old Scots pint, and about 26 in an Imperial pint. You may hear Scotsmen ask for a 'half and half' which is a half-gill (a double measure) of whisky and a half-pint of beer to wash it down.

```
4 gills = 1 mutchkin
8 gills = 2 mutchkins = 1 chopin
16 gills = 2 chopins = 1 pint
8 pints = 1 gallon
64 pints = 8 gallons = 1 barrel
```

The Scots pint and the Stirling Jug

No one really misses the ell or lippie, but the pint is another, altogether more emotive measurement. The Stirling Jug is said to have been established in 1457 by Stirling Burgh Council to regulate liquid measures, but it is mentioned in Acts of Parliament as being in the town before the reign of James II in 1437. It was the yardstick by which all other Scottish quantities were standardised and was not superseded until Imperial measures were introduced in 1707.

The last mention of the Jug is in an Act of Parliament of 19 February 1618, in the reign of James VI. No accurate experiments appear to have been made with it afterwards for fixing the legal measures until the wholly remarkable Revd Alexander Bryce, minister of Kirknewton and already well-known geometrician, decided to get involved in 1750. He tracked down the original Jug, accurately measured its volume and reset the standard.

The actual Jug itself can be seen in the Smith Art Gallery and Museum in Stirling (along with the world's oldest football, for those who are interested in such things).

GAELIC WORDS IN ENGLISH

Present-day inhabitants of Scotland are (linguistically, at least) an admixture of *Scotii* who arrived from Ireland to mingle with Picto-Celts living around present-day Fife and the north-east and British Celts in Strathclyde (speaking a language like Welsh) and the area around Edinburgh, jumbled up with the Danes who arrived from Northumbria, Scandinavian Vikings in the north and west, and later the Anglo-Normans who came to live mainly in the Lowlands. The highlanders' language evolved into Gaelic, but lowlanders have long spoken Scots, the distinctive Germanic language which developed alongside English. However, there are many Gaelic words and names in Scottish history and geography and it helps to know them. Also, there are many Gaelic inclusions in present-day language – some quite surprising.

English, like Scots, is a late Germanic language and has borrowed heavily from older languages. It therefore has more Celtic words than is commonly realised, including those that came indirectly by way of Gaulish into French and then English. Many of those Gaulish words are close to the older Goidelic (Gaelic) Celtic language spoken in Ireland in pre-Christian times. There are also Brythonic (British or Welsh) sources as well as continental Celtic and Indo-European roots.

Scots contains a great many Gaelic words unfamiliar outside Scotland – dule or dool, meaning grief or distress, comes from the Gaelic *doilgheas* (sorrow, affliction) and *duilich* (difficult, sorry, grievous). The Latin-derived words dolour, doleful and dolorous have the same meanings. But many are universally recognisable by English speakers everywhere – keelie (a self-asssured young man) and gillie (an attendant on a Highland estate) both derive from *gille* (a young man or servant).

A number of widely known words may come from either Scots or Irish Gaelic (whisky or whiskey would be a good example) and it will surprise many Americans to realise that cowboy, cracker and redneck are actually Scottish words in origin. Some words (*ceilidh*, *grotty*) entered directly into English, without necessarily first becoming widely used in Lowland Scotland, and although some are old – pet or caddie for instance – many of these are twentieth century borrowings. Examples would be smashing (Gaelic *'s math sin*) and Gaelic *sporran*.

Then there are the many cognate words, sufficiently similar, that exist because either they entered Gaelic from English or have the same influences (Latin, French, Indo-European roots etc.). They look like straight imports from one language to another but are actually developments in parallel from common origins: Gaelic *baist* (baptize) and English baste (moisten) for instance.

Table 28.

Scots/English	Irish	Scots	Meaning
airt	aird	aird	point of the compass
bannock	bonnach	bonnach	bread cake
banshee	bean-sidhe	bean-sidhe	wailing spirit, woman of the sidhe (pronounced 'shee') meaning 'fairyland'
bard	bàrd	bàrd	poet, singer
Beltane	Bealltainn	Bealltainn	Spring festival
blather	bladar	bladar	nonsense or gossip
bog	bogach	bogach	soft ground, bog
bog	bog	bog	soft
bonnyclabber	bainne-clàbar	bainne-clàbar	curdled milk
booley	buaile	buaile	Fold or pen for livestock
bothy	bothan	bothan	small hut
brae	bràighe	bràighe	hill
brat	brat	brat	unruly boy
braw	brèagha	brèagha	nice, fine, beautiful
breeks	briogais	briogais	trousers, pants
brisk	brisg/briosc	brisg/briosc	fast, bracing
brogue	bròg	bròg	shoe
brogue	bròg	bròg	accent (especially Irish)
brogue	bróg	bròg	shoe, boot
bun	bun	bun	base, bottom, posterior
burn	bùrn	bùrn	small river
caber	cabar	cabar	as in 'tossing the caber'
caber	cabar	cabar	pole, rafter
caddie	cadaidh	cadaidh	porter, golfclub carrier
cairn	carn	càrn	heap, pile
carrageen	cairgein	cairgein	moss
carrageenan	carraigín	carraigean	Irish moss seaweed
cateran	ceatharn	ceathairne, ceatharn	peasantry, freebooter
ceilidh	céilidh	céilidh	dance, party

clan	clann	clann	family
clarsach	clàrsach	clàrsach	a musical instrument
cleave	claidheamh	claidheamh	sword
claymore	claíomh mór	claidheamh mór	great sword
coleen	cailín	caileag	girl
cowboy	cowhuby		cattle drover
curragh	currach	currach	coracle
corrie	coire	coire	rocky valley
crag, craig	creig	creag	rocky outcrop
crannog	crannag	crannag	
creel	criol	criol	lobster trap
cross	cros	cros	cross
dig, twig	tuig	tuig	understand
dochandoris	deoch-an-dorus	deoch-an-dorus	a little drink
dour	dùr	dùr	gloomy
down	dún	dún	dune, hill
dulse	duileasc	duileasg	edible seaweed
dun	dun	dun	brown-coloured
gab	gobgab	gobgab	talk, jabber
Gael	Gaedheal	Gàidheal	a Gaelic speaker
Gaeltacht	Gaidhealtachd	Gaidhealtachd	the community of Gaelic speakers
galore	go leor	gu leòr	plenty, enough
gillie	giolla	gille	lad, servant
glen	gleann	gleann	valley
gloamin	glòmainn	glòmainn	dusk, twilight
glom	glám	glam	grab, clutch
grotty	grod	grod	dirty
hooligan	uilligán	uilligán	rowdy person
ingle	aingeal	aingeal	fireplace
inch (island)	innis	innis	island
island	innis	innis	island
gob	gob	gob	mouth
jabber	gobgab	gobgab	talk
kail	càl	càl	cabbage-like vegetable
keech	cac	cac	ordure, dung
keen	caoin	caoin	weep, lament
kibosh	caidhp báis		cap of death
knock	cnoc	cnoc	knock
kyles	caolas	caolas	headland
leprechaun	leipreachán	leipreachán	Irish imp
linn	linn	linn	pool
loch	loch	lough	lake
machar	machair	machair	poet (literally, 'maker')
oxter	achlais	achlais	armpit
pet	peata	peata	favourite
philabeg	feileadh-beag	feileadh-beag	short kilt
phony	fáinne	fàinne	ring (from a gilt brass ring)
pibroch	piobaireachd	piobaireachd	style of pipe music

pillion	pillín	pillean	small pad, cushion
plaid	pluid	plaide	blanket
pony	pónai	pónai	pony
poteen	poitín	poitín	distilled spirit
puss	pus	pus	face
reel	righil	righil	dance
ross	ros	ros	promontary
Sassenach		Sasunnach	English person (possibly from 'Saxon')
shabeen, shebeen	síbín	siopín	illicit drinking den
shamrock	seamróg	seamrag	shamrock
shanty	seantigh	seann taigh	old house
shennachie	seanachaidh	seanachaidh	Bard and genealogist to a Chief
shillelagh	sail éille		cudgel (also a village in Co. Wicklow)
shoo	siuthad	siuthad	chase away
skean	sgian	sgian	dagger
skiff	sgiobhag	sgiobhag	snow
slew	slua	sluagh	host, multitude
slob	slaba		mud, slovenly person
slogan	sluagh ghairm	sluggh-ghairm	call to the multitude
slug	sluig	sluig	swig
smashing	is math sin	's-math-sin	literally 'it is great'
smidgen	smidin	smidin	small piece
smithereens	smidiríní	smidiríní	small pieces
sneck	sneag	sneag	latch
soutar	sutair	sutair	travelling tinker
sporran	sparán	sporan	purse
spunk	spong	spong	courage
strath	srath	srath	land around a river
strontium		Strontian	from Strontian, a village in Argyllshire
swap	suaip	suaip	exchange
tack	tac	tac	leased farm
Tory	tóraí	tòraiche	pursuer, robber, bandit
trouser	triús	triubhas	trews, pants
twig	tuig	tuig	understand
weem	uamh	uamh	cave (as in Wemyss, Pittenweem)
whisky	uisge beatha	uisge beatha	water of life
winnock	uinneag	uinneag	window

Consult *An Etymological Dictionary of the Gaelic Language* by Alexander MacBain, and other resources, available online at www.ceantar.org/Dicts.

Gaelic pronunciation
Letters
There are eighteen letters in the Gaelic Alphabet:

- Thirteen Consonants: b, p, f, m; c, g, l, n, r, t, d, s; h
- Five Vowels:– Broad vowels: a, o, u;
  Slender vowels: e, i

– H is aspirate. After the consonants b, p, f, m, c, g, d, t, s, it forms the aspirates, bh, ph, fh, mh, ch, gh, dh, th, sh. At the beginning of a word it is written h–; as na h-uain; and has a strong breathing sound.

– The letters, sg, sm, sp, st, have no aspirated form.

Consonant sounds

Consonants fall into two categories: broad and slender

– Broad consonants are surrounded by a, o, u.

– Slender consonants are surrounded by i, e.

– The consonants p, t, and k are preaspirated – preceded by a voiceless h – in the middle and ends of words.

– There are 3 different kinds each of l, n and r which are almost impossible to understand.

– And almost every consonant is different depending on whether it comes at the beginning, middle or end of a word. But not always.

– Not only that, many are silent. Sometimes. For instance, the Gaelic for 'Gaelic' is Ghàidhlig, pronounced gay-lik.

Confused? You will be.

Table 29

			Example Translation Pronounced
B		like the English b in bag at the beginning of words, elsewhere sounds like the p in dopey	
Bh		mostly, this is pronounced like v; sometimes in the middle and at the end of certain words it is like u, and sometimes it is silent	Tapadh leibh 'Thank you' Tahpuh leeve
F		like f in English	
Fh		silent, except in the three words fhéin, fhuair, fhathast, when it has the sound of h	
M		like m in English	Tha gu math 'I'm fine' Ha goo mah
Mh		like v, and more nasal than bh; silent in the middle and end of some words, and gives a nasal sound to the vowel; in some areas it has the sound of u, e.g. samhradh, pronounced sauradh.	Glè mhath 'Very well' glay vah
P		like p in English pin.	Tapadh leibh 'Thank you' Tahpuh leeve
Ph		like f in English prophet.	
C		always hard, like cat; before a, o, u, it has the sound of c in can; after a, o, u, it has the same sound in some districts; as, cnoc, like ck in lock; but more often like chk; before e, i, and after i, like c in cane.	Ciamar a tha thu? 'How are you?' kemuhr a ha oo
Ch		before or after a, o, u, it is a gutteral sound as in loch; in contact with e or i, it has a more slender sound	
Chd		has the sound of chk; as luchd, pronounced luchk	
G		more or less like English; before and after a, o, u, it is like g in got; in contact with the slender vowels e, i, it sounds like gy; and like k as in kettle in the middle or end of a word	
Gh		before and after e, i, it has the sound of y in English yet; in contact with a, o, u, it has a broader sound like g in get; in the middle and end of certain words it is silent	

T	before or after a, o, u, the sound is like th in than; in contact with e, i, it has the sound of ch in chin	Tapadh leibh 'Thank you' Tahpuh leeve
Th	at the beginning of a word it has the sound of h; it is silent in the pronoun thu (pronounced oo) and in certain tenses of irregular verbs when preceded by d; in the middle of some words it has a slight aspiration, in others it is silent	Glè mhath 'Very well' glay vah
D	initally, like English d, elsewhere like English t, but at the end, it can be like ch or j	
Dh	same as gh	
S	in contact with a, o, u, it is like s in English; before or after e, i, like sh; after t- (with hyphen) it is silent	sidhe 'fairy land' shee
Sh	has the sound of h	
L	before or after a, o, u, and ll after a, o, u, has a flatter sound than l in English, with the point of the tongue against the teeth; in contact with e, i, the sound is like ll in million. It has a simple sound after i, and when aspirated it is like l in English hill	
N	in conjunction with a, o, u, it is like n in English new; with e, i, it has a slender sound like n in pinion; n aspirated has the sound of n in English pin; after c, g, m, t, it resembles the sound of r	
R	rolled, like r in English burrow	
	monosyllables ending in lb, lbh, lg, lm, nm, rg, rb, rbh, rm, are sounded as two syllables; thus, fearg (fearug), dealbh (dealuv), marbh (maruv)	
	the letters l, n, have an aspirated sound, though the aspirate letter is not used	
	so also has r, though much slighter	

Vowel sounds

Vowels may have a duration mark over them:

- Short-sound vowels a, o, u; e, i
- Long-sound vowels à, ò, ó, ù; è, é, ì

- Two and three vowels coming together, with the sound of the one passing into the other, are called diphthongs and triphthongs:
uan
uaigh
- ao is pronounced like the beginning of the French *oeuvre*
- Some have one simple sound, e.g. gaol (gal), ceum (kem)

Short Sounds	Gaelic Example	English Equivalent	Long	Gaelic	English
a	bas	cat	à	bàs	far
a	bata	sofa	à	làdhran	
o	mol	hot	ò	òl	lord
o	bog	smoke	ó	mór	more
u	cur	put	ù	cù	moor
u	solus	but			
e	fear	net	è	nèamh	where
e	fead	rate	é	féin	rain
e	gile	whet			
i	mil	milk	ì	trì	tree

SCOTS LEGAL AND GENEALOGICAL GLOSSARY

Scots is a separate language which developed alongside and at the same time as the current predominant dialect of English (which is by no means the only English dialect) and it is a mere accident of history that Britain, and therefore the world, does not speak Scots and read the Authorised Version of the Bible in Scots. Scots and English are about as similar as German and Dutch or Norwegian and Danish, and there are Scots words routinely used in legal and official documents up to 1710 and beyond which genealogists and family historians must be able to recognise and understand. Old documents may throw up terms which are either Scots words, or particular to the Scottish legal system.

Scots	Definition
abaid, baid	delay
abbacy	the office or position of abbot
abbot	senior monk of an abbey (pre-Reformation, Catholic or Episcopal)
abdjudication (for debt)	passing of a debtor's property to his creditors; see apprising
aboleist	abolished
absolvitor	judgement for the defender in a civil action (when the court assoilzies)
abuilyements, abulzeaments	habiliments, clothing, garments, equipment
accidents	payment when becoming a burgess
accomptant	accountant
accretion	enlargement of an inheritance when a co-heir fails to prove rights to a share
acquiet	guarantee undisturbed possession or use of land
acta and decreta	acts and decreets (decrees), specifically of the Privy Council
actis	acts, legal documents
actorney	attorney, lawyer
adeill	at all, not adeill = not at all
adjudication (charter of)	charter granted by the Crown to a creditor giving over the estate of a debtor in settlement of the debt
adjudication in implement	decision by a court to implement a faulty title to land
adjuge	sentence to pay a fine
adminicle	supporting documents and evidence for when proving the existence and details of a lost deed or testament
admoneis	admonish
adnul	annul
adnullit	annulled
adoes, adois	business (e.g. without further ado)
advise	take care of e.g. advise affairs
advocate	1. (noun) Scottish barrister 2. (verb) bring a judgement before a higher court or tribunal for review
advocate	bring a judgement before a higher court or tribunal for review
advoke	see advocate
advowson or advocation	the right to appoint someone to a church living or benefice
ae	one, only e.g. ae son, only son
ae coo's meat	sufficient land to raise one cow, or the rent or value of such
ae fur land	sloped or steep land which can only be plowed in one direction
afoir	before, in front of, prior to
aganis	against
agent	person acting for another in official, business or financial matters

agnate	related on the father's side
aide–de–camp	junior officer assistant to a senior officer
aik	oak
air	heir
air by progress	heir by virtue of the usual titles
aire	circuit court
airis	heirs
airmy	army
airschip guidis	moveable goods falling to the heir
airschipe	heirship
airth	direction from which the wind blows, a certain quarter e.g. a house open to every airth
aisle	covered burial place in or attached to a church
aits	arts
aits	oats
aitseed	the season for sowing oats
aitsen tyme	the season for sowing oats
aixies	illness, ague, fever
alba firme	Latin for blench ferme, lands held for a peppercorn rent
Albany herald	official of the Lyon Court (Albany Herald, Ilay-Herald, Marchmont Herald, Ross Herald, Rothesay Herald and Snadoun Herald)
ale	beer fermented in an open vessel using yeasts that rise to the top, but unflavoured by hops
aleuin	eleven
alhallow, allhallowtide alhallow day	All Saints' Day, 1 November
aliment	maintenance of children, wife, parent etc. (similar to alimony)
allegeance	allegations
allekay, allakay	1. bridegroom's attendant (best man) 2. footman or manservant 3. lackey
allenarly	only or exclusively
allkymist	alchemist
allyat	allied
allye	kinship, ally or associate
almeral	admiral
amand	1. compensation 2. fine
amarold	1. emerald 2. haemorrhoid
amerciament	literally, 'being in mercy', a fine imposed on an offender
amerciat	1. fined 2. a fine
amrie, aumrie	cupboard (= French, armoire)
andermess, andersmess	St Andrew's Day (30 November)
ane	one
anent	about, concerning
aneuct	enough
anis	once
annalzie	transfer of ownership
annat	initial six months or year's income paid to executors of an estate
annesis	things annexed to land, appurtenances
annex	smaller property subsidiary to a larger or more important one, pendicle
annexation	uniting lands to the Crown (polite term for 'confiscation')

annual rent	interest on money lent, or mortgage, payable yearly from land revenue (but NOT a normal rent)
annuallar	person in receipt of annual rent (interest)
ansuer, ansuere, ansueir	answer
ansuert	answered
antecessour, antecestre, antecestor	ancestor, antecedent
antiant	ancient
anticipet	anticipated
apayn of	under penalty of
apothecary, apothecarie	surgeon
apouse	spouse, husband or wife
apparent	heir to landed property, who has already succeeded
apparent (appeirand air)	where the process of succession of an heir has begun after the death of the predecessor but is not complete (not to be confused with heir apparent)
apparent heir	'apparent' meaning, in this case, 'obvious' or 'clear', the heir who will succeed to a title or land; see heir presumptive
appearand	apparent (heir)
appell	appeal
appoint	order the destination of property (in court)
apprehend	arrest, seize in the name of the law
apprentice, apprent	person working for and with a craftsman attached by formal arrangement to learn the craft
apprise	value and sell the land of a debtor to pay off a debt
apprising, apprysing	sentence of a court whereby a debtor's heritable property is sold to pay the debt, later replaced by adjudication
appurtenance	something hung on to, e.g. a small portion of land
aqua, aqua vitae	whisky, water of life
aquavite	whisky
aquavitie man	whisky distiller
arage, arrage	feudal service with avers (draught-animals)
arand	ploughing
arbiter	1. arbitrator 2. arbitration
arch-beddle, archpedell	senior church or university officer, see beddle
archbishop	senior clergyman in charge of a province (pre-Reformation, Catholic, Episcopal)
archdeacon	senior clergyman in a diocese (pre-Reformation, Catholic, Episcopal church)
archdean	clergyman attached to a cathedral (pre-Reformation, Catholic, Episcopal)
archer	bowman
archpedell	arch-beddle, senior church or university officer, see beddle
ark, arch	1. chest or trunk for storing grain, etc. 2. mill waterway
arle	take into service on payment of money
arles, arrels	payment to signify completion of the bargain, money given to servants to bind an engagement – there is no contract without payment, but it could be a token payment
arlis-pennie	token payment, see arels
armourer, armorer, armorar	1. maker of armour 2. officer in charge of arms
arrest	1. apprehend 2. seize property of a debtor held by a third party
arrestee	the person from whom a third party's assets are taken or recovered
arrestment	seizure after legal process of a person or property

arrestments	relaxing attachment for debt
art or part, art and part	'be art and part in', to be involved in or an accessory to
artailzerie	artillery
articles of roup	the conditions under which a property may be auctioned after roup
Articles, Lords of	a committee of parliament which selected what would be considered, and therefore a curb on parliament's powers
as	than, e.g. sma'er as = smaller than
as accords (of law)	agreeable to (law)
as wodinsday, ask wedinsday	Ash Wednesday, the first day of Lent, six-and-a-half weeks before Easter
Ash Wednesday	first day of the Lent fast
ashet	a large oval or round serving plate; later, a saucer
asiament	1. easement, advantage, convenience 2. euphemism for lavatory (seat of easement)
askit actis	asked to have it recorded that …
assaillie	attack
assay	attack, assault, trial of endurance
assedat	let or leased for a period
assedation	tack (let) of land for a set period
assignation	deed assigning or conveyance of a person's rights in moveable property, claim for debts, or rights in leased land, to another
assignay	assignee
assize	sitting of a jury, inquest or court
assize herring	royalty of herring paid to king from herring fishermen
assoilzie	acquit, absolve from the outcome of a legal action, decree not liable (in a civil action)
assume	to tax church property
assurance	guarantee
assyth, assythement	compensation, recompense, indemnification, money paid by the killer of someone to the relatives or friends, similar to cro or wergeld
astrenze	place under an obligation
astriction	requirement for land-holders to have their corn ground at one particular mill, for which they would pay multures and sequels; the lands astricted or thirled are the mill's sucken
atentic	authentic
athill	noble
atour	moreover, in addition, often found in a precept of sasine or a charter
atour	over, beyond
attingent	close in age or relationship
attorney-at-law	advocate, lawyer appearing in court
attour	besides
aucht	1. eight or eighth 2. owned 3. owed 4. a possession 5. anything or everything
auditor	examiner of accounts or goods
auen	own (as in 'my own')
augmentation	1. increase in feu duty 2. action by a churchman to get an increase in stipend
auld	old
auntie	1. unmarried woman who kept an inn 2. drink purchased in such a place
austral	southern, southerly
author	original owner, the person from whom a title or ownership originated by sale or gift
availl	worth, monetary value

aventayle	visor of a helmet
aver, avair	1. draught horse, old horse 2. to swear or assert as fact in legal proceedings
aw (stand aw of)	be greatly afraid of
awand (awin)	owing
award, awat	ground ploughed after the first crop from lea (ley) or fey
awblaster	crossbow
awful	terrible
awner	shipowner
awys	judgement, determined advice
ay	always, ever
aye and while	until
ayr	heir
ayris	heirs
back up	endorse, support
backman	supporter in wartime
backseats	subleases of land
baginet, beginet	bayonet
baick bread, balk breddis	kneading or baking board
bailery, bailiery	bailie's area of jurisdiction
bailie, baillie, bailer, bailze, bailzie	magistrate in a burgh or in a barony, officer employed to give sasine or formal possession of land
bailie clerk	clerk to bailies in a burgh
bailie court	a court presided over by a bailie as magistrate
bailie-depute	deputy to a burgh magistrate
baillie in that pairt (part)	representative appointed for a specific function, such as the giving of sasine
bairn, barne	1. young person (as opposed to the modern usage, child or infant) 2. schoolboy or chorister
bairn's pairt (part)	child's share of a parent's estate, patrimony
bairn's pairt of gear	child's share of a parent's moveable property on his death, also called legitim
bairntime, bairnteme	offspring, brood of children or animals
bait wricht, bait-wright	boat-wright, boat-builder, shipwright
baith, baitht, bath, batht, bayth	both
bajan	first year university student
balance	flat dish or plate
bale of fire	beacon fire
ballandis	scales for madder, a dye stuff
balulalow	lullaby
band	bond, contract
bandis	marriage banns
banerman, bannerman, bennerman	bearer of army standard
banis, bannes, baneis	banish
banisment, baneisment	banishment, exile
banket	banquet
bannest	banished
baptist	baptised, named
barber, barbour, barber-chirurgeon	apart from the usual meaning, barbers also extracted teeth and carred out basic surgery
barbican	outer gate of a castle
barded, barbed	horse accoutred with armour

bareman	a bankrupt, person in debt
bargain, bergan	dispute
bargan	struggle, conflict
barker	tanner
barnman	thresher
baron	holder of lands (barony) direct from the Crown (in baroniam), which had certain privileges, (such as the administration of justice) and duties (like military service); a barony may be only a title, with no land or rights
baron bailie, baron-bailze	law officer in a barony
baron court	barony tribunal presided over by the baron or his deputy (baillie)
Baron of Exchequer	senior officer in the Exchequer
baronet	lowest rank of nobility, essentially a hereditary knighthood, granted by the Crown
barony free	an estate of the Crown raised by crown charter into a barony, with power to hold courts, impose penalties, etc. (See sheriffdom, regality)
barony officer	baron bailie
barrack-master	non-commissioned officer in charge of an army barracks
barres	barrier, outworks of castle, enclosure for tournament
barrikin	small barrel
barrister	court lawyer (English)
basar	executioner
base right or base fee	the right of someone holding lands from a former vassal, not from the superior of the lands; the buyer was normally also infeft by the superior
bassing and lawar	basin and laver, washing-jug and bowl
bastion	cudgel
batel, battel, batailze	battle
bathe as ane and ane as bathe	jointly and equally
batoun	baton
battard	small cannon
bauchill	to denounce/disgrace publicly
bauchle	small, usually deformed person (term of abuse)
baudkin	embroidered
baxtarie, baxtrey	baking (craft name)
baxter, bakester	baker
baytht	both
be	by (e.g. by rights)
beadle, bedell, beddal, beddell	church or university officer
beand	being
bear, beir, bere	barley, specifically the once common four-rowed variety
bearer	coal carrier, often a girl or woman, who hauled coal in baskets from the face to the shaft
bear-sawing, bear-seed	1. seed barley 2. barley sowing season
bedhous, bede hous	hospital or almshouse
bee-scaifs	bee-hives
beet	bundle of flax
beetyach, bittoch, bittock	small sword or dagger
beidman, beadman, beadsman	1. person living in an almshouse, pauper 2. beggar
beitting	building
beken	admit as possessor
bell penny	money saved up to pay funeral costs

bellman, belman	bell-ringer, town cryer
benefice	a church 'living', i.e. the income from rents, produce, collections etc.
benis	beans
bent silver	money paid by children to a school to pay for 'bent grass' to cover the floor
bere fra	to dispossess someone of land or property
bereans	dissenting Protestant sect
beris	place of burial
bern	barn
bers, barse	small cannon
beschop	bishop
besom	1. brush 2. woman (term of affection or abuse, depending on context)
best aucht	the most valuable animal or other possession claimed by a superior on the death of a tenant
betuix	betwixt, between
beuk, buik	book
bibil	bible
bicker	assail
bidie-in	women cohabiting without marriage
big	build
biggen	pregnant
bigget	built
bigging, biggin	building
biker	beaker, bowl
bilget, billiet	written military order
bill chamber	court presided over by judges of Session
bill of lading	document listing the type and amounts of cargo loaded onto a ship or waggon
bind	standard barrel measure for packing goods
bing	1. funeral pile 2. spoil tip from coal or other mine workings
bink	bench, ledge, rack or shelf for dishes or at a fireplace
bird alane	only child
birl quheil	spinning wheel
birlaw court	local court for lesser disputes
birlaw man	person elected as judge in a birlaw court
birlin, birling	rowing boat or galley in the West Highlands
birning	punishment by branding
birny, byrne, byrnie, birnie	coat of chain mail
birth	crop, produce
birthful, berthy, birthy	fertile, usually of animals
bishop	clergyman in charge of a see (diocese) (pre-Reformation, Catholic, Episcopal)
blac	black
black hous	thatched Highland hut of stone and turf with a central fireplace on an earth floor
black mail	rent payable in labour, cattle or non-silver coinage
black ward	holding in ward by a subtenant of another tenant who himself is held in ward of his superior
blacksmith	smith, iron forge worker
blanter	oat-based food (e.g. porridge, bread, meal pudding)
blason	badge of authority of a king's messenger
bleacher	cloth or linen whitener

bleeze silver	gift of money to a schoolteacher at Candlemas (2 February, feast of the Purification of St Mary the Virgin and the Presentation of Christ in the Temple, chosen by the Catholic Church to coincide with the ancient Celtic feast of Imbolc)
blench ferme, blench-duty, blench holding	land-tenure at nominal or peppercorn rent, or only to be paid if asked for (*si tamen petatur*); in theory the seller would remain the granter of the land but in practice have no further rights to them
blench holding	holding of land under blench ferme
blew	blue
blockmaker	broker, trader
blok	a bargain
blokit	bargained for
blude roll	list of persons accused of bloodshed
bludewite, bludeweck	guilty of or charged with bloodshed
blue	whisky or other spirit (from the colour of the flame)
blue blanket	craftsmen's guild banner
blunderbush	blunderbuss
boat	butt, barrel, cask, tub
boatswain, boatswain-yeaman, bo'sun, bosun	officer in charge of ship's crew
bocht	bought
boday	scarlet dye
boddoch	mutchkin, the liquid measure equivalent to three-quarters of a pint
bodily	personal (e.g. bodily oath, a solemn oath personally given, or bodily harm)
boid	bid
boirdours, bordours	borders
boll	1. dry measure of weight or capacity equal to six bushels (of grain) 2. valuation of land by the number of bolls it produced annually 3. payment in kind (usually food) to a farm worker
bombardier	corporal in artillery regiment
bond	a written obligation to pay or do something
bond of caution	an obligation by one person to provide security, surety or guarantee for another
bond of corroboration	confirmation of a debt (for example, to the inheritor of the original bond)
bond of disposition in security	the most common type of heritable security in the nineteenth century, where a personal bond by the borrower was secured on land
bond of manrent	an obligation by a free person to become the follower of a protector, in turn undertaking to support the protector (quite unusual)
bond of provision	bond by a father providing for his offspring
bond of relief	an undertaking to relieve a cautioner (See bond of caution) from an obligation
bond of taillie	entail
bondage, binage, bonnage	service owed by a farm worker to the farmer
bondelsoure, bonelesew	pasture linked to bond service
bone plewis	unpaid ploughing as part of service
bone silver money	paid in lieu of service
bone wark, bonday wark	service, unpaid work as part of service
bone-setter	surgeon
bonnet laird	small farmer who owns his land
bonnet, bannet	metal helmet
bonnet-maker, bonatmaker, bonnat-maker, bonat-maker	hat-maker, milliner
book-bosom'd	priests often carried their mass-books close to their chests

bookmaker	person who takes or arranges bets and wagers
books of adjournal	records of the Court of Justiciary
books of discipline	two volumes listing the laws of the Reformed Church, adopted 1560 and 1581
books of sederunt	(literally 'those who were sitting'); records of the acts of the Court of Session
borch, broch, borowis	surety, bail
bordel, brothe bordeler	brothel-keeper, customer of brothels
border warrant	warrant for the arrest of persons and effects in England for debts in Scotland
boreaus, borreaus, burriours	executioners, hangmen
boreing	borrowing
borow, borrow	stand surety or bail on behalf of
bos	leather wine flask
bot, butt	without ('touch not the cat bot a glove', motto of Clan Chattan)
bote	wine cask
bothyn	a lordship (occasionally a sheriffdom)
botisman, boitisman, boitman, botman	boatman
bound court	district tribunal or jury
bountie	gratuity or gift in addition to wages in an employment contract
bounty	extra money paid to fishermen at the end of the season
bouster, bowster	bolster, pillow
bouthous	mill building where the flour is sifted
bow	1. herd of cattle 2. church message
bow house	cow shed
bower, bowar, bowyer, bowet-maker	archery bow-maker
bowman	archer
bowne	prepare, make ready
box master	treasurer, keeper of a cashbox or its keys
box penny	duty paid to be at market
boyart	small, one-masted vessel
boyis	leg-irons
braboner, brabonar, brabaner, brabiner, brabanar, barboner, bradboner	weaver
brae	salmon trap
braig	knife
braith	fury, fit of rage
braithly	very angrily
branks	iron face bridle used in public punishment of abusive language, slander, gossiping etc.
brasier, brass-smith, brassier	brass worker
bred	unit of measurement for hides
breek brothers	rivals for a girl's affections
breve of inquest	writ empowering a sheriff (or bailies) to investigate a claimant's title
breve of mortancestry	writ directing an inquest into a claim that an ancestor's land or property is wrongfully held by someone else
breve, brieve	brief or writ from the Chancery in the king's name, often under the Privy Seal ordering an inquiry or service
brew talloun	duty paid for rights to brew beer

brewar, browstar, browster, brouster, brewster, brewer's servant	brewer
bridle silver	small payment to a servant for leading the horse
brieve bauck	a ridge of land unploughed
brigadier	army officer leading a brigade
brigantine	1. leather armour with metal scales or plates 2. two-masted ship
brim	stream, burn
brocker	possibly stone-dresser, builder's labourer
broken	without a feudal chief, outlawed
broken men	landless men; assumed to be living by spuilzie or stouthrief
brokin	ship-wrecked, or stranded
brothers german	true brothers, children of the same father or parents
brothers uterine	of the same mother but different fathers
browd, browstar, browdinstare, browdstare, browdinster, broudinstar	embroider
brught	burgh
brusery	embroidery
bu (bow, bull)	head farm of a udal estate
buckler	small, round shield
buckram-stiffner	maker of buckram (coarse cloth pasted) for bookbinding
buggis	lamb's wool
buirde	board, lodgings
buit	compensation
bull (Papal)	a written grant of some privilege by the Pope, incorrectly used to mean any papal document
bun	small barrel
bunnet	cloth cap, bonnet
bunsucken	thirled (bound in service) to a mill
burcht	burgh
burd cloth	table cloth
burdiner	1. guarantor to a monetary transaction 2. someone who takes financial responsibility for another
burding	burden
burgage	1. burgh law 2. type of tenure under which land in a royal burgh is held by the king 3. the land itself held under burgage
burgage holding	the conditions of holding, owning or occupying property in royal burghs
burgess air	the heir of a burgess, who might normally inherit burgess status
burgess ticket	document conferring burgess status
burgess, burges, burgs, burgesser	citizen, freeman of a burgh, member of a burgh guild, person with rights to trade freely within a burgh
burgh clerk	clerk in burgh administration
burgh court	town or burgh tribunal
burgh law	town law, based on the fifteenth century 'Leges Quatuor Burgorum', the Laws of the Four Burghs
burgh rudis	cultivated land belonging to the burgh
burn	brook, stream
burn ledar, burneman	water carrier
buroustounis, burroustounis	burgh-towns
burryman	ritual scapegoat for all the ills of a community

buschement	ambush
Bute pursuivant	member of the Lyon court (Bute pursuivant, Carrick pursuivant, Dingwall pursuivant, Kintyre pursuivant, Ormond pursuivant, Unicorn pursuivant)
butterman	butter seller
button-gilder	craftsman who adds gold to metal buttons
by	beside, apart from, e.g. 'be and by the law', according to but apart from the law
by and attour	over and above
bygottin	illegitimate, by-blow
byronis	arrears
caddie, cadie, cadet	carrying servant, porter for hire, military cadet
cadger, cadgear	carrier, carter, travelling dealer
cadroun, caudron	cauldron
caduciar	subject to, by means of
caibe	cabinet maker, joiner
cair	go
caird	tinker, pot-mender
cairt	1. cart, 2. ship's chart
cairter	carter
Cait	Pictish kingdom roughly equivalent to modern Caithness
callan	girl
calsay	causeway, street
calsay-maker	road-builder
candavaig	salmon
candilmaker	candlemaker
candlemas	2 February, a Scottish quarter day (with Lammas, Martinmas and Whitsunday), the days on which contracts, leases, tacks and rents began and ended and when bills were settled
cannoner	gunner
canny	canvas
canon	clergyman attached to a cathedral (pre-Reformation, Episcopal)
canous	grey-haired
cape	privateer
capellane	chaplain
caper	1. bread or oatcake with butter and cheese 2. dance, fool about
capercailzie	black grouse
caping, capring	privateering
capitanry	captaincy
capmaker, quaiffmaker	soft hat maker
capper	copper
captain-lieutenant	army lieutenant
captain-tailor	regimental tailor and cloth buyer
caption	arrest
caption, letters of	authority to arrest (capture) a debtor, or someone who has not carried out some undertaking (such as a promise to repay a debt or to marry)
captour	officer appointed by a court to apprehend criminals, and early policeman
carage	carriage, a service on a tenant which bound him to carry for the superior a stated amount of grain, goods, coal etc., or to provide men and horses for a certain number of days per year
cardow	work or trade illegally guild or craft membership or burgh freeman status

cardower	1. unlicensed worker in a craft or trade 2. travelling tinker, tradesman or tailor
care sonday	Easter Sunday
carecake	cake eaten on Shrove Tuesday, before Lent
caroline-weaver	loom weaver
carpeter	carpet weaver
Carrick pursuivant	member of the Lyon court (Bute pursuivant, Carrick pursuivant, Dingwall pursuivant, Kintyre pursuivant, Ormond pursuivant, Unicorn pursuivant)
carrier, curriour	person who transports goods
carry	weir in a stream
cartow	cannonball weighing a quarter of a hundredweight (28lbs, about 28kg)
cartwright	cart maker
carver	wood patterner
cast	repeal, cancel, annul, nullify
castellaw	measure of cheese or flour
castellward	payment in lieu of feudal service to guard a castle
casting up the heretage	taking up peats on an estate
casualties, feudal	payments which became due to a superior when certain events happened, such as marriage, relief, non-entry or wardship
catechist	church teacher of the catechism
cateran	outlaw, Highland freebooter
causey paiker	prostitute
caution	security, surety, guarantee, bail
cautioner	guarantor, one who stands caution (surety) for another
cavel	share of property by lot
caw, ca'	pull, carry
Ce	Pictish kingdom roughly equivalent to modern Moray and Buchan
cedent	one who assigns property to another
certiorat	certified
cessio bonorum	legal process by which a debtor could avoid prison by surrendering up all his goods to his creditors
cessioner	someone in receipt of property surrendered by another to pay debts
chairbearer, chairman	carrier of a sedan chair and passenger
chair-master	overseer of sedan chair carriers
chaise setter, chaise hirer	arranger of hired passenger vehicles
chakkeraw	the Exchequer Row and by extension a chequered cloth or chess board
chalans	accuse, call to account, challenge
chalder	Scottish unit of grain measure, 16 bolls or 4–6 Imperial bushels
chalfe	chaff, used to stuff mattresses
challender	maker of coverlets
challop	shallop, a type of small light boat with a schooner rig often used for fishing
chamber iron chimney	an iron grate for a room
chamberlain, chalmerlaine, chamerlane	1. a principal officer of the Scottish Royal household 2. circuit court presided over by the chamberlain
chamlet	light cloak
champart	the share of produce due to a feudal superior
chancellor	senior legal official
Chancery	royal office which wrote charters, brieves and other documents, kept records etc.
chandler, chandlar	candlestick and candle maker
changekeeper	innkeeper, ostler

chantour	choirmaster in church
chaplain	privately appointed clergyman
chaplainry	chaplaincy
chapman, chepman, chopman, chapman traveller	pedlar, travelling salesman, shopkeeper, stallholder or trader
chaptane	captain
charge	a command in the king's name
charge des affaires, charge d'affaires	diplomat representing a country's business matters abroad
charger	plaintiff
charpenteir	carpenter
charter	document of title, grant from the Crown or a superior, conveyance of an estate
charterour	Carthusian monk
chaumer, chalmirleir	chambermaid
chaumercheild	valet
check wheel	spinning wheel with a check inserted to stop after a certain amount spun
cheesemonger	cheese seller
cheiffis	chiefs
cheinyie	chain
chekker, chakker	official auditor in court cases concerning royal revenues
Chelsea pensioner	retired soldier living at or with a pension from the Royal Hospital, Chelsea
chemist	pharmacist, apothecary
chetery	land reverting to the feudal superior if the tenant dies intestate (escheat)
chief supercargo	owner's representative on board ship
childer, childir, cheldyr	1. sailors, deck hands 2. children 3. people in general
chimney crewkes	hooks to hang pots over a fire
chimney gallowes	bar projecting from the fireplace on which cooking pots were hung
chimney raxes	See raxes
chimney speel	a roasting spit
chirurgeon, cirurgyen, chirurgian, chirugenair	surgeon
chirurgeon-apothecary	surgeon who also makes and supplies medicines
choap keeper	shop
chopeine, chopin, chappin	1. liquid measure, half a Scots pint, approximately 0.85 litre or almost an English quart 2. a container of this volume
chopis bak	back shops, where preparation took place
christin, cristin, christian, chrissenmas, christinmes	Christmas
chymna	chimney
cinquefoil	five leaves, a charge in heraldry
Circinn	Pictish kingdom roughly equivalent to modern Angus
circuit court	a court which goes round the country trying criminal cases; in Scotland called the Court of Justiciary
cisteus	Cistercian monk
citat	cited
cite	city
citinar, citiner	citizen
clag	claim against property
clais, clathis	clothes

clait, claith	cloth or clothing
clamant	demand for redress
clap dyke	turf or earth drainage wall
clare constat	'clearly appears', a writ or precept (order) granted by a subject superior to an heir, whose right to a property is obvious from documents and which orders the giving of sasine
clasp maker, clespmaker	maker of clothes fastenings
clayth, claith, clath	cloth
clearances	practice of removing tenants from land (mainly Highlands)
cled	provided, clothed
cleme	claim
clepe and call	court summons
clerk of the bills	official who manages bills of complaint presented to a court
cloot, clout	cloth or clothing
clothier, claythman	cloth worker or seller
cloth-laper	cloth finisher
clout	1. small piece of land 2. a cloth, clothes ('Ne'er cast a clout till May be out')
club	apprentice (usually in shoemaking) not yet a freeman
clubmaker	maker of golf clubs
coachman, cotchman	coach driver
coachmaster	overseer of a fleet of coaches
coad (cod)	pillow or cushion
coadwair, codwair	pillow slip, cushion cover
coal factor, coal grieve	coalmine overseer, manager
coal fauld	coal yard
coalcawer, coilbeirar	coal carrier
coal-heuch	coal pit, coalmine working
coast-waiter	coastguard
cobbler	shoe maker or mender
coble and net	symbols used in the transfer of ownership of fishing rights
coble, cobel	1. small fishing boat 2. malt-steeping vat
cocket, cocquet, coket, coquet (letter of)	certificate or seal that customs have been paid on exported goods
cod, coad	cushion, pillow
codware	cushion cover, pillowcase
cofe, coffing	an exchange
coffee-man	coffe-house keeper
coft	bought
cog	container, bowl or pail made of wooden staves
cognition	recognising an heir as entitled to a property
cognition and sasine	the process whereby an heir is accepted as having property
cognosced	formally recognised (as heir etc.)
cogster	flax dresser
coll	coal
coll bearer	female coal carrier
coll heuch	mine
collar	haysheaf maker
collation	approval given by a bishop to appoint someone to a church living or benefices
collector	revenue gatherer

collegiate church	church founded by a private person, in free alms
collep	drinking vessel
collever	coal-bearing horse
collier, colzear, colzeare, coalhewer, coliar, coalhewar, coalheaver, coilheaver	coal merchant
collum	ship
colman	furnisher
colonel	officer in charge of an army regiment
colourmaker	paint maker or seller
comburges	fellow-burgess
comite of states	committee of estates
com-maker, combmaker	comb-maker
commander	senior officer on ship
commander-in-chief	senior officer in a large army unit
commendator, commendatar	one who managed the income from an abbey benefice when vacant or who had grant of a vacant benefice for life (before the Reformation usually the abbot, after usually a layman)
commissar clerk, commisser officer, commissary clerk	clerk in a commissary office, mainly recording wills
commissar, commissary, commisser	civil official of the Commissary court
commissariot	1. registry for confirmation or probate of wills etc. 2. the district covered by the jurisdiction of a Commissary Court – these had the geographical boundaries as the pre-Reformation church courts and (more or less) the medieval dioceses, but not to the old counties
commissary	officer making a confirmation or grant in matters of inheritance, confirmation of testaments etc. Originally, this was a bishop's official, but after the Reformation an official of the Commissary Court
Commissary Court	office administering the estates of deceased persons in cases of intestacy, and confirmed testaments – submitted by parish priests to bishops pre-Reformation and after 1584 a civil office, the first of which was in Edinburgh a further twenty-one were established
commissioner	lawyer qualified to hear and record oaths
Commissioners of Supply	people appointed by the county to assess land tax due, maintain the roads, raise and provision the militia etc.
commixtion	joining property of different owners, which affects their rights differently
commodities	advantages and benefits arising from the ownership, possession or use of property
common serjand	burgh officer, law officer, town officer
commonty	a common ground used or owned by more than one person
compear, compearance	to appear in a legal proceeding
composition	payment to the superior of land by an heir succeeding to it
compositor, componitour	1. arbitrator in legal cases 2. sum paid in settlement 3. agreement to settle
compromit	settlement, agreement
comprysing	comprehending, but legally similar to apprysing
compt	account
comptroller, controller, comtreller	official in charge of revenue payments on goods
conand	covenant
condescend	to state the facts
condescendance	summary of the facts in a trial
conduce	employ, hire
conduck	conduit, water channel

confectioner	maker or seller of sweetmeats and cakes
confirmation of grant	confirmation of a charter by a superior
conjunct	1. joint e.g. conjunct fiar, joint ownership of land 2. connected by blood
conjunct fee	title to lands held jointly, by husband and wife, a number of heirs, business partners etc.
conjunct right	a right held jointly
conjunctly and severally	two or more individuals having an obligation, duty or empowerment to do something, whether singly or together
connex	appurtenance, something connected with an estate
connotar	public notary acting alongside another
conqueish, conquess, consques, conquis	1. to conquer 2. to acquire property by purchase, donation or exchange rather than inheritance
conquest, heir of	an heir succeeding by ascent, as representing an older line, e.g. if the middle of three brothers died, the youngest succeeded to the heritable property but the eldest to the conquest property, this distinction ended in 1874
consanguinean	half-sibling, child of the same father but different mother
conservator	official concerned with the privileges of a body corporate or institution
constable	law officer
contorar	contrary
contracted	betrothed – in Scotland this was legally equivalent to marriage as consent was legally binding and the marriage ceremony was introduced in order to make the contract publicly known, although it was not essential
convener	chief official of a craft or trade
conveyance	transfer of property
cookie	prostitute
cooper, cowper, cupper	cask or barrel maker (See coupar, couper)
cop	cup used as a liquid or grain measure
coper guis pan	copper pan for cooking goose
coppersmith	one who works with copper
coqueter	Clerk of cocquet
cordwainer, cordiner, cordonar, cordoner, cordinar, corduner, cordowner, cordoner	shoemaker
corkcutter	cutter of cork bark
corn–chandler	corn merchant
corn–couper	corn dealer
cornel, crownell, crowner	1. colonel 2. coroner
cornet	lowest rank of army commissioned officer, sub-lieutenant, ensign
coronell	coroner
coronicles, cornicles, corniclis	chronicles
corporal	non-commissioned army officer
corshous	building standing at right angles to others
cose, cosse	exchange, usually of land
cosnant	wages without board or lodgings
cost side	coast
cottar land	land attached to a cothouse
cottar, cottrall, cotter	tenant occupying a farm cottage, sometimes with a small piece of land in exchange for working on the farm
Council and Session	the 'books of council and session' are the Register of Deeds
councillor	1. town councillor 2. counsellor, advocate

count	English or French equivalent to earl
counter	hostile encounter
counter warden, compter-warden	keeper of accounts, treasurer
countermaister	ship's mate
countess	wife of an earl or count
coup	1. refuse tip 2. manure cart 3. basket used to catch or carry salmon
couper	herring dealer
couper-boit	a herring dealer's boat
cours	coarse (of linen)
Court of Justiciary	the main criminal court in Scotland, operating by a number of circuits
Court of Session	supreme civil court in Scotland
court plaint	feudal privilege of dealing with complaints made to a court of justice
courten roads	curtain-rods
courtesy	entitlement to income from the heritage of a deceased (See liferent)
cowclink	prostitute
cowfeeder	dairy farmer
cow's mail	the rent of sufficient land to graze a cow
cox-swain	navigator of a boat or ship
cramer, cremer	stall-keeper, pedlar
cran	barrel, barrelful of unsalted herrings
crannog	old lake dwelling, a wooden house on stilts on an island lake or earth mound standing in water
crear	small merchant vessel
credit draper	person who sells linen or clothes door-to-door on credit and collects the money weekly or monthly
creel	wicker fish basket, lobster cage
creelman, creillman, creilman, creelaman, crealman, creilmaker	maker of creels for lobster and crab fishing
creep	crêpe material, used to make hoods etc.
creve	crave, petition for a right to do something
crimpson	crimson, red
crippelt	crippled, with a physical disability
cro	financial recompense for a killing
croft	small piece of land adjoining a house
crofter	smallholder
cross dwelling	lodging
crowdie-mowdie	oatmeal and water eaten uncooked
crownes of the sun	French coins, named for the minting mark, worth about 14 shillings
crue	croy, hovel
cruives	enclosures used in salmon fishing
cruk	circle, hook, shepherd's crook, bishop's crozier
crukit hauche	low ground (hauch of haugh) or water-meadow beside a winding river
crummock	an edible tuber or rootplant
cryit fair	fair with advance public proclamation
cuch bed	couch bed
cuik, cuke	cook
cullour	colour
cultellar	cutler, knife-sharpener
culvering	1. handgun 2. cannon

culvert	drain, dewer
cummer, kimmer	witch
cumptour	money-counter, accountant
cunigar, cuningar	rabbit warren
cunnar, cunstar	ale taster
cuntra, cuntray, cuntre	country
cunyie	corner plot of land
cunzehous	the mint
cunzeour	master of the mint, coiner, minter
curate	clergyman not fully ordained, minister's assistant (pre-Reformation, Episcopal)
curator	a person appointed to act for someone unable to manage his or her own affairs, such as a minor or a lunatic
curator *ad litem*	guardian of a minor in a lawsuit or of a wife sueing a husband
curator, curat	guardian of a minor between fourteen and twenty-one years old, as opposed to tutor, guardian until fourteen (twelve if female)
curn, curne	literally, a single grain of corn, but usually appearing as 'the third curn' or with another number, indicating a proportion of the crop; small number, a few
currach	coracle, small fishing boat
currier	hide curer, tanner
currier	tanner of skins, hides and leather
currour	forest warden
curtilage	a courtyard or other piece of ground near or belonging to an occupied building
cussing	cousin
customer, custumer, customar	customs officer
custom-house officer	collecter of revenues in custom-houses
cuthill	a wood
cutler, cutlar, coilter, cultellar	cutlery maker
cutter	someone who cuts down trees for wood without permission
dagmaker	maker of mittens for fishermen
dailis	ewes fattened for slaughter, usually because they have not lambed
dale, deal	wooden shelf or container, usually for milk
damasker	damask cloth worker
dame	married or widowed lady
dative	as in testament dative or tutor dative, granted by the court and containing no will, as opposed to testamentar, done or appointed by the testator and containing a will
davach	measurement of land, about four ploughgates
dawern	a day's work
day labourer	workman paid daily
de facto	'in fact', or something which has actually been done, is a fact
deacon warner	official summoning members to a guild, court, council or church meeting
deacon, deacon convener	1. chief official of craft or trade guild 2. lay official in a church
deall	a board of deal (or pine)
dean	1. chief official of craft or trade guild 2. head of a university faculty
dean of gild or guild	president of a guildry, judge of the dean of guild's court and usually magistrate in a royal burgh
deathbed law	an heir could cancel deeds not to his advantage by a terminally ill predecessor within sixty days before the death
debatable	land and boundaries subject to dispute

debitum fundi	'debt of the land' arising out of it, e.g. arrears of rent or feu-duty
decerned	decreed to be
decimae	tithe or tenth part of the annual produce of land due to the church, same as teinds
declarator	action to have a right or interest declared by law
decree of locality	decree of the Teind Court apportioning how a stipend should be paid by each of the parish heritors
decree of modification	decree of the Teind Court altering a churchman's stipend
decree of valuation	decree of the Teind Court determining a heritor's teinds
decree, decreet, decreit	decree, sentence or final judgement of a court
decreet arbitral	award to parties in a dispute after arbitration
decreet of *cognitionis causa*	decision of a court on the amount of a debt to be paid out of a deceased's estate by the heirs; it may also confirm the creditor as executor of the estate
decreet of removal	judgment ordering defenders to leave lands
dede, deid	1. deed 2. dead 3. death
deed	formal written document in a particular format laying out the terms of an agreement, contract, obligation but not a sasine and not concerned with heritable property and its transfer or assignment
defender	Scots law equivalent of a defendant in a suit or trial
deforcement	1. occupying property belonging to someone else 2. resisting officers of the law
defunct	deceased person
deid's part, deid's pairt, dead's part	that part of someone's moveable estate they may dispose of by testament after death; the other parts are the bairn's part and the *jus relicta*
delated	accused
deliverance	judgment
demittit	demitted, dismissed, resigned, given over
demurrage	payment made to a shipmaster or shipowner if a ship is held up longer than usual while loading or unloading
depone	depose, give evidence, make an oath
deponent	someone who makes a deposition before a court
deposition	testimony of a witness put down in writing
depute	deputy
derfly	boldly
design	assign, bestow, give, grant
destination	nomination of successors to a property in a specific order (See entail)
deviding	division of lands or property
devoid and red	vacate land or property
dew service, deservice, do-service	service owed or performed by a tenant on behalf of a superior
dewitie	duty
deyman	1. day labourer 2. dairyman
diem clausit extremum	'he has closed his last day'; the name of a royal order sent to a sheriff to enquire into the death of a debtor of the Crown, and to ensure the Crown is satisfied for the debt
dight	prepared, armed, equipped etc.
diligence	1. legal proceedings in the recovery of debts, enforcement of payments etc. 2. court warrant to make witnesses attend a trial or to require the production of documents
Dingwall pursuivant	member of the Lyon court (Bute pursuivant, Carrick pursuivant, Dingwall pursuivant, Kintyre pursuivant, Ormond pursuivant, Unicorn pursuivant)

diocese	the extent of a bishop's jurisdiction, which continued to be important after the Reformation as the area determined the boundaries and jurisdiction of the Commissary Court
dirrogatione	derogation, partial repeal of a law
discharge	a written deed which cancels or extinguishes an obligation, usually one to repay a debt
disclamation	renunciation of obligation by a tenant to the superior
disheris, disherish	disinherit
dispone	dispose of, convey (land), alienate
disposition	a deed whereby a right to property (either heritable or moveable) is alienated by one person and conveyed to another
disposition in implement	a disposition granted in implement of a previous, imperfect conveyance
dispositive clause	the clause in a deed which transfers property of any sort
dissasine	dispossession
dissenting	Protestant but not part of the 'established' Church of Scotland
distitut	destitute
ditcher	digger or cleaner of ditches
dittay	the substance of the charge against a person accused of a crime
diuers	divers, various
diuidit	divided
dochtir	daughter
docquet	docket or statement of authenticity annexed to a document recording a sasine (transfer of property)
doctor	1. medical practitioner 2. school master
domestic	household servant
domicillis	domiciles, dwellings
domicills	household goods
dominical lands	the mains or principal farm on an estate, owned by the lord or dominus
dominie	schoolmaster
dominium directum	'direct lordship'; the interest a feudal superior had in property such as the right to feu duties, casualties etc.
dominium utile	'lordship by usage'; the interest a tenant had in landed property such as the right to direct usage and enjoyment of the income from it
dominus	sir, the title used by knights, chaplains and later by baronets but it can also mean laird or lord
donator	the receiver of a donation, following failure of the rightful succession
doom	a judgement or sentence
doomster	the public executioner who, at one time, pronounced sentence
dornick, dornyk	work or naperie, from cloth woven at Tournay, France
dote	give or grant lands as an endowment
dowager	widow, retaining courtesy title and privileges e.g. dowager queen
dragmaker	net maker
draper, drepper, clayth-draipper	cloth and thread seller
draw dykes	ditches for water
drest	dealt with harshly, maltreated
drover	driver of animals to market or between farms
druggist	apothecary, pharmacist, chemist
drysalter	dealer in dried, tinned or salted foods, edible oils, dyestuffs, gums, tallow etc.
dryster	grain drier
duchess	wife of duke, highest noble title under the sovereign

duke	highest noble title under the sovereign
duris	harm, injuries
dutyfeu	service or payment owed to a superior
dwell	owned or occupied by someone in particular
dyer, dyster, litster	person who makes dyes and colours cloth
dyke	wall
dyker, dykar	dyke or wall builder
dytements, dyting	poetry, writing
dyvour	bankrupt
earl	nobleman, above viscount and below marquis, equivalent to an English or French count – his wife is a countess
earn, erne	Scottish eagle
easement, esement, aisment	1. easement, advantage, convenience 2. euphemism for lavatory (seat of easement)
econimus	steward, manager, bursar
edict	public proclamation summoning persons to compear (appear) before a court
edict of curatory	edict on family from both sides to act as curators (guardians) to a minor
effeir	fall by right, as in 'as effeirs', correctly, as appropriate
effeirs, as effeirs, effeiring	correctly relating or corresponding to
eik	an addition or supplement to a deed
eik, eiking	addition, as to a will
eiked	added
eild	children, issue
elder	one of twelve laymen who administer a church along with the minister (post-Reformation)
elder, eldar, eldder, elde, elser, eldest, senior	older or oldest heir (See younger)
elderman	alderman, burgh magistrate or councillor
elemosinar, elimozinar	almoner
elide	weaken evidence
ell	measure of length, about one yard, traditionally the distance between nose and fingertips
eme	uncle or near male relation
emerode	emerald, but also haemorrhoids
emmet	ant
emphiteose	feu duty in perpetuity
end	outcome of a legal process
engel	angel, a gold coin
engeneret, engendrit	engendered, begotten
ensign	lowest army-commissioned officer rank in foot regiments, sub-lieutenant
entail	or tailzie, a deed which altered the legal succession of lands to another line, or by which the descent of lands can be secured to a specified succession of heirs
enter, inter	1. obtain or take possession of lands, property or an office 2. to put someone in possession
entres	interest
entres, entress, entry	1. entrance 2. appointment of an heir as a new vassal with his superior
entrie silver	dues paid when entered as heir in an estate
episcopal	pertaining to a bishop
equerry	attendant on a noble or sovereign, especially in connection with his horse

equipollent	equivalent, of equal authority or value
erd erthe and stane	earth and stone, figurative expression used in conveyance (transfer of property)
erer	rather
erl	earl
escheat, eschet, ascheat	forfeit, as in escheat goods or estate forfeited or confiscated on conviction for a crime, non-payment of debt etc.
eschew	accomplish, succeed
esquire	title of a gentleman, as opposed to mister or master, which indicated a university graduate
essay-master	assay master in the Royal Mint
est	east
estaitis	estates (of the Crown)
estin	eastern
ettlit	aimed (at)
evenar	arbitrator appointed to apportion lands
evidents	title deeds, documents proving ownership
examiner	auditor or inspector of business, trade etc.
excamb, excambion	exchange; the exchange of one heritable subject for another, for example, someone may have exchanged a piece of land for some agreed service, and that passes to the heir of the deid (deceased). The Montgomery Act (1770) was aimed at agricultural improvements by allowing 50 acres arable and 100 acres not fit to plough to be excambed. The Rosebery Act of 1836 allowed one-fourth of an entailed estate, not including the mansion house, home farm and policies, to be excambed, provided the heirs took no more grassum (entry fee) than £200. The Rutherford Act of 1848 applied it to the whole estate. Nowadays, the necessary consents of substitute heirs are regulated by the Entail (Scotland) Act 1882 and there were more land reforms later. If the umquhile (deceased) had exchanged something or inherited something exchanged then the right to continue this is inherited.
excise officer, exciseman	collecter of customs revenues
excrescens	interest
executor	legal administrator of the moveable property of a dead person, nominated either in the deceased's testament (executor-nominate) or by the Commissary Court (executor-dative)
executor-dative	person appointed by a court to effect a warrant
executor-nominate	person appointed by a testator to effect a warrant, as in the executor of an estate, appointed in a will
executrix	female executor
executry	moveable property of the deceased, as opposed to heritable (immovable) land, buildings, mineral and fishing rights etc.
exhorter	preacher, minister (Protestant, post-Reformation)
exoner	exonerate, free from liability
eyrn	iron
factor	person appointed by another to conduct affairs on his behalf, business agent, attorney
factory	power of attorney
factrix	female factor
fader, fadir	father
fadir-in-gode	godfather
fadir-of-lau	father-in-law
faillie, failzie	failure to comply with something, or non-fulfillment of an obligation
failzand	lacking in e.g. an heir

failzieing	failing
falcon and culver	artillery pieces
falconer	falcon and hawk trainer or handler
falsing the doom	making a protest against a doom (judgment) before taking the matter to a higher court
famyle	family, kindred, lineage, relations
farder	further
farding land	fourth part of a penny land
farrier, ferrier	farrier, horse-shoer, horse veterinarian
Fastern's night	Shrove Tuesday, eve of the Lent fast
father-in-law	step-father or wife's father (gude father)
fault	need
fayr	father (the y is the 'thorn' character, pronounced th)
fayve	five
fede	feud, blood enmity
fee	1. full right of property in heritage, as distinct from liferent 2. hire oneself out for farm work
feild	field
feill	many
fellis	fells, hills
feltmaker	maker of cloth by pressing (felting), without a loom
fence	1. escape from prison or arrest 2. seizure of goods or land
fenced court	court opened and held with all due solemnity
fencing master	teacher of fencing and sword-play
feoffment	legal giving of possession of land and the fact of being legally possessed (See infeftment)
ferd	fourth
ferd corne	fourth corn, grain for sowing
fere	friend, comrade
ferme, ferm	1. rent (See blench ferme) 2. firm, steady 3. farm
ferme, ferm	rent or annual payment
fermorar, fermourer, fermour	farmer
ferryman	ferry operator
feu, few	holding of property under feudal tenure, i.e. held of a superior
feuar, fewer, fiar, fewar, feuer	1. person who holds a feu (land or house) at a rent 2. agent who collects that rent on behalf of the superior
feu duty, feu-maills, feu-fermes	rent paid for a feu
fiall	feudal tenure
fiar, fear	owner, person holding a property in fee, e.g. an heir who has the fee (ownership) as distinct from the person in possession of the life-rent
Fib	Pictish kingdom of Fife
Fidach	Pictish kingdom roughly equivalent to modern Strathspey
fidlar	fiddler, violinist
fireman	tender of a fire, for cooking, brewing, metal working etc.
firle	ferrule, metal ring binding a knife or fork to its handle
firlot	a Scottish measure which, like the rest, differed from place to place and depended on what it was being used to measure; as far as grain was concerned, it was the fourth part of a boll (and therefore anything from about nine-tenths to one-and-a-half Imperial bushels)
firlot mell	measure of meal or other dry goods; a quarter-boll

fischer, fischerman, fisher, white fisher, fishman	fisherman or fish seller
fishmonger	fish seller
fitter	installer of machinery, furnishings etc.
flaggan, flacon	flagon
flaxdresser, flax-raiser	preparer of flax for spinning to make linen
flegeoure	fletcher, arrowmaker
flemens-firth	asylum for outlaws
flesher, fresher, flesches, flescher	butcher
fleur-de-luce	fleur-de-lys, the stylised iris used in heraldry
flit	remove, in the sense of leaving land or a house
floater	plasterer, surface leveller
foir	fore, front
foir bears	forebears, predecessors, ancestors
foirfadirs	forefathers, ancestors
foirgrandscheir	great-grandfather
foirsaid, foyrsaid	aforesaid
fold dycks	dykes or walls for enclosing livestock
foranent	up against, adjoining
foregranddame	great-grandmother, but occasionally female relative further back
foregrandfather, foregrandsire	great-grandfather, great-great-grandfather or earlier male ancestor
foreland, foirland	front tenement or house
foreman	person in charge of workers at a farm, factory etc.
foremast-man	foremost man, foreman
forester	forest worker, tree tender
forework	stone facings on the frontage of a building, often ornamental
fore-worker	stone mason concerned with forework (the frontage of a building)
forfault	1. forfeit 2. confiscation of rights or property
forsamekle	forasmuch
fort major	army officer in charge of a fort, castle, camp barracks etc.
fortalice	fortress, tower of a fortified house
Fortriu	Pictish kingdom roughly equivalent to modern Perthshire, centred on Forteviot
fostering	it was the practice among noble and royal families, and clan chiefs, to have their heirs brought up elsewhere, partly to reinforce links, partly as hostage against disagreements
fosteris	children or other dependants
Fotla	Pictish kingdom roughly equivalent to modern Atholl
foullis	fowls, chickens
founder	foundry worker, metal caster
frame smith	maker of shoulder yokes for carrying pails
franktenement	freehold
franktenementar	freeholder
fray	scare, frighten
fre lands	free lands (See barony)
free forest	forest with hunting rights granted under charter to the owner by the Crown
free-woman	woman with the right to trade in a burgh, female equivalent of freeman
freith	free
Frenchie	person from France, or one who puts on airs to appear sophisticated

freshly	briskly
frething	freeing, unburdening
fruiter	fruit seller
full	clean or thicken cloth by treading
fuller	cloth-finisher
fuller, fouller	person who cleans, thickens and finishes cloth
fulling	cleaning and thickening cloth prior to finishing
fundlin	foundling, orphan
furm	form or bench
furrier	preparer and seller of furs and fur garments
furth of	beyond, abroad, outside the borders (of)
furthputting	eviction from property
futter	fodder or straw
fyfe	small flute
Fyfe, Fyffe	the county and sheriffdom of Fife
fyft, fyift	fifth
fyftye	fifty
fyiftein	fifteen
gabart	barge, lighter
gabartman, gabertman	lighterman, bargee
gairn waird bleads	garden hedge scissors
gais	gauze material
gais scarfe	gauze scarf
gait	1. goat 2. street leading to a gate of a town, rather than the gate itself, e.g. Hiegait, Westgait, Overgait, Trongait
gallouaye	Galloway
gallowes	swing beam, e.g. on a chimney
gallus	1. gallows 2. trouser braces (gallusses) 3. comely (mainly in Glasgow, e.g. 'a gallus lassie')
gaol	jail
gaoler	jail keeper
gardiner, gardner, gairdner, gairner	gardener
garnette	siege engine used in war
garnison, garnisoun	garrison
gat	begot, gave birth to, sired
gause	fine cloth, gauze
gave in commend	made over as a benefice
gaynest	most suitable
geir, gear	1. goods e.g. household gear 2. implements used in a mill e.g. 'lyeing and goeing geir', some of which went to the tenant while others were the property of the superior
general supervisor	overseer, usually in an office, government department or business
generallity	generality, as in 'among the generallity of our people'
genitour	janitor
genoligie, genolligie, genolygie	genealogy
gentleman	someone with means, above a commoner but below a noble
german	full, related by blood as opposed to marriage (of a brother or sister, or cousin – See brother german)
gif, gyf	if, whether

gilding	applying a layer of gold to an object (button, picture frame etc.)
gird	1. child's toy, consisting of a metal hoop (gird) pushed by a hooked stick (cleek) 2. iron cartwheel cover 3. belt
girder	1. maker of hoops for cartwheels (girds) 2. belt maker
girdle	griddle, iron baking plate
girdler, girdlesmith	maker of girdles (iron baking plates)
girds, girdis	horse girths
glamour	enchantment, magical spell, delusion
glass-grinder	window glass maker
glazier, glassier, glassinwright	maker and fitter of window glass
glebe, glebeland	land attached to a parish church to which the minister had a right in addition to his stipend
glebe-house	church manse
gll'ality	contracted form of 'generallity'
glover	glove maker and seller
glufis, gluiffis	gloves
godfather	witness to a baptism
gold drawer	maker of gold wire by drawing it through a die
goldsmith	worker in gold
goodsone, gudesone	grandson or son-in-law
gossip	cousin, friend
governor	castle, prison, hospital or almshouse overseer and manager
graith	wealth
graithit	make ready
gramarye	magic
gramercy	thank you, from the French *grand merci*
granter, granger, grinterman	granary keeper
grantschir, grandscheir	grandsire, grandfather
grassum, gersum	entry fee paid by holder of a tack (rent)
gren	green
grewgren silk	gros-grain silk
grieve, greive, grief	manager, overseer, factor of a farm or estate, sometimes provost of a burgh
grissillis, grissels	grilse, immature salmon
grit	great
groom	person who tends horses
ground officer	manager or factor of an estate
gudame	grandmother
gude father	wife's father
gudeman, goodman, guidman	farm owner or tenant, gentleman; James V used to go about incognito calling himself 'the Gudeman o' Ballengeich', land adjacent to Stirling Castle
gudeson	grandson or sometimes son-in-law
gudewife, goodwife, guidwife	mistress of a household or farm, wife of a gudeman
gudsyr, guidschyr, gudscheir, gudscher	grandfather
guid, guidis	good, goods
guids and geir	possessions (moveable as opposed to heritable)
guild	band of tradesmen (sometimes craftsmen) with powers to control trade levy duties etc.
guild brother	guild member

guild officer	elected position in a guild, such as treasurer or deacon
guis, guys	goose
guther	grandfather (See gudsyr)
guyder	guide, guardian
gyle	guile
haberdasher	seller of threads, buttons, ribbons etc.
habile	1. manageable, easy to use 2. with the capacity or power (to do something)
habit and repute	criminal reputation
hackbut, harquebus	short musket, arquebus, early match-lock field gun (too heavy to be shoulder-fired but used throughout Europe from 1450–1550)
hackbuteer, hackbutter	musketeer, soldier armed with a hackbut (harquebus)
hackney-coachman	driver of a coach for hire
hag	firm ground in a bog, moss or swamp
hagbut	type of musket
haiffand	having
haill	whole
hair merchant	dealer in hair, such horsehair for stuffing chairs
halket kyne	spotted cows
hals	neck
hames, haimes	leather traces for a horse, cart, plough etc.
hamesucken	1. crime committed on a person in his or her own home 2. fine or penalty for such a crime
hammerman	smith, blacksmith, metal worker
handsell	the first payment for goods etc.
handseynzie	banner, hand-sign
hardiment	boldness
harnessmaker	maker of leather harnesses and traces for horses, oxen, ploughs, carts etc.
hatter	hat maker, milliner
haundy	handy
havand	having
haver	possessor or custodian of a document needed as evidence
hech	promise
hecht	promised
hecklemaker, heckilmaker	flax-comb maker
heelmaker, heilmaker, pantoun-heilmaker	maker of shoe heels
heiche	high
heid	head
heilsome	wholesome
heims, hemmyngs	shoes of untanned leather
heir apparent	'apparent' meaning, in this case, 'obvious' or 'clear', the heir who will succeed to a title or land (See heir presumptive)
heir general	one who succeeds to both the heritable and moveable property of a deceased person, who also happens to be that person's heir at law and heir by normal course of succession (his heir of line)
heir in heritage	(normally) the eldest son
heir male	heir descending through the male line
heir of tailzie, heir of provision	heir by virtue of a deed of entail or provision
heir portioner	one of several heirs taking equal parts, often in the case of daughters

heir presumptive	one who expects to succeed to an estate but whose right may be defeated by a birth nearer in blood to the ancestor (See heir apparent)
heir special	heir to a particular subject or thing
heirs	heirs were of various forms – heir general, the heir of provision, heir special, heir portioner, heir apparent
heirship moveables	certain moveable goods (usually the best or most valuable) belonging to the deceased, to which the heir in heritage was entitled by law
herald	royal messenger, member of Lyon Court (Albany herald, Ilay herald, Marchmont herald, Ross herald, Rothesay herald and Snadoun herald)
herald-painter	coat of arms painter
herd, hird	shepherd, stockman
heretage	immoveable property (land etc.) devolved on the heir at law as opposed to an executor
herezeld or herit	form of death tax – tribute due to the feu superior on the death of the fiar or occupier and, if not expressly stipulated in money, was usually the best horse, ox, cow etc.
herit, heriot	See herezeld
heritable	capable of being inherited; pertaining to land and houses, i.e. the property which went by inheritance to the heir at law – as opposed to moveable property; 'heritable right' meant right by inheritance
heritable proprietor	owner of heritable property
heritably	by heritage
heritage	inheritance, heritable estate, property in the form of land and houses which descended to the heir at law on the death of the proprietor
heritier	heir, inheritor
heritor	local property or land owner with financial responsibilities for parish burdens, e.g. poor relief, schools, church buildings, almshouses etc.
hesp	hasp, brooch clasp, hinge
heuch	glen with steep sides, crag
hew	hue
hind, hyne, hynder	farm servant
hint	gripped
hird, hyrd	shepherd, cattle herd, keeper of livestock
hirer	arranger of labourers, servants, animals, carts, coaches etc. for a fee
hisband	husband
hog	one-year-old sheep
hogg	pig (or one-year-old sheep)
hogstone	worsted jacket
holograph	testament written by the hand of the testator and therefore valid in law
homologate	indirectly approve of, agree with, confirm, prove, ratify
hookmaker	maker of buttonhooks
horn (at the)	denounced as a criminal, debtor or outlaw
horner	maker of horn items, e.g. combs, spoons, drinking cups
horning (letters of)	writ obtained by a creditor ordering a debtor to pay or be 'at the horn'
horning (relaxed from)	released from the effects of letters of horning
horse, master of	stable overseer
horse-cuper, horse-cooper	horse merchant
horsesetter, horse-setter	horse-hirer, owner of horses for hire
hosier	maker or seller of hose and stockings
hospital	almshouse

hospital-master	almshouse keeper
hostler	ostler, innkeeper
household master	butler, chamberlain in charge of a household
housekeeper	senior household servant, usually female
house-maills, house-meals	house-rent
house-steward	senior household manservant, butler
houshald	household
hoviss	house
howff, hough	1. inn, tavern 2. burial ground 3. place of resort
huckster	pedlar, hawker
hulster cairds	holster cards
humest	uppermost
husband-land	twenty-six acres ploughed by two oxen
husbandman	tenant of a homestead and land on an estate, keeper of stock animals
hypothecate	mortgage to secure a debt
hyrd	hird, shephers, livestock-keeper
ihone	John
Ilay herald	royal messenger, herald of the Lyon Court (Albany herald, Marchmont herald, Ross herald, Rothesay herald and Snadoun herald)
ilk	same
ilk (of that)	of that place or race, but meaning *de eodem*, where the name of the family and estates are the same granted by royal charter e.g. Durie of Durie, or Durie of that ilk – the right to be so called survives if the estate is lost but purchasing a property does not necessarily transfer the right to be called *of that Ilk*
ilke, ilkane	each, every one
implement	completion, fulfillment
in twyn	apart, asunder
incontinent after our deceiss	without delay after my death
indite	indictment
indweller, indwellar, induellar	inhabitant
infeft	1. to seize or give formal possession 2. to be in possession of
infeftment	1. investing a new owner with legal possession of land or heritage 2. action or deed recording formal possession
infeftment in security	temporary infeftment in heritable property as security against a loan, debt or other obligation
ingland	England
inglis	English
ingraver	engraver, patterner on metal or glass
inhibition	writ forbidding a debtor to part with, burden, mortgage etc. his heritage, so securing it for the next heir or a creditor
inquest, inquisition	inquiry before a jury into a person's right to succeed as heir
insicht	furniture, or household goods
instrument	legal document, often testifying to completion of an act, e.g. sasine, putting in possession of land
intendent	person in charge, keeper, superintendent
interdict	inquisition
interlocutor	strictly speaking, a judgment or order of a court, or of the Lords Ordinary, pronounced in the course of a lawsuit short of the final judgement and not finally settling the case
intermeddle	interfere without right

interrogatory	formal question requiring a reply under oath
interruption	legal action to extend the length of a period of prescription (See prescription)
intertainer	entertainer, in the sense of a guardian looking after and housing a minor
intres thairto	interest in
intrometter	person concerned in the affairs of another e.g. a trustee or executor
intromission	1. being concerned in the affairs of another 2. possession and management of property belonging to someone else – legal, when someone is designated as an 'intrometter with the goods and gear', or illegal, when it is called 'vicious intromission' when illegal or without any right
intrusit	intruded
inventar	inventory of moveable possessions, debts etc.
inventar judicial	inventory made by order of the court
Iohannis, ionnais, ioannes	John
iron bak	ash pan, iron basket
ironmonger	seller of iron goods and hardware, tools etc.
irritancy (clause of)	clause in a legal document specifying a condition to some right such as changing one's name on marriage as a condition of ensuring succession for heirs
ischear	1. usher, official who kept order in a church or court 2. assistant teacher
iuge	judge
iugit	judged
iuris-consultours	legal counsel
jailer	jail keeper
jak of bane deer	bag of deerskin
janitor	caretaker, doorkeeper
javelor	jeweller
jocktaleg	large clasp knife
joiner	woodworker
jointure	provision for a widow, usually in her marriage contract, of an annual payment during her lifetime and giving her first claim if her husband died a debtor or bankrupt
journee	a day's battle
journeyman	qualified craftsman working for someone else
junior	younger, in the sense of heir to a title or land
jus mariti	a husband's right to his wife's moveables
jus relictae	'right of the relict' (widow), the share of the moveable goods of a marriage to which a widow was entitled on the death of her husband – one-third would go to any children as the bairns' pairt or legitim, one-third would be the dead's pairt which the deceased could bequeath by a will or 'legacie'
justi-coat	vest with sleeves
kaichpeller	tennis-court attendant
kain	1. rent paid in kind (animals, grain etc.) 2. when paid along with money, the value of the payment in kind
kamys	1. combs 2. ridged ground
keill, kill	kiln
keilman	furnaceman, kiln worker
kemmyng-stok	combing stock for wool
ken, kend, kent	know, known
ker	cart or sledge for moving transport hay
kerfull	cartload
kertar, cairter	carter, maker or driver of carts

kill	kiln, oven for drying malt etc.
king's remembrancer	Crown debt collector
king's weigher	officer appointed by the court to keep official weights and measures, and to weigh and measure dry and liquid goods
Kintyre pursuivant	member of the Lyon court (Bute pursuivant, Carrick pursuivant, Dingwall pursuivant, Ormond pursuivant, Unicorn pursuivant)
kippage	disorder
kirkmaster	paid official in charge of church buildings and responsible for the upkeep
kirk-officer	church officer, beadle, church warden
kist	chest, trunk
kithes	appears, shows
knag	cask (of wine, vinegar etc.)
knapscall	headpiece of armour
Knight-Marischall, Knight-Marischal	title granted to Sir John Keith, 3rd son of the 6th Earl Marischal in 1660 for saving the Royal Honours from capture by Oliver Cromwell, and was later held by others as part of the ceremonial office of Hereditary Lord High Constable and Knight Marischal of Scotland
knock	mallet for beating linen
knycht	knight
knychthed	knighthood
kou, coo	cow
ky and followers	cow with calves
ky, kyne	plural of kou, cows
kyrk	kirk, church
laceman, lace-weaver	cord maker
lache volt	low-vaulted room
ladie	lady, woman of high birth, wife of a nobleman
ladill	ladle, large spoon
laird, lard	holder of land directly from the king, landowner, landlord or chief
Lammas	1 August – one of the quarter, or term, days (with Candlemas, Martinmas and Whitsunday) on which contracts, leases, tacks and rents began and ended and when bills were settled
land surveyor	estimator of land area
land-waiter	customs officer, especially concerned with the landing and taxing of goods at a port
lang syne	long since, long ago
lantrone, lanthorn	lantern
lapper	person who folds and wraps linen
last-maker	maker of cobbler's lasts for shoemaking
laubeir, laubir, laubyr	labour
lauberar	labourer
lauds	midnight service of the Catholic church
lau'll	abbreviation of 'lawful'
lave	rest
law-burrows	legal security, bound over to keep the peace
lawful (daughter or son)	legitimate, born in wedlock
lawn	fine linen, used to make sleeves etc.
laxfisher, laxfischer	salmon fisherman
leat	late
leather-dresser	person who prepares leather for cutting

lecens	licence
lecturer	university teacher, instructor in a church
leet	list of candidates for election
legator	the person to whom a legacy is left
legatour	only legatee
legitim	bairn's pairt of gear, child's share of a parent's moveable property on his death – one third if there was a surviving spouse, otherwise half, but only applied after satisfaction of any other prior rights
leid	folk
leillie & treullie	legally and honestly (in later testaments the word used was 'faithfully')
leispund	unit of weight for butter, oil, wool equal to 18 pounds Scots
lenth	length
let	hindrance
letter-carrier	letter deliverer, postman
letters	writ or warrant
lettrone	lectern, reading desk
ley	lea, pasture land, unploughed land
libraire	bookseller
licentiat	licensed e.g. to practise medicine or law
lie	word used to introduce local names, or any Scots word or phrase used in a Latin document
lieutenant	army or navy officer, below captain
lieutenant colonel	army rank below colonel
lieutenant general	army rank below major-general
lieutenant governor	deputy governor e.g. of a province, jail, castle etc.
liferent	ownership for life only, as opposed to fee (full ownership) and not to be passed on – it might be a sum of money paid yearly, or the income from a piece of land, or use of the land
liferenter	person who has the liferent, the right to receive revenue from a property for life, but not to sell or dispose of it
lighterman	boatman, operator of a harbour lighter or barge
lime merchant	dealer in lime for use in fertiliser, cement, paint etc.
limner	portrait painter
linen draper	linen seller
linen lapper, linen stamper, stamp-master on linen	linen printer
lint dresser, lint heckler	flax-dresser
lint-wheel wright	maker of spinning wheels for flax spinning
liquidat	debts or other due payments fixed in advance at a definite sum, or having a monetary equivalent by decreet of court
litherlie	idle
litster, litstar, litser, lister	dyer
littet, littit	dyed
lockit buik	locked book in which the names of burgesses were recorded on appointment
locksmith	maker and repairer of locks and keys
loosing arrestment	release from arrestment for debt when security is found
lord	1. title of a noble (peer) 2. honorific title given to a senior judge or administrator
Lord Clerk Register	senior judge
Lord Lyon King-of-Arms, Lord Lyon King-at-Arms	chief officer of heraldry in Scotland

Lords of Council	king's council sitting as a court of law, before the Court of Session was instituted
lorimer	maker of metal parts for horse and ox harnesses etc.
lous	loose
loused	closed (because when a shop, for instance, was 'loused' the workers were 'loosed'
ludgeing, ludgen, ludgin, ludgins	lodging, often the town house of a landed family as in Argyll's Ludgins, Stirling
luggs	1. ears 2. handles of a jug 3. hinges
lugyng	temporary lodging
lybel	1. libel 2. indictment 3. list e.g. these lybelled, items specified in a document
lyfrent	See life-rent
lymeman, lymemaker	lime worker, lime mixer
Lyon Court heralds	senior officials of the Lyon Court – they are Albany herald, Ilay herald, Marchmont herald, Ross herald, Rothesay herald and Snadoun herald
macer, messer, messor	mace bearer, usher in court or parliament
madder	dyestuff
magister	Mr (indicating a university graduate, a Master of Arts)
magistrate	local judge
mail, maills and duties	mail is the Scots word for rent; maills and duties were the yearly rents of an estate due in money or grain
maill, meall, meill	meal
maills	rent or payment (See house-maills)
mails (males)	feu duties, rents
mains, mayns	chief or home farm of an estate
mair	1. mare 2. more
maister	master
major	army rank between captain and colonel, in charge of a battalion
major-general	army rank above lieutenant-general
make menyng	lament
malis, mailings	small farms
malthouse	brewery
maltmill-maker	maker of mills for preparing malt
maltster, maltman, malter, maltmaker	brewer, person who malts barley etc. for brewing or distilling
man of weir	fighting man, soldier, warrior
manor place	main mansion of an estate
mantua maker	bonnet maker
marable, marbole, marboll	marble
marcat, mercat	market
marchant, marchand, merchan, mechant, merchand, merchant, grocer	merchant, buyer and seller of goods
marchioness	wife of a marquis
Marchmont herald	official of Lyon Court (Albany herald, Ilay herald, Marchmont herald, Ross herald, Rothesay herald and Snadoun herald)
mareit	married
marikin-maker, marinkin-maker	worker with maroquin (Morocco) leather
mariner	sailor
mark or merk	1. silver coin worth 13s. 4d. (or two-thirds of a pound) Scots and therefore just over a shilling sterling at the time of the Union 2. unit of valuation of land
marquis, marquess	rank of nobility between earl and duke

marriage contract	contract made between the husband or promised husband and the male relatives of the wife, made either before marriage (ante-nuptial) or after (post-nuptial)
marshall, marischall, marischal	officer of state or burgh official
Martinmas, Mertinmas	11 November – one of the quarter, or term, days (with Lammas, Candlemas and Whitsunday), when contracts, leases, tacks and rents began and ended and when bills were settled
mason, masoun, master-mason	stone worker
master	teacher, senior craftsman, craft guild member
mealmaker, mailmaker, maillmaker	oatmeal seller
mealman, meilman, meilmane, mealmonger	dealer in oatmeal
mealwright	mill wright
measour	measure
measurer	official who weighs and measures goods for market, often taking a tithe in duty
mediciner, medicinar	physician, apothecary
meeting house	dissenting place of worship (not Church of Scotland)
meil, meill, meall	measure of grain weight in the Northern Isles, equal to 6 settings or 1/24 of a last
meinie	company
mell	associate with, or have dealings with
memell	fork handles
mercat	market (See marcat)
mercat cross	usually the main market square of a town, with a cross or pedestal to indicate this
mercator, mercatrix	merchant (man or woman)
mercatrix	female merchant
merinell, marinell	mariner, sailor
merk	1. Scots currency and coin, worth 13s. 4d. Scots 2. land area of that value 3. measure of weight in the Northern Isles, 1/24 lispund
merk land	fourteenth and fifteenth centuries, land valued at one mark sterling (later revalued)
messinger, messanger	messenger
met and measour	mete and measure
metster	official who measures goods or land for sale
meydvyf	midwife
mickle, meikle	small amount ('many a mickle mak's a muckle')
midshipman	senior sailor
midwife	childbirth assistant, usually an older woman
millar knaife, miln-knaif	undermiller
millar, milner, mylner	miller
milliner	hatmaker
mill-wright	mill builder
miln, milne, myl	mill
milnwright, miln-wright, mylne-wright	mill-wright, mill builder
minchak, minschok	young nanny (female) goat
minister	ordained cleric (post-Reformation)
minor	below the age of majority, child older than twelve if female or fourteen if male, but still under the age of twenty-one; 'minority' also referred to the whole period from birth until twenty-one – minors often had curators appointed to look after their affairs when young

minstrall, menstraler	minstrel, musician
mis	misadventure
misprison, mispreson, misperson)	1. slander 2. conceal a crime as in 'misprison of murder'
modir	mother
monk	member of pre-Reformation Celtic, Catholic or Episcopalian religious orders
morsing-horns	gunpowder flasks
mortcloth dues	money paid for the use of the public pall (death shroud) at a funeral
mortifyed money	money left by deceased persons for charity
moss-trooper	border marauder who regularly pillaged the English
moveable property	as opposed to heritable, every type of property not land or connected with land
moyr	mother
muck	dung, manure
muckle	large amount ('many a mickle mak's a muckle')
muir	moor
muis	bushels, measures
muked	mucked, manured
muller	moulded work such as a picture frame
multure, multour dewetie	payment in grain and/or money to a mill owner for grinding (See astriction)
multurer, multerer, moulterer, moulturer	collector of multure duty in a mill
music-seller	seller of sheet music and printed songs
musitiane, musicianer	musician
muslin singer	a person employed in singeing the nap off muslin
mutchkin	pint English measure
myle	mile
mylne	mill
myre	marsh
myster	need, emergency
nacket	1. scorer or marker at tennis, billiards etc. 2. stone used in playing shinty 3. pinch of snuff or tobacco
nackety	conceited, well-dressed
nag	horse
naigis	nags, small horses or ponies
napery, naperie, naprie	table linen, napkins
neck-verse	first verse of Psalm 51 which if read by a criminal on the scaffold entitled him to have his life spared and be exiled
need-fire	signal beacon
neuo	nephew
nobmaker	maker of hard shoe tips
nolt-driver	cattle drover
noltherd, nolthird	cattleherd
nolts' tongues	cow tongues
nonentry maills (gift of)	rents of land in the possession of the superior until the heir can take possession
northt, northin	northern
northtest	northeast, northeasterly
nortuest	northwest, northwesterly
not adeill	not at all
notar, noter, notary	notary, notary public, someone licensed to record legal transactions

notarial docket	notary's certificate at the foot of a document
notarial instrument	deed drawn up by a notary
notarial symbol	sign or seal used by a notary
novodamus	renewal of a feudal grant by charter, often with some amendments or additions (eiks)
nurseryman	worker in a plant nursery
nychtbour	neighbour
oastlair	ostler, inn-keeper
obligement	bond, obligation
odal	udal, having no fuedal superior
oeconimus	steward, manager, bursar
oil leather-dresser	preparer of leather
omissa	items which had been originally omitted from the deceased's estate
on life	still alive e.g. only bairn on life, only surviving child
on-delyverit	undelivered
onleful	unlawful
ordinans, ordinance	order
ordinar, cordiner	cordwainer, shoemaker
Ormond pursuivant	member of the Lyon court (Bute pursuivant, Carrick pursuivant, Dingwall pursuivant, Kintyre pursuivant, Ormond pursuivant, Unicorn pursuivant)
oslair	ostler, innkeeper
ost	host
oukis	weeks
oure	over
our-gilt	overgilt, gilded over, gilt-edged
outbrecks	barren land not worth cultivating
outfeild	outlying and less fertile part of a farm, where the ground was hardly or never cultivated (before enclosure and crop rotation in the eighteenth century)
outred	finish off, complete
outreddar	person who fits out a ship ready for a voyage or unloads it of cargo in port
outsight plenishing	moveable property kept or lying out of doors – livestock and implements like ploughs, but not corn or hay
overman, oversman, oursman	overseer
ower	over
oxengate of land	13 acres
oxgang	measure of land generally about 13 acres
oy, oye	grandson, granddaughter, sometimes niece, nephew or other descendant
packman	pedlar, chapman, travelling merchant
pairt	part, portion, share of an estate
pairts and pertinents	what a piece of land was always granted with, everything connected with the land whether specified or not
palfurniour, palfurner	groom, person with the care of horses
pand, pane	draperies for a bed e.g. counterpane
panter	painter
pantoun-heilmaker	maker of heels for soft shoes, slippers etc.
paper stainer	paper colourer
parapris	paraphrase
parchment maker	preparer of skins for parchment
paroch, parochin	parish

parochiner, parochinar	parishioner
parson, person, farson	parish clergyman (pre-Reformation)
pasment	passement, decorative border on cloth or lace
pasment-weifar	weaver of passement, decorative border on cloth or lace
passenger	1. traveller 2. ferryman
paticer, pothisar	pastry-cook
pavier	street paver
pease	peas
peces	1. pieces, title deeds 2. any article considered alone
pedagog	teacher
pedall, peddel, beddal	beadle, a church or university officer
pekis	pecks (measure)
pendicle	appurtenance, often a small portion of land added to a larger
pendicler	tenant of a pendicle, smallholder
penny land	unit of land value for taxation purposes
penny-pie-baker	maker and street seller of small pies
pensioner	person in receipt of a pension
peper	paper
periwig, peir-weik, pirivick, peruke	gentleman's wig
periwig-maker, peir-weik maker, pirivick-maker, peruke-maker	gentleman's wig maker
pertaining in heritage	belonging to someone as heir
peste, pestelens	pestilence, plague
petar	petard, explosive charge in a box, firework
petitioner	someone who brings an action in court
pewterer, pewder-man, pewderer, pewdirer, peutherer, peuterer, peutrar, pewtherer, putherer	worker in pewter
piece, the piece	each
pieman	pie street-seller
pier-master	harbour-master
pikman	miner who uses a pick
pilgit	argument, fight, quarrel
pilot	boatman who guides vessels into or out of harbour
pinut	pint
pipemaker	maker of water or drainage pipes
piper, pyper	bagpipe player
pissanis	pisane, armour for the chest and neck (from Pisa)
pistolat	1. small pistol 2. coin (pistole)
plag	plague
plain	open, flat country or field of battle
plantation of kirks	farmland, orchards etc. providing goods and revenue for one or more parish churches (See glebe)
planter	plantation worker (tobacco, sugar or tea in the West Indies)
plenishing insight	furniture in a house
plenishing outsight	farm or estate stock, implements etc.
plenishings	furniture and other moveable goods
plet slevis	pleated sleeves
pleugh	plough

pley	plea, complaint in law
ploughgate	measure of land, 8 oxgangs or about 100 acres
ploughwright	plough maker
pm'es, promes	promise, oath
pntlie	abbreviation of presently
pnts	abbreviation of presents (meaning documents and evidence)
pocing iron	poker
pocket-book	wallet
pok	pocket
policy, policies	lands, gardens and pleasure-grounds surrounding a mansion or farmhouse
pookman	porter
port	martial music played on the bagpipes
porter	1. carrier, servant, caddie 2. stout ale
porter dealer	buyer and seller of porter stout (beer)
portion natural	the share a child has in the estate of an intestate father
portioner, portiner	owner of a small piece or share of land
portioners	heirs, those who inherit land jointly (usually daughters)
post, toun post	letter deliverer
pot iron	iron pot stand
potter	maker of clay or earthenware pots, jugs etc.
poultrie-man, pultriman	poultryman, person who takes care of hens, ducks, geese and other domestic birds and fowls
poynding, poinding	(pronounced pinding) seizing (attaching) lands or goods to discharge a debt
pranter	printer
preacher	religious exhorter
prebend	1. churchman's stipend 2. land, tithe or other source of a stipend
prebendary, prebenter	canon or member of the chapter of a cathedral or collegiate church who holds a stipend (pre-Reformation or Episcopal)
precentor, precenter, presenter	leader of singing in church
preceptor, praeceptor	teacher, instructor
prentice	apprentice
prentice-master	qualified craftsman looking after an apprentice
presbytery, presbetrie	court of the ministers and elders of a district overseeing several parishes
presenter of signatures	official in the Court of Exchequer
presents	things, usually documents, presented to make a case, as in 'by these presents'
priest	ordained churchman (pre-Reformation, Catholic or Episcopalian)
primare, primer	principal of college or university
primme	first, main, prime
principal	academic in charge of school, college or university
prinll	abbreviation of principal
print cutter	maker of printing blocks
prior	head of a priory for men
prioress	head of a priory for women
priory	religious house, monastery, nunnery
prisar	apprisor, appraiser, one who apprises and puts goods etc. up for sale to pay a creditor
prisit	apprised
privateer	private fighting ship with a commission from the government
probationer	Church of Scotland minister not yet ordained

proces	legal proceedings
procreat	begotten
procurator	1. lawyer in lower courts 2. person authorised by another to manage his affairs in the context of testaments, a solicitor, law agent or counsel
procurator fiscal	originally a solicitor with responsibility for the 'fiscal' or treasury; now the main law officer in a burgh or sheriffdom, public prosecutor in criminal cases and also coroner
professor	senior academic in a college or university
proport	purport, intend, convey
propriis manibus	by his (or her) own hand
propyn	gift or present
prosecution of signatures	following or obtaining a signature (See signature)
protocol	first copy of an instrument, written by a notary in a protocol book
protomedicus	main doctor
prove	attempt
provost	chairman and chief magistrate of a town or burgh council, equivalent to the (English) mayor
prydit, provydit	provided
puncheons	tunnel props in mining
pund	pound Scots, worth one-fifth of an English pound sterling from 1560 and one-twelfth (1s. 8d.) from 1603
pundis	pounds (monetary)
pundler	weighing machine using weights and a lever
punzoun	a small company
pupil	1. minor (under fourteen if male, twelve if female) whose affairs were managed by a tutor 2. schoolchild
pupilarity	being a pupil (a minor under fourteen years old if male, twelve if female)
purring iron	poker
purs	purse
purser	administrative officer and money keeper on a ship
pursue, persew	prosecute a lawsuit
pursuer	plaintiff, complainer in a court case
pursuivant	member of the Lyon court (Bute pursuivant, Carrick pursuivant, Dingwall pursuivant, Kintyre pursuivant, Ormond pursuivant, Unicorn pursuivant)
pynour	labourer, porter, caddie
q	abbreviation for con e.g. Qsents, consents
qrof	whereof
quaiffmaker, queffmaker	cap or soft hat maker
quair	quire, book
quarrier, quariour, quarriour, querrior	quarry worker
quarter day	Candlemas, Lammas, Martinmas and Whitsunday, the days on which contracts, leases, tacks and rents began and ended and when bills were settled
quartermaster	person in charge of supplies in the army, a guild etc.
quey, quoy, coy	heifer
quh	where this is found in words it can be read as 'wh' e.g. Cuneoquhy = Kennoway, quhar = where
quha	who
quhair, quhar	where
quhairbe	whereby

quhairin, quherin	wherein
quhais	whose
quham	whom
quhar	where
quharfor	wherefore
quhatsomevir	whatever, whatsoever
quheill, quhyle	while
quheit	white
quhen	when
quhiddir	whether
quhil	while (in the sense of 'until')
quhilk, whilk	which
quhome	whom
quhou	how
quhoubeit	howbeit, howsoever
quhy	why
quick	alive
quod	quoth, said
quondam	former or deceased
quot	twentieth part of the moveable estate of a deceased person, originally due to the local bishop but paid to the commissaries after the Reformation
quoy, quoyland	1. enclosure 2. piece of land brought into cultivation from outside a hill dyke
quyt of entry	quit of entry, having paid fees due to a superior on inheriting lands
rabut	repulse, rebate
racken	reckon
raising letters	taking out legal summons
ranking, process of	system for arranging creditors in order of precedence for payment
rase	rash, uncouth
ratsche	lock (powder tray) of a gun
raxes	chain on which a roasting spit is turned over a fire
reader, reider	1. reader in church 2. member of a university ranked between senior lecturer and professor
rear admiral	admiral's deputy in charge of a fleet
receiver general	senior customs official
record	repute, account
rector	1. head schoolmaster 2. senior clergyman in charge of a college, religious house or congregation (Catholic) and in receipt of tithes (Episcopal) 3. member of a university court elected by the students
reddendo	literally, the return – what the feu superior could expect from the vassal in exchange for the grant of land and protection, in the form of military service, provision of men and equipment, payment of rent in cash or kind (feu duty) etc. Changes in the law of feudal tenure after the 1745 Jacobite rebellion, and the growth of central government throughout the nineteenth century, diminished the reciprocal element in the feudal relationship, as the state provided protection and the reddendo was restricted to the annual payment of feu duty
rede	counsel, advice
reedmaker, reidmaker, redemaker	1. maker of reeds for musical instruments 2. arrow maker
reft	bereft
refut	defence, stronghold

regality	territorial jurisdiction granted by the Crown, whereupon the holder is styled Lord of the Regality with the power to hold courts, impose sentences etc. (See barony, sheriffdom)
regent	1. ruler or administrator of a country during the minority, or incapacity of the sovereign 2. senior teacher or administrator in certain universities 3. member of the governing body of certain schools, colleges and universities
regent	master or one of the supervising body of a school or college
registrar, register	official who keeps registers of births, marriages, deaths, wills and other documents
relict	widow or widower
remanent	remaining
renunciation	1. renouncing a right or a title to property, redeeming a debt etc. 2. deed by which this is enacted
reponit, reponed	replaced
residenter, resinder, resider	resident, inhabitant
resignation	return of a feu by a vassal to the superior, either permanently, or *in favorem*, where the intention was that the superior should make a new grant, as when land was sold
ressaver	receiver
resting	remaining due, owing
rests	arrears
retour	extract from the Chancery of the service of an heir to his progenitor in which the heir is proven to succeed or inherit
retour of inquest	report of a jury called to decide if an heir is entitled to inherit
reustrie, revestry	vestry of a church
rex dollar	German silver coin valued from 2*s*. 6*d*. to 4*s*. 6*d*. at different times
riddle	large seive for stones etc.
rig and rendell	See runrig
risp	creak
rive	rip, rend, tear
road contractor	person who oversees road building
rondle, roundall, rowndall	basically anything round, such as a shield, a table a tower, a song (rondel, rondellay)
room	space
room-setter	renter-out of rooms
Ross herald	official of Lyon Court (Albany herald, Ilay herald, Marchmont herald, Rothesay herald and Snadoun herald)
Rothesay herald	official of Lyon Court (Albany herald, Ilay herald, Marchmont herald, Ross herald and Snadoun herald)
round sheets	sheets around a mattress
rounder bed plaids	woollen bedcovers
roup	sale by auction, governed by conditions called 'articles of 'roup'
rout	company
runrig, rig and rendell	system of cultivation in which separate strips of a field were cultivated by different people
rys	twigs, small branches
sacrist	head porter and mace bearer (especially at Aberdeen University)
saddle tree, sadle-trie	wooden frame of a saddle
saddler, sadler	maker and seller of saddles
sadill of aik	seat of oak
saidis	aforesaid

saidle	1. saddle 2. wooden seat
saifand	saving, excepting
salbe	shall be
salmond	salmon
salt backet	salt tub
salt officer, salt grieve	overseer of saltworks or salt pans
salter	salt manufacturer or merchant
saltfat, saltfoot	pewter salt-cellar
saltpans	pits for boiling salt from seawater
salt-watchman	person who guards saltpans
samekle	so much
samen	same
sang	song
sasine	act giving legal possession of property and the deed recording this
sasine register	list of property sasines
sauld	sold
sawer, sawar, sawyer	sawyer, timber-cutter
say-master	person in charge of assay (at the mint)
scaur	steep embankment
schade	shadow
scheigrinder	scissor-sharpener
scheip	sheep
scheipcottis	sheep-cotes
scheiphirdis	shepherds
scheirsmith	scissors maker
scheise	cheese
schepherd, schiphird	shepherd
scho	she
schryne, scrine	shrine, desk, screen
sclaitter	slater
scribe	clerk, secretary, writer
scruittore	escritoire, writing-table
scule	school
scutifer	shield-bearer
se'all	abbreviation of severall (several)
seaman	sailor
seamstress, semstress	woman who sews
seedman, seedsman	seed merchant
selch	seal (the marine mammal)
selch's skin	sealskin
selffis	selves
senator of the College of Justice	judge of the Court of Session
senior	elder of two (brothers, heirs etc.)
sensyne	since that time
septemtrional, septentrional	northern (usually on maps, e.g. *Terres Arctiques Septemtrional et Boreales*)
sepulture	grave, burial place
sequel	See astriction
sergeant, serjeant	1. senior non-commissioned officer 2. town or court law officer

servant bailie, servitour, servitor, servitrix	domestic servant
servator, servitor	1. agent, custodian, secretary, apprentice 2. napkin, serviette
session-clerk	senior elder in a Kirk (post-Reformation)
sett	let to
setting	unit of weight for grain = 24 marks or 1/6 meil, equivalent to 1 leispund
sevine, sewln, seuyn	seven
sewster	seamstress, needlewoman
sex	six
sext	sixth
sexten	sixteen
seye	sea
shadow half	north side of land
shag lyning	cloth with rough nap
shambo	chamois leather
shambo-dresser	chamois leather-dresser
sheds of land	portions or fields of land
sheeling, shieling	shepherd's hut
sheerman	scissor-maker
sheirs, sheers, shears	scissors
sheriff	judge in a local court
sheriff clerk	clerk to the sheriff court and keeper of the court records
sheriff depute	deputy sheriff appointed by the Crown to a county or district
sheriff in that part	someone appointed by the Crown to take the place of a sheriff for a particular purpose
sheriff officer	bailiff, law officer represent in and carrying out order of a sheriff
sheriff-clerk	official in a Sheriff Court
sheriffdom	district under jurisdiction of sheriff, county (See barony, regality)
sheriff-substitute	assistant (usually part-time) sheriff
shilling-a-week man	person who sells goods on credit and collects the payments weekly
shipmaster	captain of a merchant ship
ship's mate	second in command on board ship
shod, shode, shot	separate from others
shop	originally a workshop, but later a place for selling goods
shore-man	harbour worker
shore-master	harbour master
shuttles	small internal drawers in a cabinet
sicklike, siclyk, sicklyk	suchlike, like, likewise, in the same manner
sieve wright	maker of sieves and riddles
signalman	1. operator of railway or road signals 2. signaller, person who sends and receives signals (military)
signature	warrant subscribed by the king to grant a charter
silkman	silk dealer
siller	money, silver
sillis, syllis	sills, strong horizontal timbers
skaith	hurt, damage, injury
skaithless	undamaged, uninjured
skat	various types of land tax, of Viking origin e.g. salt skat, malt skat, butter skat
skimmer	1. flat, perforated spoon for skimming fat 2. person who skims milk etc.

skinner, skyner	preparer and seller of animal skins
skipper	captain of a boat or ship
slater, slatter, sclater, sklaiter	roof slate preparer and fitter
sledder	driver of a sled or sledge
sleist, sluther	vagabond, lazy individual
sloop	single-masted sailing vessel rigged fore and aft
sloppis	bands
smith, smyth, smythe	metal worker, especially of iron
Snadoun herald, Snowdoun herald	official of the Lyon Court (Albany herald, Ilay herald, Marchmont herald, Ross herald and Rothesay herald)
soam	rope or chain pulling a plough
soap boiler	soap maker
solicitor	lawyer who does not appear in court
sommance	summons
sone, soune	1. son 2. the sun
soney	sunny
sonyeit	hesitate, delay
soumes	sums
southt	south
southyn	southern
special service	serving as heir to a special subject (property etc.)
speet, speit	1. roasting spit 2. spite
spinster	unmarried woman
spirit dealer	buyer and seller of alcohol, vinegar etc.
spiritualities	teinds due to the Church
spleuchis	splints
spoue	spouse, husband or wife
spounge	sponge
spouse	husband or wife
springzie rapper	springy rapier
spuilzie	robbery, stealing moveable goods or 'spoils' (See broken men)
spuilzied	despoiled, robbed, stolen
square wright	carpenter, joiner, cabinet maker, furniture maker
St Barnabright	St Barnaby's day, 11 June, usually bright and sunny
stabler, stabular	owner or operator of stables for horses
staff and baton	symbols used when a tenant resigns lands to the superior
staig	young horse
staithless, scaithless	skaithless, undamaged, uninjured
stamper	stamping machine operator
stamp-master	quality controller, especially of linen
stand aw of	be greatly afraid of
staner	dye maker
stapis, stoups	large pitchers or jugs
stark	strong
stationer	dealer in paper, pencils, ink, printer material etc.
statuary	1. sculptor, carver 2. sculpture
stays	corsets
stead	place

steall	stale
steddyngis, stedings	farmhouse and outbuildings
stent	tax
stentar	tax collector
steward	1. manager of an estate 2. assistant to king or noble 3. officer on a ship responsible for food etc.
steward-clerk	clerk to a steward
stewart-depute	assistant to the steward of an estate
stifing	starch
stirk	weaned heifer (two or three years old)
stot, stottikin	bullock
stoup	water pail
stour	conflict
stouthrief	robbery from a dwelling house (See broken men)
stribs, stirroubis	stirrups
stuiver	Dutch coin
subdean	assistant to a dean in a guild, university etc.
submission	See decreet arbitral
subtenant	person who sub-rents property from a tenant
sucken	See astriction
suffragant	assistant to a clergyman
sugar boiler	sugar refiner, one who prepares sugar for processing
suit	pursuit
summa	Latin for all, sum or total, usually found at the end of an inventory totalling the value of the deceased's estate
sunny half	south-facing part of land
superior	ultimate owner, person who made a grant of land in return for the payment of an annual payment (feu) or the performance of specified services (or both), the person receiving the lands becoming the superior's vassal
supervisor	overseer
surgeon, chirurgeon, chirurgean,	one who carries out medical operations, amputations, bleeding etc.
surgeon-major, surgeon-general	military surgeon ranks
surrender (decreet of)	ordering tithes or teinds to be surrendered to the Crown
surrogate	1. to appoint as a substitute 2. proxy or substitute in connection with a right or claim
surveyor	estimator of quantities and values of land, buildings and goods for reasons of valuation, construction or revenue
suspension (letters of)	order charging that bills or decrees be suspended until pleas are heard
swar	snare
swippit	supped
swith	instantly, now, without delay
swmes	sums
sword-slipper	sword sharpener and mender
swyr	sword
syd	side
sylebob	syllabub, drink made of milk mixed with spirits or cider, spiced, sweetened and served hot
symblair, somler	butler, sommelier
syne	since

tack	lease by formal written contract between landlord and tenant, renewable every nineteen years in Scotland, every three in Shetland
tack of lands	customs, lease
tacksman	lease-holder, tenant of land who sub-lets or rents (tacks)
tailor, talor, tallor, tailzeour, tailor burges	tailor of men's clothes
tailzie	older name for an entail, a deed which altered the legal succession to lands
tailzier	entailer, someone in receipt of a deed which altered the legal succession to lands
take lugyng	to camp, lodge in a temporary place
tambour	hoop used to hold embroidery fabric
tambourer	embroiderer
tanner	hide or leather curer
tapestrier	tapestry weaver
tapster	barman, server of beer
tarn	mountain lake
tas, tassie	cup
tasker	pieceworker
tavernor	innkeeper, ostler
taxt-ward	casualty of a superior for lands in non-entry (See casualty)
tayngis	tongs
teick, tick	ticking of a bed, mattress, pillow etc.
teind sheaves	tithe of grain
teinds, teindsheaves	tenth part of the annual produce of land, due to the Church
teller	bank clerk, money counter
temple lands	lands which once belonged to the Knights Templar, invited into Scotland by Robert Bruce when both were excommunicated by the Pope
tenant	renter, inhabiter of rented property, land etc.
tenement	literally, a holding, but meaning a house, flat or piece of land
tenementer	holder of a tenement
tennent	tenant
terce	the third share of heritable (immovable) property due to the relict (widow) if no other provision has been made for her; the other two shares being for the children, if any, and the rest for the deceased to bequeath as he wished
terce-pryour	prior, head of a priory
term	date when interest or rent is due
testament	grant of administration of an estate by the authorities – not the same as a will (in Scotland)
testament dative	a grant of administration by a court of a will, as opposed to probate
testamentar	done or appointed by the testator (as opposed to dative, ordered by a court) and containing a will (See dative)
thatcher, theicker, theikar, theiker	thatcher, worker with reeds or straw for roofing
theats	horse traces on plough, cart, carriage etc.
thesaurer	treasurer
thir	these
thirl	bind in service (See astriction, multure, thirlage)
thirlage	obligation on owner or tenants of land to grind their grain at a particular mill (See multure)
thirled	bound in service, obligated (See astriction, multure, thirlage)
thomie	thumb
thrid	third

throng of	full of, crowded with
throuster	trusser, hay-baler
throw	through
thwarter	athwart, crossing
tide surveyor	senior customs officer who checks cargo being loaded onto ships
tidesman, extraordinary tidesman, tide officer	tide-waiter, customs officer who checks goods and duties payable on board ships
tide-waiter, tidewater, tidewaiter, tidesman	customs officer who checks goods and duties payable on board ships
tidy or tydie ky	pregnant or lactating cow
timber merchant	dealer in rough (uncut) wood
timberman, timmerman	tree-feller and preparer of rough wood
tinplate worker	maker of tinplate goods
tinsmith	worker with tin
titellis	titles
tobacco spinner	preparer of tobacco for sale
tobacconist	seller of tobacco, pipes, matches and other smoking products
tocher	dowry brought by a wife to her husband at their marriage
tocher guid	goods or money making up the dowry
todd	fox
toft	land attached to a house (See messuage)
tolbooth	building in a burgh which served as a toll collection office, courtroom and prison
tolerance	deed granting a privilege
toll-gatherer	toll-gate guard and duty collector
toun post	town letter deliverer, postman, messenger
toun, toune	town
town	steading plus houses of cotters
town clerk	legal officer and secretary in town council
town house	administrative offices of civic authorities
town officer, toun officer	town law officer, common serjand
town-major	town's law and ceremonial officer
trader	buyer and seller of goods
trafficker	trader, buyer and seller of goods
translation	document transferring a bond from one holder to another
transumpt	official copy of a deed
traveller, travellour, traveler, chapman	travelling salesman or dealer, door-to-door or dealing with businesses
treasurer	senior financial manager in a burgh, department, organisation etc.
treasurer-clerk	clerk in the office of treasurer or treasury
tred and handling	trade and business
tressure	narrow border around a coin, token or shield
trowblance	molestation
trumpeter	trumpet player (usually military)
trumpmaker	maker of trumpets and other brass instruments
trunkmaker	maker of travelling trunks, chests etc.
tuffell cloath, taffill cloth	tablecloth
turner, turnour	wood turner
turssyt	carry, truss
tutelage	state of being under a tutor, under the age of majority

tutor	1. legal representative, guardian or adminstrator of a pupil (minor) 2. private teacher
tutory	appointment of a tutor
twidlen	twill cloth
tymous	betimes, timeous, timely
tyne and wine	lose and win
tyne, tynt	lose, lost
udal, uthell, odal	having no fuedal superior e.g. odal proprietor, udal tenure (on ancestral property)
umquhile, umqle	deceased, erstwhile, late (as in dead)
under-miller	assistant worker in a mill
uneath	scarcely, hardly
Unicorn pursuivant	member of the Lyon court (Bute pursuivant, Carrick pursuivant, Dingwall pursuivant, Kintyre pursuivant, Ormond pursuivant, Unicorn pursuivant)
unlaws	fines
upholsterer	cloth or leather furniture finisher
usher, ischear	1. court or church official who kept order 2. assistant teacher
usquebaugh, usquebea, uisge beatha	water of life, whisky
usufructuar, usufructuary	trustee who enjoys the produce or income from property he holds in trust for somebody else, e.g. an abbot
utencilis & domiceillis	household goods
uterine	children of the same mother
uthairis	others
vaik (of a tack)	vacancy of a tenancy
valent	upheld, valorised
vassal	person to whom land is conveyed by a superior for the payment of a yearly rent or feu duty, or the performance of some regular service such as military aid
vennel	narrow street or passage
verdour bed	bed with landscape or sylvan tapestry design
vicar, viccar	parish clergyman (pre-Reformation, Episcopal)
vicar-pensioner	ordained clergyman who received a living, house, land and/or salary from the income of a parish or abbey
victual dealer, victualler	grocer
victual, victuelis	1. grain 2. food of any kind 3. goods in kind
vill	village, buildings round a castle
vintner, vinther, vintiner, wintner	wine merchant, innkeeper
violer, vialer	fiddler, violin player, viol player
viscount	noble title below earl or count but above baronet and knight
viscountess	wife of a viscount, the rank below earl or count
visitor	inspector of a university, a business etc.
volt	1. vault 2. channel in which a mill stone grinds
vphaldyn	upheld
vrak (wreck) of salmon	salmon lying ashore
wad	1. dye 2. stuffing
wadset	deed giving the rent of a debtor's lands etc. to a creditor in payment of the debt
wadsetter	creditor, holder of a wadset (property mortgage)
wadwife	female wad maker (wad = dye or stuffing)
wage	reward, pledge, wage
waggoner	driver of heavy goods waggons
wagon-maker	maker of heavy goods waggons

waillyt	chosen, chose
wair and bestow	spend
waiter	watchman or guard
waled men	chosen men
walkaris craft	fuller's trade or guild (See fuller, walker)
walker, waker, waulker	cloth fuller, who cleaned and thickened cloth, often by walking on it in water
wanes	dwellings
ward lands	lands held in ward
ward superior	person entitled to take rent from the lands of a deceased vassal while the heir is not infeft or is a minor and thus cannot give military service
ward vassal	wardater, person holding lands in ward (i.e. in exchange for military service)
ward, waird	feudal land tenure rights in exchange for military service by a tenant
wardater	ward-vassal, person receiving lands held in ward from the ward superior
warden	person in charge of a hospital, almshouse, poorhouse etc.
ward-holding	tenure of lands by ward rights (i.e. in exchange for military service)
warnstore	magazine, store for provisions
warrand	warrant
warrandice	assurance or guarantee, usually in the form of a 'clause of warrandice' in a deed, against any wrong arising from a defect in a title or otherwise, in which case an alternative payment would be made
warrandice land	lands conveyed provisionally as a guarantee in case a purchaser should be evicted from the lands bought
warrison	order to attack, blown on horns
waryt	cursed, spent
wast	west
watchmaker	maker and repairer of clocks and watches
watchman	night guard
waterman	person who works near a river or harbour and possibly a boatman
waverand	having doubtful title
wax chandler	wax seller, candle maker
wax maker	preparer of wax for candles etc.
weapon-schaw	massed soldiery of a clan or county
webster, wab ster, wobstar, wobster, weivar, weifar, weiffar	loom weaver
wecht	weight
wed	mortgage
weigher	weigher of goods before market
weighhouseman	operator of a weigh house for weighing goods before market
wellar	well sinker, well builder, well borer
wenschoat, wainscoat	wainscot, oak furniture
werrament	really, verily
wesy	go to see, look at closely
weyhouse	building where standard weights and measures were held
weying	weighing
wharffinger	owner or operator of a wharf
wheelwright	maker, repairer and fitter of cart and coach wheels
whinger	large knife
white fisher	catcher of white fish e.g. cod, haddock
white-iron	cast iron containing a small amount of graphite

white-ironman	seller of white iron (cast iron) goods
white-ironsmith	maker of goods from white iron (cast iron)
Whitsunday	15 May; one of the term, or quarter, days (with Lammas, Martinmas and Candlemas) when contracts, leases, tacks and rents began and ended and when bills were settled
whoip	whip
wight	strong
will	express wishes of someone as to the disposal of their property when they die, but not the same as a testament (See testament)
win	dry (peats)
wine cooper	wine-barrel maker
with	in ownership or possession of
wmbeset	surrounded
woolcomber	preparer of wool yarn
wool-comber	one who prepares woollen yarn for use
woolfyner	woolcomber, preparer of wool yarn
woollen-draper	woollen cloth seller
wool-stapler	person who weighs wool for selling at market
worset	worsted, woollen cloth
worset-man	worsted dealer
worthis	needs
wowman	woolman, wool dealer
wraith	ghost
wrangis	wrongs, injuries, harm
wright, wricht, wrigth	craftsman
writ	legal document or writing
writer	1. clerk or scribe 2. attorney or notary (as in 'Writers to the Signet')
Writer to the Signet	highest order of writers (essentially solicitors) with the authority to prepare writs for the royal signet
writing master	1. teacher of writing 2. writer of documents for others
wroken	avenged
wuip	whip
wynd	narrow street or passage
wys	wise, advice
wyssie, wissie	inspect
yarn boiler	person who prepares yarn
yarn merchant	buyer and seller of thread
yeartak	one year's lease
yerk	twitch, as shoemakers and leather workers do in fixing stitches
yoak	yoke
younger	title given to the heir apparent of someone with a geographical designation as part of the surname or a Scottish chief, such as George Durie, Younger of Durie to distinguish him from his father, George Durie of Durie
z	the letter y was often written like a z in Scots documents – thus, the name Menzies is actually pronounced 'Mingiss'; z-words make sense when pronounced with a y (as they were)
zaird, zeard	yard
zeirs	years
zit	yet
zoungair	younger

LATIN FOR GENEALOGY AND HISTORY

Latin's a dead language, as dead as dead can be.
It killed the ancient Romans, and now it's killing me
Schoolboy rhyme

Latin terms often crop up in genealogical research, particularly in church records, legal documents and on inscriptions. Those of us who battled with Latin at school may be able to dredge up enough to make sense of documents, although it should be realised that the Roman Latin of Julius Caesar we learned at school was almost 2,000 years adrift from the late medieval Latin of church and legal documents; so it shouldn't come as a surprise that there are differences. These word lists are intended to help interpret Latin writings.

Cases and gender

Remember that Latin is 'inflected' (makes a distinction between gender and cases of nouns and adjectives). So for instance, because mensa (table) is feminine and filius (son) is masculine, one table is una mensa and one son unus filius. Cases also matter. In English phrases like 'year of birth' and 'in the year of our lord', the words 'year' and 'lord' are the same regardless of case. But in Latin, 'year' is *annus* but 'in the year' is *anno* as in *anno domini*. And where, say, land is given 'to Thomas of Durie', this would be given in Latin as *ad Thomam Durii*.

Common words and phrases

Bear in mind that:

- there is no w or y in Latin
- a u was written as a v and v usually pronounced as w, except before a consonant. Therefore '*vxor*', for instance, is '*uxor*' (wife) and '*vita*' (life) and is pronounced 'weeta'.
- other spelling variants you may encounter include:
  - i and j are used interchangeably (*eiusdem* or *ejusdem*)
  - e may be used for ae (æ) (*seculum* for *saeculum*)
  - e may be used for oe (œ) (*celebs* for *coelebs*)
  - c may be used for qu (*condam* for *quondam*)

Common abbreviations are given in brackets – e.g. *ibidem* (ib, ibid) – as are genitives – index (*indicis*).
Phrases commonly encountered in documents are also listed by first word –*ex hac mortali ad immortalem vitam* (from this mortality to immortal life).
Some male and female forms are given – *neosponsus, neosponsa* (newlywed).
Numbers are largely not included.

Roman numerals

Quite honestly, how the Romans ever managed to do sums with their daft littoral numerals (and without a zero) is a mystery. But they are commonly found in genealogy. The letters can be written in capitals (XIV) or lower-case (xiv).

The basic numbers are:	These can be combined:
I = 1	VII = 5+2 = 7
V = 5	IX = 1 before 10 = 10 − 1 = 9
X = 10	XL = 50 − 10 = 40
L = 50	LXX = 50 + 10 + 10 = 70
C = 100	MDCCII = 100 + 500 + 200 + 2 = 1702
D = 500	MCMLXXIV = 1,000 + (1,000 − 100) + 50 + (10 + 10) + (5 − 1) = 1974
M = 1,000	MMIII = 2003

D is sometimes represented by the symbol CI, and M by the symbol CIC.

COMMON ROMAN NUMERALS

1 = I	10 = X	20 = XX	100 = C	1,000 = M
2 = II	11 = XI	21 = XXI	101 = CI	1,400 = MCD
3 = III	14 = XIV	30 = XXX	110 = CX	1,600 = MDC
4 = IV	15 = XV	40 = XL	150 = CL	1,700 = MDCC
5 = V	16 = XVI	41 = XLI	160 = CLX	1,800 = MDCCC
6 = VI	19 = XIX	50 = L	200 = CC	1,900 = MCM
7 = VII		60 = LX	400 = CD	2,000 = MM
8 = VIII		70 = LXX	500 = D	2,003 = MMIII
9 = IX		80 = LXXX	600 = DC	
		90 = XC	900 = CM	

Strangely, 1999 was often given as MDCCCCLXXXIX instead of MIM. And note that 4 is IV, not IIII (except on clocks).

Latin Numbers

Numbers can be cardinal (one, two, three . . .) or ordinal (first, second etc.). These can come in a variety of forms. For instance, church records often use the ordinal form ending with an 'o' (*secundo* for second, *vicessimo* for the twentieth). And they take gender (as with masculine 'unus', feminine 'una', neuter 'unum'). Sometimes all forms are the same (e.g. sex, octo). And there are some outright stupidities – 'seventeen' is quite sensibly *septendecim* ('seven-ten'), but eighteen is *duodeviginti* ('two-less-than-twenty'). As for twenty-eighth – well, as the table shows, they just couldn't decide.

Cardinal		Ordinal			
1	unus, una, unum	1st		primus, prima, primum	primo
2	duo, duae, duo	2nd		secundus/a/um	secundo
3	tres, tria	3rd		tertius/a/um	tertio
4	quattuor	4th		quatrus or quartus/a/um	quarto
5	quinque	5th		quintus/a/um	quinto
6	sex	6th		sextus/a/um	sexto
7	septem	7th		septimus/a/um	septimo
8	octo	8th		octavus/a/um	octavo

9	novem	9th	nonus/a/um	nono
10	decem	10th	decimus/a/um	decimo
11	undecim	11th	undecimus/a/um	unidecimo
12	dudecim	12th	duodecimus/a/um	duodecimo
13	tredecim	13th	tertius/a/um decimus/a/um	tertio decimo
14	quattordecim or quattuordecim	14th	quartus/a/um decimus/a/um	quarto decimo
15	qundecim	15th	quntius/a/um decimus/a/um	quinto decimo
16	sedecim	16th	sextus/a/um decimus/a/um	sexto decimo
17	septendecim	17th	septimus/a/um decimus/a/um	septimo decimo
18	duodeviginti	18th	duodevicesmus/a/um	duodevicesimo
19	undeviginti	19th	undeviceimus/a/um	unodevicesimo
20	viginti	20th	vicesimus/a/um or vigesimus/a/um	vicesimo
21	viginti unus/a/um	21st	vicesimus/a/um primus/a/um	vicesimo primo
22	viginti duo/duae	22nd	vicesimus/a/um secundus/a/um	vicesimo secundo
23	viginti tre	23rd	vicesimus/a/um tertius/a/um	vicesimo tertio
24	viginti quattuor	24th	vicesimus/a/um quatrus/a/um	vicesimo quarto
25	viginti quinque	25th	vicesimus/a/um quintus/a/um	vicesimo quinto
26	viginti sex	26th	vicesimus/a/um sextus/a/um	vicesmo sexto
27	viginti septem	27th	vicesimus/a/um septimus/a/um	vicesmo septimo
28	viginti octo	28th	vicesimus/a/um octavus/a/um or duodetricesimus/a/um	dueodetriceimo
29	viginti novem	29th	vicesimus/a/um nonus/a/um or undeteri-cemimus/a/um	undetericesimo
30	trigenta	30th	tricesimus/a/um	tricesimo
31	triginta unus/a/um or unus/a/um et triginta	31st	triceimus/a/um primus/a/um or unus/a/um et tricesimus/a/um	tricesimo primo
40	quadraginta	40th	quadragesimus/a/um	
50	quinquaginta	50th	quinquagerimus/a/um	
100	centum	100th	centesimus	
1,000	mille	1,000th	millesimus	

DATES AND TIME

Days		Months	
English	**Latin**	**English**	**Latin**
Sunday	dominica, dies dominuca, dominicus, dies Solis, feria prima	January	Januarius, Januarij
Monday	feria seconda, dies Lunae, lune	February	Februarius, Februarij
Tuesday	feria tertia, dies Martis, martis	March	Martius, Marcij
Wednesday	feria quarta, dies Mercurii, mercurii, mercurinus, mercoris	April	Aprilis
Thursday	feria qunta, dies Jovis, jovis	May	Maius, Maij
Friday	feria sexta, dies Verenis, verneris	June	Junius, Junij
Saturday	feria septima, sabbatum, dies sabbatinus, dies Satumi, sabbati	July	Julius, Julij
		August	Augustus, Augustij
		September	Septembris, 7ber, VIIber
		October	Octobris, 8ber, VIIIber
		November	Nouembris, 9ber, IXber
		December	Decembris, 10ber, Xber

Latin records often write out dates in full and numbers within a date usually end with an 'o': For example, *Anno Dominio millesimo quinquecentesimo nongesimo octo et die viginti tre mensis Julii* – 'In the year of (our) Lord one thousand five hundred ninety-eight, and on the twenty-third day of the month of July'. Sometimes i and j are used interchangeably, and often a final ii is written as ij, thus Julii, Julij and Iulii all mean July.

LATIN GLOSSARY FOR GENEALOGY AND HISTORY

See *Beginners' Latin: Latin 1086–1733: a practical online tutorial for beginners*, The National Archives (www.nationalarchives.gov.uk/latin/beginners).

Latin	English
a (ab)	from, by
ab hoc mense	from this month on
abavia	great-great-grandmother, female ancestor in the fourth degree
abavus	great-great-grandfather, male ancestor in the fourth degree
abdormitus	died
abdormivit	he/she died
abiit	he/she died
abinde	since
abitus est	he/she died, went away
abjectarius	cabinetmaker, woodworker
abjuro	to renounce by oath

ablutus	baptism, christening
ablutus est	he was baptised
abnepos	great-great-grandson, male descendant in the fourth degree
abneptis	great-great-granddaughter, female descendant in the fourth degree
abortivus	premature birth
abs	from, by
abscessus	death
absque	without, except
abstersus	baptised
abuo	I baptise, I wash
ac	and
acatholicus	non-Catholic, Protestant
accipio	to accept, take, receive, take possession of
accola	local resident
acicularius	needle maker
acquiescat	he/she is content with, reposes, dies
acquietus est	he died
acra	acre
actum	record
ad	at, to, in, for, towards
adhuc	as yet, still
adjutor	assistant
adjuvenis	assistant
adnepos	great-great-great-grandson, male descendant in the fifth degree
adolescens	young man, adolescent
adulterium	adultery
advenit	he came, appeared
advocatus	lawyer
aeger	sick
aegyptus	gypsy
aequalis	equal
aetas (aetatis)	age
aetate	(being) in the age of, age
affines	relatives by marriage, in-laws
affinitas	relationship by marriage
affirmavit	he/she affirmed, asserted, confirmed
agentis	of the official
agnatus	male blood relative
agonia	cramps
agricola	farmer
ahenarius	coppersmith
albus	white
alemannus	German
alias	otherwise, also, or, at, another (called)
alibi	at another time, elsewhere
alimenta, alimento	provision made for younger sons or unmarried daughters
aliud (alius)	other, another
alius, alia, aliud	other

Allemania	Germany
Allutarius	tanner
altare	altar
alter	the next, the other
alter, altera, alterum	the other of two
altera die	on the next day
alutarius	tanner
ambo	stranger or foreigner
ambo	both, two together
amita	aunt (father's sister)
amita magna	grandfather's sister, grandaunt
amita uxoris	wife's father's sister
amitinus	cousin, (child of father's sister)
ancillus/a	servant
andedictus	aforesaid
Anglia	England
anima	soul, spirit
animam reddidit domino suo	he/she returned the soul to his/her Lord (died)
anni proximi elapsi	of the preceding year
anno	in the year (of)
anno domini	in the year of our Lord
anno incarnationis	in the year (since/of) the incarnation (of the Lord)
annus	year
annus bissextus (bissextilis)	leap year
anonymus/a	stillborn son/daughter
ante	before, in front of, prior to
ante meridiem (a.m.)	before noon
anti	against, opposite
antiquus	old, senior
apoplexia	stroke
aprilis	of April
apud	at the house of, at, by, near
aqua	water
arbor consanguinitatis	family tree
archicoquus	head cook
archidiaconus	archdeacon
archiepiscopus	archbishop
archivum	archive
arcularius	carpenter
arenarius	sand digger or vender
arma	coat of arms
armentarius	herdsman
armiger	gentleman, squire
armorum	of coats of arms
arragia	customs duties
at	but
atavus	great-great-great-grandfather, male ascendant in the fifth degree

atque	and
augusti	of August
aula	hall
aurifaber	goldsmith
aurifaber, aurifex	goldsmith
auriga	driver
aut	or
autem	but, however, moreover
auxentium	Alsace
ava	grandmother
avi	ancestors, grandparents
avi relicta	grandfather's widow
avia	grandmother
aviaticus	nephew
avunculus	uncle (mother's brother)
avus	grandfather
bacallarius	bachelor
baillivus	bailiff
banni	marriage banns
bannorum, liber	register (book) of marriage banns, announcements
bannum	bann, marriage proclamation
baptisatus/a	baptised
baptisatus/a est	he(or she) was baptised
baptisavit	he baptised
baptismatis	of baptism
baptismi	baptism, christening
baptismus/a	baptism
baptizatorum, liber	register of baptisms
baptizatus	christening
baptizatus	baptism, christening
baptizatus est	he was baptised, has been baptised
baptizavi	I baptised, have baptised
barbetonsor;	barber
baro	baron
beatus	blessed, deceased
bene	well
bergarius	shepherd
biduum	two-day period
biennium	two-year period
binus, bina, binum	double, twofold, two at time, two by two, two each, twice, in pairs
bona	possessions
bonus	good
bordarius	cottager, tenant, border
Borussia	Prussia
brasiator	brewer
burgensis	burgess, citizen
cadaver	dead body
caelebs	bachelor, unmarried man

caelum	heaven, sky
caementarius	stonemason
calcearius	shoemaker, cordwainer
calciator	shoemaker, cordwainer
Caledonia	Scotland (specifically the north)
caligator	shoemaker, cordwainer
Cambria	Wales
cameranius	chamberlain, groom, valet
capella	chapel
capellanus	chaplain
capilliciarius	periwig-maker
capitis	chief, head
capo	caupo, taverner
capt et jurat	taken and sworn
caput	head, chief
carbonarius	collier, coal miner
carecarius	carter
carnarius	butcher
carnifex	flesher
carpentarius	carpenter
carta	charter, deed, map
casale	estate, village
casatus	cottager
cataster	land, property record
catholicus	Catholic
caupo (cauponis)	innkeeper
causa	cause, sake, because of
celator	turner
celebraverunt	they celebrated, they were married
cellarius	vintner, butler
census	census
centenarius	a person 100 years old
cerarius	wax-worker or chandler
cerdo (cerdonis)	handworker
chartarius	paper miller
cheirothecus	glover
chir	chirurgeon, surgeon
chirotherarus	glover
chirurgia	surgery
chirurgus	surgeon
chramarius	merchant
cimeterium	cemetery
cingarus	gypsy
circa	about, around, nearly
circiter	about, approximately
civis	citizen
claith-draper	cloth-draper
clare constat	'clearly appears', a writ or precept (order) granted by a subject superior to an heir, whose right to a property is obvious from documents and which orders the giving of sasine

clausit	he/she finished, closed
claustrarius	locksmith
clausum	closed, finished
claviger	macer
clericus	clerk
clericus	clergyman
clostrarius	locksmith
coelebs	bachelor, single man
coemeterium	cemetery
cognati	maternal relations
cognationis	blood relationship
cognomen	name, family name, surname
collis	hill
colonus	colonist, settler, resident (sometimes farmer, peasant)
colorator	dyer
comes	count
comitas	county
comitatus	county
comitissa	countess
commater	godmother
commorantes	living, residing
comparatio	presence, appearance
comparere	to appear
comparuit	he/she appeared, was present
comparuit pro me	he/she appeared before me
compater	godfather
compos	in possession of
Conarius	tanner
concepta est	she was pregnant
conceptus/a/um	conceived
concessit	consented
condicillus	codicil, list
conditione, sub	conditionally
coniuges	married couple
coniunx (coniux)	husband or wife
conjugatus	married
conjuges	married couple
conjugum	of/from the married couple
conjuncti	marriage
conjuncti sunt	they were joined (in marriage)
conjux	spouse (wife or husband)
consanguinitas	blood relationship (impediment to marriage if too close)
consanguinitatis	of blood relationship
consobrina	female cousin (mother's side)
consobrinus	male cousin (mother's side)
consobrinus/a	cousin on mother's side
consors (consortis)	wife
contra	against, opposite

contracti	contracted, drawn together
contrahere	to contract, to draw together
contraxerunt	they contracted (marriage)
convulsionis	of convulsions
cooperta	married (of a woman)
coparcener	co-heir
copseller	(See capseller)
copulati	marriage
copulati sunt	they were married, joined
copulatio	marriage
copulationis	of marriage
copulatus	married, joined
copulatus/a	married man/woman
copulatus/a est	he/she was married
copulavit	he married (performed wedding)
coquus	cook
coram	in the presence of
coriarius	leather worker, tanner
corpus (corporis)	body
cotarius	cottager
cras	tomorrow
creatura dei	foundling (creature of God)
cubicularius	'chamber chyld', valet
cui impositum est nomen	to whom was given the name
cuius	whose
cuiusdam	of a certain
culina	kitchen
cultellarius, cultellar	cutler
cum	with
cuprifaber	coppersmith
cur	why
curia	court
currarius	carriage builder
custos (custodis)	custodian, guard
datum	date, given
de	of, from, by, concerning, about
de eodem	of that ilk (Scot.)
de ritu sanctae matris ecclesiae	according to the rite of the holy mother church
debilitas	illness, weakness
decanatus	deanery, section of diocese
decanus	deacon
decembris	of December
decessit	he/she died
decessit sine prole	died without issue, childless
decessit vitae patre (d.v.p.)	died in father's lifetime
decessus	died, death
decretum	decree
decubuit	he/she died, lay down

dedit	he/she gave
deflorata	deflowered, no longer a virgin
defuit	he/she departed, died
defunctorum	of the dead
defunctorum, liber	register of the deceased
defunctus est	he died
defunctus/a/um	dead, death
defungitur	he/she dies, is discharged
dei	of God
deinde	then, thereafter, next
denarius	penny, small coin, money
denatus	deceased, dead, death
denatus est	he died, has died
denunciatio	publication of marriage banns
denuntiationes	marriage banns
desponsationis	engagement
desponsatus	engaged
desponsus/a	betrothed
Deus	God
dexter	right
dictus	said, stated, known as
didymus/a	twin male/female
die	on the day
die sequenti	on the following day
die vero	this very day
diem clausit extremem	he/she finished the last day (died), the name of a royal order sent to a sheriff to enquire into the death of a debtor of the Crown, and to ensure the Crown is satisfied for the debt
dies (diei)	day (days)
dignus	worthy
dimidium	half
dimidius/a/um/	half, broken, divided
diocesis	diocese
discessit	he/she died
disponsationis	permission
divortium	divorce
doageria	dowager
dodum	formerly, recently
domi	at home
domicella	young lady, servant, nun
domicellus	young nobleman, servant (usually in a monastery)
domina	lady
dominica	Sunday
dominus	lord, rule, the Lord (Jesus Christ)
dominus, clerical title with 'miles'	sir, knight
domus	home, house, family
donum	gift
dos (dotis)	dowry

duae	two
ducatus	duchy
ducis	of the duke or leader
dum	while, when, until, as long as
dux	duke, leader
dysenteria	dysentery
e	out of, from
e, ex	from
eadem	the same
eam	her
ebdomada	week
ecclampsia	convulsions
ecclesia	church
ego	I
eiusdem	the same
ejusdem	the same
ejustdem die	of the same day
elapsus	past, elapsed
empicus	lung disease
enim	for, namely, truly
eo tempore	at this time
eod die	on the same day
eodem	the same
eodem die	on the same day
eodem mense	in the same month
episcopus	bishop
epphipiarius	saddler
equalis	equal
eques (equitis)	knight, cavalry soldier
erant	they were
erat	he/she/it was
ergo	therefore, because of
erratum	error
esse	to be
est	he/she/it is
et	and, even
etiam	and also, and even
eum	him
ex	from, out of (places of origin)
ex causa	on account of, for the sake of, because of
ex hac mortali ad immortalem vitam	from this mortality to immortal life (died)
ex illegitimo thoro	of illegitimate status
exhalavit animam	he/she breathed out his/her soul (died)
extra	outside of, beyond
extraneus	stranger, foreign
extremum	last
extremum munitus	last rites provided

exulatus	exile
faber	craftsman
faber	maker, smith
faber ferrarius	blacksmith
faber lignarius	wright, woodworker
faber muriarius	builder, mason
factis tribus denuncia-tionibus	three banns having been published
factis tribus denuncia-tionibus	three marriage banns having been published
factus	made
falso	falsely, incorrectly
familia	family
familiaris	relative, slave, friend, follower
famulus	servant
feber (febris)	fever
februarii	of February
fecunda	pregnant
feme covert	married woman
feme sole	unmarried woman
femina	female, wife, woman
fere	almost, nearly
feria	day, holiday
fermorar	farmer
ferrier	farrier
festum	feast, festival, wedding
fidelis	faithful
figulus	potter
filia	daughter
filia fratris/sororis	niece, daughter of brother/sister
filia populae	illegitimate daughter
filiaster	stepson
filiastra	stepdaughter
filiola	little daughter
filiolus	little son
filius	son
filius fratris/sororis	nephew, son of brother/sister
filius populi	illegitimate son
finis	border, end
firmarius	farmer
fluxus	dysentery
focus	fireplace, hearth, home
foderator	furrier, cloth worker, fuller
fodiator	digger
folium	page
fons (fontis)	baptismal font, spring, fountain
fons et origo	fount and origin
fossor	grave digger, miner
frater	brother

frater ex materno latere	half-brother common mother
frater ex paterno latere	half-brother common father
frater germanus	twin brother
frater naturalis	brother
fructuarius	fruit seller
fuerunt	they were
fui	I was
fuit	he/she/it was
Fullo	fuller, waulker
furnarius	baker
gallearius	sailor
garcio	boy, servant
gardianus	church warden
gemellae	twins (female)
gemelli	twins (male, or male and female)
gemellus/a	twin
geminus/a	twin
gemmarius	jeweller
genealogia	genealogy
gener	son-in-law, cousin
generis	of the type, sex, etc.
generosus	of noble birth, gentleman
genitor	father
genitores	parents
genitum	begotten, born
genitus	birth
genitus est	he was born, begotten
gens (gentis)	male line, clan, tribe, lineage
genuit	he/she was begotten
genus	type, kind, birth, descent, sex, origin, class, race
genus (generis)	sex, type, kind, birth, descent, origin, class, race
germana	sister german (sister by blood), German
Germania	Germany
germanus	brother german (brother by blood), German
gloris	brother's wife, wife's sister
glos	husband's sister
gradus	degree, grade
gratia	grace, sake
gravida	pregnant
guardianus	guardian
gubernium	domain
habent	they have
habere	to have, to hold
habet	he/she has
habitans	resident, inhabitant
habitantes	residents
habitare	to reside
habitatio	residence

habitavit	he/she resided, dwelt
habuit	he/she had, held
haec (hac)	this, the latter
haereticus	heretic
haud	not
hebdomada	week
Helvetia	Switzerland
heres (heredis)	heir
heres masculus	male heir
heri	yesterday
Hibernia	Ireland
hic	here
hic, haec, hoc	this
hinc	from here
his	this, the latter
Hispania	Spain
hoc	this, the latter
hoc die/mense/anno	on this day/month/year
hodie	today
homo (hominis)	man, human being
honestus	respectable, honorable
hora	hour
hortulanus	gardener
hospes (hospitis)	innkeeper
huius	of this, of the latter
humantio	burial
humantus	burial
humatio	burial
humationis	burial
humatus/a	buried
humatus/a est	he/she was buried
humilis	humble, lowly
Hungaricus	Hungarian
hydropsis	dropsy, oedema
hypodidasculus	schoolmaster, usher
iam	already
ibi	there
ibidem (ib, ibid)	in the same place
idem, eadem, iden	the same
ifans	child
igitur	therefore
ignotus/a	unknown
iit	he/she went
ilius	of that
ille, illa illud	that
illegitimus/a	illegitimate
illius	of that, of the former
imbrodinster	embroiderer

impedimentum	hindrance, impediment (often to a marriage)
impedimentum consanguinitas	impediment of too close a blood relationship
imperium	empire
imponere	to place upon, to impose
imponit	he imposes, places upon
impositus/a/um	imposed, placed upon, given
imposui	I placed upon
impraegnavit	he impregnated
impregnata	pregnant
in facie ecclesiae	in front of the church
in sinum maternum conditus	given into the maternal breast (buried)
incarnationis	of the incarnation (of the Lord)
incola	inhabitant, resident
index (indicis)	index
inerunt	they entered into (marriage)
infans/infanta (infantis)	child, infant
inferior	lower
infirmus	weak
infra	below, under, later
infrascriptus	written below, undersigned
iniit	he/she entered, began
initiatus est	he was baptised
injuria	injury, worry
instant, inst.	this month
institor	pedlar, cramer
inter	between
intra	within, during
intronizati	marriage
intronizati sunt	they were married, have been married
intronizaverunt	they married, have married
inuptus/a	unmarried
invenit	he/she found, discovered
ipse/a/um	himself/herself/itself
ita	so, thus
ita vero	it is so, yes
itaque	therefore
item	also, likewise
iunior	younger
iurare	to swear, take an oath
iure	legally
ius, iures	law, laws
iuvenis	young person
ivit	he/she went
januarii	of January
javelor	jailor
Jovis, dies	Thursday
judaicus	Jewish

judicium	court, judgment
julii	of July
juncti sunt	they were joined (married)
junii	of June
junior	younger
jurare	to swear, take an oath
juravit	he/she swore, took an oath
jure	legally, lawfully
juro	I swear, I testify
jus, jures	law, laws
juvenis	young person
juxta	near, beside
laborius	labourer, worker
lanarius	wool worker
lanatus	clothed in wool
laniarius (or laniator)	butcher
lanifex (lanificis)	weaver
lanio	flesher
laterarius	brick maker
lathamus, lathomus, latomus	quarryman, mason
lautus	baptism, christening
lautus/a est	he/she was baptised
lavacrum	font
lavare	to wash, to baptise
lavatus est	he was baptised, washed
lavo	I baptise, wash
legio	legion
legitimatus	legitimate
levabat	he was holding, raising, lifting up
levans (levantes)	godparent(s)
levantibus	by the godparents
levare ex fonte	to raise from the baptismal font, to act as a godparent
levir	husband's brother, brother-in-law
liber	book, register, free
liber baptizatorum	baptismal register
liber defunctorum	death register
liber matrimoniorm	marriage register
liberi	children
libra	pound (weight)
libri	books
lichnopeus	candlemaker
ligati	marriage
ligati sunt	they were married, have been married
ligatus	married, joined, married person
ligatus/a est	he/she was joined or married
ligavi	I joined (in marriage)
lignarius	cabinetmaker, joiner, woodworker
lignicidus	woodcutter

linifex (linificis)	linen weaver
loco tutoris	in the role of a tutor (custodian or a minor)
locus	place
locus sigilli	where a persons seal is placed (on a document)
long tempore	for a long time
longum morbum	after a long illness
ludimagister	schoolmaster, teacher
ludus	game, training school, jest
Lunae, dies	Monday
lustratio	baptism, christening
lustrationis	of the baptism
macellator	butcher
magis	more
magister	master
magnus, magna	great, large
maii	of May
major	greater, older
majorennis	of legal age
majores	ancestors
majoritatis	of legal age, majority
male	badly
malus	bad, evil
mane	in the morning
manu propria	by one's own hand (signed)
manus	hand
marasmus	weakness
maris	of a male, man
marita	married, wife
mariti	marriage, married couple
maritus	married, husband
Martii	of March
martimonium	marriage
Martis, dies	Tuesday
mas	male, man
masser	macer
mater (matris)	mother
mater meretrix	mother of illegitimate child
matertera	maternal aunt, mother's sister
matrica	register, record book
matrimonium	marriage
matrimonium contraxerunt	they contracted marriage
matrina	godmother
matruelis	cousin on mother's side
me	me
mecum	with me
medicus	doctor
mendicus	beggar
mense	in the month (of)

mensis	month
mercator	merchant
mercenarius	day labourer
Mercurii, dies	Wednesday
meretrix (meretricis)	harlot, prostitute
meridies	noon
meus/a/um	my, mine
miles (militis)	knight, soldier
minimus/a natu	youngest
minorennis	not of legal age
minoritatis	below legal age, minority
minus	less
modo	lately, now, presently
modus	manner, way
mola	mill
molitor	miller
moneta	money
mons (montis)	mountain
morbus	disease
more novo	(according to) the new style (of calendar)
more vetere	(according to) the old style (of calendar)
moritur	he/she died
mors	death
mortis	death, of death
mortutuus	death
mortuus	death
mortuus/a est	he/she died
mortuus/a/um	dead, deceased
mos (moris)	custom, manner
mulier	woman, wife
multus	many
munitus	fortified, provided
mutuo consensu	by mutual consent
mutuus	common, mutual
nux	nut
n.b. = nota bene	note well, notice
n.n. = nomen nescio	name unknown (I do not know the name)
nascit	he/she is born
natales	birth
natalis	natal
nati	birth
nativitas	birth
naturalis	natural, illegitimate
natus	birth
natus est	he was born
natus/a	born (adj.), son/daughter (noun)
natus/a est	he/she was born
nauta	sailor

nec	neither, nor
necessitate baptismo	by emergency baptism
necessitatis	of necessity
necnon	and also
negotiator	merchant (commerce)
nemo (neminis)	no one
neosponsus/a	newlywed
nepos (nepotis)	nephew, grandson
nepos ex fil	grandson
nepos ex fratre	brother's son
nepos ex sorore	sister's son
neptis	niece, granddaughter
neque	and not
nescit	he doesn't know
niger	black
nihil	nothing
nisi	if not
nobilis	noble
nobilitatis	of nobility
nocte	at night
nomen	name, given name
nomen nescio (n.n.)	name not known
nominatus est	he was named
nomine	by/with the name (of)
non	not, no
nonagenarius	a person in his nineties
nos	we, us
noster	our
nota bene (n.b.)	note well, notice, take heed
notarius	notary
nothus	illegitimate child
Novembris	of November
noverca	stepmother
nox	night
nudius	earlier
nudius terius, nudius tertius	three days earlier
nulloque detecto impedimento matrimonio	and no hindrance to the marriage having been discovered
nullus/a/um	no, none
numerus	number
nunc	now, at this time
nunc dies terius	three days earlier
nunc temporis	of the present time
nunquam	never
nuntius	messenger
nuper	lately (sometimes of a deceased person)
nupserunt	they married
nupta	married woman, bride

nupti	marriage
nuptias	wedding
nuptus/a	married
nurus/a	son's wife, daughter-in-law
nutritor	foster father
nutrius	foster child
nutrix (nutricis)	foster mother
ob	on account of, for, according to
ob imminens mortis periculum	on account of imminent danger of death (as with emergency baptism)
obdormitus est	he fell asleep, died
obierunt	they died, have died
obiit	death, he/she died, went away, departed
obiit sine prole	died without issue
obitus	death, died
obstetrix (obstetricis)	midwife
Octobris	of October
octogenarius	a person in his eighties
officialis	official
olim	formerly, once (sometimes of a deceased person)
omnibus sacramentis provisis	(he/she) was given all the last rites
omnis	all, every
operarius	day labourer
oppidum	city, town
orbus/a	orphan
originis	of the birth
origo (originis)	origin, birth
oriundus	birth, originating (from), born
orphanus	orphan
ortus	origin, birth
ortus	birth
ovilius	shepherd
ovis	sheep
pacatio	payment
paene	almost, nearly
pagina	page
pagus	district, village
palatium	palatinate
panifex	baker
papa	pope
parentes	parents
pariochialis	parochial, parish
pariter	equally, also
parochia	parish
parochus	parish priest
pars (partis)	area, region
partibus	part, share, portion, piece; region, direction, role, party, faction, side
partus	birth, childbirth, offspring

parvulus	very little, small
parvus	little
pastor	pastor, shepherd
pater (patris)	father
pater familias	head of family or household
patres	ancestors, forefathers
patria	fatherland, native land
patrinus/a/i	godfather/godmother/godparents
patris familias	head of family or household
patruelis	cousin on father's side
patruerlis	paternal nephew
patrui relicta	paternal uncle's widow
patruus	paternal uncle
pauper	poor, pauper
pax (pace)	peace
pedegogus	teacher
pellio	bonnet maker
pelliparius	furrier
penult	the last but one, next to last
per	through, by means of
per subsequens matrimonium legitimatus	legitimised by subsequent marriage
peregrinus	foreign, strange
perendi (or perendie)	day after tomorrow
perfecit	he/she completed, did
periit	he/she perished, died
peritus	death, deceased, dead
peritus est	he died
pestis	plague
phthisis	consumption, tuberculosis
pictor	painter
pie	piously
pigator	dyer
pilearius, pileator	hatmaker
piscarius	fishmonger
piscator	fisherman
pisces	fish
pistor	baxter, baker
pius	pious
plutus	baptism, christening
plutus	baptised, sprinkled
pomerid = post meridiem	afternoon (p.m.)
pons (pontis)	bridge
popula	people
post	after
post meridiem, pomerid, (p.m.)	after noon (p.m.)
post partum	after childbirth
posterus	following

posthumus	born after death of father
postridie	on the day after, a day later
potuit	could
preceptor	teacher, instructor
predefunctus	previously deceased (e.g. before the birth of a child)
predictus	aforesaid
prefatus	aforesaid
prefectus	magistrate
pregnata	pregnant
premissus	published previously (e.g. marriage banns)
prenobilis	esteemed, honorable, respected
presens (presentis)	present, in attendance
preter	besides, also, past, beyond
pretor	village mayor
pridie	on the day before
primus, primum	first or firstly
princeps	prince
principatus	principality
priores	ancestors
privignus/a	stepson/stepdaughter
pro	for, on behalf of, as far as
pro indiviso	undivided
pro tempore	for (at) the time
proavus/a	great-grandfather/great-grandmother
proclamatio	bann, decree
proclamationis/es	decree(s), marriage bann(s)
procurator	lawyer, monastic official
progenitus	firstborn
proles	child, issue, offspring (gender not stated)
proles spuria	illegitimate child
promulgationis	decree, bann
proneptus	grand-niece
prope	near, close to
propinqui	relations, relatives
propriis manibus	with his own hands
propter	because of, near
prosocrus	wife's grandmother
prout	as, accordingly
provincia	province
provisus	provided (with)
proximo, prox.	of the next month
proximus	previous, preceding
proximus consanguineus	nearest relation
pudicus/a	chaste, upright, virginal
puella	girl
puer	boy, child
puera	girl
puerperium	childbirth

purgatus	baptism, christening
purgatus/a	baptised, cleansed, purged
puta	reputed, supposed
quaestor	treasurer, paymaster
quam	how, as much as
quando	when
quartis	fourth
quasi	almost, as if
que	and (as a suffix, e.g. paterque, and the father)
qui, quae, quod	who, which, what
quidam, quaedam, quodam (or quoddam)	a certain person (male/female) or thing
quod	because
quondam	formerly, former (deceased person)
recognito	examination, inquest by jury
rectus	right, direct
regeneratus est	he was baptised
regimine pedestre	infantry regiment
regina	queen
registrum	index, list
regius	royal
regnum	kingdom
relictus/a	widower/widow
religio (religionis)	religion
relinquit	he/she left behind, abandoned
renanus	of the Rhine
renatus	baptism, christening
renatus/a est	he/she was baptised
repertorium	index, list
requiescat in pace	may he/she rest in peace
restio	rope maker
rex (regis)	king
ritus	rite, ceremony
rotulus	roll
rufus	red
rusticus	peasant, farmer
Sabbatinus, dies	Saturday
Sabbatum	Saturday
sacellanus	chaplain
sacer, sacra, sacrum	sacred
sacerdos (sacerdotis)	priest
sacramentis totiis munitiis	fortified by all the last rites
sacramentum	sacrament, ordinance, rite
sacro fonte baptismi	in the sacred font of baptism
saeculum	a generation, century, age, eternity, world
saepe	often
salarium	salary
saltare	salter, maker of salt

sanctus/a/um	holy, sacred, a saint
sanus	healthy
sarcinator	patcher , sackmaker
sartor	tailor
satis	enough
Saturni, dies	Saturday
scabinus	judge, lay assessor
scarlatina	scarlet fever
schola	school
scissor	tailor
scorbutus	scurvy
scorifex (scorificis)	tanner
scorta	unmarried mother, whore
Scotia	Scotland
scribo	I write
scripsit	he/she wrote
scriptus/a/um	written
secundus	second
sed	but
sellarius	saddler
semel	once, a single time
semi	half
semper	always, forever
senex (senicis)	old man
senilis	weak from age
senior	older, elder
senium	old age
sepelire	to bury
sepelivi	I buried
septagenarius	a person in his seventies
Septembris	of September
septimana	week
sepulti	burial
sepultorum, liber	burial register
sepultus	burial
sepultus est	he is buried
sepultus/a/um	buried
sequens (sequentis)	following
serdo (serdonis)	tanner
servus	servant
seu	or
sexus	sex
si	if
sic	thus, so, yes
sigillum	seal
signum	sign, mark
signum fecit	he/she made a mark, signed
silva	woods, forest

sine	without
sinister	left
sinus	bosom, breast
sive	or
smigator	soap maker
socer (socris)	father-in-law
socius	apprentice, comrade, associate
socrinus	brother-in-law
socrus	mother-in-law
socrus magna	maternal grandmother
sol (solis)	the sun
solemnicatio, solemnicationis	marriage
Solis, dies	Sunday
solutus/a/um	unmarried, free from debt
soror	sister
sororius	brother-in-law
spasmus	cramp, spasm
spirituales, parentes	godparents
sponsalia	marriage banns
sponsalis	betrothed
sponsati	marriage
sponsatus	married
sponsor	godparent
sponsus/a	groom/bride, husband/wife, spouse, betrothed
spurius/a	illegitimate
stallarius	stabler
statim	immediately
status	condition, status
stemma (gentile)	pedigree
stinarius	ploughman
stirps	origin, source
stuprata	pregnant out of wedlock
stuprator	father of illegitimate child
sub	under, beneath, below
sub tutela	under guardianship
subscripsit	he/she signed
subscriptus	undersigned
subsequentis	following, subsequent
subsignatum	marked (signed) below
subsignavit	he/she signed with a mark below
Suevia	Sweden
sum	I am
sunt	they are/were
superior	upper
superstes	surviving, still living
supra	before, above, beyond
supradictum	above written
surdus	deaf

susceptor/orix/ores	godparent (male/female) godparents
sutor	cordiner, cobbler, shoemaker
suus/a/um	his/her/its/their own
synergus	apprentice
taberna	inn, tavern
tamen	however
tandem	at first, finally
tannator	tanner
tegularius	tiler, slater
tegularius	brick maker
teleonarius	tax collector
tempus (temporis)	time
terra	land, earth
terris et baronia	land and barony (of)
tertia	third
tertia parte quartae partis	third part of a quarter part (i.e. one-twelfth)
tertius	third
testamentum	will, testament
testes	witnesses
testibus	by witnesses
testimentum	will, testament
testis	witness
textor	weaver
thorus	status of legitimacy, bed
tignarius	carpenter
tinctor	litster, dyer
tinsel, tynseil	loss
tomus	volume
tonsor	barber
tornator	turner, lathe worker
totus	all, entire
trans	across
transitus est	he died
tribus	clan, lineage, tribe
triduum	space of three days, three-day period
trigemini	triplets
tubinnator	trumpeter
tum	then
tumulatus	buried
tunc	then, at that time, immediately
tunc temporis	of former time
tussis	cough
tutela	guardianship, tutelage
tutor	guardian, tutor
tuus	your
typhus	typhoid fever, typhus (note, these are not the same disease)
ubi	where
ult., ultima, ultimo	of the preceding month

ultimus/a/um	last, final
unctio	annointing, unction
unctio extrema	extreme unction, last rites
unde	wherefore, whereupon, whence
Ungaricus	Hungarian
unigena	only begotten daughter
unigentius	only begotten son
unigenus/a	only begotten son/daughter, unique
unitis	combined into
unus	one, only, together
urbs (urbis)	city
ut	how, as, so that, therewith, in order that
ut infra	as below
ut supra	as above
uterinus	on mother's side (of family), of the same mother
uxor	wife
uxoratis	married
vagabundus	wanderer, vagabond
vagus	tramp
variola	smallpox
vassus	servant, vassal
vel (vel . . . vel)	or (either . . . or)
velle	will, testament
venerabilis	venerable, worthy
Veneris, dies	Friday
venia	permission, indulgence
vero, die	on this very day
vespere	in the evening
vester	your
vestiarius	clothier
vetula	old woman
vetus (veteris)	old
via	road, way
vicarius	vicar
vicecomes	sheriff, reeve
vicinus	nearby, neighborhood
victricus	stepfather
vicus	village
vide	see
videlicet (viz.)	namely
viduus/vidua	widower/widow
villa	farm, country home, estate, large country residence or seat, villa, village
villicanus	reeve, steward
vir	man, male, husband
virgo (virginis)	virgin, female, girl
virtuosus/a/um	virtuous, honorable
vita	life
vitam cessit	he/she departed from life (died)

vitri compositor	glassinwright, glazier
vitriarius	glassmaker
vitricus	stepfather
vivens (vivus)	living
viz. = videlicet	namely
vos	you
vulgo	generally, commonly
vxor (= uxor)	wife
zingarius	gypsy

LIST OF OCCUPATIONS

For Latin names of occupations and other abbreviations, see the table above.

adv.	advocate
advocate	lawyer appearing in court, equivalent to English barrister
ag. lab.	agricultural labourer
alewife	female owner or manager of an alehouse
annealer	finisher of metal or glass, by furnace and chemicals
annuitant	person with an annual income or pension
apoth.	apothecary
apprentice	trainee learning a craft or trade, usually bound to a master
argentier	controller of finances, comptroller, treasurer
army H.P.	soldier on half pay
assizor	juror at a trial (assize)
b.	burgess
bailie	magistrate in a Scottish burgh court
banksman	miner at the pithead unloading coal from cages
baron (or barony) officer	early policeman, who enforced the law within the barony
baxter, bagster	baker
beadle	parish or church official who assisted the minister with administrative work and acted as usher
beadman, bedeman, bedesman, bedeswoman etc.	licensed beggar
beamer	weaving mill worker who loaded yarn onto the beam of a loom
beetler	fabric embosser in a cloth mill
black litster	black dyer
blacker, berlin blacker	varnisher of ironware products
blaxter	bleacher (of cloth)
bleacher	bleacher of textiles or paper
blockcutter	carver of wooden blocks used for printing
blockmaker	broker, trader
blockprinter	printer (on paper or cloth) using wooden blocks
boatman	boat operator at loch or river crossings
bobbin turner	maker of spools (bobbins) for textile mills
bookmaker	taker of bets for gambling on horse and dog races etc.
boot clicker	bootlace hole-maker
boot closer	stitcher of boots and shoes
boot laster	shoemaker, using a metal 'last'

boot sprigger	shoemaker, using 'sprigs' (headless nails) to nail soles to uppers
bottler	bottle filler, usually in a distillery
bower	bowmaker
bowman	subtenant who looked after cows for a season
boxmaster	treasurer or deacon of a trade guild
brasener	brass-worker
brasiator	brewer
brazier	brass metal worker
brewster	brewer (of beer)
brodinster, broudster	embroiderer
brouster	brewer
brusher	coal mine worker who kept mine roofs and sides in repair
burgess	enrolleed as merchant or craftsman in a burgh
byreman	farm worker in the byre (cow-shed)
cabinetmaker	wooden furniture maker
cadger	travelling pedlar
cadie, caddie	runner of errands or parcel carrier; later, golf club carrier
caitchpeller	keeper of a caitchpell or tennis court
cal. prin.	calico printer (on cotton cloth from India)
callenderer	smoother of cloth or paper using rollers
candler	candle maker or retailer
cap seller, cop seller	seller of wooden bowls
carbonarius	charcoal maker
carder	brushed wool ready for spinning using wire 'cards'
carter	worked with horse and cart, carring goods
cartwright	maker and repairer of horse carts
catechist	instructor in religion
caulker	repaired ships' hulls by sealing with 'caulk' (tar)
causewaymaker	road (causeway) builder using stone setts
cautioner	guarantor, one who stands surety for another
cellarman	keeper of beer, wine and spirits
chairman	sedan chair carrier
chair-master	hirer out of sedan chairs
chaisemaker	carriage maker
chandler	dealer in supplies, usually for ships
chapman	stallholder or travelling salesman
chapper, chapper-up	knocked ('chapped') on doors to wake early shift workers
charwoman	female domestic cleaner
check weighman	checked a miner's production so he could be paid
chir. apoth.	chirurgeon-apothecary.
chowder	fishmonger
clagger	removed clags (dirt and clumps) clots from wool
clark	clerk
clicker	lace hole-maker (boots and shoes)
clogged	maker of wooden clogs
cloth dresser	cloth cutter in a textile mill
cloth lapper	cleaned cotton fibres before carding
coachman	coach and horse driver

coal trimmer	person who balanced coal barges or ships
coalmaster	owner and/or operator of a coal mine
cobbler	shoe maker or repairer
cocquetour	cook
collier	coal miner working at the coal face
colourman	mixer of dyes for textiles
colporteur	travelling book seller
combmaker	maker of combs for textiles or hair
compositor	setter of type for printing
conservator	guardian or custodian
cooper	maker of wooden barrels and casks for beer etc.
cordiner	shoemaker
cordiner, cordwainer	leather boot and shoe maker
cork cutter	cut and prepared imported cork bark
costermonger	street seller of fruit and vegetables
cottar	tenant with a cottage and minimal land
cotton piecer	leant over spinning-machines to repair broken threads (often small children)
cotton warper	cotton mill loom operator in weaving
cotton winder	wound the threads onto a weaving loom
cow-feeder	tenant of small farm with dairy cattle
cowper	maker of cups
creamer	occupant of a cream or kraim (booth)
creelman	carried produce to market in a creel (basket)
crofter	tenant of farm and cottage (croft), usually in the Highlands
curator	person appointed by law as guardian, e.g. for a minor
currier	person curing or tanning leather hides
customer	receiver of customs or excise
custumer	collector of customs duties
cutter	cut cloth for a tailor
dagmaker	pistol maker
dairymaid	girl who milked cows and made butter in a dairy
dapifer	steward in a royal or noble household
dempster, doomster	one who pronounces judgment, a sentencing judge
dexter	dyer of textiles
diker	builder of dry stone walls (dykes)
docker	docks worker, loading and unloading ship cargo
dom. serv.	domestic servant
dominie	school master
draper	retailer of cloth, fabrics, sewing threads etc.
drawer	mine worker who pushed or dragged coal carts
drayman	cart driver of a dray (long flatbed cart)
dresser	1. surgeon's assistant in hospital 2. stone worker in a quarry cutting rocks to shape 3. foundry worker cleaning metal after casting
drover	cattle dealer or mover of cattle to market
drysalter	dealer in salted and dried meats, pickles, sauces
dustman	street and domestic rubbish collector
dyker	builder of dry stone walls (dykes)
engine keeper	operator of an industrial steam-driven engine

exciseman	collector of taxes, especially duties
f.s.	female servant
factor	agent for land or property owner, rent collector
farm servant	farm worker under contract
farrier	blacksmith who shoes horses
fencible	militiaman, soldier recruited for war
ferry-louper	Orkney name for arriving mainlander
fethelar	a fiddler, musician
feuar	landholder who paid a feu (fee) to the superior
fireman	1. furnace stoker, e.g. on a train or ship 2. fire fighter
fishcurer	drier and salter of fish for transport in barrels
fishwife	woman selling fresh fish door to door
fitter	assembled parts for machinery
flax scutcher	beat flax fibres before dressing
flaxman	flax dealer
flesher	butcher
fletcher	arrow maker
flockmaster	shepherd in charge of a flock of sheep
forespeaker	advocate, pleader in court
founder	maker of metal items in an iron or brass foundry
freeman	not feued to a feudal lord, and able to own property and trade in a burgh
French polisher	wood finisher, using sandpaper and oils
fruictman	fruit seller
fuller	cloth worker cleaning and thickening cloth by wetting and walking on it
furnaceman	looked after furnace in a metalworks
g.	guild brother
gaberlunzie	travelling beggar
gamekeeper	kepper and breeder of game on an estate
ganger	leader of a gang of workmen
gangrel	vagrant, tramp
gaoler	jailer
gasfitter	fitted pipes for domestic gas supply
gauger	excise officer
gen. lab.	general labourer
ghillie	keeper of wild game especially deer on Highland estates
gilder	used gold leaf to adorn furniture, frames etc.
girnalman	in charge of granary or grain store
glover	glove maker
gowcher	grandfather
granger	keeper of grain store (granary)
grieve	factor who collected farming rents
groom	looked after horses in a stable
ground officer	employee on a large estate to supervise tenants
gudger	grandfather (= gudsire)
H.L.W.	hand loom weaver, weaver of cloth at home
haberdasher	retailer of small clothing wares and sewing materials
hackler	lint dresser who separated coarse flax with a toothed hackle

hammerman	metal worker, smith
hatter	milliner, hatmaker
hawker	pedlar, door-to-door seller of small items
heatherer	thatcher, roofer using heather divots or stems
hecklemaker	maker of flax combs for the hackler/heckler
heckler	See hackler
heddler	weaving loom operator in a textile mill
hedger	laid and repaired hedges around fields
herd	shepherd
heritor	large landholder in a parish, responsible for the church, school, poor relief etc.
hetheleder	person who cut and sold heather for fuel
hewer	miner cutting coal at the coal face
hind	farm servant
holder-on	rivetter's assistant in ship-building etc.
hooper	made hoops for barrels
hortulanus	gardener
hosier	seller of wool or silk stockings (hose)
hostler	looked after horses at an inn
howdywife	midwife
husbandman	farmer, farm animal keeper
iron dresser	foundry worker who cleaned sand etc. from cast metal after moulding
iron miner	miner of ironstone rock
iron moulder	foundry worker who poured molten iron into moulds
iron planer	planed flat surfaces onto cast iron
iron shingler	operated a steam hammer on wrought iron
iron weigher	weighed iron products in foundry for sale by the ton
J.P.	Justice of the Peace, magistrate
jackman	attendant or man-at-arms to a nobleman or landowner
japanner	applied black gloss lacquer to furniture
jobbing man	carried out a variety of small jobs e.g. minor carpentry
joiner	wood worker, carpenter
journeyman	qualified tradesman after serving apprenticeship
kirk-master	deacon in a church
kish maker	willow basket weaver
laird	landowner of a rural estate
lamplighter	lit the gas street lamps in towns
lathsplitter	made thin strips of wood (laths) for nailing to walls and ceilings as a base for plastering
laundress	washerwoman
lawman	officer with magisterial powers
lawrightman	controlled local weights and measures and land tax
leerie	lamplighter (gas lamps)
lengthsman	rail worker who maintained a length of track
letter carrier	delivered letters by hand (later, postman)
liferenter	had a tenancy for life
limmer	thief, scoundrel
limner, limmer	artist who decorates (limns) manuscripts
lineator	surveyor, measurer
lithographer	made printing plates from typeset paper or film

litster	cloth dyer
litster, littister	dyer
lorimer	maker of metal horse harnesses
lotter	1. batched up odd lots of wool for sale 2. croft or small farm divided into lots, usually worked by the crofter's sons
loun	young boy (north-east Scotland)
lozenge cutter	cut and prepared sweets or preserves
m.s.	1. male servant 2. merchant service (seaman)
maltster	preparer of malt for brewing
manf	manufacturer
mangler	washerwoman who wrung out clothes through a mangle
mantua maker	ladies dressmaker or bonnet maker
marikin maker	maker of dressed goat's skin or Spanish leather
mariner	seaman
mason	stone cutter and layer
master	1. head schoolteacher 2. qualified, self-employed craftsman or tradesman
master mariner	ship's captain
mendicant	beggar living on alms e.g. mendicant monks
miller	in charge of a meal or grain mill
milliner	maker of womens' hats and headgear
millwright	mechanic in a mill
min	minister (or miner)
miner	worker at a mineral mine, usually coal, ironstone or shale
minr.	minister of the Gospel
moneyer	mintmaster, maker of coins
monger	seller of goods e.g. fishmonger, ironmonger
moulder	poured molten metal into moulds
mouterer	fee received by miller for grinding corn etc.
mt.	merchant
nailer	blacksmith who made nails
navvie	'navigator', canal and road digger
night soil carrier	removed toilet waste
notary	lawyer, solicitor able to notarise documents
oakum worker	took old ropes apart for the hemp fibre (oakum) to be used for caulking (qv.)
occupation	description
orraman	odd-job man
orris weaver	maker of gold or silver lace
ostler	hostler, looked after horses at an inn
ourman	overseer
outworker	employed at outdoor work
overman	colliery supervisor
p.	'prentice (apprentice)
P.L.W.	power-loom weaver in a textile mill
pattern maker	made metal patterns and moulds for iron casting
pattesier	pastry cook
patton (or panton) heel maker	maker of heels for slippers

pauper	without money or means of livelihood
pavior	layer of pavement slabs and flag-stones
pedlar	door-to-door seller of small goods
pendicler	subtenant with some grass and arable land
pensioner	originally with an army pension after service
periwig-maker	maker of gentlemen's wigs
peuterer	worker in pewter
philosophical instrument maker	maker of scientific and astronomical instruments
piecer	mill worker who joined threads broken by spinning
pikar	petty thief
pirn winder	mill worker who threaded yarn on bobbins (pirns)
pit brusher	repaired coal mine roofs and sides
pit roadman	preparing and repaired coal mine passageways
pitheadman	coal mine (pit) worker above ground
platelayer	railway worker who laid and repaired rails
plewman	ploughman
plumber	worked with lead on roofs, water pipes etc.
pointsman	railway worker who operated points
polentarius	malt maker
pony driver	led ponies underground pulling coal hutches
porter	baggage carrier; gate keeper
portioner	owner of land previously divided among co-heirs
portioner	one of the heirs of a portion of property.
post boy	guard travelling on a mail coach
postman	delivers mail (letters and parcels)
print compositor	set up type for printing
print cutter	maker of printing blocks
printfield worker	mill worker who printed cloth with dyes and inks
procurator	lawyer or advocate
procurator-fiscal	main public prosecutor in a burgh or district
provost	elected head of town or burgh council
publican	keeper of a public house (pub) selling ales, wines and spirits
puddler	iron worker operating a puddling or ball furnace to turn cast iron into wrought iron
quarrier	worker in stone quarry
quine	a young woman (queen) – north-east Scotland
R.C.C.	Roman Catholic clergyman
R.N.	Royal Navy
ranselman	empowered by a court to search houses for stolen property
reader	teacher of law, medicine, classics etc.
red leader	painted red lead oxide paint onto metal surfaces
reedmaker	maker of reeds for weavers
reeler	mill worker who put yarns onto reels for weaving
regent	schoolmaster or professor
reidare	reader, lesser clergyman in the early Church
relict	widow
resetter	receiver, concealer or 'fence' of stolen goods
riddler	maker or user of coarse sieves (riddles) for grain, soil, etc.
riever	robber, originally of cattle (esp. in Borders)

rivetter	joining metal plates with hammered rivets
rope spinner	maker of rope by braiding yarns
running stationer	caddie (qv.) stationed to run errands
saddler	maker and repairer of horse saddles and leathers
salinator	preserver who used salt e.g. for fish
sandpaperer	See French polisher
sawbones	surgeon
sawyer	worker in sawmill or timber pit
scallag	poor farm servant of a tacksman
scavenger ('scaffie')	1. dustman, street sweeper or refuse collector 2. worker in a jute mill who picked up loose material from the floor
scholar	child at school
schoolmaster	head schoolteacher
sclater	slater, roof tiler
scourer	washed raw wool with soap or in urine before processing
scrivener	scribe employed to draft contracts, accounts, etc.
scullery maid	kitchen servant (female)
seafarer	seaman, sailor, mariner
seamstress	woman who made, sewed and mended clothes
seceder	member of Secession Church (after 1733)
sen. coll. just.	senator of the College of Justice
seriand	constable or bailiff
servitor	clerk or secretary
settmaker	cutter of stones for cobbled streets
sexton	layman guarding a church and vestments
sheriff	chief officer of the Crown in a county
shingler	roof tiler using wooden shingles (cf. slater) (See also iron shingler)
ship master	owner or captain of a ship
ship stager	built the wooden scaffolding and platforms around a ship being built
shipwright	maker and repairer of ships, ship's carpenter
sho.	shopman, i.e. employed in retail
skinner	flayer of animal skins for leather, furs etc.
sklaiter	slater
slater	roof tiler using slates
sledder	driver of a sled, used over soft ground in preference to a wheeled cart
smith	metal worker, usually a blacksmith
solicitor	lawyer, usually not in court (cf. advocate)
souter	shoemaker
spargener	plasterer
spectioner	third mate on a whaling ship, responsible for correct stowage in the hold
spinster	woman who spun textiles (also used for an unmarried woman)
spirit merchant	dealer in spirits, but also vinegar
sprigger	embroiderer of lace and muslin (See also boot sprigger)
squarewright	carpenter, but for fine furniture
stampmaster	official inspector with powers to fine for faulty or fraudulent maunufacture
station master	railway employee in charge of a station
steward	chief servant of royal or noble household
stoker	stoked fuel into a furnace or boiler, e.g. on a ship

stone hewer	1. sculptor or stonemason 2. miner who drilled holes in the coal face for dynamiting
stravaiger	a wanderer, a vagrant
sugar baker	refiner in a sugar factory
sumlier	butler (sommelier)
surfaceman	laid and repaired surfaces of roads, railways or mine passage
surg. apoth.	surgeon-apothecary
surveyor of taxes	calculated and levied taxes on property
swerde-slipper, sword slipper	sword sharpener and sheath maker
tacksman	farm tenant who sub-let rents (tacks)
tacksman (taxman)	tenant, holding the lease or 'tack'
tailzeor	tailor
tambourer	embroiderer, who used a hoop to hold the cloth
tanner	curer of leather hides
tapsman	head servant in charge
tearer	assistant to a cloth printer in a print mill
tenementer	tenant of a dwelling in a town building (tenement)
tenter	mechanic who maintained power looms
thatcher	roofer using natural cut reeds or heather thatch
tick maker	upholsterer
tick manufacturer	a weaver of various fabrics (ticking)
tidewaiter	customshouse officer who received duty from merchant ships coming into harbour
tinker	travelling tinsmith, seller of pots and pans
todman	employed to kill foxes (tods) on an estate
towsman	in charge of the halyards on a fishing boat
trencherman	cook
tronman	chimney sweep
turkey red dyer	turkey red (from madder root) was used to dye cotton
turner	lathe operator, shaping wood or metal
type-founder	printer who set out individual letters on printing blocks
vanman	driver of a light commercial vehicle
vermin trapper	employed to trap and kill rats and other pests
vestiarus	keeper of the wardrobe
victualler	supplier of food and provisions
vintner	wine merchant
vulcanite comb maker	made hard (vulcanite rubber) combs for the textile industry
W.S.	Writer to the Signet (solicitor)
wabster	weaver
wadsetter	creditor or holder of land or property under mortage
wainwright	wagon maker
walker, waulker, waker, walkster, wacker etc.	fuller
weaver	maker of cloth from yarns of wool, cotton, silk etc.
weigher	weighed goods before sale (See iron weigher)
weyverr	weaver
wheelwright	wheel maker or repairer
white-iron smith, whitesmith	worker in tin and light metals (cf. blacksmith)
wincey weaver	weaver using string cotton thread

winder	textile worker who wound the thread on looms
wobster	weaver (See wabster)
workman	porter, chiefly at weighhouse
wrecker	plunderer of a shipwreck – some lured ships to destruction for the purpose
wright	maker, joiner or carpenter
writer	solicitor
wryt	Writer (to the Signet), solicitor
Y.	Yeoman of the Guard
yarn bleacher	bleached textile fibres e.g. flax
yarn dresser	prepared flax fibres (See hackler)
yarn twister	twisted silk into threads or yarn
yauger	pedlar of local fish and produce (Shetlands)
ypor.	apothecary

ABBREVIATIONS

As found in Burgess Rolls, sasine abridgements and other documents

Act of C.	Act of Council
adv.	advocate
apoth.	apothecary
App. Reg.	Register of Apprentices
archbp	archbishop
assig.	assignation
B.	Burgess (of a burgh)
B.R.	Burgess Register
bar.	barony
be r. of	by right of
bond and disp.	bond and disposition in security
bond corrob. and disp.	bond of corroboration and disposition
bp	bishop
but	without
by, or in, r. of	by, or in, right of
c.	council
c.s.	commissioner's servant
ch. resig. G.S.	charter of resignation under the Great Seal
ch.	charter
ch. conf.	charter of confirmation (from a feudal superior)
ch. conf. and novodamus	charter of confirmation and novodamus
ch. resig.	charter of resignation (from the feudal superior)
ch. resig. and adjud.	charter of resignation (by a superior) on an adjudication
chir. apoth.	chirurgeon–apothecary
comp.	comprising
con. excamb.	contract of excambion, for the exchange of properties, for example to rationalise boundaries
con. fee and liferent	conjunct fee and liferent (joint fee in two or more persons during their lives)
con. of ground annual	contract of ground annual (form of heritable security)
conjux, uxor	wife
corslet	furnished with a corslet, needed for admission as a guild-brother

customarye	levying of customs or excise.
d.	died
D.G.	Dean of Guild
dec.	deceased
decr. arb.	decreet arbitral
dewtie	fee
disch.	discharge
disp.	disposition
disp. and assig.	disposition and assignation
disp. of tailzie	disposition of tailzie (an entail)
dominus	clerical title
dominus [name] miles	Sir [name] Kt.
dr	daughter
E.I.C.	East India Company
eld.	elder, eldest
eod. die	eodem die (on the same day)
extent	assessment, value ('stent')
extract sp. service	extract of special service
f.	freeman
fear	one to whom property belongs in reversion
feu. ch.	feu charter
feu. con.	feu contract
feu. disp.	feu disposition
fr.	father
G.	gild brother
G.fr.	grandfather
G.R.	general register (of sasines)
G.S.	Great Seal
Gnall	general
H.E.I.C.S.	Honourable East India Company
hagbuit	armed with a hagbut or arquebus
hekil	heckling comb
hr appt	heir apparent
in r. of	in or by right of
indweller	resident [in a burgh]
jack, jak	coat of mail
knock	clock
L.o.S.	Lords of Session
M. 1500	burgesses made between 2 March 1498–9 and Michaelmas 1500
M.B.	merchant burgess
M.T.C.	minutes of Town Council
mar. con.	marriage contract
messr	messenger
metstar	official measurer
minr	minister of the Gospel
mr, mgr	magister, a teacher or employer, or one who has a college degree of M.A.
mt	merchant
muskitt	armed with a musket

nat.	natural
not. instrument	notarial instrument, drawn up by a notary
novodamus	new grant of land
oblig.	obligation
oy, oye, oe	grandchild
p.	'prentice (apprentice)
P.R.	particular register (of sasines)
paenarium	pantry
paitlet, paytellat	a woman's ruff
par.	parish
paroch, parochin	parish
plegius	surety, cautioner
pnt	present
portioner	one of the heirs of portions of a property, where there was no heir by primogeniture
post nupt. mar. con.	Post-nuptial marriage contract
potticar, pottefar	apothecary
pr. chan.	precept furth of chancery (similar to clare constat where the Crown was the superior)
pr. cl. con.	precept of clare constat
pretorium	tolbooth
proc. resig.	procuratory of resignation
procr	procurator
pultreman	poultryman
quheilwright	wheelwright
quondam	umquhyle, late, deceased
r., right., be r. of	by right of
R.N.	Royal Navy
ratif.	ratification
ren.	renunciation
residenter	inhabitant [of somewhere]
resig. ad. rem.	resignation ad remanentiam
ret. gen. serv.	retour of general service
s.	son
s. and h.	son and heir
s. and h. appt	son and heir apparent
sen. coll. just.	senator of the College of Justice
seq.	sequestrated
souertie	surety or cautioner
sphaeristerium	bowling green
stob and staik	permanent residence
tacksman	lessee
Tron	beam and scales for weighing goods
umq.	umquhyle, late, deceased
Upset	fee for entering as 'prentice
w.	wife (daughter to a burgess)
W.S.	Writer to the Signet, or 'clerk to the signet'
warit	expended
Y.	Yeoman of the Guard
yor.	younger

17

Internet Resources

International websites

Ancestry.com (www.ancestry.com) and **Ancestry.co.uk** (www.ancestry.co.uk)
Simply the best and ever-growing collection of databases including many Scottish.
(Subscription)

Family search (IGI) (www.familysearch.org)
This huge database from The Church of Jesus Christ of Latter-Day Saints (Mormon Church) includes the International Genealogical Index (I.G.I.), with a few hundred million names extracted from vital records worldwide, including the Scottish OPRs and the 1881 England and Wales census. However, it also includes a great deal of unreliable and often just plain wrong information supplied by users. Also available on CD-ROM. [Primary]

Cyndi's list (www.cyndislist.com)
The most comprehensive listing of worldwide genealogy sites, and a good place to start, especially for unusual or minor records. There are 20,000 links and a specific page dedicated to Scottish Genealogical Links (www.cyndislist.com/scotland.htm)

Online Genealogical Database Index (www.gentree.com/gentree.html)
OGDI is a USA-based service which claims to have links to all known searchable genealogical databases. Mostly these refer to particular surnames and are mainly indexed by the author's name, which may or may not indicate what they hold.

RootsWeb.com (www.rootsweb.com)
The original and still the largest free genealogy website (a part of the Ancestry/MyFamily group), with access or links to many databases, mailing lists, message boards etc. The Surname List has more than 1 million surnames. The WorldConnect Project has family trees with almost half a billion names, of variable reliability.

Usenet Newsgroup (news:soc.genealogy.britain)
There is a Usenet newsgroup for British (including Scottish) genealogy. It is very active and the volume of traffic is huge. Someone may be researching a similar area to you, so it is worth checking.

Helm's Toolbox (http://sitefinder.genealogytoolbox.com) has almost 75,000 links and a surnames search engine.

Researching Your Scottish Family History (http://ourworld.compuserve.com/homepages/RJWinters/gene-faq.htm)
Helpful introduction for anyone just starting out.

Genealogy Gateway (www.gengateway.com/genalogy.htm)
This huge site (over 20,000 genealogy and resource listings) includes homepage listings for 2,000 surnames (of variable quality). There is also a search engine, essential for a site this size, but unusual.

Burke's Landed Gentry (www.burkes-landed-gentry.com)
Burke's Peerage & Baronetage has long been regarded as the authority on the British aristocracy and landowning families. Burke's Landed Gentry is a multi-volume reference

work listing all major titled and untitled families in the UK; the Scotland volume contains peers, lords, barons, knights and clan chiefs as well as senior figures in politics, the military, law, religion, education etc. The website has a searchable database.

Scotland
PRIMARY SOURCES

Scotland's People (www.scotlandspeople.gov.uk)

The searchable database of the General Register Office for Scotland (GROS) and the National Archives of Scotland (NAS), with indexes and images (in many cases) of parish registers – baptisms and marriages but not deaths – (1553–1854); Civil Registers of Births (1855–1905, with images) and Marriages (1855–1930, with images) and Deaths (1855–1955, plus images); census records (with images) for 1841, 1851, 1861, 1871, 1881 (transcripts only), 1891 and 1901; Scottish wills and testaments (1513–1901). Registration and payment for searches and image downloads.

SCAN – Scottish Archive Network (www.scan.org.uk)

Previously called SCRAN, this includes a directory of many Scottish archives, links to other websites, a section on Scottish handwriting and the SCAN public catalogue (www.dswebhosting.info/SCAN), a searchable database of over fifty Scottish archives, listed here: (www.scan.org.uk/aboutus/SCANguidelines.pdf).

NAS – National Archives of Scotland (www.nas.gov.uk)

Start here for the types of records held, then consult the public catalogue (www.dswebhosting.info/nas).

NRAS – National Register of Archives for Scotland online register (www.nas.gov.uk/nras/register.asp)

This has at least the titles, and in some cases the full catalogue, of over 4,000 private archives and collections of papers, including the records of estates, individuals, businesses etc. held in local authority, university and other archives.

LOCAL ARCHIVES AND LIBRARIES IN SCOTLAND

Historical County etc.	Contact Details
Aberdeenshire Central Library Rosemount Viaduct Aberdeen AB25 1GW	*tel*: 01224 652511 *fax*: 01224 624118 *email*: ReferenceLibrary@aberdeencity.gov.uk LocalStudiesLibrary@aberdeencity.gov.uk *web*: www.aberdeencity.gov.uk/acc_data/information/arc_main.asp Chapman: ABD
Angus Angus Archives Montrose Library 214 High Street Montrose DD10 8HE	See also Dundee *tel*: 01674 671415 *web*: www.angus.gov.uk/history Chapman: ANS
Argyll & Bute Argyll and Bute Council Archives Manse Brae Lochgilphead PA31 8QU	*tel*: 01546 604774 *fax*: 01546 604769 *email*: murdo.macdonald@argyll-bute.gov.uk *web*: www.argyll-bute.gov.uk/content/atoz/services/archives

Ayrshire 1 Local Record Office Regional Archives County Buildings Wellington Square Ayr KA7 1DR	*tel*: 01292 266922 Archives Centre Craigie Estate AYR *email*: christine.lodge@south-ayrshire.gov.uk *web*: www.ayrshirearchives.org.uk
Ayrshire 2 East Ayrshire Council The Dick Institute Elmbank Avenue KIlmarnock KA1 3BU	*tel*: 01563 554310 *fax*: 01563 554311 Chapman:TAY
Ayrshire 3 North Ayrshire Council Local History Library Library Headquarters 39–41 Princes Street Ardrossan Ayrshire KA22 8BT	*tel*: 01294 469137 *fax*: 01294 604236 *email*: localhistory@north-ayrshire.gov.uk Chapman:AYR
Ayrshire 4 South Ayrshire Council Carnegie Library: South Ayrshire Council Local History Library 12 Main Street Ayr KA8 8ED	*tel*: 01292 286385 *fax*: 01292 611593 *email*: Jcastle@south-ayrshire.gov.uk *Library Services URL*: www.south-ayrshire.gov.uk Chapman:AYR
Ayrshire – Other Libraries: Baird Institute History Centre & Museum 3 Lugar Street Cumnock KA18 1AD	*tel & fax*: 01290 421701 *email*: baird.institute@east-ayrshire.gov.uk
Banffshire	See Aberdeen City Archives
Berwickshire	See Borders Council
Borders Council Scottish Borders Archive and Local History Centre Library HQ St Mary's Mill Selkirk TD7 5EW	*tel*: 01750 20842 *fax*: 01750 22875 *email*: archives@scotborders.gov.uk Chapman: BOR, BEW, PEE, ROX, SEL Includes Berwickshire
Bute	See Argyll & Bute
Caithness	See North Highland Archive
Clackmannanshire Information Librarian & Archivist, Library Services, Drysdale Street, Alloa, FK10 1JL	*tel*: 01259 722262 *fax*: 01259 219469 *email*: libraries@clacks.gov.uk Chapman: CLK

Dumfries & Galloway Municipal Chambers Buccleuch Street Dumfries DG1 2AD	*tel*: 01387 269254 *fax*: 01387 264126 *email*: EricaJ@dumgal.gov.uk
Council Offices Sun Street Stranraer DG9 7JJ	*tel*: 01387 245906 *fax*: 01387 269605 Shirley McNeillie, Area Registrar: *tel*: 01776 888439 *fax*: 01776 889492 *web*: www.dumgal.gov.uk Chapman: DGY, DFS

Dumfries and Galloway Historical Indexes
(www.dumgal.gov.uk/dumgal/MiniWeb.aspx?id=86&menuid=921&openid=921)
Indexes of several original sources, including the 1851 census returns for Dumfriesshire, Kirkcudbrightshire and Wigtownshire; Dumfries Dean of Guild Plans 1892–1974; Dumfries Jail Books and Bail Bond Registers 1714–1810; Dumfries Kirk Session and Presbytery Minutes 1689–1838; Dumfries Poor Board Minutes; Dumfries Town Chamberlains Accounts 1793–1801; Mouswald Kirk Session 1640–59; Shipping Registers for Dumfries 1824–1904, Kirkcudbright 1824–41, Stranraer 1824–1908 and Wigtown 1836–1908; Troqueer Kirk Session Minutes 1698–1771. See also the catalogue at **Dumfries and Galloway Archives** (http://archives.dumgal.gov.uk:8814)

Dunbartonshire (East and West)	See also Glasgow City Archives
East Dunbartonshire Council Local Record Office William Patrick Library 2 West High Street Kirkintilloch Glasgow G66 1AD	*tel*: 01417 768090 *fax*: 01417 760408 *email*: libraries@east-dunbarton.gov.uk Chapman: DNB
West Dunbartonshire Council Dumbarton Public Library Local Collection Strathleven Place Dumbarton G82 1BD	*tel*: 01389 733273/763129 *fax*: 01389 733018 *email*: Dumbarton.local.history@west-dunbarton.gov.uk Chapman: DNB Local Record Office City of Glasgow Archives Mitchell Library North Street Glasgow G3 7DN *tel*: 01412 272405
Dundee City Council Dundee Central Library Local Studies Department The Wellgate Dundee DD1 1DB	*tel*: 01382 431550 *fax*: 01382 434036 *email*: David.kett@dundeecity.gov.uk Dundee City Archives and Record Centre *web*: www.dundeecity.gov.uk/archives/main.htm Chapman: TAY

Friends of Dundee City Archives (www.fdca.org.uk)
Includes a database of Wesleyan baptisms 1785–1898 and index to 80,000 burials at The Howff (Dundee City Cemetery).

East Lothian	See also Edinburgh City Council *web*: www.eastlothian.gov.uk/content/0,1094,307,00.html

East Renfrewshire Council Giffnock Community Library Station Road Giffnock East Renfrewshire G46 6JF Registrar's Office Council Offices, Eastwood Park Rouken Glen Road East Renfrewshire G46 6JF	*tel*: 01415 774976 *fax*: 01415 774978 *email*: giffnockl@eastrenfrewshire.gov.uk *web*: www.eastrenfrewshire.gov.uk Chapman: RFW See also Glasgow
Edinburgh City Council Edinburgh Room Edinburgh Central Library George IV Bridge Edinburgh EH1 3EG Other Libraries: Scottish Department Edinburgh Central Library George IV Bridge Edinburgh EH1 3EG Local Record Office Edinburgh City Archives City Chambers High Street Edinburgh EH1 1YJ	*tel*: 01312 428031 *email*: edinburgh.room@edinburgh.gov.uk *web*: www.efr.hw.ac.uk/EDC/Libraries/Reference/special.htm Chapman: SCT, AYR, BEW, CAI, CLK, OFS, ELN, FIF, INV, KRS, KKD, MLN, NAI, OKI, PEE, ROC, ROX, SEL, SHI, STI, SUT, WLN, WIG *tel*: 01315 294290
Falkirk Council Falkirk Library Hope Street Falkirk FK1 5AU Grangemouth Library Bo'ness Road Grangemouth FK3 8AG	*tel*: 01324 503605 *fax*: 01324 504690 *email*: irene.mcintyre@falkirk.gov.uk Chapman: CEM
Fife Council Archive Centre	*web*: www.archon.nationalarchives.gov.uk/archon/searches/ locresult_details.asp?LR=2105 Chapman: FIF
Fife Council – Central Area Central Library War Memorial Grounds Kirkcaldy Fife KY1 1XT	*tel*: 01592 412879 *fax*: 01592 646125
Fife Council – East St Andrews Library Church Square St Andrews Fife KY16 9NN	*tel*: 01334 412685

Fife Council Genealogy Services St Andrews Fife	*tel*: 01334 413017 *email*: tracey.blyth@fife.gov.uk
Fife Council – West Dunfermline Library Abbot Street Dunfermline Fife KY12 1NL	*tel*: 01383 312600 *fax*: 01383 624708 *email*: Anne.rodwell@fife.gov.uk
Glasgow City Council History and Glasgow Room The Mitchell Library North Street Glasgow G3 7DN	*tel*: 01412 872937 *fax*: 01412 872935 *email*: history_and_glasgow@cls.glasgow.gov.uk; GLW_ARCHIVES@cqm.co.uk *web*: www.libarch.glasgow.gov.uk/main.htm Chapman: LKS, DNB, RFW, AYR, STD

Glasgow University Archive (www.archives.gla.ac.uk) Holdings the University Archives, Greater Glasgow NHS Board Archive, Business Records Centre, Scottish Brewing Archive and more.	

Highland Council The North Highland Archive Wick Library Sinclair Terrace Wick Caithness KW1 5AB	*tel*: 01955 606432 *fax*: 01955 603000 *email*: north.highlandarchive@highland.gov.uk *web*: www.highland.gov.uk/educ/publicservices/archivedetails/ northarchive.htm Chapman: HLD, CAI, INV, NAI, ROC
Inverclyde Council Watt Library 9 Union Street Greenock PA16 8JH	*tel*: 01475 715628 *email*: sandra.macdougall@inverclyde.gov.uk Chapman: RFW
Inverness-shire	See North Highland Archive *web*: www.highland.gov.uk/educ/publicservices/archivedetails/ highlandarchive.htm
Kincardine	See Aberdeen City Archives
Kinross	See Perth & Kinross *web*: www.pkc.gov.uk/library/akbell.htm
Kirkcudbright	See Dumfries & Galloway
Lanarkshire (North and South)	See also Glasgow City Archives and Lenziemill Archives *web*: www.northlan.gov.uk/leisure+and+tourism/ museums+and+heritage/archive+centre/index2.html
North Lanarkshire Council Motherwell Heritage Centre High Road Motherwell ML1 3HU	*tel*: 01698 251000 *fax* (Local History): 01698 253433 *email*: heritage@mhc158.freeserve.co.uk Chapman: LKS

Other Libraries: Airdre Library Wellwynd Airdrie ML6 0AG *tel*: 01236 76322 *fax*: 01236 763221	Cumbernauld Central Library 8 Allander Walk Cumbernauld G67 1EE *tel*: 01236 725664/452061 *fax*: 01236 458350	Kilsyth Library Burngreen Kilsyth G65 0HT *tel*: 01236 823147 *fax*: 01236 823147	Shotts Library Benhar Road Shotts ML7 5EN *tel*: 01501 821556

South Lanarkshire Council East Kilbride Central Library Reference Department 40 The Olympia East Kilbride G74 1PG	*tel*: 01355 220046 *fax*: 01355 229365 *email*: ek.reference@southlanarkshire.gov.uk Chapman: LKS	
	Other Libraries: Hamilton Central Library 4 Auchingramont Road Hamilton ML3 6JT *tel*: 01698-452403 *fax*: 01698-286334 *email*: hamilton. reference@library.s-lanark.org.uk	Lanark Library Reference Department Lindsay Institute Hope Street Lanark ML11 7LZ *tel*: 01555 661144 *fax*: 01555 665884
Lothians (East, West, Edinburgh and Midlothian)	Lothian Health Services Archive *web*: www.lhsa.lib.ed.ac.uk	
Midlothian Local Studies Collection Midlothian Council Library Headquarters 2 Clerk Street Loanhead Midlothian EH20 9DR	See also Edinburgh City Archives *tel*: 01312 713976 *fax*: 01314 404635 *email*: local.studies@midlothian.gov.uk *web*: www.midlothian.gov.uk/Library/Local.htm Chapman: LTN, MLN	
Moray Moray Local Heritage Services Local Studies Section Grant Lodge Cooper Park Elgin IV30 1HS	*tel*: 01343 562644 *fax*: 01343 562630 *email*: graeme.wilson@moray.gov.uk *web*: www.moray.org/heritage/index.html Chapman: MOR	
Other Libraries: Buckie Library 94 High Street Buckie AB56 1HB *tel*: 01542 832121 *fax*: 01542 835237	Forres Library Forres House High Street Forres IV36 0BU *tel*: 01309 672834 *fax*: 01309 675084	Keith Library Union Street Keith AB55 5DP *tel*: 01542 882225 *fax*: 01542 882177 Local Record Offices Archives Section The Tolbooth High Street Forres
Nairnshire	See North Highland Archive *web*: www.highland.gov.uk/educ/publicservices/archivedetails/highlandarchive.htm	
Orkney The Orkney Library Laing Street Kirkwall Orkney KW15 1NW	*tel*: 01856 873166 *fax*: 01856 875260 *email*: archives@orkneylibrary.org.uk *web*: www.orkneylibrary.org.uk Chapman: OKI	
Peeblesshire	See Scottish Borders Archive and Local History Centre *web*: www.scottishborders.gov.uk/libraries/hist/history.htm	

Perthshire A.K. Bell Library York Place Perth PH2 8EP	*tel*: 01738 444949 *fax*: 01738 477010 *email*: Jaduncan@pkc.gov.uk *web*: www.pkc.gov.uk/library/akbell.htm
Local Record Offices Perth and Kinross Council Archive York Place Perth PH2 8EP	Chapman: KRS, PER *tel*: 01738 477022 *fax*: 01738 477010
Renfrewshire See East Renfrewshire	See also the Glasgow City Archives Chapman: RFW
Ross & Cromarty	See North Highland Archive
Roxburghshire	See Scottish Borders Archive and Local History Centre
Selkirkshire	See Scottish Borders Archive and Local History Centre
Shetland The main collection is held in the local collection within the library serving Lerwick. The library moved in early 2002 from the former building to the converted adjoining former St Ringan's Church. Shetland Library Lower Hillhead Lerwick Shetland ZE1 0EL	*tel*: 01595 693868 *fax*: 01595 694430 *email*: info@shetland-library.gov.uk *web*: www.shetland.gov.uk/atoz/ed3.htm Chapman: SHI, small quantity for OKI Local Record Offices Shetland Archives King Harald Street Lerwick Shetland *tel*: 01595 696247 *email*: shetland.archives@zetnet.co.uk
Stirling Central Library Corn Exchange Road Stirling FK8 2HX. Local Record Offices Stirling Council Archive Unit 6 Burghmuir Industrial Estate Stirling FK7 7PY	*tel*: (01786) 432106 *email*: central_library@stirling.gov.uk *web*: www.stirling.gov.uk/index/stirling/archives.htm Chapman: STI *tel*: 01786 450745
Sutherland	See North Highland Archive
Wigtown	See Dumfries & Galloway
Western Isles Council (Comhairle nan Eilean Siar) Stornoway Library 19 Cromwell Street Stornoway Isle of Lewis HS1 2DA	*tel*: 01851 708631 *fax*: 01851 708676 *email*: bobeaves@cne-siar.gov.uk Chapman: INV, ROC, WIS

| Local Record Offices
Registrar's Office
Town Hall
South Beach Street
Stornoway
Isle of Lewis

tel: 01851 709438
email: emacdonald@cnesiar.gov.uk | **Other Libraries:**
Community Library
Sgoil Lionacleit
Liniclate
Isle of Benbecula
HS7 5PJ

tel: 01870 603532
fax: 01870 602817
email: lionacleitlibrary@eileanansiar.biblio.net | Community Library
Castlebay Community
School
Castlebay
Isle of Barra
HS9 5XD

tel: 01871 810471
fax: 01871 810650
email: castlebaylibrary@eileanansiar.biblio.net |
| West Lothian Council
Library HQ
Connolly House
Hopefield Road
Blackburn
West Lothian
EH47 7HZ

Local Record Offices
Records Manager
4 Rutherford Square
Bellsquarry
Livingston
West Lothian | *tel*: 01506 776331
fax: 01506 776345
email: sybil.cavanagh@westlothian.gov.uk

West Lothian Local History Library
web: www.westlothian.gov.uk/content/leisure/libraries/Liblocal/localhistory

Chapman: WLN | |

Ireland

Public Record Office of Northern Ireland (www.proni.gov.uk)
General information and fairly full details of holdings. Includes Freeholders' records (www.proni.gov.uk/freeholders/intro.asp), an index to pre-1840 registers of registered voters and poll books of actual voters; and **The Ulster Covenant** (www.proni.gov.uk/ulstercovenant/index.html) with names, addresses and signatures of about half a million men and women who opposed Irish home rule in 1912. [Primary]

National Archives of Ireland (Eire) (www.nationalarchives.ie)
Information on Irish genealogy and family history including Transportation Records to Australia, 1836–57. [Primary]

Irish Genealogy (http://irishgenealogy.net/antrimgen.html)
Searchable database of what remains of the 1851 Co. Antrim census and other resources (surname lists etc.). [Primary]

Irish ancestors (www.ireland.com/ancestor)
In collaboration with *The Irish Times*, links to sources (some primary) for Irish genealogy. (Subscription) [Primary]

Ulster Historical Foundation (www.ancestryireland.com)
Rapidly growing searchable databases totalling more than 2 million records, including birth, baptismal, civil and church records from 1845. (Free search but subscription for full access.) [Primary]

United Kingdom and Ireland

TNA – The National Archives (www.nationalarchives.gov.uk)
Formerly the Public Record Office (PRO) and simply the best place to start for all England and Wales records. Details of the holdings of the National Archives, including freely searchable indexes to the 1841 to 1901 censuses for England and Wales (full access to information and images requires payment.) [Primary]

NRA – National Register of Archives (www.nra.nationalarchives.gov.uk/nra)
Indexes of the nature and location of manuscripts and historical records relating to British history. [Primary]

A2A – Access to Archives (www.a2a.org.uk)
Catalogue of over 400 English archives held outwith The National Archives.

Archives Hub (www.archiveshub.ac.uk)
Archives held by UK universities and colleges.

Commonwealth War Graves Commission (www.cwgc.org)
A fabulous and properly reverential source of information on members of the Commonwealth forces who died in the First and Second World Wars and some civilian casualties of the Second World War. [Primary]

Familia (www.familia.org.uk)
Directory of family history resources available in public libraries in the UK and Ireland.

Familyrecords.gov (www.familyrecords.gov.uk)
Information on and links to the major UK family history websites.

FreeBMD (http://freebmd.rootsweb.com), **FreeCen** (http://freecen.rootsweb.com) and **FreeReg** (http://freereg.rootsweb.com)
Free Internet access to various Civil Registration indexes mainly in England and Wales. Currently over 130 million records and growing, but far from complete and few images. [Primary]

GENUKI (www.genuki.org.uk)
Superb general information site for sources, addresses, etc. for UK and Ireland genealogy.

Society of Genealogists (www.sog.org.uk)
Only really useful for personal visits to the London headquarters, and if a member of SOG.

1837online.com (www.1837online.com)
Pay per view indexes of some BMD, census and other records for England and Wales from 1837–2004. Frustrating and sometimes expensive to use in that it often directs the user to an alphabeticised page that may or may not contain the name searched for. [Primary]

18

Scottish Monarchs: Reigns and Genealogies

A lot of Scottish history has hinged on the genealogies of its sovereigns. In the Dark Ages Scotland was occupied by a number of distinct peoples. The original inhabitants, the mysterious Picts, occupied seven 'kingdoms' in the north and east of the country, and arrived from Europe during the Celtic migrations of the first millennium BC. The Scotii were one or more tribes of Goidelic (Gaelic) Celts who came from north-west Ireland at various times up to the fifth century AD into Argyll and the West Highlands, which they named Dalraida. The Britons of Strathclyde, who were Brythonic Celts speaking a language like Welsh, were in control of the area from the Clyde to the Solway and parts of Cumbria, with a stronghold in Dumbarton (Dun Breatann, 'Fortress of the Britons'). North-east England was occupied by Angles, who migrated into the Scottish lowlands as far as the Forth, dislodging the Britons from Edinburgh in the seventh century. The Vikings – raiders and later settlers from Norway and Denmark – occupied Shetland, Orkney and the north-west of Scotland (to them, 'Sutherland' was indeed south) from the 800s and also gave rise to the Normans.

The MacAlpin dynasty united these disparate peoples into one nation – Alba – by a mixture of conquest, a few judicious royal murders and intermarriage between Gael and Pict. The Celtic system of inheritance was tanistry, the tanist being the successor to the king, but not necessarily his eldest son. The female lineage was all-important. The reigns of the MacAlpin kings were overshadowed by fierce dynastic conflicts for the next two centuries.

The Canmore dynasty secured its position at home and in relation to England by a series of marriages with the Saxon royal family (Malcolm and Margaret), and the Plantagenets. Alexander II originally fought alongside the English barons and the French against John Lackland, but after John's death he married John's daughter and Henry III's sister, Joan, in 1221. The decease of his son and his great-granddaughter ended the Celtic dynasty.

This set the stage for the disastrous two decades during which the Comyn-Balliol alliance and the powerful Bruces vied for the throne while Edward I claimed overall supremacy. Initially, Edward had been invited by the Guardians of Scotland to adjudge the genealogical claims of Balliol, Bruce and the other 'Competitors'. All of these stressed their descent, by the rules of tanistry and via female lines, from David I.

The Stewart/Stuart monarchs took every opportunity to intermarry with English, French and Danish royalty. The crucial events were the marriages of James IV to Margaret Tudor (the elder sister of Henry VIII, which made his grandson James VI heir to the English throne after the death of his second cousin once removed, Elizabeth) and the marriage of his daughter Elizabeth Stuart to Frederick of Bohemia (whose grandson would become George I after the death of Queen Anne, the last Stuart).

A family tree of the House of Macalpin and Moray

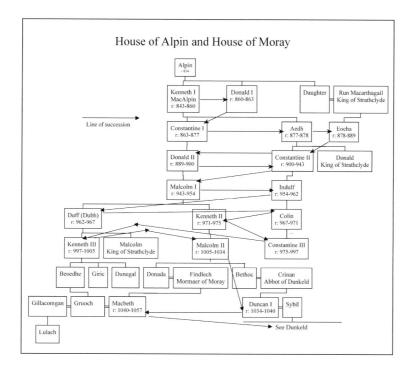

A family tree of the House of Dunkeld

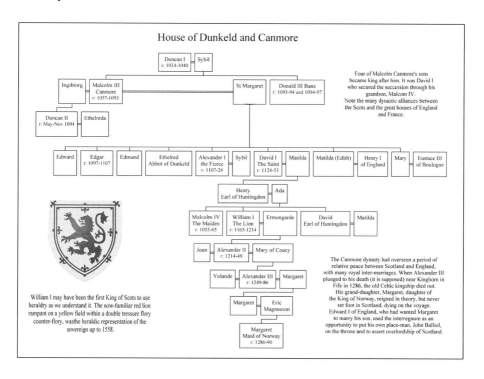

A family tree of the House of Balliol and Bruce

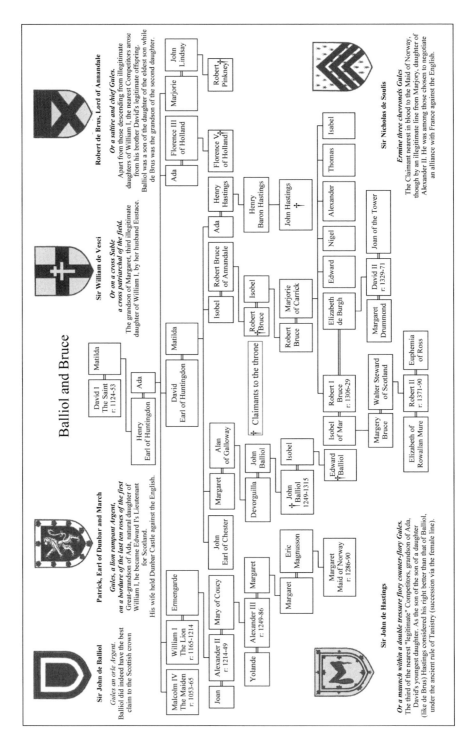

Balliol and Bruce

Sir John de Balliol

Gules an orle Argent.
Balliol did indeed have the best claim to the Scottish crown

Patrick, Earl of Dunbar and March

Gules, a lion rampant Argent, on a bordure of the last ten roses of the first
Great-grandson of Ada, natural daughter of William I, he became Edward I's Lieutenant for Scotland.
His wife held Dunbar Castle against the English.

Sir William de Vesci

Or on a cross Sable a cross patriarchal of the field.
The grandson of Margaret, third illegitimate daughter of William I, by her husband Eustace.

Robert de Brus, Lord of Annandale

Or a saltire and chief Gules.
Apart from those descending from illegitimate daughters of William I, the nearest Competitors arose from his brother David's legitimate offspring.
Balliol was a son of the daughter of the eldest son while de Brus was the grandson of the second daughter.

Sir Nicholas de Soulis

Ermine three chevronels Gules
The Claimant nearest in blood to the Maid of Norway, though by an illegitimate line from Marjory, daughter of Alexander II. He was among those chosen to negotiate an alliance with France against the English.

Sir John de Hastings

Or a maunch within a double tressure flory counter-flory Gules.
The third of the nearest "legitimate" Competitors, grandson of Ada, David's youngest daughter. As the son of the son of a daughter (like de Brus) Hastings considered his right better than that of Balliol, under the ancient rule of Tanistry (succession via the female line).

A family tree of the House of Stewart

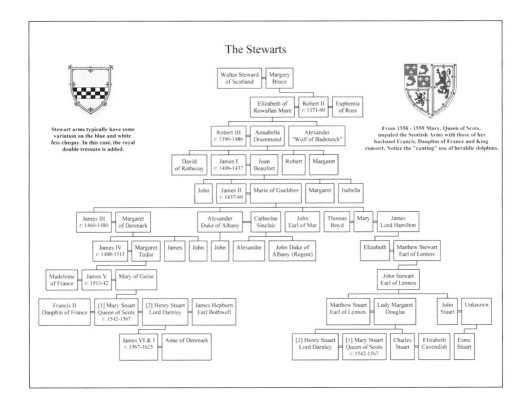

The Stewarts

Stewart arms typically have some variation on the blue and white fess chequy. In this case, the royal double tressure is added.

From 1558 - 1559 Mary, Queen of Scots, impaled the Scottish Arms with those of her husband Francis, Dauphin of France and King consort. Notice the "canting" use of heraldic dolphins.

A family tree of the House of Stuart

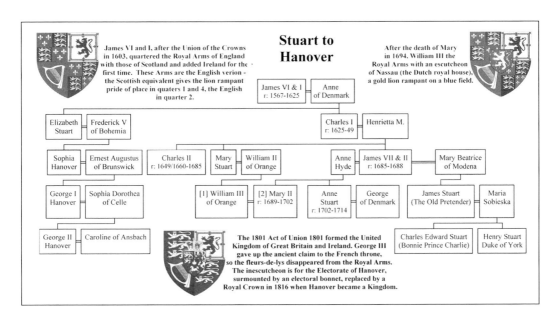

Stuart to Hanover

James VI and I, after the Union of the Crowns in 1603, quartered the Royal Arms of England with those of Scotland and added Ireland for the first time. These Arms are the English verion - the Scottish equivalent gives the lion rampant pride of place in quaters 1 and 4, the English in quarter 2.

After the death of Mary in 1694, William III the Royal Arms with an escutcheon of Nassau (the Dutch royal house), a gold lion rampant on a blue field.

The 1801 Act of Union 1801 formed the United Kingdom of Great Britain and Ireland. George III gave up the ancient claim to the French throne, so the fleurs-de-lys disappeared from the Royal Arms. The inescutcheon is for the Electorate of Hanover, surmounted by an electoral bonnet, replaced by a Royal Crown in 1816 when Hanover became a Kingdom.

19

Organising your Research

It is very easy to collect lots of notes on loose bits of paper, documents, print-outs, photographs and other information, and put it all in a drawer or a box file promising yourself to 'sort it out later'. But there will come a time when it defies organising. So, start with a structure and stick to it. The method below is only one of many, but it works in practice.

1. Write everything down!
   DO NOT rely on your memory. Everything you see written, every book you consult, every website you look at, make a brief note of it. Even if you find nothing, it is useful to know that – it will save time repeating fruitless searches.
2. Use a hardback bound notebook
   DO NOT use loose-leaf paper. Carry a bound notebook everywhere. Note everything. Later (but soon, preferably the same day), type this up into a document, spreadsheet, genealogy program or whatever method you prefer for keeping your results.
3. Make full use of Charts, Research Calendars and Family Group Sheets.
   These are three of the most useful tools for genealogists. A pedigree chart is a visual aid of (usually) three or four generations of a family. A research calendar will remind you where you have been, what you found (or didn't find) and what you intend to do next. The Family Group Sheet is all the information on one nuclear family (father, mother, children) with sources. There are examples of these included in this book, which you are free to copy and use.
4. Keep one (extended) family in a ring binder.
   Genealogists argue whether to file print-outs, documents and notes by each person alphabetically. The problem is, any one document might refer to a number of people – a birth record will have information on at least three (child, father, mother) and a census could be as many as ten, or more. Alphabetical ordering takes no account of time and there may be multiple people with the same name, often in the same generation (cousins, for instance). Therefore, set up a ring binder for each project and use tabbed dividers to separate:

   – Pedigree/Ancestral charts (useful to have at the beginning as an *aide-mémoir*)
   – Family Group Sheets (all together, in chronological order of father's birth date)
   – Births (every birth record, arranged chronologically)
   – Marriages (as above)
   – Deaths (as above)
   – Censuses (by year)
   – Wills and Testaments abstracts (chronologically)
   – Newspaper clippings etc.
   – Plastic one-page wallets for documents (use archive-standard polyester, not PVC)
   – Plastic wallets for photographs (polyester)

You can always add other categories later, e.g. Military.

5.   Give each family a number (start with 001, so SMITH001). Then number individuals from your index person (the person you start from). He/she will be 1, father 2, mother 3, paternal grandfather 4 and so on. See below for more information on numbering systems.

6.   Photocopy, photograph or scan every actual document, keep the photocopy in your file and put the document away in a safe place. Use plastic one-page wallets and a metal or acid-free cardboard file box. Your local stationery shop should be able to advise, as will your local library or archive. Some A4 photocopy-paper boxes are acid-free, come with a lid and are strong and stackable.

7.   If you store images on your computer, put the images in meaningful folders, give them filenames that tie up with the document and print out every image and store it in your file as paper. John-Smith1.jpg is meaningless as a file name; D-1905-SMITH-John-75-Scoonie-Fife456-0002.jpg will lead you straight to the paper file version (D = Death, B = Birth etc).

8.   On each document copy or image print-out, write the source and reference number, and the filename.

9.   It's OK to have the same person in different family files. Copy all relevant papers.

10.   At the beginning of the file, have two lists of everyone – alphabetically (with birth date), such as:

SMITH, Alfred b. 12 Jun 1887
SMITH, John b. 14 Apr 1890
JONES, Mary b. 10 Sept 1725

Charts and numbering systems

Genealogy uses charts and family group sheets to record data. Genealogy software programs can help, and can print out information in a variety of formats, but there is still something to be said for the old paper and pencil.

The two basic forms for recording genealogical information are ascendant charts and descendant charts. An ascendant chart starts with you and moves back through the generations of your ancestors. A descendant chart starts with you or another individual in your family tree and lists all of the descendants coming down through the generations. On these forms you record the names of your ancestors or descendants and the dates and places of the three major genealogical events (birth, marriage and death). They basically serve as a master outline for your genealogy information and make it easy to see at a glance where you have gaps in your knowledge of people or events.

Ascendant charts

The chart which most people begin with is the pedigree chart, a type of ascendant chart. The most common type of pedigree chart displays four or five generations of family data on a single page, but you can purchase paper charts which will accommodate as many as fifteen generations. A four-generation chart is useful as it fits neatly on a standard size page and leaves enough room for data. The first individual named on the left of the chart is the one whose ancestry the tree documents. The chart then branches in two to show parents, then in four for grandparents and so on. This chart only shows the index person's direct ancestors – there is no room on a pedigree chart for siblings, multiple marriages, etc.

The pedigree chart is the more graphic representation of a person's ancestors, while an ahnentafel (German for 'ancestor table') presents the information in a neat, compact manner as a table or list. Ahnentafels are not used quite as often today as they were in the past.

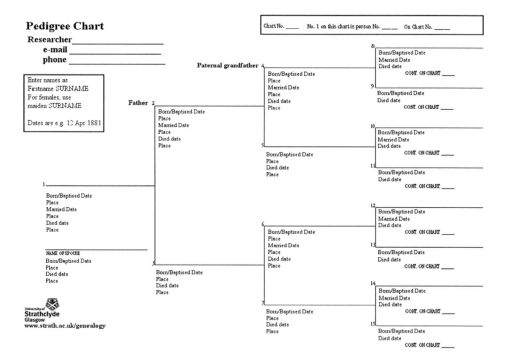

Pedigree Chart

Researcher_____
e-mail _____
phone _____

Chart No. _____   No. 1 on this chart is person No. _____   On Chart No. _____

Paternal grandfather 4

Father 2

Enter names as
Firstname SURNAME
For females, use
maiden SURNAME

Dates are e.g. 12 Apr 1881

Born/Baptised Date
Place
Married Date
Place
Died date
Place

1._____
Born/Baptised Date
Place
Married Date
Place
Died date
Place

NAME OF SPOUSE _____
Born/Baptised Date
Place
Died date
Place

8._____
Born/Baptised Date
Married Date
Died date
CONT. ON CHART _____

9._____
Born/Baptised Date
Died date
CONT. ON CHART _____

10._____
Born/Baptised Date
Married Date
Died date
CONT. ON CHART _____

11._____
Born/Baptised Date
Died date
CONT. ON CHART _____

12._____
Born/Baptised Date
Married Date
Died date
CONT. ON CHART _____

13._____
Born/Baptised Date
Died date
CONT. ON CHART _____

14._____
Born/Baptised Date
Married Date
Died date
CONT. ON CHART _____

15._____
Born/Baptised Date
Died date
CONT. ON CHART _____

University of
Strathclyde
Glasgow
www.strath.ac.uk/genealogy

Ancestors are numbered on pedigree charts and ahnentafels using a system known as the ahnentafel numbering system. You (or the person whose ancestry is being traced) are number 1. A father is twice his child's number (1 x 2 = 2) and a mother is twice the child's number plus one (1 x 2 = 2 + 1 = 3). The numbers for men are always even and the numbers for women are always odd, with the exception of number 1 which can obviously be either. Notice that the first number for each generation is equal to the number of people in that generation (i.e. paternal great-grandfather is 8, and there are 8 great-grandparents). Use the same numbering in your Family Group Sheets.

Descendant charts

Descendant charts are most often used to chart all of the descendants (or at least as many as can be found) of a specific ancestor. You won't find these very useful as you start out, although you should prepare one to include your children and grandchildren if that applies. In general, however, descendant charts begin with a progenitor – the earliest proven ancestor in a line. This means doing some research before you can create this type of chart.

These use a different numbering system, with the progenitor as 1 and all children as 1a, 1b or 1i, 1ii etc.

Family group sheets

This is the basic worksheet used for genealogical research. While a pedigree chart identifies your ancestry and serves primarily as a culmination of your work, the family group sheet is how you get there.

There are many different formats available, but each family group sheet is based on a single family unit – husband, wife and children. A family group sheet has space for the basic genealogical events for each family member, including dates and places of birth, marriage, death and burial. For each child on the list, a name of a spouse can be given, along with a date and place of the marriage. There is usually a place for notes where you should record where

FAMILY GROUP SHEET

Researcher:

e-mail:

Phone:

Family No. _____

Chart No. _____

See Pedigree Chart No. _____

Individual No. _____

Husband Sname/Fname

	d M yyyy	Place	County/State	Country	Occupation(s)
Born					Religion
Christened					Witnesses:
Married					Witnesses:
Died					Witnesses:
Buried					Cause of Death
Father			Other Wives		Date Will Confirmed/Proved
Mother					

Wife MSname/Fname

					Occupation(s)
Born					Witnesses:
Christened					Witnesses:
Died					Witnesses:
Buried					Cause of Death
Father			Other Husbands		Date Will Confirmed/Proved
Mother					

	Children Given Names	Sex M/F	Birth			Birthplace				Date/Place of marriage	Date/Cause of Death		
			Day	Month	Year	Town/City	County	St /Cty		Name of Spouse	City	County	State/Country
1													
2													
3													
4													
5													
6													
7													
8													

Strathclyde
Glasgow

www.strath.ac.uk/genealogy

RESEARCH CALENDAR

Researcher: _____ email: _____ Phone: _____

Notes

University of
Strathclyde
Glasgow

www.strath.ac.uk/genealogy

Date	Repository/Archive	Called/Visited/	Dates searched	Names searched	URL	Phone	e-mail

you got your information (source) as well as make note of any discrepancies in your findings. Family group sheets are essential because they 1) serve as a simple means of recording data; 2) make it easy to see at a glance what information is known and what is missing; and 3) serve as a means of easily exchanging information with other researchers.

Recording names

There are some important conventions which should be followed with regard to names, dates and places. These help to ensure that genealogical data are as complete as possible and cannot be misinterpreted by others.

Genealogy software programs will each have their own individual rules for entering names. Be sure to read the directions completely so that you get it right the first time!

1. Record names in their natural order – first, middle, last (surname). Use full names if known. If the middle name is unknown, use an initial.
2. Print SURNAMES in upper case letters. Example: Henry Michael BROON; Henry M. BROON.
3. Enter women with their maiden name (surname at birth) rather than their husband's surname. Example: Margaret Ellen FRASER married Henry BROON, enter her as Margaret Ellen FRASER
4. If a female's maiden name is unknown, give her first (given) name followed by empty brackets (). Example: Margaret Ellen, maiden name is unknown, married to Henry BROON = Margaret Ellen () or Margaret Ellen () BROON
5. If a women has had more than one husband, enter her given name, followed by her maiden surname (m.s.) in brackets followed by the names of any previous husbands (in order of marriage). If the middle name is known then you may enter that as well. Example: a woman named Mary CLARKE at birth, was married to Jack SMITH prior to marrying Walter LAING = Mary (Clarke) SMITH or Mary LAING previously SMITH m.s CLARKE
6. If there is a nickname that was commonly used, include it in quotes after the given name. Do not use it in place of a given name and do not enclose it in brackets. Example: Hector 'Granpaw' BROON, Margaret 'Maggie' FRASER
7. If a person is known by more than one name (due to adoption, name change, etc.) then include the alternate name or names in brackets after the surname, preceded by a.k.a. Example: Bernard SCHWARZ (a.k.a. Tony CURTIS)
8. Include alternate spellings when you find them. Record the earlier usage first. Example: Daphne BROON/BROWN
9. Use notes when you can. For example, if a female has a maiden name the same as her husband's surname, make a note of that so that you're clear in the future that you had not just entered it incorrectly.

Recording dates

It is especially important to follow genealogical standards when recording dates as the usual way that you enter a date may be different from the standard date format in another country or a different time period.

Genealogy software programs may have somewhat different standards for recording dates. Many will allow you to record them in the format of your choice and will still allow you to print out charts and forms with the standard genealogical format.

1. Use the accepted European standard of DAY, MONTH (spelled out) and four-digit YEAR. Example: 30 June, 1993

2. Americans often use dates with a number format as Month/Day (e.g. 9/11), which leads to confusion. Example: 02/01/01 – is it February 1 or January 2?

3. Spell months out, although there are standard abbreviations you can use. (June and July are often not abbreviated.) Examples: Jan. Feb. Mar. Apr. May. Jun. (or June) Jul. (or July) Aug. Sept. Oct. Nov. Dec.

4. If you only have an approximate date, add 'about' (abt.) or 'circa' (ca. or c.). Examples: c. 1851; ca. 1873; abt. November 1881

5. Use before (bef.) or after (aft.) a specific date, for instance, when you know someone was still living at some time, or was born after a certain date. Example: aft. 12 Jan. 1880; bef. 9 Apr. 1881

6. If you can, narrow it down to a specific time span. For instance, if you know the date a will was signed and the date it was recorded or confirmed, it's reasonable to assume a death between those dates. Example: bet. 3 Apr. 1869 – 12 Jun. 1870

7. If you find a date which could be interpreted more than one way, enter it exactly as it is written and give your interpretation in square brackets [ ] following the original. Example: 02/03/71 [2 Mar. 1871]. ALWAYS record EXACTLY what is given in a document, then add your interpretation after it.

Recording places

The general rule of thumb when entering place names into genealogical records is to record place names from smallest to largest location (i.e. town/locality, county/parish/district, state/province, country). You may choose to leave off the country if it is the one in which you reside and the one where the majority of your research lies, but you may want to at least make a note of this in your files. The breakdown of these locations will vary by country. Here are a few examples:

Springburn, Glasgow, Lanarkshire, Scotland
(Village/Hamlet/Farm/Area/District, Town/City, County, Country)
Calluragh, Inchicronan, Clare, Munster, Ireland
(Townland, Parish, County, Province, Country)

If you have additional place name details, feel free to include them, just be sure to make note of what they are. For example, you could add the name of the barony (Upper Bunratty) to the above location details for Calluragh, Ireland.

Many paper pedigree charts and even some computer programs do not include enough room to record full place names. Abbreviations may certainly be used as long as they are the ones in standard use. For example:

– Co. (County)
– Par. (Parish)
– Twp. (Township)

Check out this very useful List of Genealogical Abbreviations from Rootsweb for more commonly seen abbreviations (http://www.rootsweb.com/~rigenweb/abbrev.html).

Country and place names usually have accepted variations as well. The Roots Surname List of Country Abbreviations gives the three-letter Chapman codes for countries, for the counties and other abbreviations for subdivisions of many countries (http://helpdesk.rootsweb.com/help/abbrev1.html).

If you only know the town or city in which an event occurred, then you should consult a gazetteer to find the county, parish, province, etc. There are also many online sources from which you can obtain information on the county or province in which a town or city is now located. See http://www.geo.ed.ac.uk/scotgaz/scotland.html.

Population changes, wars and other historic events have caused location boundaries to change over time. It may be something as simple as a town which no longer exists or has changed names, or something a little more complex such as a town which was originally part of one county and is now part of another. It is very important to know the history of the area in which you are researching so that you will be able to make educated guesses as to where to find the records for a given time period. When recording a place name for an event, you should always record the locality as it was situated at the time of the event. Then, if space permits, you may also include the information for the locality as it exists today. Example: Beaufort Co. (now Pitt Co.), NC; Culross, Perth (now in Fife).

If you aren't sure of a location, but you have records which suggest the most likely alternative (i.e. if you know where an ancestor is buried, you may make the assumption that he probably died in that locality), then you can record the place as a 'probable'. Example: prob. St. Michael, Bristol, Gloucestershire, England.

Conclusion

This has been no more than a brief canter through some of the foothills of Scottish genealogy; there is always more to discover. As you progress in your researches you will find other sources of information, and more and more documents will come to light all the time. Genealogists can help each other by publishing their findings in Family History Society booklets, genealogy journals, magazines and on the web. The document or archive you find that is of minimal value to your researches might just be the last piece in someone else's jigsaw puzzle. Please just remember three things:

1. Never take anything at face value
2. Don't trust anything that comes without a robust reference (preferably the original document, or where to find it)
3. Be prepared to justify every assertion you make – no leaps of faith, no wild guesses, no wishful thinking

Imagine yourself to be a forensic detective and think 'Could I swear to this in a court of law?' You won't go wrong.

As E.M. Forster said in *Howards End*: 'Only connect'. But, above all, have fun.

Index